RATHFARNHAM ROADS

Topographical notes on Rathfarnham and the adjacent hills, including Two Rock and Three Rock Mountains, Kilmashogue, Tibradden, Killakee, Cruagh, Glencullen and Glendoo.

by

PATRICK HEALY

South Dublin Libraries — APRIL 2005

The material in this book was written, rewritten and updated in the period 1960 - 1985
Minimal editing has been carried out to reflect more recent developments and changes.

ISBN 0954766032

Published by
SOUTH DUBLIN LIBRARIES

Design and layout by
JOHN MCALEER

Printed in Ireland by
GRAPHPRINT LTD.

Local Studies Section
County Library
Town Centre
Tallaght
Dublin 24
Phone 353 (0)1 462 0073
Fax 353 (0)1 414 9207
e-mail localstudies@sdublincoco.ie
web site www.southdublin.ie

South Dublin Libraries Headquarters
Unit 1
Square Industrial Complex
Tallaght
Dublin 24
Phone 353 (0)1 459 7834
Fax 353 (0)1 459 7872

Introduction

by Mayor Robert Dowds

As Mayor of South Dublin, and as a History graduate, it is a real pleasure to introduce this publication. In this work Paddy Healy presents the results of his meticulous labours as a local historian. He illuminates for all, many aspects of the history of Rathfarnham and surrounding areas. Paddy Healy's work is welcome in its own right as a major contribution to the growing body of local history in Ireland. However, it is also welcome as it provides the opportunity for both the established and newer communities in the Rathfarnham and in South Dublin to delve into their great historical heritage. It is my earnest hope that people of all ages in Rathfarnham area and in South Dublin will be enriched by what Paddy Healy has presented to us.

I would like to thank the late Paddy Healy's brother, Peter for making Paddy's work available to one and all. What a wonderful legacy Paddy Healy has left us in this book and in his other writings.

Lastly I must give credit to Kieran Swords of Tallaght Library and to all others who are making Paddy Healy's work available to the public.

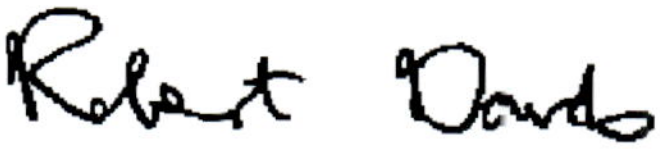

Mayor, South Dublin County
April 2005

The Crest or Coat of Arms of South Dublin County reflects the ancient history of the area, its geographic features and the work of the Council.

The motto "Ag seo ár gCúram – This we hold in Trust" is an admonition to value, to preserve and to develop the economic, social, environmental, cultural and heritage assets of the area both for our own time and for future generations.

Chamber of Commerce of Ireland
Excellence in Local Government
Economic Development Award 2004

Author's Preface

THIS booklet is not primarily intended either for the historian or for the tourist although both may find much of interest within its cover. It is hoped, however that it will prove a convenient source of information to that large body of citizens who are already familiar with the Dublin Hills and who are to be seen on Sundays and holidays travelling the roads and laneways and rambling over high summits and mountain tracks.

The writer, at an early age came under the spell of the mountains and spent many pleasant years exploring this region. A thirst for information sent him to the local and county histories, the archaeological and historical literature and to unpublished material from various sources. This volume which deals only with the area directly accessible from Rathfarnham is the result of twenty five years of observation and investigation.

The main sources of information used were Handcock's *The History and Antiquities of Tallaght,* D'Alton's and Ball's county histories and that masterpiece of decriptive writing and local information, Joyce's "Neighbourhood of Dublin". Periodicals consulted were mainly the *Journal of the Royal Society of Antiquaries of Ireland,* the *Dublin Historical Record* and *Proceedings of the Royal Irish Academy*. Information was obtained also from old guide books and topographical works and from old newspapers, maps and directories. As far as possible the material from these sources was verified on the ground and every effort was made to ensure the accuracy of local information.

Acknowledgements

THANKS are due to a number of people. Firstly, to the late Paddy Healy for his meticulous research, his informative writings and his important collection of slides and photographs which have formed this book. Initial access to Paddy's collection of manuscripts and slides was graciously facilitated and supported by a number of people, most notably Michael Fewer and Con Manning. Síle Coleman of the County Library in Tallaght was a great support in preparing the book for publication. John McAleer is responsible for the professional design and layout of the book.

The greatest debt is owed to Peter Healy who in the sharing nature of his late brother Paddy, gave access to Paddy's papers so that others could share Paddy's great knowledge and deep insights.

Rob Goodbody and the Irish Times kindly granted permission to reproduce Paddy Healy — An Appreciation.

Mrs Monica O'Connor, Mrs Kitty Keating and Mr. Pat Cooke of the Pearse Museum kindly permitted images to be used in the book. The Council of trustees of the National Library permitted the reproduction of Frizell's Map of Rathfarnham.

Details were checked with and assistance sought from a number of people who most willingly assisted: Pat Sweeney, Sean Lawless, Carol Hawkins, Maurice Bryan, Dr. Christopher Moriarty, Mary Keenan, Tommy Cowzer. Gerard Lyne, Elizabeth M. Kirwan and Bernard Devaney of the National Library of Ireland were most helpful,

If anyone's name has unwittingly been omitted, please accept an apology and a big thank you for your assistance.

Thank you all — Go raibh míle maith agaibh go léir

Paddy Healy — An Appreciation

PADDY Healy, archaeologist, local historian and friend, has died after a long life devoted to Ireland's past. Through his work on archaeological excavations in Dublin city and elsewhere, his meticulous collection of information, his support of various societies and his encouragement to younger generations, his influence has been widespread and invaluable.

Born in Canada in 1916 of Irish emigrant parents, Paddy moved with his family to Dublin at the age of five. After schooling in Haddington Road and Marino, he studied building construction in Bolton Street College, where his subjects included land surveying and technical drawing; both were to prove important in his later career. After graduation he worked as a silkscreen printer in Modern Display Artists while he took night classes under Sean Keating at the National College of Art.

During the Emergency Paddy served in the Army, then worked as a painter and decorator for a time. An important change came in 1949 when he joined the staff of the Land Commission as a surveyor. After eight years he moved to the Forestry Division, again as a surveyor.

In 1952 he began to attend Professor Seán P. Ó Riordáin's lectures in archaeology in University College Dublin as an occasional student. He joined the UCD Archaeological Society, becoming its vice-president, and his contact with the college led him to work as part of Prof. Ó Riordáin's team on the excavation of the Rath of the Synods at Tara during his annual holidays. In 1967 he joined Breandán Ó Riordáin's team on the second excavation at High Street in Dublin. At this stage Paddy made a major decision to abandon the security of his job with the Forestry Division to work full-time on archaeological excavations. He went on to work on excavations at Winetavern Street in 1969, Christchurch Place between 1972 and 1979, and from 1976 in Fishamble Street.

When the work on the Wood Quay site became controversial, Paddy stood firmly on the side of archaeology. His quiet but determined manner was a great source of encouragement to his colleagues as he sat in on the site, and he was the author of a poem written about the controversy and sold to raise funds for the campaign.

During the 1970s Paddy Healy acted as a contract archaeologist providing advice and working on excavations. Most importantly, he provided lists of monuments and sites of archaeological interest in Co. Dublin in the mid-1970s to assist in the preparation of the County Development Plan and the Action Area Plans which preceded the development of the western new towns of Tallaght, Lucan/Clondalkin and Blanchardstown.

Over the years he wrote papers and articles for a variety of publications, including several in which he described for the first time monuments and artefacts which he had discovered. Some of these were early grave slabs from the Rathdown area of south Dublin and north Wicklow and these became the topic of his MA thesis presented to NUI Galway under the supervision of Professor Etienne Rynne.

Paddy, in turn, was the subject of a publication when 29 colleagues and friends contributed papers in his honour for publication in a book, *Dublin and Beyond the Pale,* edited by Con Manning.

Among the organisations to benefit greatly from his membership were the Old Dublin Society, the Royal Society of Antiquaries, the Dublin Archaeological Society, Friends of Medieval Dublin, the Irish Architectural Archive and the Rathmichael Historical Society.

Paddy Healy was laid to rest on December 11th last in the cemetery at Mount Venus in the Dublin Mountains, close to historical and archaeological sites that he had investigated and overlooking the city which he had loved so much.

R.G. *Irish Times Monday 21st of January 2001*

Contents

Chapter 1

Rathfarnham Road, Village and Castle

THE history of Rathfarnham in so far as we can learn from existing records, began at the time of the Anglo-Norman invasion when in 1199 these lands were granted to Milo le Bret. The name Rathfarnham suggests that a habitation existed before that time but of those who dwelt therein we know nothing. They left no remains of pre-historic burial places, no early churches and no records preserved in the annals.

Even during the centuries immediately following the invasion no event of great importance occurred. The lands were, to some extent, protected from the Irish neighbours by the existence, on the southern side, of the extensive Royal Forest of Glencree, with its inevitable wardens. It was not until this great deer park was overrun by the Clan O'Toole in the fourteenth century that Rathfarnham was exposed to the danger of attack.

There was much activity here during the stormy period of the seventeenth century but early in the following century, gentlemen's residences were being erected in the vicinity. At this period also, with the harnessing of the waters of the Owendoher and other rivers a great industrial drive began, largely in the production of paper. During the early part of the last century a number of these mills changed over to the manufacture of woollen and cotton goods and later still many were converted into flour mills. The introduction of the steam engine superseded the use of water power and as the old buildings fell into disrepair they were in most cases not replaced.

Six inch Ordnance Survey map of Rathfarnham in 1843

The Rathfarnham Road

The road to Rathfarnham according to many writers follows the same route as the Slighe Chualann, the ancient highway, which in the time of St. Patrick was used by travellers from Dublin to Wicklow and Wexford. This road is believed to have crossed the Dodder at the Big Bridge, now Pearse Bridge, and re-crossed it again near Oldbawn, an unnecessarily inconvenient route, considering that a road through Templeogue to Oldbawn would not necessitate a crossing at all. The first record of a bridge being built here was in 1381 and in 1652 it was described by Boate in his *Natural History* as a wooden bridge which "though it be high and strong nevertheless hath several times been quite broke and carried away through the violence of sudden floods". After three bridges had been demolished by the river, between 1728 and 1765, the present structure of one stone arch was erected in the latter year. This was widened on the west side in 1953 when it was renamed in commemoration of the brothers Pearse.

Pearse Bridge, Rathfarnham

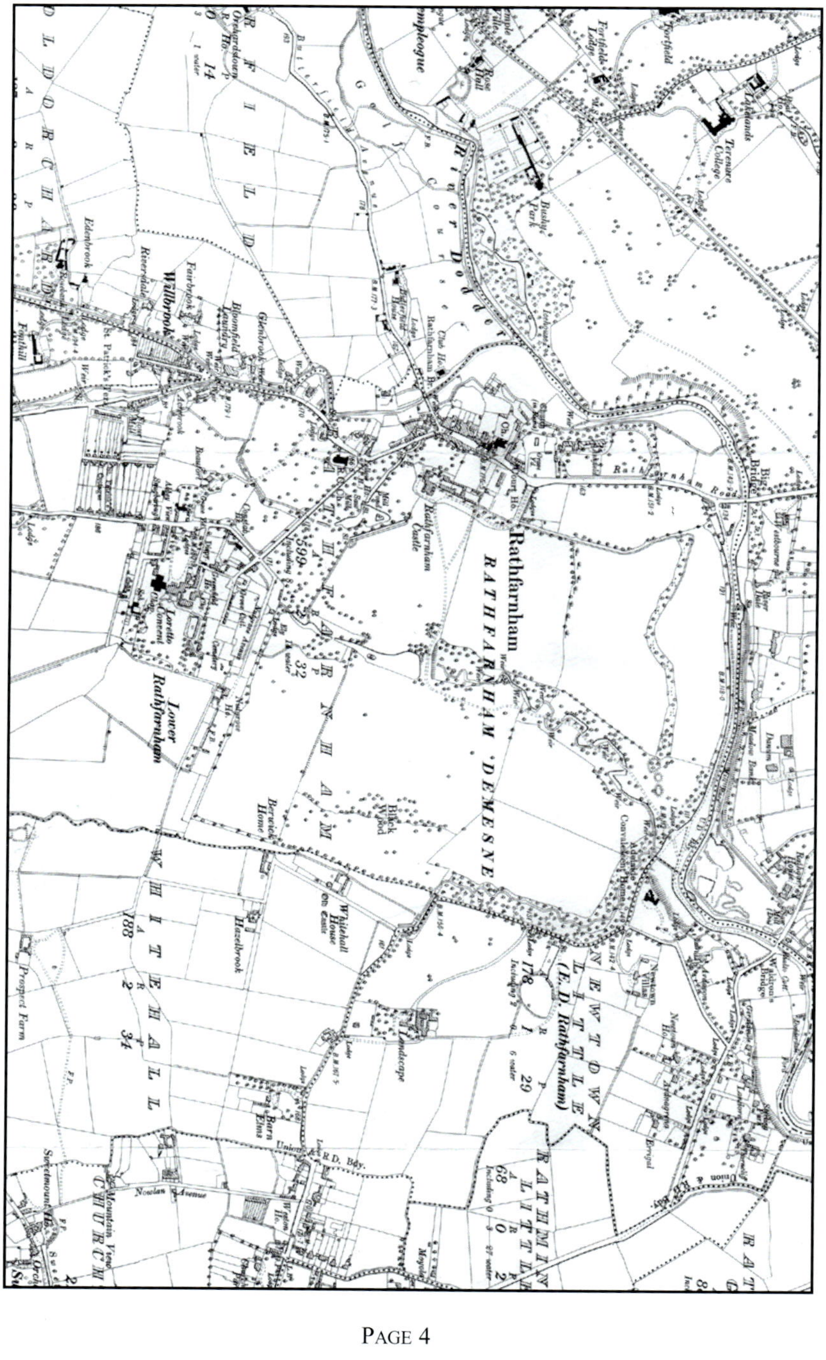

Six inch Ordnance Survey map of Rathfarnham in 1912

In 1912 when the main drainage scheme was being laid to Rathfarnham, a deep cutting was made under the road at this point. At a depth of 23ft below the road level a stone causeway was uncovered nine feet wide and built of great blocks crossing the course of the river. Cut into the surface of the stone were a number of deep parallel grooves, as from the action of wheeled traffic over a long period. This was evidence for the existence here of a busy thoroughfare before the construction of the earliest bridge.

The low-lying fields on the west side of the road, just beside the bridge were formerly occupied by a mill pond and extensive mill buildings. On a map by Frizell dated 1779 it is called the "Widow Clifford's mill and mill holding" and in 1843 it is named the "Ely Cloth Factory." It was then owned by a Mr. Murray but passed in 1850 into the hands of Mr. Nickson, who converted it into a flour mill. His family continued in occupation until 1875 when John Lennox took over. In 1880 this mill closed down, the buildings were demolished and not a trace of it now remains.

Ashfield, later known as Brookvale is an 18th Century Glebe House.

The next house on the same side, Ashfield, was occupied by the Protestant clergy during the eighteenth century. In the early part of the last century it was the home of Sir William Cusac Smith, Baron of the Exchequer and from 1841 of the Tottenham Family who continued to reside there down to 1913. After this it was occupied by the Brooks of Brooks Thomas Ltd. down to about fifty years ago when the estate was divided up and houses built along the main road. A new road was later built along the side of the house and named Brookvale after the last occupants.

Lower Dodder Road

To the east of Pearse Bridge is the lower Dodder Road, following the course of the Dodder downstream to Orwell Bridge. Facing an open green space on this road is a fine entrance gateway, built in the form of a triumphal arch and originally leading to Rathfarnham Castle. The erection of this gateway is attributed to Henry Loftus, Earl of Ely from 1769 to 1783 who also was responsible for the classical work at the castle itself. This is named "the new gate" on Frizell's map of 1779. After the division of the estate in 1913 this became the entrance to the Castle Golf Club but it was later abandoned in favour of the more direct Woodside Drive.

Lord Ely's Gate was erected around 1770.

In 1841 this place was the scene of a brutal murder, when the body of an Italian named Garlibardo was found lying on the open ground in front of the gate. Although arrests were made at the time no one was convicted of the murder. The spot was later marked with a cross.

The Motte and Bailey

To the west of this gate is a high and narrow ridge of ground about 50 feet high which is formed between the river Dodder and the stream which flows through the Rathfarnham Estate. With a certain amount of cutting and scraping this ridge has been converted into a defensive earthwork of the motte and bailey type, which were introduced by the Normans in the twelfth century and constructed as a temporary measure until such time as stone castles and bawn walls could be built. They consisted normally of a high and steep sided earthen mound, surrounded by a deep ditch and with a flat summit upon which a wooden tower was built. Against one side of this mound a larger and lower platform was made, also enclosed by a bank and ditch.

The motte and bailey in 1977.

The high mound was for the commander and the larger enclosure for his troops. In the case of the one at Rathfarnham which was probably built by Milo le Bret in 1199, the existing ridge was adopted. The narrow end was cut off by a deep cutting and the soil used to raise the top of the motte. Another cutting was made between the motte and the bailey and where the ridge widened, the bailey was formed and again isolated from the rest of the ridge by another deep cutting. The top of the motte is about 10 yards wide and the bailey is oval in shape and about 23 yards long.

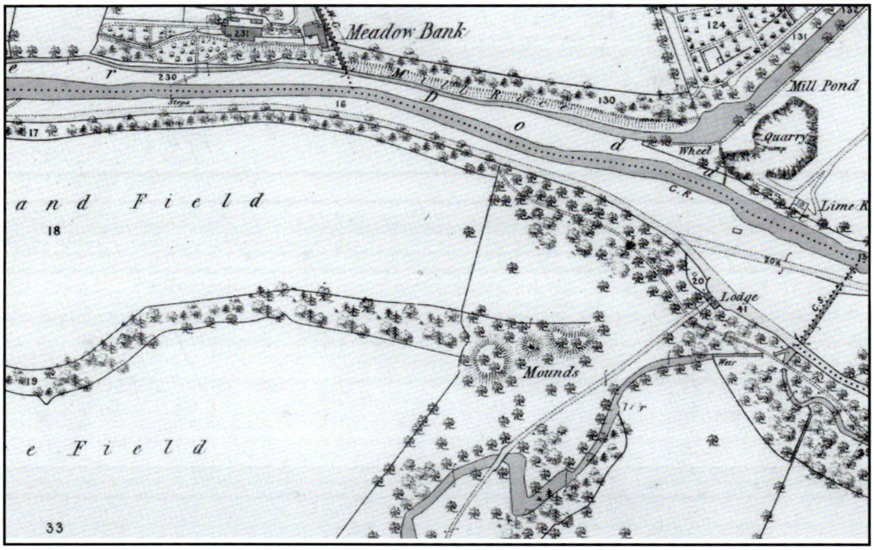

Map shows the mounds of the motte and bailey.

The Old Graveyard

Next to Ashfield is the old graveyard containing the ruins of a church which was dedicated to Saints Peter and Paul. This was a medieval church and was used for Protestant worship down to 1795 when it was found to be too small for the congregation and a new one was erected a short way off. The end walls of the old church are still standing, the west gable containing a bell turret and the east pierced by a chancel arch, the chancel itself having disappeared. The north wall is gone and all that remains of the south wall is an arched opening.

Ruins of church in Rathfarnham graveyard. Captain Kelly's grave s on the left.

Near the entrance to the burial ground is the grave of Capt. James Kelly, an old fenian who was associated with the rising of 1867. He was organiser for the Rathfarnham district and was known in the area as "The Knight of Glendoo". On one occasion when he was on the run he was hiding in the cellar of his business premises in Wicklow St. when it was raided by police. An employee named James Fitzpatrick who strongly resembled Capt. Kelly in appearance was arrested in error and was tried and sentenced to six months imprisonment, which he served without betraying his identity. Capt. Kelly died on 8th March 1915 in his seventieth year.

On the opposite side of the road are Crannagh Park and Crannagh Road, Rathfarnham Park and Ballytore Road, all built on part of the old Rathfarnham Estate. In the garden of a house formerly named "Tower Court" in Crannagh Road is an ancient circular pigeon house, a relic of Lord Ely's occupation of Rathfarnham Castle. The entrance to this curious structure is by a low door on level with the ground and the inside is lined from floor to roof with holes for the pigeons. A floor of more recent date has been inserted half way up, so as to make two rooms, and a second door broken through the wall at that level.

Circular pigeon house.

Rathfarnham Castle

On the east side of the main street and formerly approached through a rather ungraceful gothic archway is the castle of Rathfarnham, its great walls towering over the smaller houses in the village. This ancient fortress was erected by Adam Loftus, Protestant Archbishop of Dublin who was granted in 1583 what was then described as a waste village. His new castle was not long built when in 1600 it had to withstand an attack by the Wicklow clans and again in 1641 it was able to hold out against the Confederate army when the surrounding country was overrun. In 1649, a few days before the battle of Rathmines, the castle, which was garrisoned by the Parliamentary forces, was stormed and taken by the Royalists but they probably evacuated it again when Ormonde withdrew with his army to Kilkenny.

Rathfarnham Castle in 1977.

The property, of which the Loftus family had resumed possession, passed by marriage to the Whartons who sold it in 1723 to the Right Hon. William Connolly, Speaker of the Irish House of Commons, for £62,000. In 1742 the castle was sold to Dr. Hoadly, Archbishop of Armagh, and on his death four years later it passed to his son-in-law Bellingham Boyle. In 1767 he sold the property to Nicholas Loftus, second Earl of Ely, a descendant of Adam Loftus, the original builder of the castle.

This young man died within a few years, probably as an indirect result of great hardships which he had suffered in his youth, and the estate passed to his uncle, Hon. Henry Loftus, who was created Earl of Ely in 1771. This nobleman was responsible for the conversions of the medieval fortress into a Georgian mansion. The narrow loopholes were enlarged and the battlements replaced by a coping with ornamental urns. A semi-circular extension was added to the east side and an entrance porch approached by steps, on the north.

Another view of Rathfarnham Castle in 1977.

The interior was decorated in accordance with the tastes of the period and the leading artists, including Angelica Kauffman, employed in the work. Writers of the period who visited the house have left extravagant descriptions of its splendour. Henry Loftus died in 1783 and was succeeded by his nephew Charles Tottenham. He subsequently became Marquis of Ely, and later, as a reward for his vote at the time of the Union, Earl of Ely.

The entrance hall, Rathfarnham Castle from Ball's A History of the County Dublin.

Early in the nineteenth century the family sold the estate and removed their valuable possessions to Loftus Hall in Wexford. The lands were then used for dairy farming and the castle allowed to fall into disrepair. In 1852, it was bought by the Lord Chancellor, Francis Blackbourne, whose family continued to reside there until 1913. In that year the estate was sold and divided. The eastern part became a golf links. The castle and the south western portion were bought by the Jesuit Order and the north western part was devoted to housing.

The original castle consisted of a square building four stories high with a projecting tower at each corner, the walls of which were an average of 5 feet thick. On the ground level are two vaulted apartments divided by a wall nearly 10 feet thick which rises to the full height of the castle. On level with the entrance hall were the library and reception rooms and above this the former ballroom, later converted into a chapel.

To the north of the castle was a long vaulted chamber formerly known as Cromwell's Court or Fort. This was apparently a barn or storehouse erected in connection with the castle farm and like the castle itself had narrow loop holes in its 5 foot thick walls. In 1922 it was incorporated in the new retreat house, to which it formed the ground story and its character concealed from the outside by a uniform covering of cement plaster.

Cromwell's Fort, Rathfarnham Castle.

Not far from the Golf Club House was an attractive little temple built of stone and brick, another relic of Lord Ely's occupation of Rathfarnham. It was rather out of repair but if it had been restored it would have added much to the charm of this part of the links. Unfortunately, by decision of the committee, it was demolished in 1979.

1977 picture of the temple sited on the lands of Rathfarnham Castle. The structure was demolished in 1979.

In 1986 the Jesuits sold Rathfarnham Castle, but before leaving they removed the stained glass windows, made in the famous Harry Clarke studios, from the chapel.

Rathfarnham Village

In the castle grounds were several fish ponds which were supplied by a mill race taken from the stream which rises up at Kilmashogue and flows down through Grange Golf Links and St. Enda's. This served several mills before entering the fish ponds, whence it ran through the golf links while a smaller branch was conducted under the road to the flour mills which stood at the corner of Butterfield Lane. Described in 1836 as Sweetman's Flour Mills it frequently changed hands before it closed down in 1887. It was later operated as a saw mill. The dry mill race can still be seen here on the north side of Butterfield Avenue.

Rathfarnham Protestant Parish Church on the Main St. was built in 1795 to replace the church in the old graveyard which had become inadequate for the congregation. Beside the church is the old school house which dates from early in the nineteenth century.

Lower Main Street Rathfarnham in the early 1900s.

Immediately adjoining is Church Lane at the corner of which is a bank built on the site of an R.I.C. barracks which was burned down during the Troubles. In the lane is an old blocked up doorway of an early eighteenth century type.

Blocked up doorway in Church Lane in 1977.

Church Lane leads to Woodview cottages which are built partly on the site of an old paper mill. The mill race previously mentioned passed under Butterfield Lane to the paper mill and continued on below Ashfield to turn the wheel of the Ely Cloth Factory. It was later turned into the Owendoher river at Woodview Cottages but down to recent years when the new road was made to Templeogue the old mill race could still be traced through the grounds of Ashfield where its dry bed was still spanned by several stone bridges.

The paper mill, of which some old walls and brick arches still survive, has been described as the oldest one in Ireland but there does not appear to be any evidence to support this. The earliest reference to a paper mill here was in 1719 when a petition for financial aid was presented by William Lake of Rathfarnham but we hear of one at Milltown as far back as 1694. In 1751, paper was made here by William and Thomas Slater whose works were destroyed by fire in 1775. Archer's survey of 1801 mentions two paper mills here, Freemans and Teelings, and both D'Alton in 1836 and Lewis in 1837 state that one paper mill was still working and from 1836 to 1839 the name Henry Hayes, Rathfarnham Mill appears in the directories. If this can be identified with the mill at Woodview cottages it must have become idle soon afterwards as it is designated "Old Mill" on the 1843 edition of the O.S. map. In 1854 when this mill had neither water wheel nor machinery, an attempt was made to re-open it for the manufacture of paper but it came to nothing.

Ruins of old mill, Rathfarnham c. 1977.

At the end of the main street the road to Lower Rathfarnham passes on the right the site of the earliest Constabulary barracks which closed down in 1890 when the establishment was transferred to a house named Leighton Lodge near Loreto Abbey.

Chapter 2

Rathfarnham Lower and Whitehall

THE Catholic church of the Annunciation was erected in 1878 to replace the old chapel in Willbrook Road. Outside the church door is a primitive type of font on a pedestal bearing the inscription:

FONT USED IN MASS HOUSE OF PENAL TIMES
IN PARISH OF RATHFARNHAM FROM 1732

The appearance of this font would suggest that it was originally a stone bullaun and dated to a period much earlier than the penal times.

Font outside the Church of the Annunciation.

On the opposite corner is the well-known Yellow House, a licensed premises built on the site of an inn of the same name which is marked on Taylor's map of 1816. A tradition has been recorded by Mr. Hammond that in 1798 it was owned by a Michael Eades, who sheltered wanted men in his house. It was also frequented by the soldiers of the Rathfarnham Guard whose careless talk was carefully noted by the United Irishmen hiding on the premises. In 1804 when the truth came to be known, the place was wrecked by the same military.

Yellow House and Church of the Annunciation, Rathfarnham in 1977.

The Yellow House was in the news again in the 1940s when two men broke into the premises on Little Christmas night. When the alarm was raised they took refuge in the low-lying gardens beside the bridge over the Owendoher river. When two gardaí spotted them and vaulted over the wall in pursuit they opened fire and seriously injured the nearest pursuer. Despite this the gardaí continued in the chase and coming to grips they were attacked with a carpenter's brace and battered into unconsciousness, while the culprits escaped down the river. The two gardaí eventually recovered and a man was later arrested, charged with attempted murder and sentenced to twenty-one years imprisonment. The two gardaí Michael Flynn and John Tighe who were promoted to the rank of sergeant were very properly awarded the Scott Gold Medal for their courage.

Nutgrove Avenue

A short distance past the church is Nutgrove Avenue, widened and extended in the 1950s to link up with Churchtown. The old quiet tree shaded avenue has been completely swept away, along with the

Nutgrove school.

"narrow lanes" a cramped passage bounded on both sides by towering walls and full of right angled bends, which wended its crooked course between Loreto Convent cemetery and the garden of Nutgrove House. A massive gateway stood at the entrance to this avenue down to about 1911 which bore the inscription "Nutgrove School Established 1802".

In 1839 this school was under the supervision of Mr. Philip Jones, who continued to hold the post of principal until 1866 when the position was held by Mrs. Anne Jones. In 1876 the school closed down and the house was occupied as a private residence by various tenants down to recent years when it became the headquarters of the parish council. The new avenue was laid through the former school grounds and the house shorn of its ornamental gardens stood with its front against the footpath. At some time this house had been disfigured with a rather unsightly concrete porch and the old brickwork covered with cement plaster, which concealed the fact that this was a very interesting eighteenth century building containing a fine stairs and coved ceilings with good plaster decoration. Unfortunately the house was allowed to fall into very bad repair and eventually had to be demolished.

Joyce in his *The Neighbourhood of Dublin* states that this house was at one time the dower house of Rathfarnham Castle but in this he is almost certainly mistaken, as Frizell's map of 1779 shows that it was outside the estate. It is possible that he confused it with the other old house on the opposite side of the avenue which was formerly named Ely Cottage, later altered to Ely Lodge, and which was shown as within the boundary of the estate. This house was in very bad repair but was restored in the late 1970s in a very tasteful manner. The house is now named Ely House.

Ely House, Nutgrove Avenue was formerly known as Ely Lodge.

Whitehall

The Bottle Tower from Whitehall Road.

The first avenue on the left, beyond Nutgrove House, is Whitehall Road where stands that curious structure known as the Bottle Tower or Hall's Barn. This was built by Major Hall in 1742 in imitation of the better constructed Wonderful Barn erected about the same period near Leixlip. The floors and other timber work have long disappeared and the winding stone steps are not considered safe to ascend. While the ground floor may have been used as a barn, the first and second floors appear to have been residential as they are both fitted with fireplaces. A smaller structure behind the barn, built on somewhat similar lines was a pigeon house.

The Bottle Tower and Pigeon House

The old house named Whitehall which was demolished some years ago stood adjacent to the barn. It was also built by Major Hall about the same time.

Whitehall.

In 1778 it was the residence of Rev. Jeremy Walsh, curate of Dundrum, and in 1795 it was converted into a boarding house by Mr. Michael Kelly. A newspaper advertisement in 1816 invites enquiries from prospective visitors. In a description written in the last century the old fashioned kitchen and panelled staircase are specially noted.

Berwick House

The tall house at the bend in the road, until recently occupied by the De la Salle Brothers, seems to be identical with a house named Waxfield where the death is recorded in 1766 of Mr. John Lamprey. In 1836 it was known as Hazelbrook, a name which was later transferred to the nearby milk bottling plant and ice cream venture. From 1844 to 1899 it was known as Bachelor's Hall, after which it became the headquarters of a charitable institution under the name of Berwick Home. In 1944 it again became a private residence and the name was changed to Berwick House.

Berwick House in 1977.

Loreto Abbey

The imposing buildings of Loreto Abbey in Lower Rathfarnham form a landmark visible for many miles south of the city. The mansion which now forms the centrepiece of the group was built by Mr. William Palliser about 1725. No expense was spared in its construction and decoration, as can still be judged by the beautifully preserved interior, the polished mahogany and, in one room, embossed leather wallpaper. William Palliser died in 1768 without issue and Rathfarnham House passed to his cousin the Rev. John Palliser, who was rector of the parish. After his death in 1795 the house was purchased by George Grierson, the King's Printer, who resided here for a few years. When Grierson removed to his new abode in Woodtown the house remained unoccupied for some years until in 1821 it was purchased by Most Rev. Dr. Murray for the newly founded Loreto Order.

Rathfarnham House is part of the Loreto Abbey complex.

The foundress Rev. Mother Mary Frances Teresa Ball made many improvements to the place. She is said to have added a storey to the old house although there is no evidence from the exterior to support this. Many additions have been made over the years, the church was built in 1840, the novitiate in 1863 and six years later the part named St. Joseph's wing which contains the concert hall and refectory. St. Anthony's wing was erected in 1896, St. Francis Xavier's in 1903 and the Lisieux building in 1932 for the accommodation of visiting prelates to the Eucharistic Congress. In 1999 the boarding school closed down and on the 15th August 2000, the last sisters left and moved to the newly constructed Loreto House.

The drawing room, Loreto Abbey from Ball's A History of the County Dublin, was preserved in its original condition by the Loreto Order.

The Ponds

Loreto Terrace on the north side of the Abbey was formerly known as The Ponds, a name originating apparently from the large pond which two hundred years ago occupied the low lying field between Loreto Terrace and Nutgrove Avenue. This area was described in

The Ponds, Rathfarnham (Courtesy of Mrs. Monica O'Connor).

Joyce's *Neighbourhood of Dublin* in 1912 as "the dilapidated locality known as the Ponds" but it has since been largely rebuilt. An old photograph from Mr. Larry O'Connor's collection shows what it looked like at that time.

The last of the old houses was demolished in the 1950s. It was a very early eighteenth century gabled residence named Grove Cottage and was probably the oldest occupied house in Dublin.

This place was the scene of a skirmish at the outbreak of the rising of 1798. The insurgents of the south county assembled at the Ponds on 24th May 1798 under the leadership of David Keely, James Byrne, Edward Keogh and Ledwich. The two latter had been members of Lord Ely's yeomanry but had taken to the field with the United Irishmen. The insurgents were attacked by the local yeomanry corps but were able to defend themselves and the yeomanry were forced to retreat. A party of regular troops were then sent against them and a stiff encounter took place. A number of the insurgents were killed or wounded and some prisoners taken including Keogh and Ledwich. The survivors retreated to join up with a party from Clondalkin and a further engagement took place at the turnpike on the Rathcoole road where the enemy were successfully repulsed.

Grove Cottage, The Ponds, Rathfarnham.

Church of the Annunciation and the Yellow House, Rathfarnham in the early 1960s.

The site of Nutgrove School c. 1977.

Chapter 3

Grange Road to Harold's Grange and Taylor's Grange

THE road to Harold's Grange continues southward from Loreto Abbey past some very old houses. The first is Washington Lodge, its attractive eighteenth century facade hidden by a shrubbery. On the opposite side on Convent Lane stood Snugborough which had its gable end to the road. In recent years new avenues have been laid out here on both sides of the road.

Snugborough, Grange Road in 1977. This house was recently replaced by an apartment block.

Washington Lodge, Grange Road in 1977.

Barton Drive, on the left, occupies the site of a house named Barton Lodge.

On the other side is Silveracre, once the home of Dr. Henthorn Todd, Professor of Hebrew in T.C.D., who was connected by marriage with the Hudson family of the adjoining estate of

Silveracre in 1977.

Hermitage. He was well known as an Irish scholar and was the editor and translator of a number of Irish documents as well as the author of a life of St. Patrick. He died here in 1869. About the middle of the last century the name of the house was changed to Silverton but it was later changed back to the original Silveracre. Most of the land is now built on. It was also the home in the early part of twentieth century of Surgeon Croly, who founded Baggot St. Hospital.

St Enda's

The next estate on the same side is Hermitage or St. Enda's, the former home of Padraig Pearse and later of his sister Miss Margaret Pearse. The house, which is entirely faced with cut granite and has an imposing stone portico, was occupied in the eighteenth century by Edward Hudson, an eminent dentist. He had a passion for Irish antiquities which he demonstrated in an unusual way by the erection of a number of romantic ruins around the estate. Inside the boundary wall near the entrance gate he built a small watch tower and further along, a hermit's cave, a dolmen, a ruined abbey and beside a deep well, a tiny chamber with stone bench and narrow

Pictured left: Watch Tower and right: Hermit's Cave and Dolmen.

fireplace. At the corner of the road to Whitechurch the loopholed and crenellated structure known as the Fortification, or Emmet's Fort was another of his creations.

South of the house he put up a grotto surmounted by a tall pillar stone, a Brehon's chair and a fanciful construction consisting of two great boulders, one balanced on top of the other, which has since been demolished.

Just inside the boundary wall he cut an inscription in Ogham on the two faces of a large rock. When the letters are translated they read:

RIDENT VICINI GLEBASETS A KH A MOVENTEM
EDUARDUM HUDSON

Picture left: Ogham Stone and right: Obelisk

Picture left: Emmet's Fort and right: Temple-like structure.

In the pretty glen adjoining the Whitechurch road he erected a sort of temple with several small chambers and flights of steps. The estate was at that time known as the Fields of Odin and is so called on maps of the period.

Within the grounds also, at the corner nearest to Whitechurch is an obelisk, stated to have been erected by a former owner, Major Doyne, over the grave of a horse that carried him through the battle of Waterloo. The date however of Major Doyne's occupation does not support this. Unlike the constructions of Edward Hudson, which were purposely of the roughest material, this monument was of cut

St. Enda's, formerly known as Hermitage is now the home of the Pearse Museum.
Courtesy of the Pearse Museum

stone with small moulded pillars. Unfortunately the heavy hand of the vandal descended on it, toppled it from its base and smashed the supporting pillars. It has since been re-erected, leaving out the pillars.

Edward Hudson was succeeded by his son William Elliot Hudson, who was born here in 1796. A distinguished scholar, he was a friend of Thomas Davis and Gavin Duffy and was a patron of Irish literature and art. Shortly before his death in 1857 he endowed the Royal Irish Academy with a fund for the publication of its Irish Dictionary and he also left the Academy Library a valuable collection of books.

From 1840 to 1858 Hermitage was the home of Richard Moore, Attorney General, and in 1859 it came into the possession of Major Richard Doyne, stated to be a veteran of Waterloo. From 1872 to 1885 it was occupied by George Campbell, merchant of 58 Sackville St., and after lying vacant for a few years it was tenanted by Major Philip Doyne of the 4th Dragoon Guards. In 1891 Colonel Frederick le Mesurier, barrister is returned as occupier and in 1899 Mr. William Woodburn.

St. Enda's College was founded by Padraig Pearse in 1909 and was at first housed in Cullenswood House, Ranelagh. Pearse felt that the confined surroundings of this house gave no scope for the outdoor

Drawing room, St. Endas.

life that should play so large a part in the education of youth, so in 1910 he leased Hermitage from Mr. Woodburn and moved his college here. A long billiard room was converted into a study hall and chapel, the drawing room became a dormitory and the stables opening off an enclosed square became class rooms.

In *The Story of a Success* Pearse tells of the realisation of one of his life's ambitions and it was from here that he set off for the city on his bicycle for the last time on Easter Sunday 1916. After the rising the college continued to function under the care of Miss Margaret Pearse until it finally closed down in 1935. After the death of Miss Pearse in 1968 St. Enda's passed into the hands of the state and has since been opened as a public park.

Priory

Directly opposite to St. Enda's was Priory, the home of John Philpot Curran, at the time of Emmet's rising. The house was formerly named Holly Park but when Curran bought it in 1790 he changed the name to Priory. Here he lived for 27 years at the peak of his fame and here he was to endure the tragic events which cast a shadow on his private life. First, the untimely death of his daughter Gertrude, followed by the loss of his wife, who left him for another man, and lastly the discovery of the association of his daughter Sarah with Robert Emmet.

Gertrude Curran died in 1792 at the age of 12 as the result of a fall from a window. Curran had her buried in the grounds of the Priory and over the grave he placed a recumbent slab on which was fixed a metal plate bearing the inscription:

Here lies the body of Gertrude Curran

fourth daughter of John Philpot Curran

who departed this life October 6th 1792

Age twelve years.

Priory, Grange Road, from Footprints of Emmet by J.J. Reynolds (1903).

Gertrude Curran's grave, Priory from Footprints of Emmet by J.J. Reynolds (1903).

The position of the grave was clearly marked on the early editions of the Ordnance Survey maps. It was about midway along the northern boundary of the corner field facing the Fortification, on the north side of the boundary bank and a few yards from it. It was formerly enclosed by a grove of trees, which can be seen in J. J. Reynold's photograph of 1903 but these were cut down about 1928. Some time later the stumps were dug out and the stone slab broken up and thrown on the adjoining bank. The metal plate had already been taken by souvenir hunters.

Fragments of Gertrude Curran's grave slab in 1979.

It was Sarah Curran's desire to be buried here also but to this her father would not agree as he had come in for criticism on the previous occasion for burying his daughter in unconsecrated ground.

In this district nearly every ancient site is associated in tradition with either Sarah Curran or Robert Emmet and it is not surprising therefore to find that this burial place has been suggested as the last resting place of Robert Emmet. This tradition goes back for well over a century and it is rather surprising that this site was not investigated when the search for Emmet's remains was being made at places a great deal less accessible and no less improbable.

In October 1979 the opportunity offered itself to carry out this investigation. The Priory estate was being developed and heavy machinery moved in to lay the roads and sewers. Mrs. Bernadette Foley of nearby Barton Drive drew attention to the need to carry out this work before the site was buried for ever under a concrete jungle. With the cooperation of Messrs Gallaghers, the developers, a small group undertook to investigate the site. First the exact location was checked on the original large scale manuscript map in the Ordnance Survey, next the field was carefully chained and the site marked to within a few feet and then a narrow trench 3 feet deep was dug through where the burial should have been. The result was a complete blank. A second and a third trench were cut at intervals until a large area had been investigated without finding any burial, timber, brick or stone.

The developers then offered to investigate further with the excavator and carefully cleared an area of 20 yards long and 10 yards wide to a depth of 4 feet without finding any sign of disturbance. They then deepened this area by another two feet with no better result. All the accounts of the burial state that it was made in a vault and it is therefore surprising and disappointing that no evidence whatever was found and there does not seem to be any obvious explanation for it. I would like at this stage to pay tribute to the interest shown in this work by the staff of Messrs Gallaghers Ltd. especially the foreman Mr. Leslie Black.

The author pictured with spade was part of the team which undertook an archaeologiical investigation at Priory in 1979 in search of Gertrude Curran's grave.

Priory was occupied by the Curran family down to 1875 and subsequently by the Taylors until 1923. At the beginning of the century the house and gardens were still in good repair but after the Taylor's time the place was neglected. And all that remains of the house are the ruins on the green in Hermitage Estate.

Adjacent to Priory was a mound with a tree growing out of it.

In one of the fields behind Priory was an artificial mound with a tree growing on top of it. There is no information available about this and it may have been a prehistoric burial site. This mound was demolished in 1986 when houses were being built on an adjoining site. An underground passage was exposed which was followed for a considerable way by local children.

Harold's Grange

Beyond Priory and the Fortification are a number of old residences, Eden, Rathfarnham Park, Highfield Manor and Grange House, and on the other side of the road the well wooded demense of Marlay. All these properties are in the extensive townland of Harold's Grange, which in former times comprised part of the lands of the powerful Harold family. The Harolds were settled here in the thirteenth century and occupied it, first as tenants of St. Mary's Abbey and later of Lord Upper Ossory. They became responsible for the protection of the Pale in the neighbourhood of their home but they were an independant and often lawless family and did not hesitate to use violence against those whom they were expected to protect. In the reign of Henry VIII they had a small thatched castle and a watermill on these lands. Early in the seventeenth century they severed their connection with Harold's Grange but continued to hold Kilmashogue until dispossessed of their rights after 1641.

Marlay

At the beginning of the eighteenth century many improvements were carried out on the lands of Harold's Grange by Mr. Thomas Taylor. After his death in 1727 the place was occupied by his sons, one of whom, Alderman Thomas Taylor, was Lord Mayor of Dublin in 1750. Soon after his death in 1763 the estate passed to the Right Hon. David La Touche, whose wife was a daughter of Rev. George Marlay, Bishop of Dromore, in whose honour the name of the place was changed to Marlay. The Taylors had built a mansion and laid out ornamental gardens and had enclosed an extensive deer park on the northern slope of Kilmashogue Mountain. The house was enlarged by La Touche in 1781. There was formerly in the grounds a mausoleum and monument to the memory of Elizabeth, Countess of Lanesborough, a sister of John David La Touche. This was situated to the south east of the lake, it was in ruins in 1871 and has since been removed. In the first quarter of the present century Marlay was the home of Robert Tedcastle of the well known Dublin business house and for the thirty years prior to its sale had been the property of the Love family. Marlay Demense was purchased by Dublin County Council in 1972 and opened as a fine public park in 1975. The adjoining house named Marlay Grange was erected in 1874 by Hon. Hercules Rowley J.P.

Marlay House today.

Glensouthwell

Grange Road continues for nearly a mile to skirt the boundary wall of Marlay as far as the cross roads at Taylor's Grange beyond which it terminates at a group of farmhouses where there was formerly an old passage leading to Stackstown. Prior to the development of the M50 motorway, the road to Kilmashogue along College Road, passed the entrance to Glensouthwell which is now known as Danesmoate. Within the grounds is a delightful glen known as Little Dargle, watered by a brook which rises near the Ticknock rifle range. This house was built in the eighteenth century by the Southwell family and in 1787 was the residence of Capt. William Southwell. Throughout the following century it was occupied by the Ponsonbys, down to 1896 and later by Professor Stanley Lane

Glensouthwell, now known as Danesmoate.

Poole, the author of a number of works on Oriental art and numismatics. For many years down to 1946 it was the home of Lieutenant Algernon Gainsford of the Seafort Highlanders.

An ancient monument known as the Brehon 's Chair, consisting of three tall slabs about nine feet high enclosing a small square space was located in a field which was visible from College Road. It is now located within the housing development on the site. There was formerly another large slab supported by smaller ones lying to the north east but this was unfortunately destroyed about 1876 by blasting. The existing remains are apparently the portal portion of a dolmen type of tomb and the stones which were removed would have been part of the destroyed chamber. A similar type of portal can be seen on a dolmen at Haroldstown in Co. Carlow.

Brehon's Chair.

Beside the stream in the Little Dargle were the remains of a tall narrow tower of which only one wall composed of one jamb of a doorway with a pointed arch was standing in 1977. This building was about nine feet square and around 1900, the remaining wall with its battlements was about twenty five feet high. A little over a hundred and twenty years ago this tower was in a better state of preservation and was surrounded by the old walls of other buildings from which it has been suggested that this was the site of the original Grange of the Harolds. The remaining portion however was of very light construction and quite unsuitable for a building of that period and location, whether intended for domestic or ecclesiastical use. It was probably built in the eighteenth century for the better enjoyment of the view over Dublin Bay.

Remains of tower at Glensouthwell c.1900 and in 1977.

Beside the house is an octagonal building with a cellar underneath. In 1977 it was filled up with boughs and brushwood to prevent cattle falling through but is said to be elliptical in shape and was apparently an ice house. On the other side of the brook there is a fine arched gateway in cut stone leading into the pasture land.

St. Columba's College

Next to Glensouthwell is St. Columba's College, a boarding school for Protestant boys which enjoys a well deserved reputation for the high standard of its students. The fine mansion which now forms the front of the college was formerly named Hollypark and was built toward the end of the eighteenth century by Geffrey Foot of the well known snuff manufacturing family. St. Columba's was founded in 1843 and was at first located at Stackallen House in Co. Meath. In 1849 the college was transferred to this situation and the chapel and other necessary buildings erected. The old house contains some fine panelling, tapestries and antique furniture. In a grove of trees near the tennis court is St. Sabh's holy well about which no information seems to be available. It is in a deep hole faced about with masonry and approached by a flight of steps.

Hollypark is now part of St. Columba's College. (c. 1960).

Cross found on Kilmashogue Mountain.

Nearby is an ancient ice house with its entrance blocked up.

In the chapel is an ancient stone cross which was found about fifty years ago somewhere on the lower slopes of Kilmashogue mountain behind the college. It was brought into the college chapel and has been there ever since. Unfortunately there is no record of the spot where it was found and enquiries have so far failed to elicit any information. This is a great pity, as it must certainly have come from the site of the ancient church of Kilmashogue, which was mentioned by P.W. Joyce and the location of which is now unknown.

Above the back wall of St. Columba's College is a memorial to Volunteer Sean Doyle, erected on the spot where he was shot in 1920. It is against a low masonry wall at the side of a laneway and bears the following inscription:

In Memory of
Sean Ua Dubhgaill Volr.
4th Batt. Engineers I.R.A.
who was shot at Kilmashogue
Co Dublin
19th Sept 1920
by the armed forces of the
British Crown
Aged 19 years
R.I.P.

Memorial to Seán Doyle, Stackstown.

Sean Doyle was the son of Alderman Peadar S. Doyle of Inchicore. On Sunday morning 19th September 1920, he was assembled with a party of No. 3 and No. 4 Coys and 5th Batt Engineers for a demonstration of the use of home made explosive known as war flour. Many of them were unarmed and when a party of military and police surrounded them and called on them to halt, some surrendered and others escaped over the mountain. About forty prisoners were taken and Volunteer Doyle was shot dead. This was one of the first activities of the newly recruited Black and Tans.

From behind the lands of Glensouthwell and St. Columba's College the ground rises with increasing gradient towards the top of Kilmashogue Mountain. Elrington Ball, in his history of the county, states that the barrier of the Pale ran across the north end of

Kilmashogue Hill where remains of it were to be seen in the eighteenth century. This is apparently indicated on Rocque's map of 1760 where the description "old stone wall" is written against a line on the Stackstown side of Kilmashogue.

As far as can be judged from this map, which is not strictly to scale, this line coincides with a stone faced ditch which lies on the east side of the boundary between the townlands of Stackstown and Kilmashogue and which is now within a young forestry plantation. If the identification is correct this must be one of the few remaining portions of the rampart of the Pale.

Portion of the Pale ditch, Kilmashogue.

Chapter 4

Butterfield Avenue

TO the southern end of Rathfarnham village, Butterfield Avenue leads to Templeogue and Firhouse. Formerly known as Butterfield Lane, it retained its rural character down to the middle of this century but housing development, road widening and the removal of dangerous bends have now altered it beyond recognition. In this connection it is interesting to note that on the map made by John Rocque in 1760 only 4 houses are shown on the entire length of the avenue. These four houses are still standing. Down to 1912 the only addition to these was a pair of council houses beside the bridge.

Butterfield Lane from Footprints of Emmet (1903).

Rocque's map of 1760, showing Butterfield Lane.

The fairs of Rathfarnham were formerly held in Butterfield Lane on May 15th, July 10th and October 7th. The former was a cattle fair and that in July for horses and sheep. The fair green was beside the bridge and stretched along the west bank of the Owendoher river but as is the practice throughout the country, the business was not confined to the green but overflowed along the main street and into every lane and alley. At the edge of the green was a lime kiln which is marked on Taylor's map of 1816. Mr. Charles Bunn of Butterfield House owned the lime works here from 1836 to 1848.

Old Orchard House

On the same side of the avenue is Old Orchard House, one of four already mentioned. This name does not appear before 1845, previous to which there were apparently two houses named Butterfield House. It would appear, however, that in 1836 Old Orchard was named Brasvailanne, which was recorded by the Ordnance Survey that year. It is believed by many that this was the house occupied by Robert Emmet in 1803 but historical evidence does not support this.

Old Orchard House.

Butterfield House

On the opposite side of the road and a short way further on is Butterfield House, identified by most historians as the house occupied by Robert Emmet. In order to avoid being arrested before the rising took place, Emmet rented the house in April 1803 under the name of Robert Ellis and lived here with Dowdall, Hamilton and others. Some of the meetings arranged here were attended by Michael Dwyer and some of his men from Glen Imaal. In charge of the housekeeping was Anne Devlin, whose father Brian Devlin had a dairy farm nearby.

On the night of July 23rd, after the rising had been abandoned, Emmet and his party returned to Butterfield Lane but later in the night moved into Brian Devlin's where they remained for a few days.

Butterfield House in 1977.

In the meantime a party of military arrived at Butterfield House to search for Emmet and finding only Anne Devlin at home questioned her about her master, Mr. Ellis. Not getting any satisfaction they tried to force her to speak by prodding her with bayonets and half hanging her but with no better success. Due probably to the uncertainty of their information they let her go but she was later to suffer many years of imprisonment and hardship for her loyalty on this occasion.

In 1843 when Dr. Madden was writing his life of Emmet he brought Anne Devlin, then old and feeble, out in a cab to identify the house. According to his statement she did not at first recognise it as the entrance had been altered but once she identified it and obtained admission she was able to point out the bedrooms occupied by each person. This house was on the right hand side of the lane going from Rathfarnham Road. From here she was also able to see, at some

Probable ruins of Brian Devlin's house, Butterfield.

distance, the house occupied by her father. Many years later another writer, J. J. Reynolds communicated with the owner, Mr. J. Hely Hutchinson, concerning the identification of this house which had been leased to Mr. Ellis in 1803. The house was renovated and partly altered about 1900 and in 1952 the lower portion was extensively damaged by fire.

The farm occupied by Brian Devlin has never been positively identified. The map of 1843 shows only two farms near Butterfield Lane and since it was still standing in that year it must have been one of these.

One was beside the lane 150 yards from Butterfield House and the other was out in the fields and approached by a passage from behind the Yellow House. This would appear to be the most likely one and the historian Dr. Dickson has stated that there is good reason to believe that this was the house. The ruined walls were still standing about 10 years ago but the whole area is now built up and all the old features gone.

Washington House and Orchardstown House

The other two old houses on Butterfield Avenue are close together, near the far end. Washington House, formerly known as Washington Lodge and also as Oulart House is beside the road. It was occupied by a family named Grimwood from the middle of the last century down to 1916. It still retains the original curvilinear gables but the porch appears to be a later addition. A case has also been made identifying this house as the one occupied by Emmet. Orchardstown House which is entered from a byeroad was used as a private lunatic asylum from 1858 to 1892 under the supervision of the Stanley family.

Chapter 5

Rathfarnham to Whitechurch and Kilmashogue

WILLBROOK Road commences beside the Yellow House and passes on the right the parochial house St. Mary's, where the old chapel stood which was replaced in 1878. This was described by the historian D'Alton as a "cruciform edifice with galleries disproportionately low." Just beyond this the first bridge over the Owendoher led to an old house named Glenbrook which was occupied by Thomas A.A. Kirkwood, the dispensary doctor from 1836 to 1847. Adjoining the house was the old dispensary for the sick poor which was founded in 1801. Subscribers of one guinea had the right to nominate one patient and any member out of work through sickness was entitled to 3/- per week and free medical attention. Both house and dispensary were demolished when the area was built upon.

Glenbrook House

The next house was a very old one named Bloomfield. This name dates back at least 170 years. The house became the headquarters of an extensive laundry business and it provides another example of an old country residence giving its title to a great industry. This house has been identified by some historians as the one occupied by Thomas Addis Emmet which is mentioned in Wolfe Tone's diary. Tone records that with Russell he walked out to Rathfarnham to meet Emmet. He was shown a little study of an elliptical form which Emmet was building at the bottom of the lawn, which he said he would consecrate to our meetings if we lived to see our country emancipated. Tone suggested that he should not omit the inclusion of a small wine cellar and he was assured that this amenity was considered to be essential. Before this house was demolished I searched without success for the remains of the elliptical study.

Bloomfield House.

The next house on this side was Fairbrook which has also been demolished and Fairbrook Lawns now occupy the site. In the field outside the house was a curious structure like a little temple with a pillar at each corner. This of course is now gone along with the house.

Temple, Fairbrook House.

Fairbrook House.

Whitechurch Road

At Willbrook the Whitechurch road branches to the east and follows the course of a little river which flows down from Kilmashogue Mountain. On the other side of the road is a partly choked up mill race which was taken from the river higher up to serve the Silveracre Mill. This was named Brooklawn Mill on both Taylor's map of 1816 and on Duncan's of 1821. In 1836 Mark Flower had a pin and wire factory here which was then named Silveracres Mill. This closed down in 1853. The place was then converted into a flour mill by Robert Gibney who also owned the nearby Willbrook Mills. From 1864 to 1893 it was operated by Patrick Gibney, after which it was taken over by Mr. J. E. Madden. Subsequent to 1899 it changed hands frequently and the last tenant was Mr. Murray from 1922 to 1933. The mill has since been demolished but the Mill House and some out offices still remain.

Willbrook Street today.

St. Gatien's, on the other side of the road occupied the site of Willbrook Flour Mills already mentioned. This was Egan's Flour Mills noted by D'Alton in 1836. From 1847 to 1872 it was held by the Gibneys and from 1873 to 1882 by John Garvan. After lying idle for a few years it was incorporated with a dwelling house in 1885 by Mr. J. E. Madden and named St. Gatien's.

Cliff House, some distance further along the road, was formerly named Willmount and in 1847 was the residence of Frank Thorpe Porter, a magistrate and the author of a most entertaining book about Dublin called "Gleanings and Reminiscences".

Mill House and cottages, Whitechurch Road, c. 1960.

Taylor's Lane

The next road on the west side, Taylor's Lane, links up with Ballyboden and about midway along it was Newbrook Mill, where extensive paper manufacturing was carried on for many years. The two nearby residences Newbrook House and Kingston were usually occupied by those engaged in the industry. Mr. John Mansergh who

Kingston, Taylor's Lane.

Taylor's Lane, Ballyboden, c. 1960.

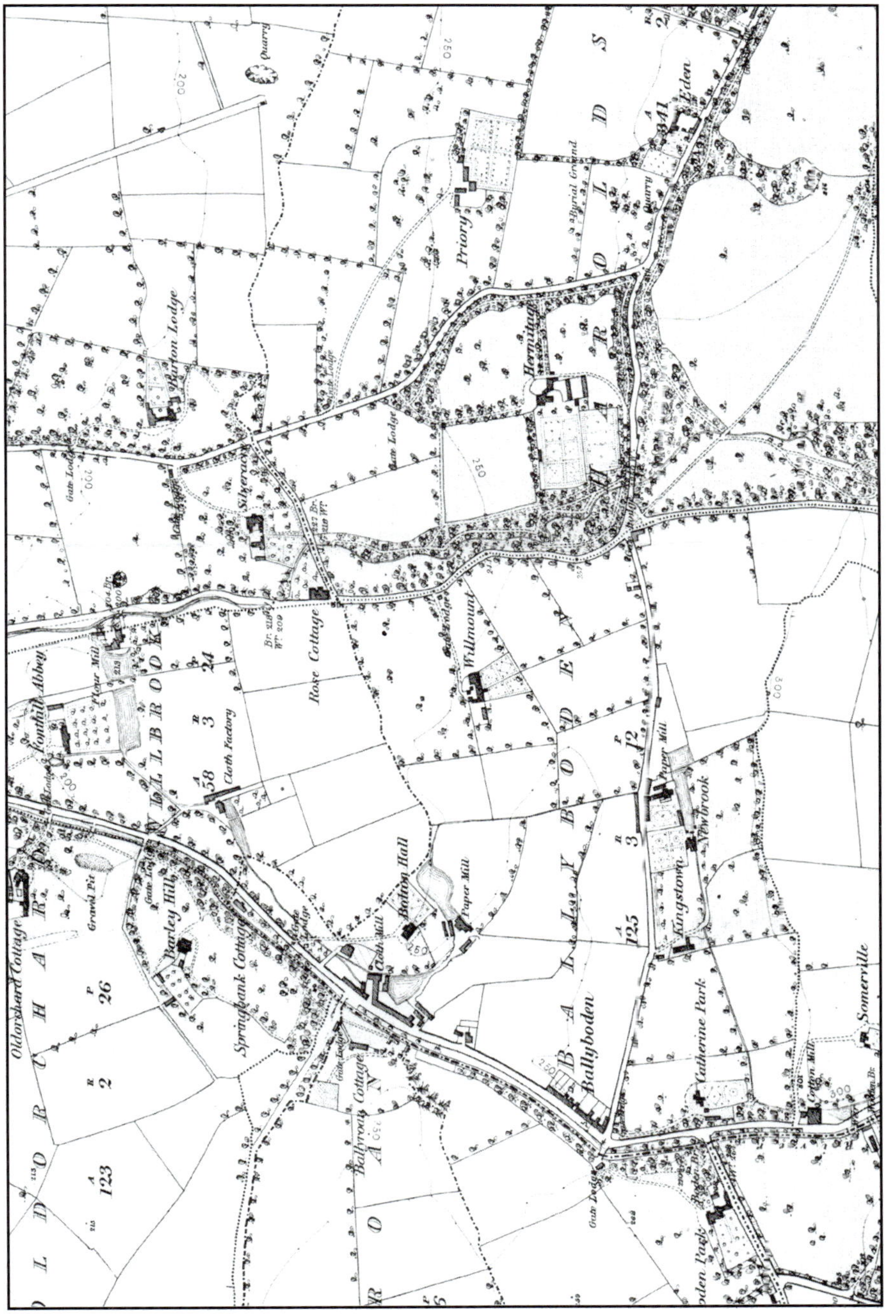

1843 6 inch Ordnance Survey map of the Ballyboden area.

started the business died in 1763. It continued to operate under his name down to 1846 when it was taken over by John McDonagh, in whose family it remained until 1897. At that time James McDonagh, J.P., was residing in Kingston House, since demolished, and Richard and Thomas McDonagh in Newbrook. From 1901 to 1935 the industry was operated by Sir John Irwin who lived during this time at Newbrook House. The mill was extensively damaged by fire in 1942 and has since been demolished.

Chapter 6

Ballyboden Road

BETWEEN Willbrook and Ballyboden there were a number of very old houses, some of which still survive. Edenbrook and Riversdale are both over 160 years old. The latter was the home of W.B. Yeats.

Riversdale, Ballyboden Road in 2000. Riversdale was once the home of W. B. Yeats.

On the other side of the road was Fonthill Abbey, the lands of which were originally built on without interfering with the old house, but unfortunately, it has since been demolished and four houses built on the site. Rosebank which was originally named Old Orchard Cottage has been demolished and the next house Orchardton, formerly named Barley Hill which was enclosed in the middle of a housing estate was vacant and derelict. It was demolished in 1979 and Orchardton Estate built on the site.

Fonthill Abbey.

On the opposite side of the road to Orchardton was the Millbrook Mills otherwise known as the Little Mill. This was shown as a cloth factory on the first Ordnance Survey map of 1837. The diameter of the water wheel was 16 feet. By 1848 this mill was operated as a flour mill by Michael Nicholson or Nickson.

Owners of Millbrook Mills

1851-52	William Evans
1853-54	Michael Nickson
1854-63	James Loughery
1864-79	James Whelan
1880	James Dempsey
1881-82	R.H. Fenwick, engineer, miller and patentee of mill machinery. Worked as an iron mill.
1883-86	Richard Dempsey returned it to a flour mill.
1887	Recorded as dilapidated
1900	Recorded as a ruin of no value

In 1935 Mr. Sean Keating R.H.A., one of our most distinguished painters, had a house built on the site of the mill. Some pieces of old masonry survive including the housing for the mill wheel. The mill stream still runs through the garden, where a small mill wheel for generating electricity has been erected by Mr. Keating's son.

Top: Mill wheel for generating electricity erected by Michael Keating and below: housing for mill wheel of Millmount Mills. (Courtesy of Mrs. Kitty Keating).

In Ballyboden village there were two very old houses. The first, Everton is now demolished. The second, Bolton Hall, which was built in 1837 is still standing. A house is shown at this location on John Rocque's map of 1760.

Bolton Hall.

At the northern end of the village was a woollen cloth mill which belonged to John Reid from at least as far back as 1836 when D'Alton in his *History of the County of Dublin* states that this mill gave employment to about 40.

1874	John and James Reid. Valuation was reduced because of disuse.
1874-96	Woollen cloth mill idle.

The ruins of this mill were demolished in 1950 when the entire village of millworkers' cottages was cleared away and a brand new village of council houses was built on the site.

Within a stone's throw of Reid's Mill and behind Bolton Hall was a paper mill belonging to Nicholas Ryan which is shown on the map of 1837. In 1854 the name is changed to Simon Brown and in 1863 to Joseph P. Brown. The value was reduced in 1876 because of disuse and from that year it was not worked again. Each of these mills had a mill pond and they were all fed by the same mill stream, which was taken from the Owendoher river at Edmonstown where it operated a paper mill and a cotton mill and also Newbrook Papermill in Taylor's Lane before reaching Ballyboden. It continued below the Millbrook Mills to turn the wheel of the flour mill at St. Gatien's before discharging into the Glin stream coming from St. Enda's.

Just south of the village is Boden Bridge, crossing over the Owendoher river. This name was recorded in 1836 but at present it is known only as "Billy's Bridge" and has been so called as far back as can be remembered. None of the local people can say who is commemorated in this title but a tradition which was collected in 1936 by the Irish Folklore Commission may throw some light on it.

Boden Bridge or Billy's Bridge

According to this record an old man named Billy Martin lived in a hut beside the bridge. He used spend his days leaning over the parapet listening to the river. He lived to a great age and when he died people used to say that his ghost was to be seen there.

A hundred years ago there was a continuous line of mill ponds as far as Rockbrook. First on the left was Sherlock's Cotton Mill which was converted into a laundry in 1873 and closed down before 1920. Next, beside the row of mill workers' cottages, was a paper mill operated by Messrs. Dollards from 1848 to 1896. It was later run by the Edmonstown Paper Co., down to about 1912. Reckitt's well known factory, now occupied by Chemserve Ltd., is on the site of another woollen mill which was also operated by John Reid of Ballyboden down to 1892 and by Frederick Clayton & Sons down to 1900.

The Mill House, Edmondstown in 1998 just before its demolition.

On the other side of the river, the new school is built on the site of Newtown Great Paper Mill, founded early in the last century by Mr. Pickering of the London House of Magnay Pickering. He was working it in 1836 but some years later it was operated by Mr. Brown, down to about 1866 when he closed down and went to America. Next are the ruins of Newtown Little Paper Mill, for the building of which Robert Randel got a grant of £300 in 1757. This was converted into a cloth mill before 1836 and seems to have ceased production soon after.

A short distance further up are the remains of Millmount Mill which was mentioned in the will of Benjamin Nunn in 1773. It is mentioned under the same name in Archer's Survey of 1801 but passed later to Messrs. Dollards who operated it in conjunction with their paper mill lower down the river. Here the rags were processed and made into the raw material from which the paper was manufactured. This mill closed down in 1899. The last mill race was the paper mill of Mr. Fry which closed down sometime before 1836. Extensive remains still survive, however, beside the avenue to Rockbrook House.

Rockbrook Village.

The ruins of Fry's Mills, Rockbrook lie beside the avenue to Rockbrook House.

Chapter 7

Rockbrook to Cruagh

THE village of Rockbrook, three miles from Rathfarnham, was formerly an industrial centre and early in the last century had no less than six mills on the stretch of river below the village. With the decline of water power these mills fell into disuse and their ivy covered ruins are all that remain scattered along the banks of the Owendoher. Adjoining the village is Rockbrook House, formerly the home of Lord and Lady Glenavy and now a school.

Rockbrook House.

At Cruagh graveyard a by-road branches off on the right into Killakee estate. This was one of the main avenues but the massive piers of the entrance gateway were taken down in 1941 when the lands were divided. D'Alton states that it was also the original entrance to the Military Road.

The ancient portion of Cruagh graveyard behind the old schoolhouse is surrounded by a high wall and is now closed to burials. It contains the remains of a church and a small watchtower. The few fragments of the church that still survive show that the nave was 39' 4" long and the walls 2' 8" thick. One jamb of the chancel arch is still standing but the chancel itself and both side walls of the nave have disappeared. The stones from the church were probably used in the construction of the watch tower, which is built partly on the site of the church, and is obviously of much later date. It is two stories high with a separate entrance on each level and like the watch towers in Prospect Cemetery, Glasnevin, was for the

The Old Schoolhouse, Cruagh with the Watch Tower in the background.

Cruagh Watch Tower.

protection of new interments from the attentions of the body snatchers. According to local tradition it was many times the scene of violent conflicts between the relatives of the deceased and the sack-em-ups and the marks of bullets could formerly be seen on the stout doors of the tower.

An ancient slab inscribed with concentric circles was seen here by George Petrie in 1816 but no trace of it can be found. From here the road descends to cross a narrow bridge, and from there onwards is a stiff climb for the next mile to the entrance of the famous Glendoo Valley.

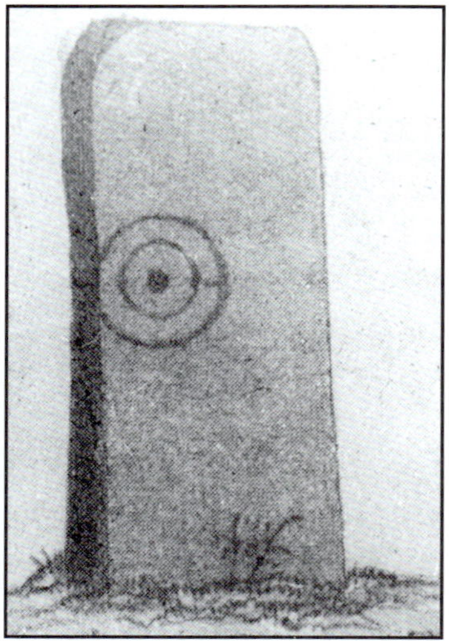

Left: Old baptismal font at Cruagh and right Petrie's drawing of an ancient slab at Cruagh.

Portion of the ruins of the ancient church of Cruagh.

Chapter 8

Taylor's Lane to Whitechurch and Kilmashogue

FROM Taylor's Lane the Whitechurch Road continues southward past some council houses and with the boundary wall of Grange Golf Club on the left. In the garden of the house stood Jackson's Cotton Mill, of which extensive remains still existed in 1836. This may also have been the site of one of the two paper mills which operated here in the eighteenth century. In 1756 William Mondett and Moses Verney came from England and built a paper mill at Whitechurch at a cost of £1,400. By 1763 they had built another mill at the same place for making press and purple papers. The laundry mill on the other side of the road, and some distance further on, may possibly occupy the site of the other mill. This laundry was started about 1830 by Mr. Bewley in whose family it remained until 1880. It was then operated by Caroline Thacker and from 1899 by Mr. Willoughby. It closed down around 1930.

On the same side of the road and approached by a short avenue is the old graveyard of Whitechurch, in which are the ruins of a medieval church. This church consisted originally of the nave only 21' 6" x 36' 6" and with walls an average of three feet thick. A later extension was added to the east end and an existing pointed doorway in the east wall enlarged on one side to form an opening eight feet wide. In 1615 this church and chancel were in good repair but by the following century they were in ruins. A large font mentioned in 1837 by the historian D'Alton cannot now be located.

Ruins of Whitechurch Medieval Church.

Whitechurch Church.

A short distance further and on the other side of the road is the Moravian cemetery which dates from the beginning of the last century. A map of this cemetery made in 1840 sets out the names of those buried therein and it is remarkable that they nearly all belong to the three families of Porter, Harly and Davis.

Moravian Cemetery, Whitechurch.

The earliest burials were in 1808, in which year five children were interred there. It is the custom with this sect to inter the coffin in an upright position. On the same side of the road is the schoolhouse, built in 1824, and beside it the parish church with the tall spire which is so prominent a landmark for miles around. This church was built in 1826. Beside the wall to the east of the church is the grave of Annie M. P. Smithson, the novelist, who died in 1948. On the opposite side of the road facing the church is a large flat slab of rock in which is cut a rectangular basin 15' 9" by 5'5" deep. Beside the hole there is a small incised cross of an early type with expanded ends and two letters difficult to decipher. The hole was apparently a socket for a cross, about which no tradition survives but the water which accumulates in it is believed to be a cure for warts.

Kilmashogue mill in 1992.

At Kilmashogue House there was formerly a corn mill, the mill race of which can still be seen. The road here crosses Kilmashogue Bridge and branches to the left past the ruins of a mill where woollen cloth was manufactured down to about 1880 by Thomas Thorncliff. Jenkins' Laundry was another local industry from 1882 to 1917.

Here commences a steep ascent which continues for the next mile and a half. At first confined between banks and thick hedges, as the higher portions of the road are reached, the prospect of the city and suburbs extends until the swing of the road around the hill cuts off the view.

To the left of the road is the house and grounds of Hillcot and above this a large area under young forestry. Here an ancient burial place was excavated in 1953 by members of the Royal Irish Academy. It was found to consist of a megalithic tomb of the gallery grave type comprising two chambers and originally covered over with a cairn of stones. At a later period parts of the chambers had been dismantled and the stones used in the construction of stone lined

Kilmashogue Mountain in 1978.

cists which were inserted in the cairn material. In comparatively recent times the stones of the cairn had been removed for the purpose of building boundary walls and the covering stones of the cists left exposed. There were no finds associated with the megalithic tomb but the cists were found to contain two middle Bronze age food vessels and a late Bronze age cinerary urn.

Higher up on the hill above this site is a large circular enclosure bounded by a wall of large irregular stones. It is sixty yards in diameter and is situated in a slight hollow on the hillside. The summit of Kilmashogue Mountain, which is 1,339 feet high, is not marked by any ancient landmark but a little to the north is a large pile of stones put there in recent years by boys staying in the neighbourhood. The view from here is really magnificent. Despite the fact that it is the nearest summit to Dublin, the panorama is uninterrupted from Mount Pelier on the left to Dalkey Hill on the right.

Ringfort, Kilmashogue in 1977.

Some time in the last century Dr. P.W. Joyce found the remains of a small church on the northern slope of the hill. Unfortunately the exact position of the remains was not recorded and repeated searches by interested parties have since failed to locate the site. The cross already mentioned under St. Columba's College probably came from the site of this church.

Kilmashogue Megalithic tomb in 1977.

Larch Hill

As the road continues to twist and climb around the western flank of the hill the view back over the city becomes obscured but to the south glimpses are obtained of Kelly's Glen, with Tibradden Mountain rising behind and the small triangular plantation known as Guinness' Wood high up near the summit. Below the road the well wooded demense of Larch Hill with its extensive farm buildings comes into view. Larch Hill was built towards the end of the eighteenth century by Cllr. Calbeck. Early in the last century this house was the residence of John O'Neill J.P. who erected the sumptious marble monument in Whitechurch burial ground in memory of his wife who died in 1835. The house later became the property of the Clarke family but subsequently passed by marriage to the Walshes. From 1907 to 1914 it was used as a sanitorium. In 1939 it was taken over by the trustees of the Catholic Boy Scout movement and is used by the members of that organisation as a training and camping centre.

Larch Hill.

In one of the fields to the south of the house is a large dolmen. The stones are much out of position due to the supporting stones on one side having fallen inward causing the cap stone to slide down with one edge on the ground. An unusual feature is the ten foot high pillar stone at one end. Surrounding the monument are a number of large boulders almost completely buried in the ground, which seem to have at one time formed a ring of standing stones.

Larch Hill Dolmen.

Ice House, Larch Hill

Half a mile further on the road reaches its highest point having risen seven hundred feet in a little over a mile. Here it is barred by a gate beyond which is private property. In one of the fields below the road is a small ring fort 32 yards in diameter.

Calbeck Castle

In the saddle between Kilmashogue and Two Rock Mountain is a ruined building known as Calbeck Castle. It is nothing more than a rather roughly constructed dwelling house and it is on record that it

Calbeck Castle.

was built about the year 1800 and according to Duncan's map it was in ruins in 1821. Mr. Calbeck was a progressive landowner who held a large area hereabouts. In a survey made for the Royal Dublin Society in 1801, Cllr. Calbeck was commended for having planted 200,000 forest trees of various types at Kilmashogue and for improving the mountain land by roads, building, enclosures and drainage. These improvements can still be seen on the north west slope of Two Rock Mountain where an area of over two hundred acres is divided into a great number of small square fields with roads laid out to serve the various enclosures. The area now shows no evidence of reclaimation and is a wilderness of swamp and heather. The remains of the cottages can also be seen but it is very doubtful if they were ever tenanted. On Duncan's map of 1821 this is named Calbeck's Hill.

Kelly's Glen

The valley lying between Kilmashogue and Tibradden mountains is known as Kelly's Glen and the avenue which passes the farmhouse with the elaborate stone porch is Kelly's Lane. This lane crosses the brook by a high cut stone bridge which shows evidence of having been widened at some period.

The original part which is nine feet wide bears a tablet with an inscription in well cut classical lettering

DI LA SOPHANNIE

The additional portion has the date faintly incised on the keystone

C.C. MDCCCL

which I understand represents "Charles Calbeck 1850."

The upper bridge in Kelly's Glen.

Just above the bridge is a spa well which over two hundred years ago enjoyed a period of popularity with wealthy invalids and others who could either journey to Kilmashogue and drink the water fresh from the spring or purchase it bottled in the city.

It was first noticed about 1748 and was considered to be superior to that of Templeogue which at that time was losing its curative properties. Kilmashogue spa however was never accorded the popularity of Templeogue, probably because of its remote situation and difficult access. The spa is easily located by the brown deposit left by the water as it flows into the adjoining brook.

Lower bridge in Kelly's Glen.

A few hundred yards upstream is another smaller bridge which bears the inscription

DI SVORE AMABILI

On the former bridge the date 1850 refers apparently to the alteration but the original bridges with the Italian inscriptions are older and were probably erected at the beginning of the century as part of the improvements scheme of Mr. Calbeck. The translation of these inscriptions reads

DI LA SOPHANNIE

— To my Sophannie, and

DI SORE AMABILI

— To my beloved sister.

According to Weston St. John Joyce they were intended as memorials to Calbeck's deceased sister. I was informed by the late Mrs. Calbeck of Pembroke Rd. that they were always known as the sisters' bridges.

Spa well, Kilmashogue.

Chapter 9

Cruagh to Glendoo and Glencullen

THE most direct route to Glendoo is that from Rathfarnham through Ballyboden and Rockbrook but for those who do not object to a more roundabout approach at a higher altitude the road across Cruagh Mountain is recommended. This branches left from the Glencree road at the point where the latter emerges onto the windswept Featherbed Bog, just five miles from Rathfarnham and drops for over a mile across the face of Cruagh Mountain with magnificent views northward over the Dublin plains. Whichever route is followed the way leads to the site of the tea rooms named Fraoc Halla opposite to which is the road to Glendoo and Glencullen. This road immediately crosses the Owendoher River by a bridge which was widened and straightened recently but which was formerly a most dangerous hazard on this long steep hill. It has been the scene of several fatal accidents which are commemorated by rough crosses set in the parapet. Much of the timber in this area was cut down during World War I and at that time a tree also disappeared which bore the initials of a number of Abbey actors who had visited here in the early days of that theatre and left this memento of their visit.

For over a mile from here the road ascends between steep wooded or heather clad slopes. On the right and separated from the road by a pleasant green sward flows the mountain stream of Owendoher, beyond which rises the steep flank of Cruagh Mountain with its plantation of larch and spruce. This road through Glendoo and Glencullen was constructed in 1840 by Mr. Fitzsimons, a local landowner, previous to which there was no means of access to

Glencullen from this side of the mountains. There was indeed a track of sorts which lay on the other side of the stream but this led only to the cottage which can still be seen high up on Glendoo Mountain and which was then occupied by a gamekeeper employed by Mr. White of Killakee. I was informed by Colonel Fitzsimons, a descendant of the man who built the road, that it cost all of £127 for 3 miles of road including culverts and walls.

Half a mile beyond the bridge the plantation on the right terminates at a point where the brook comes splashing down from the heights above, defining the boundary between Cruagh and Glendoo mountains. A track follows the course of this stream upwards and is the most convenient route for the ascent of Cruagh Mountain. This track can be followed until the gradient becomes somewhat easier, when it is advisable to cross over to the other bank and continue along the cleaned firebreak outside the forestry fence. This fence presently turns off at right angles and after following it for another three hundred yards a small pile of stones will be seen nearby on the left, marking the highest point in this extensive heatherclad upland.

From this spot, 1,714 feet high, there is a fine distant view northward of the city and suburbs but the area lying nearer to the mountains is obscured by the slope of the hill. In the foreground to the east are Kilmashogue and Tibradden and the Three Rock and Two Rock mountains. To the west is Mount Pelier and further away the high summits which bound the far side of Glenasmole.

To the south west and only half a mile away is Killakee Mountain, another great flat area, where the turf is gradually being eroded away by the elements, leaving islands and hummocks of heather-clad bog in a sea of weathered quartz and gravel. The highest point here, 1,761 feet, is also marked by a small pillar of stones. The view from Killakee hardly justifies a special visit, except for those who intend to continue on the further half mile down an easy dry gradient until they strike the Feather Bed Road. The view to the south of Cruagh is cut off by the high ground sloping away towards Glendoo Mountain. This elevation is a little less than a mile away across a great flat bog which is very easy to cross in dry weather but a much easier approach to Glendoo Mountain is from the new bog road in Old Bolies on the Glencree side of the Feather Bed. If it is not proposed to visit either Killakee or Glendoo mountains the return to Glendoo valley should be made by the same route.

Tibradden Mountain

Lying along the left-hand side of the glen is the long ridge of Tibradden Mountain rising to a height of 1,540 feet. The fine old timber which covered the lower slopes of this mountain was nearly all cut down during The Emergency but much of this has since been replanted. The ascent of Tibradden can be made either by leaving the road just past the cottage or following the track in the belt of old trees, three quarters of a mile further on. The area in between is not recommended as it is covered with deep heather which conceals a treacherous rocky slope dangerous to the most careful climber. In addition it is now cut off by forestry fences erected for the protection of the young plantations. A well defined path traverses the entire length of this ridge, with fine views into Kelly's Glen on the far side and over Kilmashogue to the city and bay.

The highest point of Tibradden Mountain is marked by a circular grassy mound composed of stones in which is an ancient burial place known locally as Niall Dhu's Grave. This site was opened up in 1849 by members of the Royal Irish Academy when it was found to contain a pottery vessel in a stone lined cist. A fragment of another vessel was found among the stones of the mound. The

Tibradden mountain.

existing remains, which were recently restored by the Board of Works, now comprise a circular compartment ten feet in diameter, open to the sky, and entered by a very narrow passage. Around the wall of the compartment is a narrow shelf or seat and in the middle of the floor is the rectangular cist which contained the burial. This was formerly covered with a flat stone which is now missing. The circular compartment which is neatly built of small stones is an unusual feature and it is not at all clear that this was part of the original monument.

A little to the south is an area of huge tumbled rocks which can provide shelter from wind and rain on the worst of days. On a vertical face of one rock is carved a cross and a crowned figure with upraised arms. The cross is seventeen inches high and has expanded terminals of a type commonly used in early Christian times but the figure is rather unusual. It suggests the figure carving found on early slabs but may possibly be quite recent work done by local stonecutters in the last century.

A report made in 1837 describes a number of small circles to the south of the cairn but a detailed examination over a wide area has failed to locate any trace of them.

Rock carvings, Tibradden.

This hill is called Tibroden on many old maps and documents and on Taylor's Map of 1816 it is named Garrycastle. In documents of the seventeenth century it is named Tibroden alias Killmainham Begg because it was formerly held by the Priory of Kilmainham.

At the upper end of Glendoo is a high granite rock upon which an inscription was cut in recent years. This reads "O'Connell's Rock 23 July 1823". According to Col. Fitzsimons, who got this work done, the local people of that day were celebrating Garland Sunday in the usual way, by an excursion to the mountain to pick fraughans followed by a dance at the dance floor and a few barrels of stout. Daniel O'Connell was visiting his daughter, who was married to a Fitzsimons of Glencullen House. When he saw the assembled crowds he addressed them from this rock.

O'Connell's rock.

Glencullen Valley

The road through Glendoo continues to wend its way, confined between steep rocky slopes and with pinewood obscuring the view in front, but once this plantation is passed it emerges into an open green valley with a view extending over Glencullen village to the

Glencullen valley.

hills beyond. To the left of the road the ground rises away towards the great flat top of Two Rock Mountain nearly a mile away. The highest point of this mountain, 1,763 feet above sea level, is distinguished by a great cairn of stones called the Fairy Castle, thirty yards in diameter and about ten feet high. No enclosing kerb can be seen and there is no evidence that it has ever been opened. It probably contains a chamber built of large stones similar to that on Seefin Mountain. Southward of this is a large outcrop of rock and further to the south the two smaller ones which can be seen from the Glencullen side and give the mountain its name. On the lower slope of the Two Rock Mountain formerly known as Slieve Gearr, there is an oval enclosure sixty four yards long and containing in the centre the foundations of a small square building. Against the inside of the enclosing bank are remains of two more structures.

The author with friends at Fairy Castle, Two Rock Mountain.

A little more than a hundred years ago this district was noted for its barren aspect and the extreme poverty of its inhabitants. There was no road or lane of any description between here and Glencullen village and no arable land except little patches between the rocks which scarcely repaid the labourer for the immense trouble of cultivating them. The principal occupation was the manufacture of brooms or besoms from the heath of the adjoining mountain and even this they had to procure in spite of the strict watch kept to prevent them. Conditions have changed much since then. The road built by Mr. Fitzsimons is now a main tourist highway and the many new houses and well cultivated plots are evidence of a contented and industrious community. It is remarkable that the fields on both sides of the Glencullen river are divided into very small plots and strips by fences and low baulks, a remnant of the ancient and uneconomic system called rundale, which was the result of repeated subdivision of the original holdings. This was probably the only place in Leinster where these conditions still existed.

On the far slope can be seen the compact village of Boranaraltry which is reached by a steep byroad branching off on the right and descending to cross the bridge below. This road continues on across the face of Glencullen Mountain to serve the old granite quarries which are such a conspicuous landmark on the far side of the valley. These quarries which once supported so many families are now almost deserted and the hillside, both above and below them, is rapidly disappearing under a blanket of afforestation. To the west of the quarries a passage has been left through the plantation to give access to the higher part of the mountain for turf cutting and other purposes. In one of the fields below the quarry is a small ringfort. In 1836 when O'Curry was collecting place names in connection with the Ordnance Survey he recorded a place called Baile an Araldaigh in Glencullen. This is probably identical with Boranaraltry and would indicate that this place was associated with the family of Harold who held large areas in County Dublin down to the seventeenth century.

Bornaraltry village.

The village of Brockey is next passed, situated in a hollow below the road and approached by a laneway on the right. The arrangement of this group of thatched houses and outoffices surrounded by little gardens and loose stone walls is very suggestive of the villages along the western seaboard. On the

Brockey village.

southern side of this village there was formerly a fine ringfort which was known from time immemorial as Old Glencullen House but no remains of it can be traced on the site and not even a memory of it survives. The same fate, unfortunately, befell a megalithic tomb which was situated on a little summit over the main road and just past Brockey village. This was known as Leaba na Saigh (The Hound's Bed) and was covered with a large stone ten feet long and eight feet wide. A drawing of this ancient monument was published by the Royal Society of Antiquaries in 1855, some years before it was completely cleared away. It is now regarded as a natural formation of boulders.

Leaba na Saigh or The Hound's Bed in 1855.

The next laneway on the right leads down by some farmhouses to Glencullen River and was part of an old road leading to Boranaraltry. In a field beside this land was a holy well known as the Butter Well, which was visited by those suffering from stomach disorders. In former times dairy vessels were washed with its waters as a precaution against the loss of butter by witchcraft, which no doubt accounts for the title of the well. Another well known as Fanny's Well, used only for domestic purposes, is at the side of the lane, outside the field.

The Butter Well in 1985.

A short way past this laneway is Glencullen Village from which roads lead to Stepaside, Kiltiernan and Kilmalin. The lands of Glencullen were at one time the property of the Abbey of St. Mary the Virgin. After the Reformation they were held by the Fitzwilliams of Merrion who sold them about the end of the seventeenth century to Mr. Thos. Fitzsimons whose descendants continued to reside there down to recent years. Glencullen House is situated in a picturesque setting on the south side of the village. Here resided during the last century Christopher Fitzsimons D.L. who was clerk of the Crown and Hanaper and a Member of Parliament. He was married to a daughter of Daniel O'Connell.

Beside the entrance to Glencullen House on the site later occupied by the dispensary was the constabulary barracks which was attacked and captured by the Fenians on 6th March 1867. The party, under Capt. Patk. Lennon, had assembled at Rathgar the night before and marched through Dundrum and Stepaside where they had successfully attacked the barracks. On approaching Glencullen, rifle men were deployed to surround the barracks. The police were called upon to surrender and refused, whereupon an exchange of rifle fire commenced, which did little damage to either side. When a party got onto the roof and opened up a hole in preparation for an attack from above the inmates surrendered. Enriched by the arms and ammunition from the barracks, the Fenians then marched over Glencullen Mountain taking the prisoners with them. Capt. Lennon, on seeing one of his men urge on a straggler with the butt of his rifle, drew his revolver and threatened to kill the first person he found insulting or abusing a prisoner.

Old R.I.C. barracks, Glencullen.

In a field beside the road opposite to Glencullen House is a large pillar stone of white quartz about 6 feet in height.

In the village is a fine granite church built in 1908 and a short distance away in the burial ground is the old church, now roofless, which fell into disrepair when the new one was built. This bears a tablet with the inscription "St. Patrick's Chapel erected A.D. 1824 to the Honour and Glory of God".

Pillar Stone, Glencullen.

Remains of St. Patrick's Chapel, Glencullen.

Before the erection of this church Mass used to be celebrated in a thatched barn which was located about half a mile to the north, in the townland of Newtown. This old barn is still standing and the field in which it is situated is known as the Chapel Field. On the corner stone of the wall is the inscription "1737 T.L.". It is still remembered locally that Mass was celebrated here in penal times and that the initials are those of Tom Langeran. *(see picture page 114)*. This was marked as a "chapel" on Taylor's map of 1816. The old schoolhouse was built about 1835 under a bequest from Lord Castlecoote, previous to which there was no school building and classes had been held in the chapel.

The field directly behind the burial ground, and at present the property of the parish, is known as the monastery field. Here in 1835 a small monastery for Cistercian monks was founded on land given to them by Mr. Fitzsimons. This was known as Mount Saint Bernard and was occupied by some of the community from Mount Mellary. Only four years before this all the Irish and English monks had been expelled from France and they were at this period seeking a suitable location in which to reorganise their community life.

Mount Saint Bernard was described as a neat house and a farm of about 20 acres. Two monks resided here and worked uncommonly hard and for long hours on very meagre fare. In addition they used to go around soliciting help to build a school. It was intended at first to increase the numbers of the community, but the project does not appear to have been successful, as by 1845 the house had been evacuated by the Order and was occupied by the curate of the parish, Rev. P. Doyle. By 1856 it had become ruinous and was apparently demolished soon afterwards. It does not appear on the Ordnance Survey map of 1871. Not a trace of this house has survived but against the boundary fence is a roofless carthouse or barn which was there during the occupation of the monks and was likely built by them. One of the monks was Bro. Macarius Moore, a tailor by trade.

The Monks' stables, Glencullen.

To the north of the village is Newtown Hill, a rough stony height on which were noted a number of stone circles and alignments. Some of these must be regarded as doubtful, since the hill is so covered with boulders and stones that it would be possible to group many of them into lines and circles that they were never intended to form. There are three monuments however which are definitely ancient and these are in line on the slope of the hill, just above the monastery field.

The first is a very fine ring fort known as the Raheen. This is 27 yards in diameter and has a high bank around it with a ditch outside. The space within is divided by crosswalls and along one side is the foundation of a rectangular building containing three rooms and the remains of a circular hut.

Circular enclosure, Newtown, Glencullen in 1977.

To the north of this is a low circular enclosure of loose stones 19 yards in diameter. Higher up, on the summit of the hill, is a prehistoric burial place of the bowl barrow type, a circular mound 5 feet high, surrounded by a fosse and low bank. Beside it is a single standing stone 5 feet 6 inchs high.

Hut sites, Ballybrack, Glencullen in 1977.

Chapter 10

Ticknock, The Two Rock Mountain, The Three Rock Mountain, Barnacullia and Ballyedmonduff

THE summit of the Two Rock Mountain, 1,763 feet above sea level, is the highest point of that group of hills which comprises the Two Rock and Three Rock, Kilmashogue and Tibradden Mountains. This highland area is bounded along the southwest side by the long deep defile of Glendoo and Glencullen valleys, on the west by the valley of the Owendoher River and on the east by the road from Barnacullia to Glencullen village.

On the northern side the mountain block is divided into three separate hills, Kilmashogue being in the centre while to the east across the Ticknock valley is the Three Rock Mountain and to the west is Tibradden on the far side of Kelly's Glen. All the roads from these valleys lead towards the north, following the slope of the valley bottoms and all are linked together by the road leading from Rockbrook on the western side to Sandyford on the east.

The higher portion of this vast area, bounded approximately by the 1,000 feet contour, is covered by a uniform blanket of heather-covered peat, interspersed with bracken and furze and dotted over with grey boulders of the underlying granite. Across this desolate moorland the pale green of young forestry plantations is beginning to make itself apparent.

On the lower slopes of the hills and in the sheltered valleys are the farmhouses and cottages of the hardy folk whose ancestors were such a scourge to the English settlers and the great walled demesnes of the landlords and gentry who were not slow to appreciate the attractions of this region. Sir George Carew complained in 1590 that "those who dwelled within sight of the smoke of Dublin were not subject to its laws."

The Ticknock area has always been a popular one with the Dublin people, not only on account of the convenience with which it can be reached from the city but also because of the variety of scenery it offers and the magnificant prospects which can be obtained from the adjoining heights. Ticknock cross roads is reached from Rathfarnham by the Grange Road. The portion of this road from Harold's Grange through Ticknock to Sandyford was not constructed until about 1840.

In a prominent position just below Ticknock cross roads is an old house named Kingston, where in 1892 an interesting find of ancient coins was made. Mr. Shiels, the owner, was erecting a shed when he uncovered a granite slab under which was an earthen pipkin full of money. This comprised 650 coins of the brass money of James II dated 1689 and 1690 of which about 440 were shillings, 6 were half crowns and the remainer sixpences. The pot was of old tortoise shellware and was unfortunately smashed at the time of discovery. About eight years previous to this, another hoard of coins was found on the same farm. This consisted of 200 half crowns of the same period which were found in a recess inside an old wall and were neatly stacked in piles. This had protected them from corrosion except around the edges. It is not known in what way this place was associated with the cause of the Stuarts or if any significance can be attached to the townland name of Kingston.

Ticknock

From this point the Ticknock road trends away in a southerly direction rising all the time until it terminates at the rifle range not far from the top of Three Rock Mountain. To the right of this road and situated in private land is the holy well popularly known as Grumley's Well. This name is at least as old as 1836 but these lands have not been occupied by any one of that name for over 170 years. Within living memory rounds have been done here and pieces of cloth left tied to the bushes, in accordance with the old custom. Cures have also been claimed, especially for complaints of the eyes. The date on which the pattern was held each year, which might supply a clue to the patron saint of the well, is no longer remembered but is believed to have been during the month of August. The existing covering, on which are carved two chalices, was constructed about 70 years ago by the landowner. As the water which flows from this well is used for domestic purposes, the indiscriminate visits of people suffering from every type of disease had to be discouraged.

Grumley's well, Ticknock in 1977.

Further up the glen and on the same side of the road is a small rocky hill known as Telshaun behind which is a row of council houses in a very secluded situation. A spa well was discovered at Tiknock about 1787 and was pronounced to be the most efficacious remedy against scorbutic disorders. This was stated by a writer as recently as 1917 to be situated on the upper slopes of the eastern side of the glen and to be surrounded by the remains of some kind of protective structure. No well or spring can be located in this area now and no information can be obtained from the local inhabitants concerning it.

Telshaun Hill.

The road leading to the rifle ranges forks to the left and in one of the furze covered fields just below the road is a ring fort 30 yards in diameter. It is built on the slope of the hill but the area inside is levelled. The stream that flows through, the Little Dargle, rises in a hollow known as Lugdoo. Beside the ranges a number of pits here were made in former times by people looking for freestone which was then in demand for scouring purposes and provided a livelihood for several families in Ticknock. According to local tradition General Holt hid his arms about here before surrendering to Lord Powerscourt in 1798.

Three Rock Mountain

To the east of the ranges and less than half a mile away is the top of the Three Rock Mountain, 1,479 feet high and easily identified from the city and suburbs by the large outcrops of granite on the summit. These masses of rock are weathered by exposure into great horizontal blocks which appear to have been superimposed one on top of the other. This deceptive appearance led the eighteenth century antiquary Gabriel Beranger to write a description of the sacrificial altars on the Three Rock Mountain.

The upper faces of the rocks are covered with initials and names carved by visitors over the years and on the top of the centre block are four shallow bowl shaped hollows, of the type known as bullauns, believed to have been used for grinding purposes in early Christian times.

On the eastern side of the centre outcrop are the remains of a house 40 feet long, 17 feet wide, and with walls only a few feet high. Local tradition is very definite that this was a public house. Near the rocks, the mearing ditches of the three townlands of Ticknock, Barnacullia and Ballyedmonduff meet at a point on the ditch. About 250 yards south of the junction is a small ring fort 20 yards in diameter. In the saddle between this and the Two Rock Mountain are a number of old overgrown passages, slightly below ground level, and cleared of loose stones. These old passages are to be found in many places on the mountains and were probably used in former times for the hauling of either stone or turf using slide carts.

Three Rock Mountain

Barnacullia

Around the eastern side of the Three Rock Mountain is the road from Ticknock through Barnacullia to Ballyedmonduff. This road passes the popular premises known as Lamb Doyle's which have been in the possession of this family for well over a century. A short distance to the east and approached by a narrow lane is the remains of the house which was occupied by Countess Markievicz up to the time of the 1916 Rising. This cottage was taken by Countess Markievicz about 1907 and was visited by many whose names were later to become by-words in the national movement. During Easter Week 1916, the wife and children of James Connolly stayed here. The cottage was occupied down to about 1945 when the last tenant was moved to a council house. It was then condemned and the roof removed. A committee was later formed to restore the cottage as a memorial to the Countess but when they were informed that they would be required to rebuild the walls, the project was abandoned.

Barnacullia village in 1977.

Markievicz cottage in 1977.

From Lamb Doyle's the road rises to the scattered village of Barnacullia, formerly occupied by stonecutters, whose craftmanship can be seen in masonry of cottages, walls and gate piers. Over a hundred years ago the bulk of the orders for cut stone came from the Dublin Corporation Paving Board. In Fulham's Glen, high up above the village there is a small cave in an old quarry, known as the soldier's cave. This name originated in olden times when a soldier, to avoid corporal punishment, came out and hid here. He died of exposure and his body was later found in the cave. During the War of Independence a camp was established in Barnacullia by the 6th Battalion of the Dublin Brigade. This was raided on the same day as the round up in which Seán Doyle was killed.

The 6th Battalion of the Dublin Brigade camp in Barnacullia during the War of Independence.

An old road leading from Barnacullia to Kilgobbin graveyard is shown on Taylor's map of 1816. It is now represented by a footpath through the estate of Fern Hill which is used by local people as a short cut to Stepaside. This passage was the cause of litigation in the nineteenth century when an attempt was made by Judge Darley of Fern Hill to close or divert it. It is now enclosed on both sides and the avenue of Fern Hill is carried across overhead. The extension of the road from Barnacullia to Ballyedmonduff was made subsequent to 1843. On the hill above this part of the road is a very interesting group of five ring forts surrounded by small enclosures and with traces of house sites. Running up the hill from here are remains of an ancient field system, consisting of narrow stripes divided by low stone walls. Two hundred yards to the south is another ring fort. This area is now planted with trees and these structures are gradually disappearing from sight.

The road now passes below an extensive granite quarry and joins the main road from Stepaside. A short distance further, on the left hand side, is a ruined house with the unusual name of Taylor's Folly. Over the front door is a stone bearing the inscription "W. T." 1817. This house was described soon after it was built as having been erected at a great expense but with little regard for convenience or comfort. The house was occupied by the Taylors down to the middle of the century and by the Moores in the latter half of the century. It fell into ruins early in the twentieth century.

Taylor's Folly.

On the opposite side of the road and situated on top of a round green hill is a small circular structure 16½ yards in diameter with low walls about nine feet thick. Although superficially of the ringfort type the small size and unusually thick walls would suggest that it may be the remains of a circular house.

Half a mile further on, a short byroad on the left leads to Newtown, where it terminates at a large farmhouse with extensive outbuildings. Behind the house, in a field known as the Chapel Field, are the remains of an old barn where mass was celebrated before the erection of Glencullen chapel in 1824. *(see page 102)*.

Ruins of Penal chapel.

To the right of the road a heather covered hillside rises away towards the top of Two Rock Mountain. At a point about a quarter mile from the road is an interesting megalithic tomb known locally as the Giant's Grave. This was originally covered with a cairn of stones and was opened up as far back as 1832 by Alderman Blacker of St. Andrew Street but unfortunately no record was left of the excavation. The tomb lay in this open condition for a century and from time to time the larger stones were removed by stone cutters. In 1935 the site was investigated by Professor De Valera and in spite of its wrecked condition yielded up a considerable amount of information.

Giant's Grave, Ballyedmonduff in 1988.

The tomb was of the northern wedge shaped gallery grave class and contained a gallery divided into three chambers. The cutline of the cairn was defined by a kerb of large stones and was horseshoe shaped with a straight facade at the west end, in which was the entrance to the ante-chamber and central chamber. There was no means of access to the eastern chamber before the roof was

Soldier's Cave, Fulham's Glen, Barnacullia in 1978.

removed early in the last century. Buried underneath the accumulated soil there, were found a stone hammer, some pieces of worked flint and many fragments of pottery. Some of these belonged to the Neolithic or late stone age tradition but most of them belonged to the early Bronze Age beaker class. This type of tomb was in use down to the middle Bronze Age or about 1,000 B.C.

For the next half mile the road drops gradually to Glencullen village. The road on the right here goes by Glendoo to Rathfarnham and that to the left leads to Kiltiernan on the Enniskerry bus route.

Chapter 11

Firhouse Road

FROM the western end of Butterfield Avenue the Firhouse Road continues straight ahead towards Firhouse and Oldbawn. On the right where a sweep of the river Dodder touched the road was a deep pool known as Pussy's Lep, a popular swimming place with boys of the neighbourhood.

Further along on the same side is an old house named Cherryfield, formerly known as Cherrytree. A proprietor named George Fowler who lived here prior to 1865 enlarged the house and reclaimed an area of waste land along the bank of the Dodder. This portion of the road was laid out about 1800 when Templeogue bridge was built. Previous to that the road from Templeogue crossed the river by a ford directly below Cherryfield and joined the existing road about a quarter of a mile further on where it could be seen, overgrown and closed by an iron gate. The Templeogue Ballad which describes the entertainment at the chaleybate spring at Spawell was printed at the Cherrytree in 1730 and dedicated to the worthy manager, which suggests that it was an inn or guest house.

On the opposite side of the road was Delaford. In the eighteenth century this was a carman's inn and was known as Clandarigg. The road then ran past the front door and out by the present avenue but was subsequently altered by a Mr. Birmingham, who lived here about 1800 so as to leave a lawn in front of the house. He also built two fine rooms and a hall in front of the inn, constructed fish ponds and otherwise improved the place, the name of which he changed to Springfield. In 1820 Mr. B. J. Ottley, then a commissioner of Public Works, took the place and called it Delaford. In the middle of a field opposite to Delaford is a stone cross erected about 1849 to secure immunity against cattle plague.

Field Cross, Firhouse Road.

On the left is the road to Orlagh and just beyond it the village of Firhouse, formerly consisting of a long row of cottages which have been replaced recently by fine new houses built on an adjoining site. A narrow lane leads down past the new houses to the City Weir on the Dodder where a considerable body of water is diverted into the old City Watercourse. This weir was built in 1244 in order to ensure a constant suppy of water to the city and continued to serve this purpose down to 1775. Prior to 1846 there was a shallow ford below the weir and this was then the direct route to Tallaght and Greenhills but the force of the water subsequently cut out a deep channel at this point undermining the toeing of the weir and making the river impassable to vehicular traffic. For many years pedestrians continued to cross by wading along the top of the weir, a dangerous practice when the river is in spate as a false step could result in a fatal accident. A wooden footbridge was later put up by subscription

The City Weir.

Firhouse footbridge.

below the weir but was soon washed away in a flood. This was replaced about 1860 by an iron lattice-work footbridge which was raised about twenty feet above the bed of the river. This footbridge was replaced by the current bridge which was officially opened in 1995.

Sally Park.

Behind a high wall on the left of the road is Sallypark, the home of William Domville Handcock, the learned author of *The History and Antiquities of Tallaght*. The house at one time belonged to the Earl of Clanwilliam and was purchased in 1796 by Handcock's grandfather, who in 1801 was praised by the Royal Dublin Society for having planted 7,000 trees of various kinds on his lands. William Domville Handcock was born in 1830 and was educated at Nutgrove School, Rathfarnham and at Trinity College. He took a keen interest in local history and collected a great store of local information from inquiries among the old inhabitants, from notes left by his grandfather and from recollections of his father, together with extracts from annals, newspapers and unpublished sources. His book *The History and Antiquities of Tallaght* preserves much valuable information concerning old houses, mills, roads and local characters.

Bibliography

The assumed bibliography of works consulted is detailed below. In most cases the latest or most accessible editions of a source have been listed, especially where an edition of the source is held in the Local Studies Collection at the County Library in Tallaght. Some sources could not be definitely ascertained.

Anonymous. "Guide to antiquities in the Dublin District." Journal of the Royal Society of Antiquaries of Ireland 44 (1914) 223-296.

Anonymous. "The mills on the Dodder and the City Watercourse." Dublin Historical Record 12 (1950): 93-95.

Archer, Joseph. *Statistical survey of the county Dublin with observations on the means of improvement drawn up for the consideration and by order of The Dublin Society*. Dublin: printed by Graisberry and Campbell, 1801.

Ball, Francis Elrington. *A history of the county Dublin*. Vol II. Dublin: Gill and Macmillan, 1979. (6 vols, reproduced by photo lithography from the 1st. impression of 1902). Available:
http://www.chapters.eiretek.org/books/ball1-6/Ball2/ball2.4.html, 1st April 2005.

Boate, Gerard. *Ireland's naturall history. Being a true and ample description of its situation, greatness, shape, and nature; . . .* London: for John Wright at the Kings Head in the Old Bayley, 1652.

Boylan, Lena. "Robert Emmet's House at Rathfarnham." Dublin Historical Record 31 (1977-1978): 55-58. (Pictures 6 and 7 between pages 60 and 61 relate to this article).

Breen, T.C. "A pre-Norman grave-slab at Rathfarnham, County Dublin." Journal of the Royal Society of Antiquaries of Ireland 111 (1981): 120-123.

Cooper, Austin. *An eighteenth century antiquary; the sketches, notes and diaries of Austin Cooper (1759-1830) Printed by direction of his great grandson, Albert Damer Cooper.* Ed. Liam Price, M.R.I.A. Dublin: J. Falconer, 1942.

D'Alton, John. *History of the county of Dublin*. Cork: Tower Books, 1976. Originally published: Dublin: Hodges and Smith, 1838.

Farrington, A. "The prehistoric burial cairn on Tibradden Mountain, Co. Dublin." Journal of the Royal Society of Antiquaries of Ireland 53 (1933): 252-254.

Fleetwood, John. (Dr.) "The Dublin body snatchers." (part 1). Dublin Historical Record 42 (1988-1989): 32- 40.

Fleetwood, John. (Dr.) "The Dublin body snatchers." (part 2). Dublin Historical Record 42 (1988-1989): 42-52.
Fleetwood, John. *The Irish body snatchers, a history of body snatching in Ireland*. Dublin: Tomar, 1988.

Frizell, Richard. *A MAP of Rathfarnham Park in the County of Dublin for the Right Honourable Henry Earl of Ely Containing 213.2.33 Plantation Measure laid down by a scale of Ten perches in one Inch in October 1779 by Richd Frizell*. Richard Frizell, 1779. (This manuscript map belongs to the National Library, call number 16 G 40 (20)).

Hamilton, G.E. "Rockbrook, Co. Dublin: its name." Journal of the Royal Society of Antiquaries of Ireland 41 (1911): 182-183.

Hammond, Joseph W. "Behind the scenes of the Emmet insurrection". (part 1) Dublin Historical Record 6 (1943-44): 91-106.

Hammond, Joseph W. "The Emmet insurrection". (part 1) Dublin Historical Record 9 (1943-44): 153-154.

Hammond, Joseph W. "Behind the scenes of the Emmet insurrection". (part 1) Dublin Historical Record 6 (1946-48): 21-28.

Hammond, Joseph W. "Behind the scenes of the Emmet insurrection". (part 2) Dublin Historical Record 6 (1946-48): 59-68.

Hammond, Joseph W. "Behind the scenes of the Emmet insurrection". (part 3) Dublin Historical Record 6 (1946-48): 84-89.

Hammond, Joseph W. "The King's Printers in Ireland, 1551–1919." (part 1). Dublin Historical Record 11 (1949-50): 29–31.

Hammond, Joseph W. "The King's Printers in Ireland, 1551–1919." (part 2). Dublin Historical Record 11 (1949-50): 58-64.

Hammond, Joseph W. "The King's Printers in Ireland, 1551–1919." (part 3). Dublin Historical Record 11 (1949-50): 88-96.

Handcock, William Domville. *The history and antiquities of Tallaght in the county of Dublin*. 2nd ed. revised and enlarged. Dublin: Hodges Figgis,1899. Facsimile edition. Cork: Tower Books,1976. Facsimile edition. Dublin: Anna Livia Press,1991. Available: http://www.chapters.eiretek.org/books/Handcock/tallaghtindex.htm, 1st. April, 2005.

Irish Manuscripts Commission. T*he civil Survey, A.D. 1654-1656 Vol. VII County of Dublin, prepared for publication with introductory notes and appendices by Robert C. Simington*. Dublin: Stationery Office, 1945.

Joyce, Weston St. John. *The neighbourhood of Dublin*. Dublin: Gill and Macmillan,1977. (originally published,1912, text of the 1977 edition is a photographic reproduction of the 1939 edition. Available: http://www.chapters.eiretek.org/books/Neighbourhood/contents.html, 1st April,2005.

Joyce, Weston St. John. *Rambles near Dublin*. 2nd ed. Dublin: Evening Telegraph Office,1890.

Kilbride-Jones, H.E. "The excavation of an unrecorded Megalithic tomb on Kilmashogue Mountain, Co. Dublin." Proceedings of the Royal Irish Academy 56 Section C (1953-1954): 461-479

Lewis, Samuel *A topographical dictionary of Ireland, comprising the several counties, cities, boroughs, corporate, market, and post towns, parishes, and villages, with historical and statistical descriptions* . 2 vols. London: S. Lewis &Co. 1837.

Madden, R. R. *The Life and Times of Robert Emmet, with numerous notes and additions, also a memoir of Thomas Addis Emmet*. New York, P.M. Haverty, 1868.

Mallet, Robert. *River Dodder district report to the commissioners on the proposed formation of reservoirs on the river Dodder for the prevention of sudden floods and an accumulation of water for the constant supply of mills on that river and on the water-courses*. H. M. S. O., 1844.

Maxwell, W. H. *History of the Irish rebellion in 1798; with memoirs of the Union and Emmett's insurrection in 1803*. London: George Bell and Sons, 1887.

McMahon, Fr. T. S.J. "Old Rathfarnham days." Dublin Historical Record 41 (1987-1988): 21-23.

Morris, Henry: "The Slighe Cualann." Journal of the Royal Society of Antiquaries of Ireland 68 (1938): 113-123.

Ó h-Éailidhe, P. "Early Christian grave slabs in the Dublin region". Journal of the Royal Society of Antiquaries of Ireland 103 (1973): 51-64.

Ó hÉailidhe, P. "The Rathdown slabs." Journal of the Royal Society of Antiquaries of Ireland 87 (1957): 75-88.

Ó hÉailidhe, P. "An unrecorded wedge-tomb at Killakee, County Dublin." Journal of the Royal Society of Antiquaries of Ireland 108 (1978): 101-103.

O hÉailidhe, P. "Three unrecorded early grave-slabs in county Dublin." Journal of the Royal Society of Antiquaries of Ireland 112 (1982): 139-141.

Ó hÉailidhe, P. and Ellen Prendergast. "Two unrecorded graveslabs in County Dublin". Journal of the Royal Society of Antiquaries of Ireland 107 (1982): 139-142.

Ó Ríordáin, Seán P. and Ruaidhrí de Valera. "Excavation of a megalithic tomb at Ballyedmonduff, Co. Dublin". Proceedings of the Royal Irish Academy 55 (1952-53), Section C: 61-81.

Ordnance Survey. *Fair Plan Rathfarnham Parish Co. Dublin* (1837). Held at the National Archives. Reference No. OS 105E/279

Ordnance Survey letters Dublin (letters containing information relative to the antiquities of the County of Dublin collected during the progress of the Ordnance Survey in 1837). Ed. Michael Herity. Dublin: Four Masters Press, 2001.

Ordnance Survey. *Name books, Parish of Rathfarnham, Co. Dublin*. Held in the National Archives of Ireland, Bishop Street, Dublin 8.

Ordnance Survey. *Memorandums, Co. Dublin*. Held in the National Archives of Ireland, Bishop Street, Dublin 8.

Ordnance Survey. *Parish of Rathfarnham Co. Dublin*. 1:2,500. Surveyed in 1864 by Captain Martin R. E. and zincographed in 1865 under the direction of Captain Wilkinson R. E. at the Ordnance Survey Office, Phoenix Park. Ordnance Survey.

Pearse, P.H. The Story of a success, being a record of St. Enda's College September 1908 to Easter 1916. Ed. Desmond Ryan. Dublin: Maunsel & Co., 1917.

Petty, William. *Hiberniae Delineatio: atlas of Ireland*. Newcastle upon Tyne: Frank Graham,1968. (original maps drawn c. 1660, engraved c. 1663, published 1685, based on the Down Survey maps).

Poe, J.W. *The cromlechs of county Dublin*. Dublin: Carraig Books, 1979. Originally published Dublin: Sealy, Bryers [1900].

Porter, Frank Thorpe. *Gleanings and reminiscences*. Dublin: Hodges, Foster & Co., 1875.

Price, L. "Boranaraltry, Co. Dublin." Journal of the Royal Society of Antiquaries of Ireland 70 (1940): 62.

Price, Liam. "The antiquities and place names of south county Dublin." Dublin Historical Record 2 (1940): 121-133.

Redmond, M. "A promontory fort at Rathfarnham, County Dublin." Journal of the Royal Society of Antiquaries of Ireland 127 (1997): 125-126.

Reynolds, J. J. *Footprints of Emmet*. Dublin: M.H. Gill & Son, 1903.

[Rocque, John]. *The A to Z of Georgian Dublin: John Rocque's maps of the city in 1756 and the county in 1760*. Ed. Paul Ferguson. Lympne Castle, Kent: Harry Margary in association with Trinity College Library Dublin, 1998.

Rocque, John. *An actual survey of the county of Dublin on the same scale as those of Middlesex, Oxford,Barks and Buckinghamshire by John Rocque*. (4 sheets)1760.

Scantlebury, Rev. C. S.J. "Rathfarnham Castle." Dublin Historical Record 12 (1950-1951): 20-30.

Taylor, George and Andrew Skinner. *Maps of the roads of Ireland*. Shannon: Irish University Press,1969. (originally published 1778, second edition 1783).

Taylor, John. *Taylor's map of the environs of Dublin extending 10 to 14 miles from the castle, by actual survey,on a scale of 2 inches to one mile*. Dublin: Phoenix Maps,1989. (single sheet facsimile of the two sheet edition of 1816).

Thom's Irish almanac and official directory. (various years). Dublin: Alexander Thom, various dates.

Turner, Kathleen. *If you seek monuments, a guide to the antiquities of the barony of Rathdown* 2nd ed. Shankill, Co Dublin: Rathmichael Historical Society, 1984.

A MAP of Rathfarnham Park in the County of Dublin for the Right Honourable Henry Earl of Ely Containing 213.2.33 Plantation Measure laid down by a scale of Ten perches in one Inch in October 1779 by Rich<u>d</u> Frizell.

Dennis
Farrell
Lower
Rathfarnham
Alderman
Horans Demesne
Total of the whole

Writing Cyprus

Bahriye Kemal's ground-breaking new work serves as the first study of the literatures of Cyprus from a postcolonial and partition perspective. Her book explores Anglophone, Hellenophone and Turkophone writings from the 1920s to the present.

Drawing on Yi-Fu Tuan's humanistic geography and Henri Lefebvre's Marxist philosophy, Kemal proposes a new interdisciplinary spatial model, at once theoretical and empirical, that shows the power of space and place in postcolonial partition cases. The book shows the ways that place and space determine identity, where together these places, spaces and identities are always in production. In analysing practices towards writing, inventing, experiencing, reading and construction, the book offers a distinct 'solidarity' that captures the 'truth of space' and place for the production of multiple-mutable Cypruses shaped by and for multiple-mutable selves, ending in a 'differential' Cyprus, Mediterranean, and world.

Writing Cyprus presents not only a nuanced understanding of the actual and active production of colonialism, postcolonialism and partition that dismantles the dominant binary legacy of historical-political deadlock discourse, but a fruitful model for understanding other sites of conflict and division.

Bahriye Kemal is a lecturer in postcolonial and contemporary literatures at the University of Kent. Her teaching and research engage with postcolonial and partition studies, comparative Ottoman and British imperialism, spatial studies, migration, comparative literature, the postcolonial Eastern Mediterranean, postcolonial islands, solidarity and activism. Her articles on anticolonial gendered nationalism, the postcolonial partitioned diaspora and the East Mediterranean have appeared in various postcolonial journals. She is co-editor of *Visa Stories: Experiences between Law and Migration* (2013), and *Nicosia beyond Barriers: Voices from a Divided City* (2019). She is currently writing about postcolonial Mediterranean, with focus on literature and arts from Cyprus, Palestine, Syria and beyond.

Routledge Research in Postcolonial Literatures

Series editors: Donna Landry and Caroline Rooney

Edited in collaboration with the Centre for Colonial and Postcolonial Studies, University of Kent at Canterbury, this series presents a wide range of research into postcolonial literatures by specialists in the field. Volumes will concentrate on writers and writing originating in previously (or presently) colonized areas, and will include material from non-anglophone as well as anglophone colonies and literatures.

65 **Caring for Community**
Marijke Denger

66 **A Century of Encounters**
Writing the Other in Arab North Africa
Tanja Stampfl

67 **Rethinking the Victim**
Gendered Violence in Australian Women's Literature
Anne Brewster and Sue Kossew

68 **Politicising World Literature**
Egypt, Between Pedagogy and the Public
May Hawas

69 **Poetics and Politics of Shame in Postcolonial Literature**
Edited by David Attwell, Annalisa Pes and Susanna Zinato

70 **Postcolonial Animalities**
Edited by Amit Baishya and Suvadip Sinha

71 **Writing Cyprus**
Postcolonial and Partitioned Literatures of Place and Space
Bahriye Kemal

For more information about this series, please visit: https://www.routledge.com

Writing Cyprus

Postcolonial and Partitioned Literatures of Place and Space

Bahriye Kemal

Routledge
Taylor & Francis Group
NEW YORK AND LONDON

First published 2020
by Routledge
605 Third Avenue, New York, NY 10017

and by Routledge
2 Park Square, Milton Park, Abingdon, Oxon, OX14 4RN

First issued in paperback 2021

Routledge is an imprint of the Taylor & Francis Group, an informa business

Publisher's Note
The publisher has gone to great lengths to ensure the quality of this reprint but points out that some imperfections in the original copies may be apparent.

Library of Congress Cataloging-in-Publication Data
A catalog record for this title has been requested

ISBN 13: 978-1-03-224000-8 (pbk)
ISBN 13: 978-0-367-42794-8 (hbk)

Typeset in Sabon
by codeMantra

Contents

Acknowledgments

The idea for this book began in 2009 with a journey from Kyrenia in the north through the Nicosia buffer zone to Limassol in the south, when I joined a *Cadences* reading event. The book would not have happened without the support and guidance of many people. I'm deeply indebted to Lyn Innes and Donna Landry: Donna commented on every version of the book, from its first inception in 2009 until the last clean up in 2019. Lyn picked it and me up every time we fell, reading early proposals, early drafts and final drafts of the book. I am very thankful to Ziad Elmarsafy, Abdulrazak Gurnah, Alex Padamsee and Caroline Rooney, who read and commented on the early drafts and proposals. I thank Norbert Bugeja, Filippo Menozzi, Tinashe Mushakavanhu, Maria Ridda and Ben Worthy for commenting on the first stages of the project. I thank Nafiya Guden, Ole Laursen and Ariane Mildenberg for commenting on final drafts of chapters. I thank Neophytos Loizides and Andrekos Varnava for reading the final draft, so as to confirm I have successfully border-crossed disciplines. I am indebted to all the authors – especially Alev Adil, Claire Angelides, Aydin Mehmet Ali, Emine/Fikret Demirag, Stavros S. Karayanni, Gurgenc Korkmazel, Montis family, George Moleskis, Nihmet Yasin, Nora Nadjarian, Miranda Hoplaros, Stephanos Stephanides – in the book for their support throughout the process. I thank the teachers and inspectors of literature from the Ministry of Education in the north and the south. I thank Pembe Ozocak for her translations.

I am grateful to Ruth Keshishian of Moufflon Bookshop and to Nahide Merlen of Isik Bookshop for providing me with the reading material, the knowledge and ongoing support that shaped the book. Thanks to my brother Kemal G. Kemal for introducing me to this and other literary scenes in Cyprus and thinking me an inspiration – you are a true inspiration, Kem.

Thanks to Vinita Joseph and Holly Hutchins for keeping me focussed. I thank the Routledge team, especially Jennifer Abbott for her guidance throughout. I also thank the reviewers for their valuable comments.

I thank those energies past and present for teaching me about being and becoming a person out of Cyprus and the UK: Giorgos Ailiotis,

Senel Bilal, Deger Djemal, Utku Cagda, Sifa Capli, Bircan Findik, Seran Niyazi, Necati Ozbeyli, Tahir Sonara, Ipek Ulug, Nurten'ba, Nu, Yil, Pembe Yenge, Nuri, Nes and Yakup abi.

I thank my family, especially my mum Meryem Kemal, dad Zekai Kemal, my sister Nafiya Kemal as well as in-laws Huseyin Guden, Macide Aganoglu, Umran Kardelen, for always supporting and believing in me, so that I believed in myself and my work.

I thank my grandmothers, Bahriye Kemal and Nafiya Necati, their great-grandsons, Kayra Zekai Guden and Tugra Devrim Guden, and my Hakki Aslan Aganoglu for giving me the energies to never give up so as to finish this book – I dedicate this book to you – nenes, teyzem and H.

1 Introduction of a Postcolonial and Partitioned Place, Space and Identity

> ...[S]pace thus produced also serves as a tool of thought and of action; that in addition to being a means of production it is also a means of control, and hence of domination, of power; yet that, as such, it escapes in part from those who would make use of it. (Lefebvre, *Production*, 26)

> Like a wanderer, I hang around aimlessly
> In homes that belong to others.
> [...]
> They say,
> You are a Maronite,
> they gave you your home
> Napoleon, you are lucky...
> [...]
> You will live in Kormakitis
> You will forget Agios Pavlos
> Nicosia will no longer see you
> If in the end Cyprus is divided
> Would you choose to live in the south
> Or would you choose the north?
> (Terzis).

> The most disturbing thing about being a Cypriot is that one can only be a Greek or a Turkish-Cypriot. Postcolonial Cypriot identity is quintessentially and inescapably hyphenated. [...] [T]he only genuine postcolonial Cypriot, is the Linobambakoi. (Constantinou, 248, 266)

Why is it that the concept of place in postcolonial discourse differs from the definitions of place provided in partition studies? As stated in the *Postcolonial Studies Reader* and *Postcolonial Studies: The Key Concepts*, place is a crucial concept in colonial and postcolonial discourse, in which it does not simply figure as a landscape or geographical territory, but a complex interaction between the self, language, history and the environment. Place is the 'concomitant of difference, the continual reminder of the separation, and yet of the hybrid interpenetration of the coloniser and colonised' (Ashcroft et al, *Reader*, 391), and self and place – always interacting and in a state of invention relevant to all the colonised and colonisers of the world. In partition studies, place has not been conceptualised or theorised as such, but instead points us towards specific geographical territories, focussing on the moment of a break, a 'violent territorial and political separation of groups' (Jassal and Ben-Ari, 21) and the traumatic consequences this break has on the society. There has been limited enquiry into the conflation between place within postcolonial discourse and place within partition studies, because partition studies are a relatively new area of study in explorations of colonial and postcolonial contexts. The complexities of place offered in postcolonial discourse are most commonly depicted and must be enhanced through place in partition studies. It is through comparing and combining the two that one can fully understand the complexities and agency of place, and how this determines the formation and flux of identity. Such a comparative approach provides new ways of experiencing, reading and constructing place, revised as a crucial concept for both postcolonial and partition studies. This concept will be interrogated to show that 'place' must meet 'space', together making them the most significant concept in postcolonial and partition discourse, so much so that it must be taken beyond just being an abstract concept and understood as a concrete concept. In this chapter and book, I propose a new model, at once theoretical and empirical, that will acknowledge and can carry the actual weight, agency and power of place and space in both postcolonial and partition discourse, using Cyprus as a significant example.

Cyprus is a postcolonial partitioned case, and to understand it a spatial understanding is crucial, whereby the island's political and cultural history of colonisation, partition and conflicting identities is an issue of place and space; the complexities of place and space that determine identity fluctuation have become its legacy. Between west and east or north and south, Cyprus is a strategically located 'Mediterranean'[1] island that has had a distinct experience of major world events. It was once a transit site for western pilgrims on route to the holy land, later an essential passageway towards conquest for western and non-western imperial regimes, more recently an overdetermined tangential area of the Arab uprising, of Islamic state action, and mass migration. The island's position between the geopolitical world divide is also reflected in its own status; Cyprus has the only divided capital in the world with the south a recognised European state inhabited mostly by people who speak Greek and identify with Christianity, and the north a de-facto entity with people who speak Turkish and are identified as Muslims. Because of this spatiality, Cyprus is simultaneously at the centre and periphery of various positions that disturb fixed categorisations, thus serving to blur the dominant geopolitical binaries within the world and the island. Hence Cyprus has always been in the process of competing productions – for example, Strabo's Greek world within a Byzantine geography (18–24 CE), Piri Reis' Ottoman-Cyprus map in *Kitab-I-Bahriye* (1521), Herbert Kitchener's first comprehensive 1878–1881 British-Cyprus map, the 1950–1960s competing anticolonial movements that remapped a Greece-Cyprus or Turkey-Cyprus, and the 1964/74 partition that was/is an affair of enclaves, lands and properties – which each aims to gain control by providing fixed definition and total knowledge of this paradoxical island. This processual status shows Cyprus' pivotal significance to those experiences with place and space that have come to define postcolonial and partition discourse, yet Cyprus has been neglected by postcolonial and partition scholars.

The case of Cyprus has been overwhelmed by historic-political works in Greek or Turkish about one ethnic group, works that reinforce binaries. Recently works in English focus on all the people in Cyprus. There has been a cross-disciplinary turn with enriching collaborations focussing on core moments, starting with new theories of comparative nationalisms,[2] followed by work on post-1964/74 island patriotism,[3] and then intercommunal and conflict resolution studies.[4] These studies are mostly in the social sciences by scholars connected to Cyprus who reclaim these moments, adopting approaches resonating with postcolonial discourse and partition studies used by historians and literary scholars. Works on Cyprus from a (post)colonial perspective are mostly by historians focussing on the Greek heritage and by anthropologists.[5] Similarly, studies on partition are mostly anthropological and geopolitical.[6] Literary scholars have been largely excluded from this fruitful interdisciplinary conversation; however, literary studies from an inclusive postcolonial and partition perspective are emerging, especially in edited collections.[7] Although a common theme between all these initiatives is place and space, this theme has not been addressed directly or comprehensively.

My study draws from, adds to and is shaped by this body of work on Cyprus, so to initiate a new cross-disciplinary approach, where history, politics and anthropology will finally meet literature within a postcolonial partition spatial framework. In this way this book also fills a gap in postcolonial and partition studies.[8] *Writing Cyprus* is the first study of the literatures of Cyprus from a postcolonial and partition perspective, combined with spatial considerations as related to humanistic-geography and Marxist philosophy. It is the most comprehensive exploration of English, Greek and Turkish writing in the context of the island's cultural and political history of colonialism, partition and conflicting identity via spatial considerations. Parts of this chapter and book relate Cyprus to key postcolonial partition cases. Comparative partition offers a gateway for new cases, like Cyprus, to be included; provides ways of knowing and learning a specific postcolonial partition case; and presents mutual understanding with enriching possibilities between postcolonial partition territories – thus enhancing a definition of postcolonial partition studies. This approach is not only a tool to write Cyprus on the postcolonial partition map, but a tool to write, rewrite, make and break the postcolonial partition map via Cyprus. Through this comparative partition, I have learnt, as Gyanendra Pandey states for postcolonial partitioned India: 'what the historians call a "fragment" – [...] literatures of India – is of central importance in challenging the state's construction of history, in thinking other histories and marking those contested spaces through which particular unities are sought to be constituted and others broken up' (Pandey, 'Defence', 50); I have learnt, as Panama Roy states via Pandey: 'the literary has been assigned the place of the preferred other to the historical narrative by many Indian historians' (Roy, 366). This book has embraced the literary as the preferred means to write Cyprus because it can negotiate between the historical-political competing narratives, thereby providing a complementary narrative that captures and goes beyond the dominant binary legacy of historical-political deadlock discourse. This study attempts to inspire new grounds for the meeting of postcolonial discourse and partition studies combined with spatial considerations, and also enable new ways of experiencing, reading and writing a different Cyprus for Cypriot-selves, diasporic-selves, Mediterranean-selves, my-selves, and all other-selves who have breathed the pain of partition and lived the disorder of displacement.

The section 'Spatial Model: Postcolonial Partitioned Place and Space via Tuan and Lefebvre' focusses on the central topic of this book – place and space – to introduce the spatial model. Beginning with place in postcolonial discourse, I engage with what I call layers of invention through drawing from key texts generally accepted as representing the postcolonial canon, because it is my wish that representatives of postcolonial discourse will allow a gateway whereby Cyprus will have a platform via these texts from which to speak. Place in partition studies will be discussed through core motifs shaped by territories accepted as key to partition studies. Investigating postcoloniality and partition will confirm the intersection pivotal for understanding the power of spatiality, which prepares the way to bring together Yi-Fu Tuan's humanistic-geography and Henri Lefebvre's Marxist philosophy. In this way I introduce the three-part spatial model, wherein postcolonial partitioned 'inventions' of place are illuminated through Tuan's perspective of 'experiencing' closed place and open space, and Lefebvre's 'spatiology' and 'rhythmanalysis'. This spatial model captures the power of place and space in postcolonial partitioned cases, including Cyprus.

The section 'The Case of Cyprus: Complex, Distinct, Bypassed Deadlock' offers foundational terms required to write and read the book. Cyprus is introduced via complexities this study is/was subject to, its distinctiveness and relevance to postcolonial partition studies, and reasons that Cyprus has been bypassed by these studies. This will lead the way to 'Competing Narratives of History: A Deadlock Production', which will read and write Cyprus through a chronology of four different historical moments: the 'Ottoman Winds', 'Becoming Mrs British-Cyprus', 'Independence Failures', and '1964/74 Partition', considering Cyprus within the discourse of historiography, politics, colonialism, postcolonialism and partition. This broad approach is essential because Cyprus has not been the object of analysis within postcolonial partition studies, and as a result its relevance to these discourses, pivotal for understanding literary Cyprus, is relatively unknown. This historical-political discussion will not be a straightforward account but a complementary performance between the dominant 'competing narratives' – a partition studies motif – from across the divide. Here I will trace the deadlock, whereby the divided historical-political narratives will partially speak whilst mostly contesting each other, so as to point to the need for new narratives – the literary other – that can negotiate with this binary. This dialogue, dialectic and deadlock will first show how the people of Cyprus, who have been partitioned for decades, if not centuries, have shared 'identities' determined by places and spaces throughout history. Second, it will show Cyprus is relevant to postcolonial and partition discourse, which provides a new gateway to reading and writing it beyond the binary. Third, it demonstrates the power of place and space in all postcolonial and partitioned cases. All three of these points operating via the dialectic, dialogue and deadlock are captured most fully through literary narratives that perform with but move beyond the historical-political deadlock, which will be the focus of the book.

Spatial Model: Postcolonial Partitioned Place and Space via Tuan and Lefebvre

Postcolonial and Partition Place

Postcolonial discourse responds to the effects that European colonisation has on places and people, which point most often to the colonised, yet the coloniser territory and society are equally pivotal. This is a responding that deals with the complex interaction and separation between coloniser-colonised and place-self, within colonial and postcolonial contexts. Postcolonial studies engage with the layers of knowledge and representation inscribed onto a place by the imperialist imaginary, as well as those produced by colonised subjects, which, in turn, determines the identity of the coloniser and the colonised. This process makes it possible for place to be understood as 'language' (Ashcroft et al, *Reader*, 391) or text, which is in a constant complex process of invention and becoming.

Postcolonial discourse is inescapably about place and the playful process of invention: an un-invention that wipes out and puts an end to existing constructions; a pre-invention that is to return to a past primordial construction; and a re-invention that is to start anew for future constructions.

The significance of place in postcolonial discourse has been displayed in the most influential works by pioneers of the field. On *Orientalism* and *Culture and Imperialism* Edward Said writes:

> [These books]are based not only on the notion of what I call imaginative geography – the invention and construction of a geographical space called the Orient, for instance, with scant attention paid to the actuality of the geography and its inhabitants – but also on the mapping, conquest, and annexation of territory both in what Conrad called dark places of the earth and in its most densely inhabited and lived-in places, like India or Palestine. (Said, 'Inventions', 181)

Said shows that the invention of geography was a process used by imperial powers both before and after colonisation and conquest; here the imperialist imagining subjects the geographies to layers of Orientalist construction, by which the imperial powers un-invent, wipe out and release them of all rational knowledge and civilisation in order to mark them as backward, irrational, Oriental others of the west. This imaginative geography is, as pioneered by Frantz Fanon in *Black Skin, White Masks* and *The Wretched of the Earth*, based on a dualistic principle: 'the colonial world is a Manichaean world', whereby 'This world cut in two is inhabited by two different species' (Fanon, *Wretched*, 30–31) in 'two camps' (Fanon, *Black*, 2) – black-white, colonised-coloniser, east-west, barbaric-civilised. This Manichaean world or Manichaeism, as developed further by Abdul JanMohammed, is a concept for the uncompromising binary within imperialist imagining – the colonised world is conceived as inferior, uncontrollable and ultimately evil, and the coloniser world is conceived as superior, in perfect control and the embodiment of good – confirming the coloniser 'will not be inclined to expend any energy in understanding the worthless alterity of the colonized' (JanMohammed, 'Economy', 65). It is in fact this 'imaginative geography' of the imperialist, developed prior to colonisation, which justifies the necessity for colonising and conquering the territory. It is upon colonisation that this imperialist imagining goes beyond the imperialist text, and starts to figure physically on the colonised territory; here making territory a central site of the most complex process of invention and extreme contention during the colonial and postcolonial period.

In the colonial period this process of invention continues with, as Said confirms, the colonisers' 'mapping territory', which can be understood through Paul Carter's notion in *The Road to Botany Bay* of 'transforming [empty] space into place' (Carter, xxiii). Here the territory is imagined as empty space, whereby existing colonised constructions are un-invented, wiped out and released of all meaning, so to be re-invented via cartographical investment that name and claim it into an enclosed place for themselves. They physically and mentally map a colonial place that is, as Fanon confirms: 'divided into compartments' with a 'zone inhabited by the colonial settler' that is powerful, spacious, bright, clean, well fed and full of good things, and a 'zone where the native lives' that is powerless, ill, evil, confined living, hungry and on its knees (Fanon, *Wretched*, 29–30). Through this mapping, the imperialist invests a new language into the geography, by which the coloniser locates, knows and gains total control of its colony, whilst the colonised are dislocated from, and lose all understanding and command of their colonised home and themselves in the process.

By this imperialist investment, the colonised undergo a 'lack of fit' between the language and maps used by the coloniser to describe the place, and the place actually experienced by the colonised. Often pointed out via settler experiences as confirmed by Robert Kroetsch: 'there is in the Canadian word a concealed other experience, sometimes British' through which the inhabitants 'recognizes that something doesn't fit' (Ashcroft et al, *Reader*, 394–95), and Dennis Lee: 'Try to speak the words of your home and you will discover – if you are a colonial – that you do not know them' (Lee, 163). However, as Ashcroft et al. confirm, 'whether the speaker is the settler, the indigenous occupant of invaded colonies, [or] a member of a colonised and dominated African or Indian society [...] language always negotiates a kind of gap between the word and its signification' (Ashcroft et al, *Reader*, 391). In all colonial encounters, the subject undergoes this 'lack of fit', and they do not have the agency to withdraw, resist or write back to the imperialist mapping, compartments and zones until the decolonial moment of nationalising.

By these nationalising moments the colonised subjects try to reclaim their relationship with place in multiple ways, where they enter a fresh process of invention by, as Fanon suggests, 'approach[ing] [...] the colonial world, its ordering and its geographical lay-out [...] to mark out the lines on which a decolonised society will be reorganised' (Fanon, *Wretched*, 29). Here the geographic, cartographic and compartmentalising significance in the colonial moment paves the way for it to be a crucial player in the decolonial and postcolonial moments. Here, as Fanon suggests, the colonised often imitate the coloniser by setting out to break existing texts – the imperial texts. Now it is the colonised who empty the territory of the coloniser's inheritance, to turn it into a place for themselves that they can know and command.

This process of recovery often starts, as Kroetsch states, with the colonised aiming to 'un-name' and 'un-invent the world' invented by the coloniser, so that they can 'uncreate themselves into existence' (Ashcroft et al, *Reader*, 394–96). In most cases, the colonised un-invent the colonisers' mappings by a pre-invention, which is a 'nativism' as in the negritude movement, that attempts to return to a pre-colonial pure territory by using an archaic language and symbols. Thus, place is imbued with primordial names, ancestors, ancient myths as Nhlanhla Maake shows in 'Inscribing Identity on the Landscape: National symbols in South Africa' and Liz Gunner suggests in 'Names and the Land: Poetry of belonging and unbelonging, a comparative approach'. Such an un-invention and pre-invention is a dangerous imaginative fallacy: first, because colonial inheritance is an inescapable incurable palimpsest in the land; second, fixating on a pre-colonial moment can result in validating the Orientalist binary of backward irrational colonised as opposed to civilised rational coloniser. In *The Wretched of the Earth*, Fanon warns the subject against such pre-invention, and in *The Empire Writes Back*, Ashcroft, Griffiths and Tiffin state 'It is not possible to return to or rediscover an absolute pre-colonial cultural purity' (Ashcroft et al., *Empire*, 220). Furthermore, this pre-invention or pre-mapping prolongs and intensifies the 'lack of fit', because the archaic language and maps used to interpret a place and the actual daily experiences in that place have no resonance. In this process of pre-invention or re-invention gendering becomes significant, which continues to imitate colonial modes of investment – the coloniser linguistically and cartographically gendered the colony into a female in need of protection from the imperial mother, son or father – to confirm total knowledge, duty and command of place. In most nationalising cases, the territory is a woman – endangered chaste virgin, seductive lurer, mother, the goddess – and in some it is a man – fatherland or the land of martyred sons – as a means to mobilise and return command to the de/colonised nation.[9]

Postcolonial discourse also offers a process of recovery beyond such nationalist practices – un-inventing imperial inheritance to pre-invent and re-invent original heritage – to contain place. This is shown in Graham Huggan's 'Decolonising the Map' that defines territory as 'shifting ground' between a 'de- to reconstruction', between mapbreaking the colonial texts to mapmaking postcolonial texts (Huggan, 'Map', 126) using Gilles Deleuze's and Felix Guattari's map as a rhizome: 'open and connectable in all of its dimension; it is detachable, reversible, susceptible to constant modification. It can be torn, reversed, adapted to any kind of mounting, reworked by an individual, group, or social formation' (Deleuze, 12). Here the postcolonial territory is a 'rhizomatic ("open") rather than [...] a falsely homogenised ("closed") construct' (Huggan, 'Map', 126), depicted as a shift 'away from the desire for homogeneity towards an acceptance of diversity[...] not as a means of spatial containment or systematic organisation, but as a medium of spatial perception' (Huggan, 'Map', 124). This rhizomatic process blurs the binary between colonised and coloniser territorial inventions; it relocates perceptions and inventions to transgress in both colonised and coloniser territories, and revises the binary between colonised subjugation and coloniser domination.

Through this rhizomatic process there is entry into that perfect Fanonian space: 'Zone of occult instability' (Fanon, *Wretched*, 183) that can truly contaminate the divided world, through a practice that can – borrowing Said's point on *The Wretched of the Earth* – 'bridge the gap between the white and non-white' (Said, *Imperial*, 326), or the coloniser and colonised. This is a zone where 'The two cultures can affront each other, enrich each other [...] to recognize and accept the reciprocal relativism of different cultures' (Fanon, *African*, 44). Here, the colonised responds to the colonial encounter through appropriating as opposed to abrogating the investment, enabling entry into what Leela Gandhi defines as a 'mutual transformation of coloniser and colonised' (Gandhi, 140). This is an entry into a zone where the binary is blurred, as in Homi Bhabha's 'The Commitment to Theory', where colonised and coloniser differentiation is contaminated, via a 'third space' for the translation, hybridisation, negotiation and ambivalence between them, and in 'Mimicry and Man' via the colonised 'imitating' the coloniser to be 'almost the same but not quite' (Bhabha, *Location*, 89). These concepts pave the way for mutual transformation to figure in both colonised and coloniser territories.

The processes of mutual transformation are enhanced when considering spatial mobility and migration of the (formerly) colonised within and between the empire, including: colonised persons as indentured labourers between colonies; colonial soldiers mobilising in the west to fight Europe's war; the formerly colonised economic migrants from the colonial periphery moving to help rebuild the metropolitan imperial centre. These considerations provide for a spatial move away from the binary between the colonised-coloniser inventions in the colonial world, and towards contaminating different binaries in the postcolonial world(s), which continues to be 'cut in two' or three between first world and third world, powerful and powerless, global and local.

This spatial-world-turn gave way to focus on uneven developments through Marxist approaches, often related to world systems or world cultural theory offered by sociologist and political economist, which provides new concerns with positionality and representability of/in the world. This can be understood through the Subaltern Studies Collective, and especially Gayatri Chakravorty Spivak's contribution on first world-third world inventions, and more recently through Warwick Research Collective (WReC) that cuts the world into three portions – core-semiperiphery-periphery – so to understand combined and uneven developments through comparative systems of inequality. Through Spivak the focus turns to ways the 'so-called "Third World" [...] *produces* the wealth and the possibility of the cultural self-representation of the "First World"' (Spivak, 'Practical', 96). Here confirming the third world cannot be represented as powerless because it is a necessary ingredient, without which, the western hegemony and capitalism of the first world could not have taken its force and course. This inspires grounds to interrogate a person's positionality and representability in the world, where direction moves away from the dominant political forces and intellectual elites to marginal groups of the third world who are disempowered and outside of the hegemonic power structure. This is a move to marginal zones or spaces occupied and invented by the world's Other – subaltern women, farmers and labourers, migrants, diasporas and refugees, to list a few – who lack power and are excluded from socio-political production. This suggests a positionality whereby the worlds' Other have a stand from which to speak; however, as Spivak famously utters in 'Can the Subaltern Speak?', this is a crisis of representation, because the third world elites considered the 'authentic inhabitants of the margin' (Spivak, 'Margin', 224) cannot speak of/for the disempowered, because these elites have limited knowledge of the marginal space the Other occupies and invents.

These concerns simultaneously pave the way for global and local dynamics operating through transnational and transcultural inventions, which cannot, as Arjun Appadurai points out, be understood 'in terms of existing center-periphery models', first world-third world, powerful-powerless models, but instead as a 'complex, overlapping, disjunctive order' (Appadurai, 'Disjuncture', 33) or disorder. This invention figures in the former imperial centre as depicted in studies that can be defined as a postcolonial city turn.[10] Here, as Saskia Sassen confirms, the city is a complex site where the global and local, and the powerful and powerless actors from different worlds meet. This enables the world's excluded Other to emerge as a new force, where, manipulating the complexity, they invest new names – i.e. the diasporic mini homelands in London – in the global city to invent or 'make' social and political spaces they know and control, whilst the powerful agents of the first and third world are dislocated from and lose command of the imperial city, the country and worlds in the process.

Further to this the city's Other is both a person and a site enabling such transnational and transcultural invention. Here Raymond Williams' model of the country and city can be adapted to the imperial centre and its postcolonial periphery, or postcolonial peripheral city and its countryside. Here the complexity of the postcolonial territory, like the imperial city, is exposed in multiple ways, including: unveiling the colonial legacies in the independent state; unearthing the historical layers in the land; revealing the 'mutual transformation' between the formerly colonised and coloniser; highlighting the relationship between the official native elites and the former coloniser and capturing the network between the postcolonial periphery and the former metropolitan imperial centre. In this process, two categories are the excluded Other that exploit the complexity: first, the postcolonial territory itself is peripheral Other to the imperial centre, often governed by official native elites who smooth out the uneven developments so to invent an imagined equality. The second excluded Other is the unofficial people of the postcolonial territory – especially the subalterns who remained in the periphery as well as their family members who departed to the centres – who become political actors and a collective force by exploiting the relations within and between the postcolonial periphery and the imperial city.

Such inventions can be enhanced via postcolonial islands that are based on – borrowing Iain Chambers' term on the Mediterranean – a multiple mutability: here the island is the world's Other, considered a debris site excluded from being a global political and economic power, yet in a position that can manipulate the complexity to emerge as an unofficial distinct force. The island or islands, whether those in the Mediterranean, the Caribbean or the Pacific, have always been sites between highly complex networks – as example: the connective medium between islands controlled by the Ancient Greeks; the channels for crusaders in quest of the holy land; shipping lanes for explorers in search of newfound land; maritime trade routes for western imperialist in search of wealth via colonies – within the sea.[11] The island's positionality between these complexities in the sea makes it a site for indefinite arrival, transit and departure with multiple conceptions and construction by actors from across the world. For foreign forces that sail by or stopover, the island is/was conceived as a natural territory or utopia that is, as Rod Edmond and Vanessa Smith confirm in *Island in History and Representation*, defined by its boundedness, it fits within the retina of the eye, making it an object, like property, that can be grasped, owned and is complete. Through the arrival and departure of these forces, however, the island disrupts this imposed completeness by transforming into a hybrid territory or dystopia, defined by its unboundedness, making it a subject of constant foreign occupation and implementation that is ungraspable and incomplete. This positionality confirms that the island is a permeable fluid site subject to layers of historical, cultural and political encounters and exchange, constantly moving and transforming in difference and disorder that it can cope with, ending in it having a doubling paradoxical[12] character that is an open fragment and a closed unity. First, for example, each historical encounter is a single fragment of reality, where multiple fragments co-exist in a closed unity within the island. Second, the island is a fragment of land in the sea, imposed with an imagined unity by the western minds, whilst naturally acquiring an actual unity through connecting and communicating with other islands, thereby producing a complex 'global' – transnational and sociocultural – archipelago.[13] In light of this, the island can exploit the complexity to emerge as a force and make a political space in different ways. It freely performs with neighbouring islands to produce a global archipelago in a part of the world that they can control, and it grants itself the freedom, like the foreign explorers, to raid and select from the globe – that cultural and historical palimpsest – figuring in the island to (re)produce these parts of the world and itself anew. In this process, the island can be established as a key player that shapes the economic growth of the powerful nations in the world, disrupts the world powers and rewrites dominant western imaginings that produce the island as a property that can be owned and controlled. Instead, if the postcolonial island is to be addressed as a property, then it is a thing of/for the globe with a worldly exchange and use value that is an uncontrollable force always in the process of becoming.

Postcolonial studies have more recently attended to the ecological and environmental effects caused by colonialism and globalism. First conceptualised by Alfred W. Crosby as 'ecological imperialism', which explores ways colonised environments have been physically devasted and transformed, more recently there has been a 'green turn' and 'animal turn' initiated by Graham Huggan and Helen Tiffin, and subsequently developed by various scholars,[14] whereby ecocriticism meets postcolonialism to suggest all colonial issues are environmental issues. Such ecological and environmental destruction once caused by imperial visitors are now caused by new visitors as related to postcolonial tourism.[15] More recently geo-destruction is caused by wars and mass migration as in the east Mediterranean, ending in a turn to studies on postcolonial borders and Europe.[16]

This hyper-complex process of invention within colonial and postcolonial contexts leads Ashcroft, Griffiths and Tiffin to claim: 'place *is* language, something in constant flux, a discourse in process' (*Reader*, 391). This discourse provides for place to be understood as, what Carter calls 'spatial history', a palimpsest that is constantly in a process of being read, written, experienced and invented. Place is a 'shifting ground', and, as Lefebvre states, it is a 'disjointed unity' that is at once a homogeneous measurable closed zone, and a fragmentary immeasurable open zone, which 'divides and rules' a country and people; this invention of closed zone and open zone is the concept of place that defines the postcolonial curriculum.

The postcolonial concept of place thus discussed has pointed broadly to either colonised or coloniser territory, without specifying a geography or type of colonial context. In many studies, however, postcolonial placemaking and its complexities are discussed through prioritising settler colonies, like Canada and Australia: Huggan states that they have a 'multiplication of spatial references resulting not only in an increased range of national and international locations but also a series of "territorial disputes"' (Huggan, 'Map' 123). Similarly, in the *Postcolonial Studies Reader*, Ashcroft, Griffiths and Tiffin claim: 'It is perhaps no accident that the most overt agonising over place occurs in the settler colonies' (392), supported through articles relevant to settler experiences in the settler colony. The examination of postcolonial place through such claims is flawed, because it dismisses the colonies that have undergone partition[17]; partitioned colonies are more intensely outfitted with a range of spatial and 'territorial disputes', and are central sites that experience the most overt and agonising processes of invention and re-production.

Partition studies enhances an understanding of place because it deals with territories that have experienced the most traumatic processes of spatial invention. These territories have not only undergone all the aforementioned complex inventions between closed zone and open zone that define postcolonial discourse, but they have also experienced an actual physical, social and mental partitioning in the colonial and postcolonial moment. Partition studies can be understood through 'comparative studies' between the three key territories – India-Pakistan-Bangladesh, Israel-Palestine and Ireland – explored mainly in social sciences,[18] and focussing on core 'motifs' they offer.

Though my understanding draws on these key partitioned territories with focus on the motifs, particularly in relation to the decolonial moment when a new state transformed from a single to two entities, here I confirm that partition studies should go beyond this moment and these key territories. Partition is central to the foundation, formation and fall of various empires, which has created and is creating postcolonial partition territories. Therefore, I argue that partition studies should begin when Europe began conquering and cutting the globe: starting with the Americas and Asia partitioned between five European empires, including British, French, Dutch; then 1881–1914 with the Scramble of Africa, ending in its partition between seven empires, including British, French and Portugal; followed by the 1916–1920 Middle East partition, when the Sykes-Picot Agreement then Treaty of Sevres divided the Ottoman Empire's territories between France and Britain. In addition, partition studies should engage with former colonies that entered a process towards partition; here I mean territories like Lebanon that experienced division and conflict, or Syria, Yemen and Myanmar that are experiencing it. This partition study shows the continual presence of the British who created the key partition territories.

That said, in this book the meaning of partition is shaped by studies on key partition territories and motifs including: 'geographical partition', 'competing narratives', 'name games', 'number games', 'divide and rule', 'ethnic-nationalism', 'ethnic-cleansing', 'population transfer/exchange', 'border-line partition disorder (BPD)', 'property', 'violence' and 'conflict resolution'. Place – especially spatial practices and experience – is crucial to each motif, which I will define in a stylistic form resonating with partition – a fractured disjointed style to discuss a fractured disjointed territory and people.

Geographical Partition: reproduces the territorial boundaries and borders of a state from a single to two or more units, which separate conflicting groups into a new homogenous majority unit and arrangement. This moment of territorial binary and break becomes the main focus of partition studies: for Israel-Palestine focus is 1948, Ireland 1919–1921 and India 1947. In *Literature, Partition and the Nation State*, Joe Cleary studies the partition of Israel-Palestine and Ireland when these original partition settlements were challenged after 1960. In *Remembering Partition*, Gyanendra Pandey states that, 'historians belonging to both India and Pakistan continue to write of the partition of India, or of British India, in 1947' (Pandey, 13). Pandey rightly interrogates the limitations of subjecting the study of partition to the geographical break by stating: 'How many partitions did it take to make the Partition of 1947?' (Pandey, 19). Pandey studies three partitions.[19] It is apparent from Pandey's explanation that the official '1947 Partition' – note capitalisation of the 'P' – is considered most significant, where the 'three different conceptions of "partition"' – note the lower case 'p' – are discussed as going into the 'making of the 1947 Partition' (Pandey, 25). This helps highlight Pandey's own misconceptions by confirming that in partition territories the most studied physical geographical break – I correct this as the 'official partition' – is just one layer in partition production. This production is relevant to all cases, which include actual and imagined layers of partition operating via various binary groups – the ethno-religiously divided inhabitants, as well as the official and the unofficial minds – who invent their side as a safe controllable closed zone, and the other side as a dangerous uncontrollable open zone. Examining the actual and imagined layers enables a new kind of shared narrative, identification and geography of partition to be produced, so multiple partitions that can blur binaries, boundaries and deadlocks.

Competing Narratives: this is based on the ways the inhabitants speak about what happened, so how they address the process that created partition, as related to dominant historical and political records, which are actual and imagined, official and unofficial, and oral and written narratives; this creates the historical-political deadlock. This competition is mostly between the survivors of partition on opposing sides of the ethno-religious divide, who each aim to invent a closed territorial zone for themselves that contests the threatening open zone across the divide. This competition is also between players from the same side, which diversifies the narrative mappings. Thus, this multiplicity of competing narrative mappings manifests itself in a language game, a 'shifting ground', where the territory is consistently under invention and re/production, so the dominant binary legacy of historical-political deadlock can be blurred.

Name Game: the rival system of names, particular place names and people names, operating between languages, religions, ethnicities and traditions. This is demographic and cartographic cutting and compartmentalising of people and place through naming; it is a mental and physical invention that enables the namers to have total knowledge and power. The namers and names consistently change. In the colonial moment, this game is between the colonised and coloniser, where the latter have total power through naming and claiming the territory, as in the 1824 Ordnance Survey in Ireland that Anglicised Gaelic place names. In the decolonial moment, this model is appropriated by the colonised inhabitants, who compete against each other to rename and reclaim their places through reverting back to pre-colonial names. This model is also widespread in the postcolonial moment, as seen when the state of Israel wiped out Palestinian place names from 1948.

Number Games[20]**:** the rival system of numbers that compartmentalises people and place, which is always under negotiation. This may include census recordings, mapmaking, and the representative government. Such practices start with the coloniser's mental and physical construction that carves the colonised people and land into a numerical system, so to enable them to have total knowledge and power. The colonised later appropriate these methods against each other, as a weapon to obtain power; here they compulsively play with quantities, a game of majorities and minorities, to imply in excess that the human condition and its geography is a mathematical mental abstraction.

Divide and Rule: the colonial policy to control people by sharpening difference and dissent between them, so to prevent the possibility of the colonised unifying against the coloniser. This difference and division between the groups is reinforced through the colonisers' demographic and cartographical compartmentalisation, meeting their inconsistent support and moulding of the demands and devotions of each group towards inventing a territory. This causes the conflict to be between the separate groups over the production of territory rather than between the coloniser and the colonised.

National Identity and Nationalism: the mental devotion and construction of a relatively large group of people, organised and united by common narratives and symbols of descent, ethnicity, religion, history or language under a single usually independent place. The organisation and division of groups who share a common narrative for the territory is the first stage of partition; the strengthening of the aspiration to invent this shared territory divides the groups even further; once the aspiration of each group is transformed into a mobilisation it is often here when conflict reigns, ending in partition. Paul Brass' instrumentalist model in *Ethnicity and Nationalism* sheds useful light to locate the ethno-national development in partitioned territories. Brass explores the elites' role in selecting and manipulating symbols, which transform some primordial categories into an ethnic community and later into modern national and nationalist groups. Here if the elite protagonists are from different categories, they select different symbols that generate a divided ethno-religious community and nation. Brass' model shows how nations and nationalism are mental constructions determined by identifying with symbols from the array on offer, resulting in a 'slide' from one identification to other,[21] which confirms 'Human beings have multiple collective identifications, whose scope and intensity will vary' (Smith, 175). This identification intensifies into a nation through symbols that are always in deep connection with place, space and geography.

Ethnic-Cleansing[22]: the policy of a particular group systematically to eliminate another group from a given territory on the basis of religious, ethnic or national origin. Such a policy involves violence and is usually connected to military operations. It is a physical expulsion and eradication of a people and their inscriptions from a place. The ethno-national devotion of the group to map a homogenised closed zone for themselves gives way for them to invent open zones of conflict, massacre, genocide and outrageous violence. This cleansing process often ends with geographical partition as a means to solve the bloody conflict in the territory.

Population Transfer/Exchange: the moment that breaks a group into separate homogenous territorial units, where journeys, border-crossing, hostage exchange, missing people and refugee status reign. In this process, the victims experiencing the transfer or exchange invent the home they depart from as a closed zone of belonging and safety, and the home they will arrive to as an open zone of foreignness, longing and danger.

Border-line Partition Disorder (BPD): this is a mental and physical experience resulting from the invention of a fresh border that divides the territory and people into two or more entities. The border often initiates with a line drawn on a map as in Green Line in Palestine-Israel (1949), and the Radcliffe Line in India and Pakistan (1947). The line materialises from mental to physical territory via the construction of military barriers and checkpoints. This gives way for crossing lines, so border-crossing experiences to be a central preoccupation for partition survivors, resulting in shifting attitudes, moods, behaviour and interaction as related to each side – thus generating what I call the border-line partition disorder (BPD).

Property: this is related to the houses, grounds and lands the survivors of the population transfer departed from and arrived into, which enhances

BPD as related 'returning home' and 'key fetish'. Here there is a maddening invention with a slippage between the present property 'here' that they physically live in, which is owned by someone else; and the past property 'there' that they mentally conceive in loathing or longing, which is lived in by someone else. It is a play whereby the past property is, as in nostalgia, conceived as a safe site the victim inhabited, and a dangerous site that the other across the divide occupies. This property motif is a 'much neglected dimension of partition' (Daiya, 115), which is the most powerful and dominant force, and it is my experiences of growing-up and living with testimonies about property by survivors that inspired the central topic of this book – the study of place.

Violence[23]: this is the narrative that is monumentalised, institutionalised and nationalised in different ways. Sometimes a noisy outbreak of competing narratives, with each side blaming the other for the atrocities; other times a silencing and retreat from the narratives, so to claim, a form of escapism at best, that violence does not and cannot belong to the narrative of the nation. In this process, the survivors of partition are at once heroic victims and agents of the violence, who aid the complex invention of the partitioned territory.

Conflict Resolution: this relates to various plans proposed to resolve the conflict, which takes place both before and after geographical partition, and between different bodies. This may include: territorial partition plans discussed between the coloniser and representatives from both communities as in India; United Nations partition plans discussed between leaders across the divide.

Place and Space via Tuan and Lefebvre

This significance of spatial invention in postcolonial and partition cases, whereby various people claim their rights to experience, read and construct a specific territory, can be illuminated through making use of Tuan's humanistic-geography developed in *Space and Place: The Perspective of Experience*, and Lefebvre's Marxist philosophy in *The Production of Space*. Even though Tuan and Lefebvre do not mention colonial, postcolonial or partition moments,[24] together they provide an all-inclusive worldly approach that can be adopted and adapted to illuminate the forces of place, space and geography in such context.

Tuan and Lefebvre show the forces of spatiality by prioritising human, social and/or political agency to create a different world. Tuan offers a universal approach to understand human 'experience' of being in the world, inclusive of all people without distinguishing socio-political, historical and/or geographical positions. Through this Tuan pioneered humanistic-geography, when attention turned to the creativity of humans to shape the world as related to material, emotional and spiritual 'experiences'; Tuan locates the experiences of the tenants of the world at the centre of geography and proposes that to have a healthy relationship with the environment we need a balance between the 'experience' of 'space' and 'place'. Lefebvre focusses on specific positions, with emphasis on ways people subject to capitalist geographies – often the modern city via Paris or the western country, yet adaptable to non-western locales – struggle with diverse spaces so to have socio-political agency. In this way Lefebvre initiated Marxist-philosophical approaches to the politics of space and time as related to everyday life; he committed to changing life and society so we can live better and differently, especially through emphasising the rights of all people to claim, control and construct centres and peripheries within the world. For this, Lefebvre proposes a 'spatiology' based on a method with a tripling-triad that people, especially 'inhabitants' and 'users' who are 'underprivileged and marginalized' (391), can 'use' for the actual production of a different world.

Tuan provides a humanistic perspective on experiencing 'space' and 'place', which illuminates ways of understanding the 'invention' of binary zones in postcolonial discourse and partition studies. Through Tuan we can interrogate the interchange and complex shuttling between the experience of open zones and closed zones in colonial, postcolonial and partition moments; and see how the term 'place' often deployed in postcolonial discourse is limited as a label. As stated, Tuan confirms that to have a healthy relationship with the environment, we need a balance between the experience of 'place' and 'space'. Place is closed, complete and bounded, it is a humanised text invested with memories, traditions, achievements and values that humans are attached and belong to (Tuan, 3); thus, providing permanence, security and reassurance to humans, who see frailty in themselves and chance and flux everywhere (Tuan, 154). Space is chance and flux that is an open incompleteness, which has no controllable pattern of established meaning, it is like a blank sheet on which meaning may be imposed; consequently, it is a freedom that humans long for, and an exposure generating danger, threat and vulnerability (Tuan, 50–54). Tuan points out that humans must acknowledge the dynamics between 'place' and 'space', where these are distinct experiences with distinct definitions, yet interrelated and simultaneous:

> Human beings require both space and place [...] a dialectic movement between shelter and venture, attachment and freedom. [...] A healthy being welcomes constraints and freedom, the boundedness of place and the exposure of space. (Tuan, 54)

Unlike in Tuan's humanistic-geography, in postcolonial discourse and partition studies these experiences of 'place' and 'space' are merged and used interchangeably losing their distinctiveness, which hinders a proper understanding of the environment. Tuan enables us to overcome this hindrance so to acknowledge that the colonial, postcolonial and partition territory undergoes a complex invention experienced as a closed zone or 'place' and an open zone or 'space', where the experiences are inconsistently separated with one selected as prime. In most cases, particularly in early colonial implementation, and the decolonial or partition stage of territorial recovery, the experience of 'place' is selected as primary. Here, the (formerly) colonised and coloniser aim to invent a nationally, politically and linguistically closed complete exclusive 'place' for themselves that they can know and control. In other cases, particularly in the early imperial perceptions of the colony, and more so in the postcolonial perceptions of partitioned territory and the world, 'space' is selected as primary. Here, the territory is experienced as a 'space' of freedom and threat through the adoption of imaginings such as 'empty space' in imperial perceptions, and realities of rhizomatic shifting ground, hybridity, marginal space, spatial history, migration, border-crossing, population transfers and name games in postcolonial perceptions. Thus, Tuan enhances understanding actual 'experiences' within colonial, postcolonial and partition cases: aiding us to interrogate the risks of prioritising 'place' as practised in postcolonial discourse, which gives way to an unhealthy relationship, instead showing that prioritising both 'place' and 'space' offers a gateway towards un/healthy relationships that enable new understandings to emerge. Whilst Tuan provides a useful way to examine the actual 'experiences' with 'place' and 'space' as related to colonial, postcolonial and partition inventions, Lefebvre provides a way to examine the actual process and practice of invention that controls people. Lefebvre only uses the term 'space', yet engages with multiple 'spaces' that negotiate with Tuan's 'place' and 'space', thus going beyond the binary by exploring the active-actual dialectic between spaces operating via production.

As shown in the epigraph, the production of space is a tool of thought, action, control, domination and power, but it escapes from those who would make use of it (Lefebvre, *Production*, 26). Here Lefebvre focusses on production as related to the authority and people, where space produced is powerful because it is shaped by the people, so the 'users' of space – space is a social production; however, the 'users' fail to make use of the production because the authority controls it. This production is controlled through contradiction – 'Power aspires to control space in its entirety, so it maintains it in a "disjointed unity", as at once fragmentary and homogeneous: it divides and rules' (Lefebvre, *Production*, 388) – and confusion – power 'divides, then keeps what it has divided in a state of separation; inversely, it re-unites yet keeps what it wants in a state of confusion' (Lefebvre, 358). In light of this, Lefebvre proposes a way to acknowledge the contradiction and confusion in the production, so people can take back control. Tuan's method is helpful here, showing the production is experienced as open disjointed fragmented space, and a closed homogeneous united place. Lefebvre exposes the actual production as a social production, declaring fully the agency of the people.

Lefebvre calls this approach a *spatial code* that 'allow[s] space not only to be "read" but also to be "constructed"' (Lefebvre, *Production*, 7); it 'does not aim to produce a (or *the*) discourse on space, but rather to expose the actual production of space by bringing the various kinds of space and the modalities of their genesis together within a single theory' (Lefebvre, *Production*, 16–18). Lefebvre coins this spatial code or single theory 'spatiology' (Lefebvre, *Production*, 404), which has an empirical-theoretical method that adapts Karl Marx's approaches: spatiology offers a method, defined as a 'regressive-progressive' approach, with a tripling-triad – nine interrelated spaces – that enable people to capture the 'concrete abstractions' within the actual production of space. Here regressive-progressive is a modus operandi proposed by Marx (*Grundrisse*, 105), which informed Lefebvre's work, and which he argued should be used by all researchers; it informs my work and most works on postcolonial partitioned territories. The approach is defined by Lefebvre as a spatio-temporal shift comprising a movement starting from the realities of the present to the past, then retracing our steps to the yet-to-be; here one acts retroactively upon the past, disclosing moments of it incomprehensible and in a different light, so that the process whereby that past becomes the present also takes on another aspect (Lefebvre, *Production*, 65–67). It is this regressive-progressive movement as related to the tripling-triad that captures the 'concrete-abstraction', where Lefebvre does with space what Marx does with commodity, so as to reveal the force of human and social practices in production.[25]

Lefebvre's spatiology allows people actively to read and construct via the tripling-triad, where nine spaces collide and flow, interfere and aid, and blur and crystallise one another; this process captures space as a socially produced concrete-abstraction. The first spatial triad is between the field: 'physical space', 'mental space' and 'social space', this is a process that absorbs the cosmos and material physicality, combined with mental logical and formal abstractions, and gains concreteness through human interaction and social practices. To enhance this, Lefebvre fuses another triad with space 'perceived' (physicality), 'conceived' (in the head and idealistic), and 'lived' (experiential); here again the production of 'physical space' 'perceived' through the body, combines with abstract 'mental space' idealistically 'conceived' in the mind, which gains concreteness through 'social space' that is directly lived, dynamically alive, and actively experienced. Finally, Lefebvre adds the 'representations of the relations of production', which captures fully the tripling-triad. First 'spatial practice', a 'physical space' based on 'perceived' realities with daily routines, networks and interactions connecting people and their environment; this space aids or deters, and controls or frees people's sense of location and the way they act. Second is 'representation of space', a 'mental space' conceived through arcane signs and plans of officials and specialist – politician, cartographer and archaeologist; this space dominates. Third is 'representational space', a 'social space' directly lived and with actual experiences of inhabitants and users; this 'space is dominated and passively experienced' (Lefebvre, *Production*, 33–39).

Lefebvre shows that authorities or agents of the hegemonic structure acknowledge fully the tripling-triad within the production, so as to construct space – 'abstract space'– that controls and dominates all users. Whilst the users fail to acknowledge this production, especially unaware that this domination is successful because they, who are a force that shapes it, unconsciously submit to space. Lefebvre states that to capture fully the actual production of space against this domination, we must use spatiology to examine the tripling-triad in the following ways:

> The more carefully one examines space, considering it not only with the eyes, not only with the intellect, but also with all the senses, with the total body, the more clearly one becomes aware of the conflicts at work within it, conflicts which foster the explosion of abstract space and the production of a space that is *other*. (Lefebvre, *Production*, 391)

> truth of space thus leads us back (and is reinforced) by a powerful Nietzschean sentiment: "But may the will to truth mean this to you: that everything shall be transformed into the humanly-conceivable, the humanly-evident, the humanly-palpable!". (Lefebvre, *Production*, 399)

Here the exposure of the conflicts, contradictions and confusions – disjointed unity – within dominant abstract space, paves the way for an *other* concrete space, which is made possible through the 'truth of space'. 'Truth of space' is tied to social and spatial practices as related to the tripling-triad, which expose the similarities and differences between dominant abstractions – i.e. mental space – and dominated concrete realities – social space – so to prioritise the latter severely compromised spaces related to Nietzsche's 'truth'. This 'truth of space' operates via the right to city and difference, which acknowledge the right of all people to construct a world without discrimination. This then enables for the production of an *other* – 'differential space' – which is created by 'users' who are *other*, resisting all hegemonic and ideological structures; this space is different, and '[w]hat is different is, to begin with, what is *excluded* [...] the spaces of forbidden games' (Lefebvre, *Production*, 373, 396, 397). These 'users' create this 'differential space' through acknowledging the tripling-triad so as to prioritise the lived and social spaces with all the senses and body. This relates to Lefebvre's *Rhythmanalysis*, which is concerned with enabling users to analyse, experiences and grasp rhythms – formed by repetition, movement and interaction between a time, a place and an expenditure of energy – with all the senses and body through a distinct positioning, both in terms of disciplines – as biologists, ethnologists, psychologists and especially as poets (Lefebvre, *Rhythm*, 13), as well as position and presences of the body to capture the truth of space for a differential space.

Thus, Lefebvre provides a means to examine spatial-temporal operations between various moments, including the pre-colonial, colonial, anticolonial, postcolonial and partition inventions, which are based on diverse experiences, readings and constructions by multitude of users and agents. Here is a closed and open shifting ground with spatial conception, perception and lived experiences that are produced-reproduced by users and agents overtly divided between ruler-ruled and powerful-powerless; these are coloniser official agents and colonised users in the colonial moment, and the official political agents and unofficial users in the postcolonial partition moment.

The spatial model I propose for the book is, like Lefebvre's spatial triad, determined by 'three' spatial understandings: the postcolonial and partition 'inventions' of open zones and closed zones, illuminated through Tuan's humanistic perspective on 'experiencing' place and space, and enhanced through Lefebvre's spatiology. This spatial model is fitting because it provides an inclusive critical approach that can carry the weight of and interrogate the powerful 'truth' of space and place as related to all 'identifications' in/of the colonial, postcolonial and partition world. It captures and critiques the 'invention' between open and closed zone in various geographies and shifting temporalities, as related to diverse 'experiences' and 'readings and constructions' in and for the actual-active re/production of colonial, postcolonial and partitioned territories. The territory is always in the process of creation by various people – i.e. users or agents performing as coloniser and colonised, officials and unofficial, powerful and powerless – illuminated via Tuan's and Lefebvre's spatial approaches, whereby the people claim their rights to invent, experience, read and construct a specific territory for a specific self. For this, the people make tacit but full use of the spatial model, in which the various approaches are always disrupted, often adapted and rarely fully adopted. Here the process of 'invention', Tuan's experiences and Lefebvre's spatiology remain the same; however, because the territory and people constantly change, the approach used also changes, when the people select practices from the 'inventions', place and/or space, and tripling-triad so as to produce a specific territory for a specific identification. In this book though I engage with inventions of 'place' and 'space' as related by Tuan and Lefebvre, I will mostly use the term 'place': first, because it is this term, in spite of its limitations, that has been most deployed within postcolonial discourse; second, it is this experience of closed 'place' that is often employed by the colonised and colonisers. Readers should, however, note that the meaning of place and space will change as the invention, experience, reading and construction of it changes, which gives way for the identification of the people also to change.

As this chapter and book will show, Cyprus' geographical significance or cursed place on the world map has been responsible for all the aforementioned colonial, postcolonial and partitioned spatial encounters. Cyprus has and will always be in a process of production: it is a place or gift needed and desired; necessary enough to conquer and control; prized enough to commit to games; valuable enough to kill and die for; precious enough for competing massacres; central enough to break apart. Like all postcolonial partitioned cases, the inventions, experiences, readings and constructions of place and space are key to Cyprus. This spatial production has determined the inescapable *hyphenated* 'identity' shown in the epigraph, as well as all the 'identifications' beyond the hyphen, which this book will explore.

The Case of Cyprus: Complex, Distinct, Bypassed, Deadlock

Complex, Distinct, Bypassed

A study of Cyprus cannot begin without interrogating what to name the people and the meaning of being 'Cypriot'. Therefore, I begin, in solidarity with the philosophers and cultural theorist of our time, with a weariness concerning using proper names and discussing 'identity'. In this book, I use Jacques Derrida's, Paul Gilroy's, Stuart Hall's, Edward Said's and Raymond Williams' approach to identity, where 'there is no identity, there is identification' (Derrida, *Taste*, 28). With them I make a nonsense of the term 'identity' by replacing 'foolish' notions like 'problems of identity' – foolish because identity is not resolvable – with 'disorder of identity' (Derrida, *Mono*, 10, 14) bounded with invention and supplementarity (Derrida, 'Psyche', 61), a production in a constant unpredictable mechanism of identification with many names we give to different ways we position ourselves (Gilroy, xi; Hall, 394). I address this 'identification' through Williams' model proposed in 'Dominant, Residual and Emergent' and 'Structure of Feeling' that provides cultural and national definition.

The names used to define the people in Cyprus are political. The current name used to define and divide the people *inescapably* uses a hyphenation that prioritises the dominant ethnic identification – Greek- or Turkish- – over the country of origin – Cyprus/Cypriot: the binary names 'Greek-Cypriot' and 'Turkish-Cypriot'. The identification of the people varies to include Greek, Turkish, Armenian and Maronite. For this study, I focus predominantly on inhabitants who identify with a Greek position and are currently the recognised majority, and those with a Turkish position who are the unrecognised minority compared to those with a Greek position, but a majority in comparison to the other groups. The inhabitants with Armenian and Maronite positions do not as yet have a body of literary works. However, as shown in the epigraph by Maronite-Cypriot Napoleon Terzis in the opening and closing of my book,[26] it is their diasporic displaced positionality that framed my understanding of becoming postcolonial Cypriot and Cyprus throughout this study. Though I, unfortunately, have not the room to study fully all identifications in Cyprus, I hope this book will kindle interest within postcolonial partition academics to study them.

Throughout colonial and postcolonial history different binary names have been used to divide and define the inhabitants of Cyprus[27] – at times these names were given by the ruling regimes, and other times chosen by the inhabitants. During Ottoman rule, the people were named through religious attributes, they were either Muslims or Non-Muslims. In late Ottoman rule and particularly during British rule, the name changed from religious to ethnic attributes – 'Greek' or 'Turkish' became dominant. During British rule, 'Cypriot' emerged against the dominant names in various ways. In the early stages of British rule, 'Cypriote' was used by the British, then in the anticolonial periods 'Cypriot' was imposed by the British, thus ending in a contest between the colonisers and colonised with the name 'Cypriot' being rejected. In the same period, 'Cypriot' was proposed by the left-wing political parties as an unofficial 'structure of feeling' towards uniting Cyprus. During the decolonial and independence moments ethno-national identifications were central; however, an island identification via the name 'Cypriot' linked to left values gained significance, but never became official. During independence and upon partition, the island identification gained precedence; however, the contest with 'Greek and Turkish' dominance over 'Cypriot' emergence created a third name – 'Greek-Cypriot and Turkish-Cypriot' – now official and standardised mostly with a hyphen.

Thus, throughout Cyprus' history the people were named via separate religious, ethnic and/or national positions, which solidified the binary. There was, however, an alternative identification named the Linobambakoi – the linen-cottons – who identified with both ethno-religious positions, which blurred the binary. The Linobambakoi took form during Ottoman rule, this is a historical identification that made-up a small community excluded by the people in Cyprus as well as the historical record. The Linobambakoi mocked the order of naming and knowing the people, which discomforted the Ottoman and especially British imperialists, who named them as a hybrid minority – defined as the Christians who converted to Islam, making them a 'Muslim-Christian-sect' or 'chameleon-like-sect' (Michell, 758) – of exotic abnormal traitors. Consequently, they were pressured by the British to declare one position – through which they have been confirmed extinct.

Though considered extinct, this book will show the Linobambakoi exist in Cyprus: first, the people of Cyprus use the Linobambakoi, their 'abnormal hybridity', as a tool in their competing narratives to define each other; second, as in the epigraph, the 'genuine postcolonial Cypriot is the Linobambakoi', a hybrid between ethnicities, geographies and cultures because of the postcolonial partition legacy. Unfortunately, however, most people in Cyprus fail to acknowledge their Linobambakoi identification by forbidding names or positions that blur the binary.

Postcolonial Cypriots cannot be understood through a binary because positions or naming indefinitely change when self and spatial conception change. This process of production between place, space and identification is the primary focus of this study; therefore, in each chapter of the book the name used to define the people will change as self and spatial conception change. In this way, the book highlights the significance of naming, whilst playing the name game commonly practised by people from partitioned territories. Here I adapt Costas Constantinou's statement: the most disturbing thing about being a Cypriot is that one refuses their Linobambakoi identification, instead surrendering to an escapist imaginary that there can only be a Greek or Turkish-Cypriot – accepting the foolish fallacy that Postcolonial Cypriot identity is quintessentially and inescapably hyphenated (Constantinou, 248). And so, in solidarity with the Cypriots, I expose and make a nonsense of such naming by performing with it; here showing there is no identity with one name, there is only identification with many names. In *Writing Cyprus*, though my preferred name would be 'cypriot' or to do away with all these names, I unwillingly surrender to using binary names for clarification purposes. In this name game, I disturb and deconstruct the official binary names, where I play between 'Greek-Cypriot and Turkish-Cypriot', 'Greek-cypriot and Turkish-cypriot', 'Cypriotgreek and Cypriotturk' and 'cypriotgreek and cypriotturk' depending on who speaks. The latter is my preferred name, where island identification precedes the ethnic one, and the formations are dehyphenised and decapitalised because for me such identifications should not be proper names as they lead to improper consequences. It is those imaginings that prioritise ethnic identification over being an islander, or that prioritise 'identity' to make it the higher upper case, that have been the central culprits for the legacy of bloody binary conflict in partition cases like Cyprus.

In this book I use a political model, principally Neophytos Loizides' model in 'Ethnic Nationalism and Adaptation in Cyprus', to understand conflicting identifications in Cyprus. Loizides focusses on the shifting process of 'identity' in Cyprus operating through three poles of address shared by cypriotgreeks and cypriotturks: Motherland Nationalism, Cypriotism, and Turkish-Cypriotism and Greek-Cypriotism. Motherland Nationalism is determined by 'a sense of primary loyalty' to the 'national centre' as related to 'perceptions of common origin and history with Turkey or Greece' (Loizides, 173–74). Cypriotism is an island patriotism in which Cypriot identity is the primary identification 'strengthening the attachment of citizens (regardless of ethnicity) to Cyprus, and its common tradition and symbols' (Loizides, 178). Turkish-Cypriotism and Greek-Cypriotism is:

> attachment to one's ethnic community [...] [that] appropriates themes, symbols and rhetoric both from Motherland Nationalism and Cypriotism, thereby performing a middle [wo]man role, it pays more attention to the aspirations of the ethnic community in the island than to the interests of the national centre or Cyprus as a whole. (Loizides, 180–81)

The first two identifications have been a major pole of address in Cyprus for decades, where Cypriotism is the emergent formation that writes back to dominant Motherland Nationalism. Both identifications have been examined in numerous political studies on 'identity' in Cyprus, surveyed thoroughly by Loizides[28] with commentary that each study 'aimed to deconstruct the primordialist attachment to the motherlands [by] highlighting alternative paths of identification with Cyprus across civic and constitutional lines', ending in 'attachment to motherland [Motherland Nationalism] and Cypriotism appear[ing] to be in two opposing poles often de-emphasising the various forms of adaptation and fusion' (Loizides, 173). Loizides' model offers a distinct approach that emphasises the fusion between Motherland Nationalism and Cypriotism, which gives way to Turkish-Cypriotism and Greek-Cypriotism, the dominant identifications in Cyprus. Thus, I use Loizides' political model of 'identity' formation in this book by deconstructing it into a postcolonial literary and spatial framework, especially acknowledging the actual transformative process of 'identity' as 'identification' with multiple positions determined by place, space and geography.

In official and dominant contexts, the literatures of Cyprus are ethnolinguistically divided and defined. Literary critics on each side compete amongst their ethnic selves over using the emergent name 'Cypriot Literature' and dominant names 'Turkish Literature' or 'Greek Literature', framed around ethno-linguistically excluding and dividing the Cypriots. Beyond this, literary critics on each side come together to propose the emergent plural name 'Cypriot Literatures' that is a compromise between these three names, inclusive of Greek and Turkish writings by Cypriots.[29] My usage draws and extends these dominant and emergent names. I use 'Literatures of Cyprus' to mean Greek, Turkish, English and Arab writings by cypriotgreeks, cypriotturks, cypriotarmenians, cypriotmaronites, as well as by Greeks, Turks, Britons and beyond. Here uncanonised minor Cypriot literatures – the cypriotgreek and cypriotturkish emergent writings – meet four major canonised literatures – dominant canons of Turkey, Greece and Britain, as well as the counter-canon of postcolonial literatures. Thus, through this plural name 'Literatures of Cyprus', I assert that the literatures of Cyprus or literary Cyprus is a transnational world literature (WReC), wherein all the texts are (post)colonial diasporic writings because they are about the cultural and political history of colonisation, partition and conflicting identifications as related to place, space and displacement; these writings operate through combined and uneven development connected to a system of inequality in relation to literary, cultural and language centres, semi-peripheries and peripheries that are outside, including, for example, Cyprus, Greece, Turkey, Britain and other postcolonial territories. This is writing across literary, language and geopolitical boundaries, where places, spaces and identifications are a central thematic. I have arrived at this definition through a comprehensive study of official and unofficial, and dominant and marginalised literary and cultural activities, mostly from the twentieth and twenty-first centuries, including pedagogy, publication, translation and movements. These literary activities have been shaped by authors and texts considered pioneers, makers and breakers of various generations or moments, which are linked to the aforementioned dominant and emergent, and major, minor and counter-canons. I focus on four generations or moments,[30] three of which appropriate Loizides' identifications that have been standardised as literary generations in the official curricula and emergent canon; the final one is the marginalised diaspora identification concealed from the curricula and canon. I focus on the ways these four identifications are determined by writing, reading and constructing place and space.

This is a study of literatures from both sides of the divide. Although I have cypriotturkish heritage, it is not my aim to give the cypriotturkish minority equal international recognition to that attained by the cypriotgreek majority. I am neither a politician nor historian with such an agenda, but a cypriotbritish daughter to diasporic parents uprooted from Kofunye and Pile to London, attempting impartially, with respect for all sides, to understand and share an alternative way of *Writing Cyprus* through its literatures in the light of postcolonial and partition studies. The primary literary texts explored in this book are a wide selection – mostly poetry but also short stories, life writing, plays, novels, novellas, memoirs and experimental forms published as full-length books or in anthologies and magazine/zines, meeting official documents such as the curricula – in Greek, Turkish and English. Because of my limited Greek skills, I read the cypriotgreek texts in translation, whilst reading the cypriotturkish and English texts in their originals. I tried to compensate for this problem, however insufficiently, by interviewing all cypriotgreek authors or their representatives, in an attempt to make sure the authors' intent has not been lost in translation.

There are limited translations of the literatures of Cyprus; therefore, some cypriotgreek texts have been translated by Pembe Ozocak, and the cypriotturkish texts have been translated by me. Cypriot literatures are short of translation for various interrelated reasons: they have mostly been published by local or small publishers; they lack recognition within a national and international domain; and they do not figure in a canon, department or research collective in a conventional western sense. The primary texts are difficult to access, and the usual or conventional formal processes used for literary interpretation – secondary reading and contextualisation – have not been fully applied to the texts. Consequently, to have knowledge of the literatures, I had to create new criteria of analysis.

To understand the broad and diverse scope of the literatures I did a comprehensive survey, then grouped the literatures, which may seem similar to a kind of canonisation contrary to a postcolonial emphasis on deconstructing canons and grand narratives. This was, however, a necessary part of the process, because as Spivak states, 'it's absolutely on target to take a stand against the discourse of essentialism [...][but] *strategically* we cannot'. And so, remembering Spivak's idea on the usefulness of essentialist formulations for postcolonial discourse, and employing her advice: 'we have to choose again strategically[...] essentialist discourse' (Spivak, 'Criticism', 11), I attempt to rectify any offences. In employing a strategic essentialism, the colonial, postcolonial and partitioned literatures of Cyprus can finally achieve a sense of value and assertion; they can finally demonstrate the dialogue and dialectics across the divided island and world. For this, I expose the dialogue and dialectics between four literary moments – four identifications and Cypruses – to give way to a meeting between multiple authors, texts, and contexts always in contradiction, defined-redefined, fixed-unfixed, fragmented-united, closed-open to the process of de/construction and becoming. This quadrigeminal grouping has, however, meant some pioneering figures who do not fit the terms of identification may not be addressed fully, and other literary figures may be addressed within a set of terms that limits their distinction and individuality. I use this approach because my goal is for *Writing Cyprus* in conflict and contest to meet *Writing Cyprus* in solidarity.

'Comparison' is the other form of analysis I use. I compare literatures written by Cypriots, Turkish literatures by citizens of Turkey, Greek literatures by citizens of Greece, and postcolonial and/or partition literatures by citizens of the world. Even though there are limitations to these comparisons, this approach has allowed new ways of understanding postcolonial partition to emerge.

Distinct Imaginative Geography: Oriental Ottoman East or Occidental West

Between west and east or north and south, Cyprus is a strategically and distinctly located Mediterranean island that has been subject to multiple western and non-western imperial regimes, each of which invented, experienced and constructed the island – un-inventing the previous rulers' unit to re-invent a new territory – as a closed 'place', thus enabling each imperial power to have total knowledge and command. The imperial powers that will be the focus in this book are the western regime via British rule (1878–1960), and non-western regimes via Ottoman rule (1571–1878). The case of Cyprus interrogates the dominant mode in postcolonial discourse that prioritises western imperialism by showing that British and Ottoman comparative imperialisms are paramount to understanding colonial, postcolonial and partitioned production of east Mediterranean cases like Cyprus.

Cyprus at once resonates and complicates Said's claims in *Orientalism* on 'imaginative geography', for British imperial imaginings of Cyprus are ambiguous and inconsistent. At first glance the British Empire represented Cyprus as an Oriental unit because of Ottoman governance and settlers; this enabled the British to lay claim to an Orientalist project, with a civilising mission to un-invent the backward Ottoman traces and re-invent Cyprus as civilised. There are many British imperialist texts that invented Cyprus as Oriental, in need of western knowledge and development. For example, Samuel Baker's *Cyprus As I Saw Her* (1879) and William Dixon's *British Cyprus* (1879) depict their actual experiences of travelling around Cyprus soon after the beginning of British rule, when they wrote accounts of 'What are the Cypriotes?' and 'What is Cyprus?' Dixon writes:

> With neither beauty of body nor sense of beauty in mind – with neither personal restlessness nor pride of origin– with neither large aspirations [...] they live on in limpid state, like creatures of the lower types [...] holding on by simple animal tenacity. (28)

Similarly, in 1922 the High Commissioner, Malcolm Stevenson, imagined 'Cypriotes' as uncivilised primitive 'types', stating: with 'an attractive childlike simplicity of thought and expression, he is at heart an *Oriental*'.[31] Through such representations the British bear out Said's claims about the 'Orient'; however, unlike in other colonies, the imperialists struggled to invent a conclusive Oriental Cyprus because of the western affiliation of some of the colonised. Whilst the Muslim-Turks fit the Orientalist category, the Orthodox-Greeks, who carry the root of civilisation and knowledge considered pivotal for western civilisation, especially according to the new Hellenic ideology popular during the nineteenth century, cause a problem for such Orientalist reading. To overcome this Hellenic presence, the British often renamed these 'types':

> Except in name, they are neither Turks nor Greeks [...] We must classify. Apart from creed, there are Cypriotes and Cypriotes: Cypriotes dark, and Cypriotes fair; Cypriote horned, and Cypriotes oval. (Dixon, 19–20)

Dixon attempts to un-invent both groups of ethnic meaning by re-inventing them into a 'Cypriote' or 'Oriental Cypriote', which is some kind of exotic breed between a Greek and Ottoman-Turk. Such depictions support Robert Young's claims in *Colonial Desire* regarding 'hybridity' in colonial discourse shot through with racism. This hybrid definition is, of course, an imagined fallacy because the Ottoman-Turkish and Greek identifications were visible in late Ottoman and British history. Furthermore, these imperial imaginings of a 'Cypriote' island that is 'neither Turk nor Greek' are problematic for the Orientalist project, because they invented Cyprus with Ottoman-Turkish traits by silencing the actualities of the Hellenic Greeks. This was an unsuccessful attempt because throughout British colonialism the Greek inhabitants firmly held and voiced their Hellenic identification, without surrendering to the Orientalist project: 'The Greek Cypriot press never tired of reminding the British Administration that Cyprus had been a centre of civilisation and culture at a time when Ancient Britons were still living in huts and daubing themselves with woad' (Reddaway, 22). The British Empire was unable to invent a fixed Oriental Cyprus, as it had done with its other colonies in Asia and Africa, ending with inconsistent shifts between moments when it represented the Oriental Cypriote, as above, and moments when Greek and Turkish difference was prioritised.

The aforementioned difference prepared the way for the Saidian binary – the civilised western imperialist and the uncivilised eastern colonised – to be localised between the inhabitants, the cultured Greeks as opposed to the barbaric Turks.[32] The Turk and Greek binary gained prominence during British rule, where they would inconsistently support and invent each group in succession: sometimes supporting the Hellenic Greeks because the Orientalist mission to civilise could only come from them; other times supporting the Turks because as a majority the Greeks put the Empire's control over Cyprus at risk. The Empire would also inconsistently release its hold on this binary by regressing to representation, like Dixon's and Stevenson's, of the hybrid 'Oriental Cypriote'; this is most notable after the 1931 revolt. As example, the British historian George Hill argued Cyprus was never part of Greece, and emphasised the lack of racial affinity between Cypriot and Hellenic stock through footnoting anthropological evidence that Cyprus' primitive population are an offshoot from Asia minor and north Syria (Hill, 488). The British Empire used this Oriental complication for the benefit of its hold on Cyprus, whereby both representations inconsistently figure in colonial and postcolonial moments, becoming an imaginative legacy for Cyprus. These inconsistent representations did not Orientalise Cyprus as intended; however, the British did invent a grand Oriental Cyprus via tourism, representing a romanticised paradise with hospitable inhabitants, an image that dominates postcolonial Cyprus. This Oriental Cyprus via tourism, which may seem less coercive and violent than other Orientalist projects, is the most dangerous, deceitful and powerful kind of Orientalism, because, through it, the truth of Cyprus' colonial, postcolonial and partition legacy has been internationally bypassed.

Being the third largest Mediterranean island located between Europe and Asia, Cyprus has always been a site of visiting and transit for travellers and ruling regimes. A significant traveller who initiated British foundations of Oriental Cyprus is King Richard I:

> [He] took all the castles, towns and ports which [were] found empty, and having garrisoned and provisioned them and left guard ships, returned to Limeszun [...] On the 12th day of May [...] Richard, King of England, took to himself in marriage Berengaria. (Cobham, 8)

In 1191 during the third crusade, whilst King Richard was on route to the holy land, a tempest forced him to stop in Cyprus, where he explored its charms, married his fiancée Berengaria, and conquered it for a year; he then passed Cyprus over to Guy de Lusignan. King Richard's exploration suggests he was the first to animate Cyprus via a romanticised tourism, the transit passenger of his time, who conquered, orientalised and exchanged it. Nearly a millennium and many colonisers have now passed; however, like King Richard, present tourists visit and explore the island with a similar attitude of appropriating 'her' tranquil charms in an international marketplace.

From the outset of the British Empire's second acquisition of Cyprus in 1878, the imperialists refurbished King Richard's travelling and matrimonial adventures. The first image depicting British-Cyprus is a caricature entitled 'Wolseley Courts Venus' accompanied by the poem 'Venus Loquitur' (*Punch*, 3 August, 1878); here Cyprus is depicted as Venus/Aphrodite, a chaste woman wrapped in a British flag. Courted by the British official, Wolseley, she poetically welcomes British rule. Similarly, the first British map is a caricature entitled 'Marriage of the Earl of Beaconsfield and Miss Cyprus observed by Mr Gladstone' (Shirley, 36), which is a map of Cyprus filled with the newlyweds and an observer: Miss Cyprus' body lies on the north-west, with her perky bottom shaping Tilara; the British prime minister (1874–1880), Benjamin Disraeli's body marks the centre, with his right foot extending to fill the outline of Akrotiti, today's British base. His opposition, William Ewart Gladstone's tiny head voyeuristically observes with torch from the north-east tip of Cyprus. This illustrates Disraeli's optimism in acquiring Cyprus, considered an imperial asset, an economic-military watch tower to safeguard the routes between India and Egypt. Upon becoming Mrs British-Cyprus, improvements to mark this strategic role began, all promoted as a means to enhance Cyprus' tourist potential.

From 1878 to 1960, as Governor Stevenson wrote, 'enormous advances [made]... resources of the island developed and tourist traffic encouraged' (Georghallides, 391). Cyprus' ports – Limassol, Famagusta and Larnaca – said to be the infrastructure for tourism, were really strategic points requiring amelioration for a British stronghold. The 'revival of the forests'[33] (Dunbar, 112) and 'protection of crown forests' were 'highly necessary' (Baker, 179): David Hutchins, Chief Conservator of Forests, wrote in 1909, 'Cyprus lies on the edge of the tourist stream [and the forest] should help to attract tourists and their gold' (Hutchins, 5), increase firewood, and generate therapeutic effects. More importantly the forest served in World War I, 'cut over to supply 100,000 tons of fuel and timber to the Allied armies' (Dunbar, 116) in Egypt and Palestine. Roads and railways were built, hotel resorts erupted, tourist guidebook publication flourished. Thus, the tourism infrastructure Orientalised and romanticised Cyprus, whilst masking the fact this was for the benefit of the Empire's economic-military hold.

This Orientalised tourism has been maintained throughout (post) colonial and partitioned Cyprus: during the decolonial periods, British tourists poured into Cyprus yet were shielded and oblivious to inter-ethnic bloody carnage. The tourist sector dismisses postcolonial actualities, leaving Cyprus to be Orientalised by deceptive luring images – Aphrodite's birthplace; family holidays to unite on sandy shores; 'Ayia Napa Ayia Napa' to dance the night away. The latest tourism trends construct Cyprus as a popular destination for Brits to marry and be merry –an inadvertent re-enactment of the adventures of Richard the Lion Heart and the Earl of Beaconsfield's acquisition.

Bypassed in Postcolonial Partition Discourse

The postcolonial academic sector also bypasses Cyprus' actualities, which may be because the tourist 'identity' dominates. But there are other possible reasons for this bypass: it is considered a progressive wealthy country, especially since its partial (Christian Western) accession into the European Union. It is recognised via its Greek heritage with limited address of its Ottoman, British and cypriotturkish inheritance. British rule is not considered because Cyprus was ruled as a protectorate under Ottoman suzerainty. Moreover, Cyprus' small size means thousands not millions were affected by partition. And the final reason for Cyprus being bypassed: there is no prominent postcolonial academic writing about it; prominent postcolonial academics connected to a geography write about it, enabling these geographies to enter and shape the postcolonial canon – i.e. Australia via Tiffin, Palestine via Said, India via Spivak. Most of these reasons can, however, be problematised because other geographies with similar characteristics have entered the postcolonial canon. For example, Ireland and Australia are western wealthy geographies; the Caribbean consists of small island tourist entities; Palestine and Egypt are invested with Ottoman-British legacies. Myopia towards colonial, postcolonial and partitioned Cyprus results from tourism, European and Hellenic Cyprus leading postcolonial readers to bypass Cyprus. The differing reasons listed for Cyprus' dismissal will be reconciled in this book to show it is paramount for Cyprus to be read in a postcolonial partition frame because it has relevance and much to contribute to these discourses.

Competing Narratives: Historical-Political Deadlock Production of Cyprus

The dominant historical-political 'competing narratives' are nationally and pedagogically fixed in the mental, social and physical practices of the people residing in Cyprus and the diaspora, infiltrating their environment, everyday life and their bed-time stories. I grew up with and through them, such that I did not need to pursue conventional research sources – books and archives – to provide me with some understanding; however, according to scholarly protocols, I have sought out documented evidence for these narratives. I found myself re-reading and searching for documents of historical-political Cyprus not to learn something new, but to find a reference that would support a nationalised and institutionalised narrative I already knew. That is to say, I was open to new findings and did come across fresh historical-political narratives for Cyprus[34]; however, my focus here is not on new or alternative arguments, but on old dominant narratives monumentalised into the Cypriot's Cyprus experience. In light of this, there may be times when the reader will question sources for claims; I select two interrelated sources often used in partition studies: first, oral history, especially personal testimonies and experiences by victims and agents of colonial, postcolonial and partition moments; second history education with schoolbooks for cypriotturks by historian Vehbi Zeki Serter, and those for cypriotgreeks compiled by Katia Hadjidemetriou in *A History in Cyprus* – here Yiannis Papadakis' *Report* has also been helpful. In what follows I trace the dominant historical-political competing narratives operating via a dialectic and dialogue, always ending in deadlock. This paves the way for the chapters, which assign the literary as the preferred other to the historical-political narratives, thereby capturing 'solidarity' and 'truth' within and beyond the dialectic, dialogue, deadlock production of colonial, postcolonial and partitioned Cyprus.

Ottoman Winds (1571–1878)

The Ottoman Empire arrived in Nicosia in 1570 and fought against the Venetian until the fall of Famagusta in 1571, which marked total conquest. cypriotturks claim the Ottomans were called by the inhabitants suffering from Venetian exploitation: 'To help the Orthodox Greeks in 1571, they gave 80 thousand martyrs' (Serter, 7; Ismail, 1). Without reference to the call or martyrs, the cypriotgreeks claim Ottoman conquest was because Cyprus' location sustained Ottoman expansionism and stopped pirates raiding their ships. In this narrative, they characterise the Ottoman sultan as 'Selim, the Drunkard' (Hadjidemetriou, 236) and 'Selim the Sot' (Panteli, 54). Between these competing narratives, there is some common ground in that first, both communities define the Ottoman Empire via the metaphor of the wind.[35] Second, both communities agree that this wind took over Cyprus to maintain a geographic stronghold between the Arab and African worlds, and to guard against the pirates in the eastern Mediterranean The inhabitants' willingness to rid Cyprus of Venetian religious subjugation paved the way for the Ottomans to be considered an alternative.

MAPPING SPIRIT AND BLOOD: WHO IS *OF* CYPRUS?

The competing narratives continue with debates over 'who is *of* Cyprus?' via primordial symbols – spirit and blood[36] – that map Cyprus. The cypriotgreeks write Cyprus via an Orthodox-Greek spirit invested 3,000 years ago by the Cretans and Mycenaeans, confirming the people *of* Cyprus can only be Greek (Vanezis, 28–29), whilst the 'Turks are, and always have been, a population *in* Cyprus but not *of* Cyprus' (Vanezis, 33). For cypriotturks the land and people are *of* Ottoman-Turkish blood – because of 80,000 martyrs, and because the original population were Hittite and non-Aryan Mongoloid tribes from Anatolia absorbed by Ottoman-Turks – so they have a rightful ownership of Cyprus. Both groups act as nativists by using primordial symbols to pre-invent Ancient-Greek or Ottoman-Turkish-Cyprus.

NUMBER GAMES AND FIRST PARTITION

The Ottoman Empire did not intend to conquer Cyprus as a settler colony; however, it did implement a population, which is subject to inconsistent number games for various reasons. First, there was population mobility between Ottoman colonies. Second, Ottoman census-taking[37] was based on counting households/families not individuals, and prioritised the columns of non-Muslim taxpayers; it is claimed that this formed the Linobambakoi, the Christians – either the Orthodox-Greeks or the remaining Latin-Christians – who converted to Islam to avoid faith-based taxes. Third, there are diverse estimates by European and Ottoman bodies that used different census methods – i.e. in 1640 the Ottoman superintendent estimated 'the entire population [at] 25,000'; in 1821 the French Consulate cited 90,000; in 1861 the Greek ambassador estimated 165,000 (Hadjidemetriou, 259, 293). One of the main discrepancies between Cypriots regards Ottoman military officials, which resonates with current debates over Turkish presence: cypriotgreeks claim '3000–4000' were implanted (Hadjidemetriou, 247) to suggest Cyprus only experienced a Turkish military presence in the twentieth century; cypriotturks state '20,000' officials (Ismail, 2) to suggest Ottoman-Turkish military governance is rooted in Cyprus history. Thus, inconsistent number games prevail with regard to Ottoman-Cyprus; however, what is constant is Ottoman rule un-invented the demography of Cyprus from an Orthodox-Greek to an Orthodox-Greek and Muslim-Turkish inhabited island, ending in the first partition, whereby the native Greeks and Ottoman settlers constructed separate entities for themselves. Between this binary the Linobambakoi were formed.

UN-CIVILISING MISSION: OTTOMAN ORIENTAL AND NATIVE OCCIDENT

For cypriotturks, this was an era of prosperity that improved the shattered economy and administration with serious attempts to raise standards of education (Gazioglu, *Turks*, 75, 196); plus 'Orthodox Greeks regained their religious freedom and privileges' (Ismail, 1). For cypriotgreeks, this is the moment of absolute decline, incompetence and corrupt governance (Hadjidemetriou, 246), resulting in the Ottomans giving the church and local inhabitants some privileges so to help them govern Cyprus (Vanezis, 45). The cypriotgreeks claim that learning from the Orthodox-Greek pedagogy established in '1754–1821' by mirroring Greece's secular curriculum, the Ottomans encouraged Muslim inhabitants to establish schools, which were lacking because 'the children were made to learn the Koran by heart' (Hadjidemetriou, 296–98).

Here the orientalist binary is reversed: the colonised cypriotgreeks 'represent' themselves via progress, and 'represent' the imperial Ottoman rulers as regressive Orientals learning about governance and pedagogy through them. In this process, the backward Muslim and civilised non-Muslim binary is maintained. Thus the 'backward Muslim'[38] shaped during Ottoman-Cyprus served to produce the 'modern Kemalist Turk' in post-Ottoman-Cyprus, which is most notable in British rule.

NATIONALISM'S BEGINNINGS: FROM RELIGIOUS TO ETHNIC IDENTIFICATION

Identification during Ottoman-Cyprus mirrors Brass' model: the elites selected spatial symbols that divided and defined the inhabitants, transforming them from religious categories based on Islamic or Christian identification into self-conscious ethnic communities with potential to be modern nations.

The cypriotgreek slide to ethnic consciousness gained ascendance in the mid-nineteenth century, when religious elites selected the *Megali Idea* (Great Idea) map that revives the Byzantine Empire's geography – i.e. Greece, Cyprus, Constantinople and so on – to unite all Greeks; this map was inspired by the imaginings of Strabo, the Ancient Greek philosopher, proposed in *Geography*. Greece was the first to adopt it as a national symbol to imagine a geography for 'Greeks, now and earlier, [who] *felt* that their "Greekness" was a product of their descent from the ancient Greeks (or Byzantine Greeks), and that such filiations made them *feel* themselves to be members of one great "super-family" of Greeks' (Smith, 29). The cypriotgreeks subsequently adopted the *Megali Idea* to confirm membership to this super-geography, with the additional 'enosis' – a unionist demand aspiring to unite Cyprus and Greece. This ethnic awareness is not considered an imagined geography, but a 3,000-year-old ineluctable history 'given' to them by the ancients. Adopting an antique map to define ethnic boundaries is a pre-invention, which parallels Zionist devotion to precovering the holy lands of ancient Israel.

This cypriotgreek development reflects Brass' claims that 'Ethnic categories develop self-consciousness [...] when persons of that category perceive that persons from another category are getting a disproportionate share' (Brass, 276), triggering conflicts such as between 'native religious elite and alien aristocracy' (Brass, 26). The cypriotgreek religious elites opposed the alien Ottoman conquerors; recognising that the native Greeks had fewer privileges than the settlers, they interrogated boundaries of 'us', the descendants of civilised Greeks, and 'them', the barbaric Ottoman Muslims – thus arousing mass ethno-religious awareness to mobilise so as to recover the glorious Greek age and become the privileged group in a united Greek region. Greece's war of independence (1821–1829) triggered this awareness to unite against the Ottoman: in 1820, for example, representatives of the Philike Hetaireia, an organisation formed in Greece to overthrow Ottoman rule, 'came to Cyprus [...] to convince Cypriot leaders to rise against the Turkish masters. The Archbishop became a member' (Hadjidemetriou, 274) as did others, resulting in the 9th July 1821 execution and exile of several hundred involved; second, 'several hundred [cypriotgreeks] join[ed] the revolutionary force' (Panteli, 68) in Greece. The idea of a united Greek state, and especially enosis, advanced in 1828, when 'modern Greece's first president, Count Kapodistria, called for union of Cyprus with Greece' (Mallinson, 10). As a result of these transformations, the cypriotturks claim the cypriotgreeks were cowardly for siding with Greece when the Ottoman millet system gave them the freedom the Venetians denied. cypriotturks claim that intercommunal conflict and division, which ended in 'The Cyprus Problem, originated from the "*Megali Idea [and Enosis]*"' (Gazioglu, *Crisis*, i) conceived by the cypriotgreek. cypriotgreeks claim that this aspiration provided for all people to struggle side-by-side, resisting Ottoman exploitation.

Throughout Ottoman rule, cypriotturks did not worry about ethnic identification because they had privileges, and because they imitated the Ottoman Empire who maintained Muslim affiliation with a slide towards increasing ethno-religious awareness during the *Tanzimat* (1836–1876), a period of reform working towards transforming the Empire into a modern state. Hence, cypriotgreeks imitated Ancient/Modern Greece with spiritual maps confirming Orthodox-Greekness; the cypriotturks imitated the Ottoman Empire with reference to Turkish blood watering the land to confirm Muslim-Turkish potential.

Becoming Mrs British-Cyprus

In 1878, by agreement with the Ottoman government, Britain ruled Cyprus as a protectorate until 1914; in 1925 Cyprus became a British colony. Regarding British rule, both groups 'agree' that cypriotturks were discontented and cypriotgreeks pleased, and these differing attitudes are represented via a maternal principle with ethnic symbols as related to Turkey or Greece. cypriotturks state they 'were crying blood when being ripped apart from their Mother' (Ismail, 11); cypriotgreeks focus on 'Greek-Christian spirit', whereby, it is claimed, the first comment by the Bishop of Kition to the British commissioner was: 'We accept the change of government inasmuch as we trust that Great Britain will help Cyprus, as it did with the Ionian Islands, to be united with Mother Greece, with which it is naturally connected' (Hill, 297). The cypriotturks frequently refer to this anecdote, claiming cypriotgreeks were happy because they believed Britain would give them enosis, as in former British Ionian Islands 'given' to Greece. The cypriotgreeks claim satisfaction with British rule, not for enosis but because 'They expected their conditions to improve under their Christian European master' (Hadjidemetriou, 305).

CIVILISING MISSION

The British imperial civilising project aimed to un-invent Ottoman-Cyprus so as to re-invent British-Cyprus: cypriotgreeks welcomed this in anticipation it would improve conditions; cypriotturks noted British-Cyprus potential yet without mentioning failures of Ottoman-Cyprus. As stated by pioneering historian Andrekos Varnava, however, the British Empire 'failed to forge a role for Cyprus' envisaged by the inhabitants and Empire, making it a neglected useless 'pawn' and problem for the Colonial Office (Varnava, *Imperial*, 235, 265). Britain nevertheless invested in Cyprus' economic-strategic and tourist potential, so as to name, know and command this colony.

In 1881 the British completed the first comprehensive census[39] that divided the inhabitants into multiple columns, especially exploiting the difference and strengthening the binary between the ethno-religious categories, ending with the following: total population 185,630, with '73.9% Christian-Greek and 24.4% Muslim-Turkish' (Hadjidemetriou, 293). This estimate is one of few where the divided groups agree on the numbers; however, because of this recording that solidified the binary, disagreements over number games dominate(d) Cyprus. Through this census, the Linobambakoi were forced to select one ethno-religious category, resulting in their extinction from official records, and a colonial legacy towards hybridity that each community used to define the other: cypriotgreeks define cypriotturks as hybrid Linobambakoi Latin-Christian or Orthodox-Greek who converted to Islam; the cypriotturks define cypriotgreeks via hybrid-mixed blood types. Thus, hybridity is addressed via the racist colonialist discourse critiqued by Young, rather than via the kind of mutual transformation celebrated by Bhabha, because the latter threatens cleansed definitions of being Cypriot in Cyprus.

As well as this demographic cleansing, the British completed the first comprehensive Cyprus map.[40] From 1878 to 1885, Lieutenant Kitchener converted Cyprus into numbers and names, and solidified the ethno-religious binary by marking all 'empty-spaces' into Muslim crescent or Christian cross 'places'.

Another pivotal British venture was the endorsement of pedagogies that imitated Greece or Turkey, which provided divided schools throughout Cyprus.

IDENTIFICATION THROUGH COMPETING RELIGIOUS AND SECULAR ELITES

> [O]nly those ethnic groups that do engage in recurring internal argument and struggles for control over the meanings of the values and symbols of the group and over its boundaries are likely to have sufficient dynamism to persist through time. (Brass, 278)

By the late nineteenth and early twentieth century, the intragroup competition between the elites over adopting a religious – Orthodox or Muslim – or secular dimension – Greek or Turkish – gave way for the inhabitants to recognise they were not just religious colonial subjects but members of an ethnic community with potential to be national citizens.

The cypriotgreek awareness was more forceful and took form decades before because of their affiliations with Greece: mirroring the model in Greece that occurred in early nineteenth century,[41] in 1899 the contest between 'the paternalist faction [who] struggled to maintain the dignity of the church' and the populist faction who 'appropriated discourses of [...] nation', ended in the secular populist approach gaining majority support, whereby the same symbols – the *Megali Idea* and enosis – were solidified (Bryant, *Imagining*, 80). Similarly, the cypriotturkish debate was between the elitist kadi who 'used religion to appeal to the masses' and the mufti who believed 'it was only through Enlightenment that the state would be saved' (Bryant, 103). The cypriotturks' competition was less forceful because British-Ottoman agreement meant they maintained privileges without worrying about self-definition or being coerced. Second, they imitated Ottoman formations, which were undergoing their own un-resolved transformative period – the *Tanzimat* – that did not appropriate an ethno-national imagining until the Republic of Turkey was formed in the twentieth century (Lewis, 3).

Throughout British rule each community emphasised their identification with Greece or Ottoman-Turkey, and by the twentieth century they separately transformed from ethno-religious categories to self-conscious members of a Greek or Turkish nation with ethnic-nationalist movements that shaped dominant definitions. The British sharpened this ethno-national difference, devotion and division through their administration.

BARBARIC DEGENERATES: DIVIDE AND RULE

The colonial office considered Cyprus as a 'sanatorium where officials whose health ha[d] been impaired by long services in tropical climates [were] sent' (Orr, 179). If we read this through Said's commentary – 'the essence of Orientalism is western superiority and Oriental inferiority [...] no Oriental was ever allowed to see a westerner as he aged or degenerated' (Said, *Orientalism*, 42) – it is suggestive that Cypriots saw the British officials as impaired degenerates without claiming them, as in other colonies, as Imperial Mother. Instead the motherland became Turkey or Greece because officials from there were young energetic Generals in their prime who could protect the Cypriots.

British governance is also considered impaired because of the administrative attitudes towards the divided groups. cypriotgreeks argue the British were pro-Turkish, claiming cypriotturks 'enjoyed the constant favour of the English' (Hadjidemetriou, 313) with more administrative powers via a collaborative system. For example, in the 1882 representative government introduced by Gladstone, the legislative council consisted of seven British officials, three cypriotturks and nine cypriotgreeks, whereby the British and cypriotturks could outvote the cypriotgreeks. On the other hand, cypriotturks claim the British were pro-Greek and strengthened enosis, often evidenced by quoting colonial officials:

In 1897, Gladstone wrote:

> [T]he satisfaction I should feel, were it granted to me, before the close of my long life, to see the population of this Hellenic Island placed by friendly arrangement in organic union with their brethren of the Kingdom and of Crete.[42]

In 1907, Winston Churchill reiterated:

> I think it is only natural that the Cypriot people, who are of Greek descent, should regard their incorporation with what may be called their motherland as an ideal to be earnestly, devoutly and fervently cherished.[43]

In 1926, Sir Ronald Storrs, the Governor of Cyprus claimed:

> No sensible person would deny that the Cypriot is Greek speaking, Greek thinking, Greek feeling, Greek. (Storrs, 555)

cypriotturks also refer to how in '1915 Britain offered Cyprus to Greece in exchange for support in the World War' (Ismail, 13), and to 1919–1922 when weapons were sent from Cyprus to support Greece in the Greco-Turkish war.

Thus, in Cyprus as in Israel-Palestine and Ireland, the British Empire supported each group in sporadic succession, so as to mould 'ethnic identities', manipulate intercommunal conflict and strengthen ethnic aspiration, as a 'means to maintain its own power' (Cleary, 25). For example, the British supported the cypriotgreek ethnic-national demand until 1931, first because of British anti-Ottoman rivalry; second, the cypriotgreek 1931 revolt confirmed how ethno-national aspiration had strengthened and could disrupt the Empire's control. The British enhanced a 'collaborator system' (Cleary, 25) with the cypriotturks to sharpen their ethno-national demands against the cypriotgreek majority, so that by the 1950s they served as colonial police fighting the cypriotgreeks' anticolonial and enosis demands.

This divide and rule policy resulted in the British Empire first maintaining and subsequently losing all power, when the divided ethnic-motherland nationalisms overwhelmed Cyprus.

DECOLONIAL IDENTIFICATIONS

Ethnic-motherland nationalisms:[44] by the 1950s the islanders perceived themselves as citizens of an ethnic nation, which developed into what Loizides calls 'motherland nationalism' determined by Greece or Turkey.

The cypriotgreek political, religious and military elites upheld the primordial symbols *Megali Idea*, enosis and the Greek spirit to define national identification as given: they are the offspring of Ancient Greeks. The cypriotturkish political and military elites upheld the 'blood' of the Ottoman and Modern Turkey martyrs to define national identification as progressive; they did not select primordial symbols because this showed 'backwardness', 'what we were' and 'what we need to overcome' – they are the offspring of the Ottoman Empire made new.

The cypriotturkish ethno-national identification developed because of two events: in 1925 Cyprus was declared a British colony, whereby cypriotturkish anxiety over self-definition generated ethnic-national consciousness; from 1924 to 1938 the Republic of Turkey and Mustafa Kemal Ataturk's reforms resulted in a modernised and westernised Turkish identification; thus, cypriotturks appropriated a new Turkish self through Turkey as its mirror.

Even though cypriotturks and cypriotgreeks used different rhetoric – modern Kemalist and primordial Greek – to define national boundaries, both used identical models to invent a homogeneous ethnic Cyprus that was determined by a maternal principle – 'where we came from'. The cypriotgreeks reclaimed an ancient map and 'spirit' to create Greece-Cyprus, and the cypriotturks turned to 'blood' to claim a more recent Ottoman history renewed into Modern Turkey-Cyprus. These competing spatial constructions gave way to anticolonial ethnic-motherland nationalist movements.

The first cypriotgreek anticolonial mobilisation was in 1931, which ended in policies of total coercion by the British. The second anticolonial move erupted fully in 1955 through 'National Organisation of Cypriot Fighters' (Ethnik Organosis Kiprion Agoniston – EOKA) formed by the religious elite Archbishop Makarios III and the military elite Colonel Georgios Grivas. From 1955, EOKA campaigned against the British and for enosis, which generated competing narratives for Cyprus[45]: the cypriotgreek nationalists claim EOKA struggled justly for freedom, whilst the British and cypriotturks state EOKA was a 'terrorist[...] organisation' that attempted to ethnically cleanse Turkish-Cypriots from the land to fulfil enosis' (Tansu, 13). A year into EOKA's campaign the British exiled Makarios III, whilst maintaining a collaborative system with the cypriotturks.

In the 1950s the cypriotturkish taksim ideology – a separatist demand aspiring union with Turkey – was formed. As Brass suggests, when a minority group realises that 'access to power and the right to self-determination [...] [are closed,] political elites are likely to raise secessionist demands' (Brass, 345). In 1958 the cypriotturkish military elites joined forces with Turkey's to form the 'Turkish Resistance Association' (Turk Mukavemet Teskilati – TMT), which secretly resisted until they mobilised fully on '21st December 1963' (Tansu, 7–8). cypriotturks do not acknowledge the taksim ideology, and TMT is defined as a rival national movement created to resist British colonisation and to defend the cypriotturks from EOKA massacre (Tansu, 13). cypriotgreeks always associate TMT with taksim, claiming it a terrorist organisation that showed the cypriotturks' demand for partition and their habitual violence. On Turkey's support for TMT both groups agree; on British support they disagree: cypriotturks claim the British were unaware of it, where TMT secretly resisted by deceiving the British administration

(Tansu, 14); the cypriotgreeks claim it was 'covered up by the British' (Hadjidemetriou, 348) who collaborated with cypriotturks. I define both TMT and EOKA as anticolonial movements. Some may claim TMT is not an anticolonial movement because it was not founded, like EOKA, to remove British rule; cypriotturks preferred British colonialism over EOKA's enosis, considered Greek colonialism; British and cypriottutrks collaborated. Though the anti-Greek sentiment dominated over the anti-British one, TMT's plan was always to remove the British because they prevented Turkey's involvement, leaving cypriotturks without taksim and at the mercy of the British, who treated them like second-class citizens (Tansu, 19).

Thus, cypriotgreeks and cypriotturks separately developed anticolonial ethnic-nationalisms, whereby the military elites from each group competed against each other for power and privilege. Both nationalisms gained mass membership because the elites selected ethnic symbols with which the people developed emotive ties; here was a nativism for a pre-Ottoman indigenous Greek or a pre-British revised Turkish identification determined by Mother Greece or Mother Turkey, respectively. Together they failed to notice that this anticolonial ethnic-motherland nationalism replaced British rule with a new dependence and ruling unit, a new type of colonialism that prohibited the formation of an independent nation determined solely by the people of Cyprus.

Cypriotism:[46] during this decolonial period 'Cypriotism' emerged to replace the dominance of ethnic-motherland nationalisms' Greekness or Turkishness with a Cypriot-centric patriotism. Cypriotism is framed around two distinct political agendas: Communist-Cypriotism was formed during the late 1920s by the cypriotgreek left – 'Communist Party of Cyprus' (CPC) then 'Progressive Party of Working People' (AKEL) – as an unofficial 'structure of feeling' aimed at united independence for all. Colonialist-Cypriotism was a British move from the 1930s, aiming to force Cypriotisation by de-ethnicising the people into Anglo-Cypriot loyal subjects. In this process the British supported and sharpened the difference between ethnic-motherland nationalist and Cypriotist identifications, shifting between both aspirations for the benefit of the Empire. This resulted in Cypriotism having some standing in the official national narratives; however, it failed to become a dominant voice because of its associations with a colonial agenda, and because the ethnic-motherland nationalisms were more successful in selecting symbols that generated mass membership to define Cyprus.

Cypriot Diaspora:[47] British rule also generated the diasporic identification as related to various waves of economic and political migration to different regions. This includes the colonised cypriotgreek diaspora to other British colonies, especially Egypt, Africa (Zimbabwe) and Australia from the late nineteenth and early twentieth centuries, as well as the colonised cypriotgreek and cypriotturkish to colonial centres, Britain,

Turkey and Greece, as part of the largest migrations during the troublesome years from 1925 to 1960.

Independence Failures: Second Partition (1963–1964)

In 1960 Cyprus gained independence via the Zurich-London Agreement with Treaties incorporated into the Republic of Cyprus constitution. Here the competition was for the first time framed around Cyprus as an independent entity, yet ethnic affiliations were maintained, ending in intense contest over an independent or ethnically motivated model for nation-building and state-formation. Such contest was because of state-formation, which, as in many partitioned countries, 'did not inherit[...] the boundaries of the previous colonial units' (Cleary, 16), meeting divide and rule policy which solidified ethnic boundaries. This paved the way for postcolonial failures with mass conflict on an intra-group and intergroup scale, ending in the second partition.

The failure and contest were based on interrelated factors. First, the people of Cyprus had no choice: for example, Makarios III, first president of the Republic, was 'forced to accept the Zurich agreement' (Vanezis, 137) by an ultimatum to sign it or abide by the Macmillan Plan (1958) to partition Cyprus between Turkey and Greece. Second, the agreement was based on 'Consociationalism [...] a device for freezing existing division and conflicts' (Brass, 342); however, the competing ethnic-motherland nationalist demands once strengthened by the British were dominant. Third, the constitution united two groups to form a bi-national state, an impossible task because 80 years of colonial moulding left the groups in total hostility. This gave way to minority-majority number games, including: competing over population statistics – the cypriotgreek count 78.9% cypriotgreek | 18.4% cypriotturk (Panteli, 338), and the cypriotturks count 74.7% cypriotgreek | 24.6 % cypriotturk (Denktash, 17); presidential regime of cypriotgreek president and cypriotturkish vice president, where the latter had right to veto; legislative division with a ratio 70 cypriotgreek and 30 cypriotturk elected officials. The cypriotgreek officials felt the agreement gave the cypriotturkish minority rights and power disproportionate to its size; cypriotturks found this distribution fair in light of their estimates. A further contest was over the Treaty of Guarantee between Greece, Turkey and Britain: cypriotgreek officials claim it was inconsistent with sovereignty and infringed independence because it subjected the Republic to the will of the guarantors; cypriotturks suggest it was a necessity to protect 'the Republic and Turkish community from complete destruction' (Denktash, 28).

The contest and challenge over these terms of independence began from its outset: here cypriotturks claim independence was undermined by Makarios III and his followers, who tried to create enosis by scheming against Turkey's guarantee, the fair distribution, and by forcefully expelling them from all governmental functions (Denktash, 34) into enclaves, ending in devastation that forced partition as the sole solution. To prove this, they list quotes from Makarios' public speeches:[48]

> Until this small Turkish community forming part of the Turkish race which has been the terrible enemy of Hellenism is expelled, the duty to the heroes of EOKA can never be terminated. (Sept 1962; Reddaway 194)
>
> No Greek who knows me can ever believe that I would wish to work for the creation of a Cypriot national awareness. The agreements have created a State but not a Nation. (Cyprus Mail, March 28, 1963; Reddaway, 194)

The cypriotgreeks argue Makarios III supported independence, struggling for a true sovereignty without enosis, whereby he trusted the 'Turks' who schemed against the agreement for taksim:

> Turkish Cypriots terminated their participation in the government and set up their own 'General Committee'. (Hadjidemetriou, 357)
>
> They have, in fact repudiated the Zurich Agreement and Treaty of Guarantee and have been demanding the partition of the island. (Vanezis, 179)

Regarding this 1963–1964 moment, when the State was destroyed, inter-ethnic massacre increased, and the 'Green Line' Agreement that partitioned Nicosia was drawn, each side blames the other: the cypriotturks claim it to be the beginning of their ethnic-cleansing, when a Greek land – enosis – was becoming reality; cypriotgreeks claim the cypriotturks caused the devastation for taksim. Adding to this was the intra-ethnic conflict starting in 1964, when Colonel Grivas became angered by Makarios III for failing to create enosis, so together with the Greek junta led by Niko Sampson, he set up 'National Organisation of Cypriot Fighters B' (Ethnik Organosis Kiprion Agoniston B – EOKAB) in 1971 to exterminate the 'Turks' and Makarios III. cypriotgreeks refer to this as evidence that Makarios III fought for independence without enosis; cypriotturks claim Makarios III progressed slowly in creating enosis, which incited Grivas to work against him (Denktash, 61).

From 1963 to 1974 inter-ethnic and intra-ethnic conflict reigned, during which Turkey threatened intervention/invasion in Cyprus more than three times. cypriotturks claim Turkey was threatening intervention to protect all Cypriots who were suffering under EOKAB terrorism (Denktash, 19). cypriotgreeks argue Turkey's threats were an excuse to partition Cyprus for expansionism, which was on the agenda decades before.

These postcolonial failures ended in each group blaming the other, producing total deadlock; however, the documentation confirms that both groups are both victims and culprits; together they destroyed independence, subjected each other to total violence, and failed in multiple ways. They failed to acknowledge that the British colonial 'divide and rule' policy nourished and was responsible for this conflict; they failed to drain rather than maintain colonial legacies; they failed to address the fact that though Britain was a guarantor, it left the mess it created to Turkey and Greece; in short they failed to blame the British rather than each other. They also failed to recognise mutual Cypriot experiences: a high death toll, hostages taken, missing people, refugees and diaspora, migration to Greece, Turkey and Britain. Chaos reigned. Acknowledging all these failures might have enabled the Cypriots to enter a process of recovery in which as citizens they could have constructed an independent Cyprus rather than continuing to serve as native elite accomplices to a former imperial Cyprus, resulting in partition.

Third Partition: 1974

On 20 July, 1974, Turkey became physically present in Cyprus. Cyprus' geographical borders were re-invented through an extension of the Green Line that partitioned the groups into ethnically homogeneous units, with cypriotgreeks transferred to the south, and cypriotturks to the north. For cypriotturkish officials 1974 is a peace-operation, avowing that as guarantor Turkey had legal right to settle so as to maintain peace and protect all Cypriots, especially the cypriotturks, from EOKAB's violence. For cypriotgreeks, 1974 is an invasion, through which Turkey illegally used its guarantor powers to generate a military occupation, thereby triggering ethnic-cleansing and a war of terror. I will call 20 July 1974 the '1974-partition' moment, a geographic partition that was to breed fully a partitioned place, space and identification, this time through borders that concretely divided the people and Cyprus; this 1974-partition induces people to forget the layers of partition from Ottoman and British-Cyprus that produced it. The 1974-partition, which was considered a temporary solution, has now become a permanent uncertainty; the 1974-partition was – unlike the 1947 India/Pakistan partition that was discussed for over a year and agreed by leaders with awareness by the people – both unexpected and forced.

POST-1974 PARTITION LEGACY

Upon partition 'at least one of the new units claims a direct link with a prior state' enabling them to be 'sole legitimate successor to the territory of the divided administrative unit and have asserted constitutional title to that territory' (Waterman, 117; Cleary, 19). Since the 1974-partition the south has had a direct link to the Zurich-London agreement by which the Republic was formed, whereby cypriotgreek officials make claims to the total community and territory beyond its borders, which is occupied by another unit; it is this imaginary state that is internationally recognised. As for the north, the cypriotturks created a new state in 1983, the Turkish Republic of Northern Cyprus (TRNC), which was established by Rauf Raif Denktash, who was president from 1983 to 2005. Denktash claims that because the cypriotgreek officials refuse to negotiate and to relinquish their sole legitimate existence, the TRNC is a means to give cypriotturks a legitimate, although still illegal and officially as yet unrecognised, existence in the international domain. The TRNC governs territory in the north, recognised only by Turkey.

Since the 1974-partition, leaders from both sides have met to create a solution, but the meetings have been unsuccessful because each side blames the other through contest over partition motifs, including population transfer/exchange and missing people, property, number games and attitude to violence.

Population transfer/exchange and missing people hinder resolution in Cyprus. Shortly after the 1974-partition, Makarios III and Denktash met to discuss missing people, which led to an exchange of hostages held by both sides, and competing narratives between the leaders that reverberate today. For Makarios III the cypriotgreeks taken hostage by Turkey remain missing, which prevents the families from having closure; for Denktash the 1974 hostage exchange is closure, and cypriotturks and cypriotgreeks are missing because of EOKAB not Turkey. In light of these competing narratives, the cypriotgreeks set up a committee, which searches for missing people. Whilst, the cypriotturkish officials accepted that those missing are untraceable. Though contested the fact is that between 1960 and 1974 many thousands went/are still missing because of all parties, and though there was a population exchange many were unaccounted for and mass graves have been/are being recovered since 1999.[49]

Property prevents resolution. The north adopted a point-based system, whereby cypriotturks received points for the property they left behind in the south with which they purchased property in the north; cypriotgreeks hold the official deeds and legally own this property under EU laws, cypriotturks own them under TRNC's illegal and unrecognised laws. In the south the cypriotgreeks were transferred to new properties, whilst cypriotturkish properties remained vacant. Thus, cypriotturks have adopted their post-1974 properties in the north, living in fear they will lose them, and dread of returning to the pre-1974 property in the south; cypriotgreeks long for the pre-1974 property in the north, living in hope of return.

Number games hamper resolution. cypriotturks consistently disengage themselves from being a minority, and obsessively demand more rights and equality; cypriotgreeks repetitively deploy themselves as the majority, believing the cypriotturkish minority should have only those rights that are in proportion to their population. The minority-majority complex has also led to competing narratives concerning post-1974 Turkish settlement. Since 1974 numerous Turkish citizens, both soldiers and civilians, have settled and become TRNC citizens: cypriotturks argue these post-1974 citizens should be integrated into a solution because they ensure safety; cypriotgreeks argue the settlers should not be involved in the agreement because they are not Cypriots. The exact number of Turkish settlers in north Cyprus is unclear, but the increase resonates with Said's comments on Palestine-Israel: the Israeli government issued citizenship to the Jewish diaspora on an ethnic-religious or racial basis, so as to force a Jewish majority on the country in contrast to the original majority of Palestinians (Said, *Palestine*, 18). The TRNC issued Turks citizenship to increase the population; however, cypriotturks were still a minority, both in comparison to cypriotgreeks and the new Turks. A cypriotturkish counter-narrative is that cypriotgreeks are granting Republic of Cyprus citizenship to cyprioturks living in the north so to prove themselves the sole legitimate successors.

Attitude to violence prohibits a solution. The Cypriots' attitude to violence contrasts with Pandey's argument on the ways Indian historians claim violence is not part of their history, silencing or *forgetting* it so as to envision unity (Pandey, *Remember*, 60). Cypriots make violence inherent to their history, voicing and *remembering* it so to prevent unity. This difference is because of the 'location' of people and violence: Indians of various ethnic heritages live side by side, locating the violence 'here', an ever-present threat; therefore they must elide it. Pandey argues against this silencing because the violence is part of the nationalisation and institutionalisation of India. Cypriots, on the other hand, are separated into homogeneous units, where the violence is 'there' across the border, not a direct threat on home turf, and therefore can be faced. Here the violence committed by the savage other over 'there' not 'here' dominates the national narrative, where, with constant outbursts, Cypriots immortalise horrifying experiences through real and exaggerated stories. Thus, the Cypriots, like the Indians, are simultaneously victims and agents of violence (Daiya, 111), who have nationalised and institutionalised it in Cyprus, making it part of Cypriot culture, daily life and bedtime story, which prevents peace and reconciliation.

The 1963–1974 violence committed by the other side has been nationalised especially in the divided history curricula in Cyprus.[50] The cypriotturkish curriculum commemorates the 1963–1964 violence committed by the 'savage' cypriotgreeks blamed for partition, and shows Turkey as the great motherland who saved the cypriotturks via the 1974 'peace operation' without mention of cypriotgreek suffering. This curriculum was endorsed by the right-wing government, National Unity Party (Ulusal Birlik Partisi, UBP), that administered the north for over three decades through an ethnic-motherland nationalist ideology; in

2004 the left-wing government, Republican Turkish Party (Cumhuriyetci Turk Partisi, CTP), supporting 'Cypriotism' came into power and transformed the curriculum to project Cyprus reunification and critique of Turkey with limited focus on 1963–1964, and more focus on 1974 cypriotgreek suffering (Papadakis, *History*, 17–18). This history curriculum was short-lived because in 2009, UBP and its history curriculum resumed. Thus, the TRNC national history changes itself with each political party. The cypriotgreek history curriculum is fixed, commemorating 1974 violence alongside the Ottoman violence to display the indefinite invasion and exploitation cypriotgreeks have suffered because of cypriotturkish and Turkish savagery, with no mention of cypriotturkish suffering in the 1960s. This history curriculum was called into question by Europe in 2001 with the recommendation that it must change to respect difference, support reconciliation and mutual trust between peoples, open debate on controversial sensitive issues, and not be an instrument of ideological manipulation, propaganda or xenophobia. As Papadakis confirms, however, the history curriculum books oppose these recommendations (Papadakis, *History*, 11).

These history curricula have monumentalised partition's violence so as to produce a deadlock that prohibits solution. To go beyond this deadlock, the 1963–1974 violence must be rewritten in a different narrative that institutionalises and nationalises the violence committed by both sides. Educational curricula should adopt the literary as a preferred other to existing historical narratives on partition.

Conflict resolution had been on the agenda for years with many meetings between leaders across the divide and multiple proposals by the United Nations (UN), yet no solution has occurred. The Annan Plan V[51] that endeavoured to resolve the 'Cyprus problem' before its accession into the European Union marked some change; in 2003 with the intention to build-up relationships in preparation for the plan to be taken to referendum in 2004, the borders opened. All Cypriots were able freely to border-cross to the other side to see places and people prohibited from sight for three decades, and a new collective narrative floated across Cyprus. cypriotgreeks crossed to the north and visited their homes that had been inhabited by cypriotturks or Turks since 1974; and many cypriotturks crossed to the south and saw their houses empty, in ruins, or rebuilt. 2003 became a moment when Cypriots partially replaced the 1963–1974 nightmarish stories with more positive 2003 stories of reconciliation.[52] However, such stories have not as yet been institutionalised or nationalised. In 2004 the Annan plan that proposed a single Cyprus Republic with two constituent states was taken to referendum, and the results were as follows: 64.9% cypriotturks, and 24% cypriotgreeks voted 'yes'. These results were determined by the competing narratives: President Denktash opposed the plan, stressing that it was pro-Greek; the prime minister, Mehmet Ali Talat (2004–2005), and the president of Turkey, Recep Tayip Erdogan, supported it. Thus a majority of cypriotturks voted 'yes' both because of this intra-ethnic debate and because they were willing to accept anything so as to end their prolonged international isolation and minoritisation. Most political leaders in the Republic opposed the plan, referring to it as pro-Turkish; thus cypriotgreek majority voted 'no'. Consequently, partition has been maintained, with the south successfully gaining EU membership, and the north continuing to be a largely unrecognised illegal unit.

POST-1974 PARTITIONED IDENTIFICATION

Cypriotism advanced because Cypriot identification was at risk, but it did not replace ethnic attachment. In the 2000s the left-wing parties affiliated with Cypriotism came into power, suggesting the masses conformed to a united Cypriot identification; unfortunately, this was not the case because of the fickle legacy of these parties. The cypriotturkish left-wing CTP party was established in 1970 as a rival to ethnic-motherland nationalism, which supported a Cypriotist unification highly critical of Turkey. CTP gained political power in 2004, bringing to light its inconsistencies by collaborating with Turkey without adopting policies to enhance Cypriotism. cypriotgreek's CPC then AKEL identified with 'Communist-Cypriotism'; however, they too filtered out communist and Cypriotist principles. From 2008 to 2010 when the CTP and AKEL leaders were presidents of north-south Cyprus, there were hopes of a Cypriotist solution, but this was not established and partition was maintained. The left-wing parties failed to provide a Cypriotist solution, and it can be agreed that Cyprus has passed, or was 'left' in the past, an all-inclusive united Cypriotist national identification. Though Cypriotism never became official, it was a structure of feeling that disrupted the dominant ethnic-motherland nationalisms, resulting in the third identification Loizides coins 'Turkish-Cypriotism and Greek-Cypriotism'. This constitutes the official and dominant partitioned identification based on a hyphenated unity between an ethnic dimension determined by Greece and Turkey, and a Cypriot-centred dimension determined by Cyprus. The ethnic-motherland nationalists, Cypriotists, and Turkish-Cypriotists and Greek-Cypriotists have some standing within official and dominant narratives of Cyprus; they are all types of patriotism, determined by operations between self, place and space.

Another identification pivotal to colonial, postcolonial and partitioned Cyprus is the Cypriot diasporic hybrids. By diaspora, I mean the identification resulting from internal and external displacements in the 1930–1940s, 1950–1960s, and mostly 1960–1974 carnage. In these moments, the Cypriot diaspora departed from their birth-country to arrive in adopted-countries, including the British imperial centre, the ethnic centres, various other centres or peripheries, as well as to the other side of the divide. Thus, diasporic identification includes those who physically departed from and those who remained within Cyprus' geo-borders, where together they provide new ways of understanding partition. By hybrid, I intend postcolonial concepts such as Bhabha's that move beyond racist colonial attitudes, relating to the Linobambakoi. In dominant British and Cypriot narratives the Linobambakoi[53] are commonly defined as Christians who converted to Islam, where they become a 'Muslim-Christian' community of 'crypto-believers', 'traitors' and/or 'crude opportunists' whose ethno-religious normalisation was forced during British rule, ending in them being an extinct historical community excluded from official narrative. However, Constantinou redefines the Linobambakoi as a cross ethno-religiously hospitable community, who are true postcolonial Cypriots:

> They live in Cyprus, yet without identifying with the monumental nationalist histories [...] [they] remain faithful to the secret that their identity exceeds imperial categories and limits, exceeds the conventional representations of political discourse [...] [–they] corrupt the purity of ethno-national identity. (266)

In support of Constantinou, I call all Cypriots the post-Linobambakoi understood via the postcolonial Cypriot diaspora, who negotiate with multiple ethno-religious, national, political, historical and cultural positions shaped by the official and unofficial, and dominant and marginalised narratives. Because of colonialism, postcolonialism and partition the true Cypriot identification can only be a mutable diasporic hybrid within and beyond monumental boundaries. Consequently, the Cypriot diaspora, like the former Linobambakoi, have been marginalised, forbidden and eradicated from Cyprus' grand-narratives. This identification has, however, silently endured, and I have understood it, from, through and with its relegated legacy, thereby enabling the post-Linobambakoi Cypriot diaspora to have a concrete site from which to speak to and with the different positions determined by different places, spaces and times, which contribute in different ways to *Writing Cyprus*.

Writing Cyprus examines Anglophone, Hellenophone and Turkophone works by Cypriots alongside English, Greek and Turkish authors through an empirical-theoretical spatial model, which interrogates the powerful truth of space and place in postcolonial and partition discourse. For this, each chapter discusses a different identification shared by the displaced people of Cyprus who have been geographically divided for decades and ideologically divided for centuries. Each identification uses precise practices from the spatial model to read and construct Cyprus, ending in an inclusive range of marginalised and dominant, and official and unofficial identifications with positions between Cyprus and Britain, Turkey, Greece and beyond within colonial, postcolonial and partition moments. Thus, enabling the production of multiple-mutable Cypruses in the multiple-mutable Mediterranean[54] for multiple-mutable selves – including Cypriot-selves, Greek-selves, Turkish-selves, British-selves, and various other-selves. In this way the book captures the force between multiple identifications with positions determined by spatial constructions, which enables not only a nuanced understanding of the actual production of colonial, postcolonial and partition territories, but the best possible solution and model to deal with sites of ongoing conflict, like Cyprus.

Chapter 2 interrogates the official Turkish-Cypriotist and Greek-Cypriotist identification and spatial construction, with emphasis on pedagogical imperialism and its ideological implications on the postcolonial partitioned literary curricula on both sides of the divide. Chapter 3 engages with the dominant ethnic-motherland nationalist identification, elaborating on divided anticolonial moves via a common decolonial gender nationalism meeting Tuan's national place and Lefebvre's abstract nation for the production of an ethnically pure mental place. Chapter 4 walks with the less official emergent Cypriotists via its three-stage development, from a colonialist, communist and mainly the post-1964/74 partition Cypriotist that rewrites ethnic-motherland nationalist and partition production. Focus will be on the post-1964/74 partition Cypriotists receptive to postcolonial invention of spatial palimpsest and difference, Tuan's place and space and Lefebvre's concrete-abstraction, enhanced through romantic-communism and restorative nostalgia. These literary figures habitually border-cross with a structure of feeling towards peace beyond dominant ideologies, successfully to produce a pre-partitioned order. Whilst Chapters 2–4 focus on Hellenophone and Turkophone writing, Chapter 5 engages with all three languages via the Cypriot diaspora. In the concluding chapter, the diaspora is discussed from colonial to postcolonial moments, including migratory waves within and beyond Cyprus. Particular emphasis is on the diaspora who departed from and then returned to Cyprus; I call them post-Linobambakoi rhythmanalysts who perform with all identifications and constructions discussed in the book alongside new ones, operating via margins, experimental genres, nostalgia, hybridity, local border-crossing and global broader-crossing.

Writing Cyprus offers a new 'diasporic solidarity' that captures the 'truth of space' and place for the production of a 'differential' transnational island, Mediterranean, world we can all inhabit.

Notes

1 By Mediterranean here and throughout I mean Iain Chambers's definition based on mutual interactions between cultures with 'overlapping territories and intertwined histories', which make a mutable-multiple Mediterranean (3–5, 9–10). This Mediterranean can be understood through the island of Cyprus.

2 On comparative nationalism, see Anthias and Yuval-Davis; Attalides; Bryant *Imagining*; Bryant and Papadakis; Loizides 'Adapt'.
3 On post-1964/74, see Loizides 'Adapt'; Mavratsas; Papadakis and Peristianis.
4 On intercommunal studies, see Hatay's work at PRIO; Loizides *Peace*.
5 On colonial history, see Georghallides; Katsiaounis; Holland and Markides; Peristianis and Faustmann; Varnava *Imperial*; Rappas. On postcolonial anthropology, see Papadakis *Postcolonial*.
6 On partition Cyprus, see Papadakis and Peristianis; Bianchini et al; Deschaumes and Ivekovic; Calame and Charlesworth; Khumar; O'Shea; Samaddhar.
7 On literary Cyprus, see Calotychos *Cyprus*; Colette; Ioannides; Karayiannis; Layoun; Pèrcopo; Stephanides *Cultures/Memory*; Yashin *Stepmother*; Wisker.
8 On postcolonial literary place and space, see Dutton et al; Teverson and Upstone; Upstone; Noyes; Thieme. On Postcolonial geography, see Blunt; Gregory; Nalbantoglu.
9 On gendered nations, see Innes; McClintock; Ramaswamy.
10 On postcolonial city, see McLeod; Ball.
11 On the Meditereanean, see Horden and Purcell; Braudel.
12 On the Caribbean island as paradoxical sites, see Benítez-Rojo; Hall; Bongies.
13 On the sociocultural archipelago, see Benítez-Rojo.
14 On postcolonial eco-criticism, see Carrigan; Dimock; DeLoughrey; Huggan and Tiffen; Heise; Mukherje; Roos.
15 On tourism, see Carrigan.
16 On Postcolonial Europe, see Huggan.
17 These claims on postcolonial place are also flawed when considered within a settler colony framework: the chapters in the *Reader's* (First Edition) section on 'Place' (Carter, Kroetsch, Lee, Huggan) prioritise settler experiences in North America and Australia with scant attention attributed to the indigenous inhabitants' overt agonising over place. My aim is to interrogate the definition of place in postcolonial discourse through introducing partition territories; however, this points to enriching comparative possibilities between places in the settler colony via indigenous practices, meeting the partition colony.
18 On comparative partition in social sciences, see Bianchini; Fraser; Greenberg; Goddard; Harel-Shalev; Khumar; Jassal; Hochberg, Scaeffer; Stanley. On India, see Bhalla; Butailia; Hasan; Daiya; Sarkar; Pandey; Kaul; Tharu. On Ireland, see Dawson; Laffan; Morgan; Bew. On Palestine, see Said's *Palestine*; Shlaim; Pappe. On partition literature, see Cleary; Kirkland; Bernard; Padamsee.
19 On multiple partitions, see also Samaddhar.
20 On number games, see Appadurai; Cohn.
21 On sliding identities, see Armstrong.
22 On ethnic-cleansing, see Pappe; Petrovic.
23 On violence, see Pandey; Daiya.
24 By moments I mean Lefebvre's motif, which are instants of dramatic change of daily routine, and unforeseen circumstances buried within the everyday, especially immanent subversion like a committed struggle; it relates to dialectical relations between society with itself, and between social life and environment. It is a theory of presence and a practice of emancipation, without duration that can be re-lived (*Critique*, 634–52).
25 On concrete-abstraction, see Stanek.
26 I thank Neophytos Loizides for bringing this poem to my attention.

27 Another binary name globally broadcasted is the inhabitants with a Greek position are referred to as 'Cypriots', and those with a Turkish position are either non-existent, or if they must exist then they exist as 'Turks'.
28 On Cypriotism, see Ch. 4.
29 On Cypriot literatures, see Ch. 2; Yashin 'Three' 'Cypriot', *Stepmother*; Kappler.
30 By moments I am referring to Lefebvre's motif.
31 Stevenson to Devonshire, confidential, 24 December 1922.
32 This bears comparison to other partition cases as in the Muslims and Hindus of India, or the Palestinians and Jews of Israel, where the former is backward. See Seth; Said's *Palestine*.
33 On the forest, see Baker; Dixon; Dunbar; Thirgood.
34 On new historical-political perspectives, see Loizides; Papadakis; Varnava A.
35 See Ch. 3.
36 On blood and spirit, see Ch. 3; Bryant 'Purity'. On primordial inhabitants, see Hadjidemetriou; Hakeri; Vanezis.
37 On Ottoman census methods, see Karpat.
38 This has direct links to Sanjay Seth's argument on Indian Muslims' backwardness against the Hindus, because of their disassociation from Western pedagogy, wherein 'the figure of the "backward Muslim" served to produce not one, but many identifications' (Seth, 70) to overcome negative affiliation.
39 On British census methods, see Appadurai; Baines; Cohn; Hooker.
40 On British-Cyprus map, see Given; Gole; Shirley.
41 See Frazee.
42 Gladstone, Papers and correspondence, British Library, Manuscript collection, MSS 44337.
43 Churchill's Reply to Greek elected members, 12 October 1907, C.3966.
44 On Ethnic-Motherland Nationalism, see Chs. 2 and 3.
45 On dominant narratives about EOKA, see Gazioglu; Tansu; Vanezis.
46 On Cypriotism, see Chs. 2 and 4.
47 On Cypriot Diaspora, see Ch. 5.
48 Drawn from Reddaway's Appendix II, which consists of 36 statements by Makarios supporting enosis from 1959–1977.
49 On missing people, see Cassia; Uludag.
50 See Papadakis *Report*.
51 On Annan Plan, see Varnava and Faustmann.
52 Here I share the story of my paternal grandmother; this is not a marker of my political and legal position on property. Unlike the nightmarish bedtime stories my paternal and maternal grandmothers narrated to me as a child – on 1960s bloody massacre, their sons being taken hostage, the murder of her father whilst herding his sheep, being locked up in a car boot, and being saved by Mother Turkey – this new story had a less violent and angered tone. In 1974, upon the arrival of Turkish soldiers, a cypriotgreek family living in Lefkoniko in the north hurriedly departed their home without collecting their belongings. Subsequently, my grandmother transferred from her home in Kofunye in the south to this house in the north, and has lived there since, in possession of the family's belongings, which she held onto, unlike other cypriotturks. In 2003, the legal owners of my grandmother's home arrived to their home, and grandmother welcomed them in, shared a Cypriot coffee with them and returned all their belongings. During the family's forced uprooting they were unable to take their gold planted under the large lemon tree in front of the house, and 30 years later they recovered their gold. Since this date the family, who are medical doctors, regularly visit the house and

my grandmother with medicine from the south. The year 2003 became an event that enabled me to replace my grandmothers' 1960s nightmarish story with a 2003 reconciliation story. My grandmother refused to cross over to her pre-1974 home and collect her possessions that were left behind, but I went with the door keys she held on to, and saw the grounds in ruin without trace of my grandmother. The government in the south states that cypriot-turks can be compensated for this material loss.

53 There is limited study on the Linobambakoi. On dominant definitions, see Baker; Dixon; Gunnis; Hill; Sayar and Percival and Michell. On counter definitions, see Aymes and Constantinou.

54 Here again by Mediterranean I mean Chambers' definition based on mutual interactions between cultures with 'overlapping territories and intertwined histories', ending in a transnational complexity where 'borders are both transitory and zones of transit' that make a mutable-multiple Mediterranean (3–5, 9–10). This Mediterranean can be understood through the island of Cyprus

2 Literature Education Across Dominant-Emergent (Post)Colonial Partition Positions

Hyphenated Official Turkish-Cypriotists and Greek-Cypriotists

Literature should complement the historical-political narratives on partition because it has always been a great force in (post)colonial context, and literature education in Cyprus confirms this. Literature pedagogy in colonial and postcolonial Cyprus should be understood as the playing out of a complex contest ending in partition, which is not so much between Turkish-Cypriots and Greek-Cypriots,[1] but more between colonised and coloniser, with divisions between Cypriots within the same ethnic unit looming large. Literature pedagogy is an official record that demonstrates the colonial and postcolonial stages of partitioned formation, and documents the practices and identifications shared by Turkish-Cypriots and Greek-Cypriots to shape themselves and Cyprus.

The most significant studies on Cyprus' pedagogy across the divide are by anthropologists Rebecca Bryant on education shaping nationalisms, and Yiannis Papadakis' reports on history curricula shaping political ideologies. In addition, the historian Andrekos Varnava has important work on the politics of education as hindering cultural diversity and resolution.[2] There is no study on literature education, and so this chapter will do with literature education, what Bryant has done with education and nationalism, what Papadakis has done with history textbooks, and what Varnava has done with diversifying the textbooks and curricula. I will show that literature education defines and divides the people, yet with the potential to re-define and unite them. The literature curricula have proved crucial in making and breaking (post)colonial and partition Cyprus. This chapter explores literature education in Cyprus to show how it documents, defines and divides the official identification and Cyprus, showing that even though literature education, and through it Turkish-Cypriots and Greek-Cypriots have always been partitioned, the pedagogical models have mirrored and spoken to each other so as to shape the literatures, the people and Cyprus.

This chapter begins by introducing the literatures of Cyprus through the dominant and official name games and identifications, which are reflected in the partitioned pedagogy. The focus then turns to Ottoman and British pedagogical imperialisms to demonstrate that these moments set the foundations for pedagogy to partition and define Cyprus and its people, and set the stage for the complex contest over pedagogical production. Pedagogy was at once a tool used by the imperialists to control and document a partitioned official identification and Cyprus, as well as a vehicle used by the colonised Cypriots separately to write back to imperial definitions, so to document an official identification and Cyprus for themselves. Throughout pedagogical imperialism, there has been colonised-coloniser contestation, and the most significant is the competition between the British colonisers and Cypriot colonised during the last decades of colonial rule. This was a contest over two positions determined by 'place': one side was the ethnic position, the dominant tool used by Cypriots against the imperial regimes that imitated the pedagogical models of Greece or Ottoman-Turkey, so to generate an Orthodox-Greek or Muslim-Turkish Cyprus. On the other side was the Cypriot position, a British pedagogical tool forcefully implemented by the colonial office but overtly refused by the Cypriots, which focussed on generating a Cypriotness distinct to Cyprus. Throughout this pedagogical contest between the British and Cypriots the ethnic position has always dominated over the Cypriot position to provide a divided Turkish or Greek definition for Cyprus.

This study of colonial pedagogal implementation will pave the way for the primary focus, an analysis of postcolonial pedagogy, especially the recent secondary school national literature curricula on both sides of the divide, so to demonstrate how Turkish-Cypriots and Greek-Cypriots share the same model preserved from the imperial moment. The postcolonial literature curricula continue to be partitioned and maintain a contest over the two positions that shows how national and cultural definition operate in Cyprus; this will be analysed through Raymond Williams' 'Dominant, Residual and Emergent' (*Marx*, 121–28). Here the curricula give substantial standing to the 'dominant' ethnic position and the 'emergent' Cypriot position, which generate the official Turkish-Cypriotist or Greek-Cypriotist identification, by continuing ethnically to cleanse the voice from across the divide, whilst considering these two positions as in a perfect balance. However, such balancing is an imaginative fallacy because the official identification is based on a contest and dynamic relationship between the often-silenced emergent Cypriot position and the dominant ethnic position determined by mutable places and spaces that blur the boundaries, ending in identifications and Cypruses that are inconsistent and processual.

This chapter offers a different approach to the other chapters in this book. Though I will address place and space during the analysis of the literary texts in the curricula, this chapter is not about the actual practices of postcolonial partition 'invention', Lefebvrean 'spatial tripling-triad production' and Tuan's 'place and space', but instead the actual process of identification with two positions as determined by the literature pedagogy of different places. These places are Greece and Cyprus or Turkey and Cyprus, which are read and constructed as a Lefebvrean 'mental space' and experienced as Tuanian enclosed 'place' in perfect balance to generate a perfect identity fusion. This process is documented fully in Cyprus' literature education, and if considering Lefebvre's 'space' (*espace*), which corresponds to the English word 'sector', one could say that the Cypriots produce a pedagogical sector for themselves. And so, this chapter will analyse the actual production of literature pedagogy, which determines official identification of Cypriots and Cyprus. This exposure brings hope that if in this current stage Cyprus and its emergent Cypriot position have been recovered from its relegated history to interrupt the Greek or Turkish dominant position, then maybe in the next stage the ethnically cleansed voice from across the divide will have some standing in the literatures of Cyprus.

Defining the Literatures of Cyprus: Naming, Pedagogy and Publication

My definition of the literatures of Cyprus is based on a comprehensive study of activities, including pedagogy, publication, translation and movements shaped by pioneering authors and texts, linked to dominant and emergent, official and unofficial, and major, minor and counter-canons. In this section I focus mainly on the more official dominant perspective so as to pave the way for the less official emergent. This chapter expands the official definitions via literature education, and subsequent chapters move from the official to less official via various literary activities.

For this definition we must start with interrogating the name game as related to the literatures of Cyprus, which shows that the model dividing Cypriots via two positions figures fully in debates and definitions related to the literature. Greek-Cypriots and Turkish-Cypriots use different official names amongst themselves to define and distinguish their literature, and these have always been subject to internal contest over an ethnic or a Cypriot position. Greek-Cypriot literary critics are divided regarding using the name 'Cypriot Literature' and 'Modern Greek Literature'.[3] The critics supporting 'Cypriot Literature' argue that this writing is an expression of life in Cyprus, and other names have the risk of excluding or eliminating the Cypriot position; here 'Cypriot Literature' is Greek and the name 'adds nothing and subtracts nothing from its Greekness, nor cuts it from neohellenic literature' (Papaleontiou, *Hellenic*, 39). The Greek-Cypriots critics supporting 'Modern Greek Literature' argue that writings from Cyprus – like Cretan literature, the Phanariots and Athenian School, or the Generation 1930... – are a generation within the Greek literary canon; they refuse 'Cypriot Literature' because the Cypriot position moves away from the body of Modern Greek Literature, and because this name echoes British imperial policies – to replace identification with Greece's Greekness with an island Cypriotness – forcefully implemented into pedagogy, which will be analysed in later sections. The Turkish-Cypriot literary critics[4] employ parallel arguments, staging a contest between the name 'Turkish-Cypriot Literature' and 'Turkish Literature': some argue for 'Turkish-Cypriot Literature' because it separates Turkish-Cypriot from Greek-Cypriot literature, it prevents the risk of losing the Cypriot position, and it appropriates a Turkish position; other critics supporting 'Turkish Literature' argue writings from Cyprus belong to Turkey's canon, and there is no room for a Cypriot position.

Beyond this dominant literary debate, some critics, like Matthias Kappler and Mehmet Yashin, argue against both these literary names and instead support the plural name 'Cypriot Literatures', which include both Turkish-Cypriot and Greek-Cypriot literary production without depending on Greek or Turkish codes. Here two Cypriot literatures become one multilingual uncanonised literature distanced from Hellenism and Turkishness that excludes the other ethnic Cypriot.[5] My own usage draws on and extends this plural term: I use 'literatures of Cyprus' to mean Greek, Turkish, English and other writings by Cypriots of all different backgrounds, as well as by Greeks, Turks, Britons, and beyond. This is a compromise or comparative between exclusive national literatures and inclusive transnational literatures; here the uncanonised minor Cypriot literature – Greek-Cypriot or Turkish-Cypriot emergent writings – meet four major canonised literatures – dominant canons of Turkey, Greece and Britain, as well as the counter-canon of postcolonial literatures. Thus, through this plural name, I assert that the literature(s) of Cyprus or literary Cyprus is a transnational world literature, wherein all texts are (post)colonial diasporic writings about the cultural and political history of colonisation, partition and conflicting identifications as related to place and space; these writings operate within a system of inequality and displacement in relation to literary, cultural and language centres, semi-peripheries and peripheries that are outside, including, Greece, Turkey, Britain and other postcolonial territories.

Such a plural literary name with a diverse definition like mine, Kappler's and Yashin's is marginalised by the more dominant debates, which are based on maintaining an ethnic position or incorporating a Cypriot position. It is in fact as a result of ideas like Kappler's and Yashin's of a united Cypriot identification, combined with memories of British pedagogical policy, that the title with a Cypriot position is rejected, because it puts the ethnic identification of the Cypriot in danger, as it would have to contain and be contaminated by the other ethnic literature that most Cypriots refuse to accept as a literature of Cyprus. For a majority of literary critics, the aim is to generate an ethnically exclusive name for the literature, thereby ethnically cleansing the other Cypriot, whilst confirming that the literature of Cyprus is either Greek or Turkish, written by Greek-Cypriots or Turkish-Cypriots who live in Cyprus but are part of the literatures of Greece or Turkey.

As a result of this ethnically exclusive aim, the names 'Modern Greek Literature' and 'Turkish Literature' have always had more standing and been more often officially recognised. This is reflected in the names of the literature pedagogy, whereby in the Republic of Cyprus the title is 'Modern Greek', and in the TRNC the title was always 'Turkish Literature' until the pedagogical reforms of 2006, when the term 'Turkish-Cypriot Literature' was introduced and has been maintained. Both official names show that the ethnic position is more victorious than the Cypriot position, and an analysis of the literature curricula shows that both positions are simultaneously in play such that both curricula are at once records that extend this literary contest over the positions, and are documents that mirror the dynamism in the official 'Turkish-Cypriotist' and 'Greek-Cypriotist' identification.

This name game also figures in publication as will be discussed in later chapters. To briefly summarise, Cypriot authors often aim(ed) to publish in Greece or Turkey because readership in Cyprus has always been small. Though literary outputs and readership were negligible in size, there have been developments: for example, the British moment introduced the first printing press in 1880,[6] aiding local literary outputs in Greek, Turkish, English and translation. The decolonial moments, especially 1950–1964, enhanced Hellenophone or Turkophone writings by Cypriot ethnic-nationalists identifying with Greek or Turkish literatures shown through much welcomed local publications like literary magazines and zines[7]; and a few Anglophone writings sponsored by the colonial official, including magazines such as *Cyprus Review*, which a majority of Cypriot writers refused to be part of. After independence and partition, mainly from 1965 to 1986 when Cypriot identification was at risk of elimination, many state-sponsored initiatives such as publication of anthologies and literary magazines used 'Cypriot literature', with Greek-Cypriot releases in Greek and English translation,[8] and Turkish-Cypriot outputs in Turkish with translations,[9] meeting a handful of bi-communal/-lingual initiatives.[10] Recently, publications on 'Cypriot Literatures' – including anthologies, literary magazines and translation projects[11] – are multi communal/-lingual inclusive of all Cypriots. Throughout this post-partition period local publishers in support of 'Cypriot Literature' written in English, Greek and/or Turkish have emerged.[12] These developments foster the emergence of a moment and movement that defines the literatures of Cyprus in my terms, transcending dominant Turkish-Cypriot and Greek-Cypriot literary binaries, whilst exposing that Cypriot positions and literature(s)are marginalised when compared to the ethnic ones. Such emergent moves and moments are considered illegitimate in the official context, and are excluded from the official national curricula that will be discussed in this chapter.

Pedagogical Imperialism

Education in Cyprus has been at the forefront of dividing and defining the Cypriots into two units, a process that has evolved from religious to ethno-religious to ethno-national groupings. Consequently, education has always been a major subject of contention, not only between the ruling regimes and Cypriot subjects but also between the Cypriots in the same ethnic unit. During Ottoman rule, this definition was based on religious groupings with religious foundations authorised to be the regulatory institutions of education; both institutions had the same goal with different ends: 'how to make the student good Orthodox or Muslim subjects?' During the last stages of Ottoman rule and into British rule, the divided education continued but the institutions focussed on modern secular definitions, whereby the Cypriots gradually transformed from being self-conscious ethno-religious subjects to ethno-national citizens. This paved the way for contest between the Cypriots and British colonisers: the Cypriots fully adopted the teachings of the ethnic centres, Greece and Turkey, to form 'good Greek' and 'good Turkish' citizens; whilst the British imperialists attempted to replace this ethnic position with a Cypriot position and consciousness to form 'good Cypriot subjects'. These definitions operated in all subjects; however, literature had a major role in documenting and determining the stages and contest in colonial Cyprus.

During Ottoman rule, the Greek-Orthodox Church had the authority to form pedagogical institutions.[13] There is limited address by Greek-Cypriots on pedagogy in the first few centuries of Ottoman rule, other than criticising the pedagogical poverty and religious values of the 'backward Muslim-Ottomans'. Instead, pedagogical discussion begins around 1815, when the first 'Hellenic School' was established, through to 1860 when 'there were [secular] schools in almost all the towns and quite a number of villages' (Hadjidemetriou, 296–97) rich with a progressive Greekness. Here the Church adopted Greece's education[14] as a vehicle to generate ethnic awareness and values, where Greek or Greek-Cypriot teachers educated in Greece carried these pedagogical definitions to Cyprus. As Panayiotis Persianis writes in *Church and State in Cyprus Education*: 'the more [ethnic]nationalist the Bishop was, the greater number of schools he tried to establish' (Persianis, *Church*, 130) [...] 'the teachers and the Church leaders appealed usually to the [ethno-] national feelings [...] without any great effort to appeal to the religious feelings of the pupils' (Persianis, *Church*, 185). The Church acknowledged ethnicity over religion for several reasons: first, they adopted Greece's pedagogy, yet, it must be noted that though ethno-national formations were priority in Greece, religion and the Church were always an ethical force that provided the 'spiritual and moral development of the youth [whereby] love of God and country were inseparable and [...]

the foundation of all education[…] [Both were always] in close alliance with classical national humanis[m]' (Kazamias, 12). Second, Ottoman presence meant religious definitions were less at risk, than were the new Hellenic Greek self-definitions of emergent nationalism. In light of this, the Church enhanced Hellenic definitions that aspired to enosis via the Ancient Greek Language and Literature subject: the most essential curricular subject that taught Greek-Cypriots the consciousness of their Greek origins and its relationship to modern Greeks; a powerful strand in confirming Greekness of Cyprus, a Greece-Cyprus kinship (Persianis, *Church*, 185; Koutselini-Ioannidou, 396). Thus, Ancient Greek studies enabled Greek-Cypriots successfully to mobilise the ideological move within emergent ethno-nationalism so to resist Ottoman coercion and rule; this powerful study was not prohibited or a subject of contention during Ottoman rule.

The Turkish-Cypriot education was modelled upon the Vakf[15] system – 'religious foundations or pious endowment […] to support religious, cultural and social development' (Gazioglu, *Turks*, 189) – established shortly after the Ottoman conquest of Cyprus. The Vakf, like the Church, used education as a vehicle to define the people, where schoolmasters from the Ottoman imperial centre came to Cyprus to deliver Islamic values via Qur'anic, Persian and Arabic studies, which taught Turkish-Cypriots how to be 'good Muslim' subjects (Gazioglu, *Turks*, 196–98). Turkish-Cypriot schools maintained only a religious character until the *Tanzimat* reforms (1836–1876) of the Ottoman Empire, when 'education in Cyprus went into a transformation period of modernisation […] parallel to the mainland' (Gazioglu, *Turks*, 199). By 1862 *medrese* elite secondary and higher education advanced, when the first lower secondary *Rushtie* (Rustiye) schools and upper secondary were founded to produce a modern education for 'elite Turkish-Cypriot intellectuals' (Gazioglu, *Turks*, 199); by 1871 new methods were introduced into elementary schools, when geography and history were added to the curriculum' (Gazioglu, *Turks*, 197). The nineteenth century was a period when secular education was gaining ascendance over religious education; however, unlike the Greek-Cypriots, Turkish-Cypriots maintained Ottoman-Muslim definitions.

Thus, throughout Ottoman rule, the people were pedagogically partitioned, yet the pedagogical models were largely parallel. Both communities addressed education through religious institutions, which adopted the pedagogy of different places to define the people: The Church adopted Greece's pedagogy and prioritised Ancient Greek studies to define Greek values for Greek-Cypriots, whilst the Vakf adopted the Ottoman Empire's pedagogy to emphasise Islamic values for Turkish-Cypriots.[16] This partitioned pedagogy was strengthened during British rule: from 1878 to 1933,[17] the colonial government did not have an education policy, and instead Cypriot subjects separately controlled their education via identification with Greece's or Ottoman/Turkey's pedagogy.

The British encouraged Greek-Cypriot pedagogical enhancements that adopted Greece's Ancient Greek studies, which they considered a model of civilisation that played an important role in elite education in Britain; however, it did become a subject of contest between colonial offices. In 1880, at the suggestion of the first Director of Education, Josiah Spenser, the High Commissioner of Cyprus, Robert Buddolph, attempted to make English a general vehicle of education; in response the Secretary of State for Colonies, Earl of Kimberly, rejected the plan, stating:

> considering the rich and varied literature of ancient Greece and the great progress which modern Greek has made in [...] education [...] Greek [...] affords ample means not only for an ordinary education but for the attainment of a high degree of mental culture. (Persianis, *Lending*, 48; C2930, 1881; Varnava, *British*, 165)

This colonial attitude towards pedagogy in Cyprus differed greatly from those pursued in other British colonies. The British Empire's general pedagogical practice can be traced in Thomas Macaulay's 'Minute on Indian Education 1835', which claims they had to

> educate a people who cannot at present be educated by means of their mother tongue [...] [Instead by knowing] our literature and English tongue [...] [that] abounds with the works of imagination not inferior to the noblest which Greece has bequeathed us [,the native] has ready access to all the vast intellectual wealth, which all the wisest nations of the earth have created. (Macaulay, 349–50)

In light of this imperial attitude, the colonial office did not Anglicise Greek-Cypriot education because their Greek origins meant they could educate and represent themselves as they had ready access to the vast intellectual wealth with a high degree of mental culture that the noblest and wisest men on earth created.

By the twentieth century, some decades after the Greek-Cypriots, Turkish-Cypriots also developed an ethno-national pedagogy by imitating Turkey's education, particularly via the reform (1919–1924) introduced by Mustafa Kemal Ataturk, which prioritised secular subjects so to teach the nation a narration of Turkishness. This Kemalist pedagogy was framed around 'the concept of general culture (*genel kultur*) [influenced by France's model] defined in terms of humanistic studies' and taught through 'language, literature and history' (Kazamias, 21–23). Thus, both Turkish-Cypriots and Greek-Cypriots received pedagogical models, materials and teachers from elsewhere, where they read the history, culture and society of someone out there, someone else's life and location as their own.

Adopting an education that is not one's own is a characteristic associated with many colonised people, whereby the colonial power, as shown in Macaulay's speech, institutionalises an educational system in the colony derived directly from the metropolitan centres of Empire. In *The Colonizer and the Colonized*, Albert Memmi exposes the function of colonial education as teaching the colonised someone else's culture: 'The memory which is assigned him is certainly not that of his people. The history which is taught him is not his own. [...] Everything seems to have taken place outside of his country. He and his land are nonentities' (Memmi, 105). In Memmi's study it is the Empire's culture the colonised is forced to learn; however, in Cyprus the colonised Cypriots willingly made their respective ethnic centres their Empire. The Cypriots institutionalised an education, where everything took place outside, making their own history, land and the 'Cypriot' a nonentity, whilst Turkey or Greece was the sole entity. By the 1930s, however, this changed, when the Cypriots – like the French colonial subjects of North Africa Memmi described, or the British colonial natives of India Macaulay describes – were condemned to have an education that inculcated British imperial culture, and emptied them of the definitions they valued and were free to select up until this moment.

The 1931 revolt was the trigger that made the British realise the need for education policy 'to help them either to maintain their political control over the Cypriots or to make their "civilising" role in Cyprus better understood and appreciated by the colonised' (Persianis, *Lending*, 56). The British recognised education's significance in generating Cypriot ethno-national loyalty, which they had to interrupt because it was putting their authority at risk. Consequently, from 1933 to 1949 British implemented a new policy[18] to maintain control, eliminate the risks of anticolonialism and master the colonised Cypriots' loyalty. Maintaining control and instilling loyalty through education were a strategy used in other British colonies, as shown in Gauri Viswanathan's *Masks of Conquest* on literary pedagogical imperialism in India. The colonial pedagogy incorporated in other colonies, particularly in India, Africa and Palestine,[19] was now appropriated with revisions for colonial Cyprus; the Cypriots, particularly Greek-Cypriots, were no longer considered different with a 'high mental culture', but were now treated the same as other colonised subjects of the British Empire – they had to be educated and emptied of ethno-national meaning.

This new policy de-centralised and de-ethnicised the education, now framed around 'one' education that sought a 'Cypriotisation of the two communities' (Persianis, *Lending*, 57) with a Cypriot-centred pro-British ethos. This policy aimed to empty the Cypriots of ethno-national feeling to claim they were neither Greek members of Greece nor Turks of Turkey, but instead Anglo-Cypriot loyal subjects of the British Empire. This policy was implemented by replacing the board members, teachers and models from Greece or Turkey with a new board of Cypriot and English teachers responsible to re-write the pedagogical framework, which had to be authorised by the colonial Director of Education. This pedagogy was built on the illusion of a de-ethnicised Cypriot-centric collectivity – Turkish-Cypriot and Greek-Cypriot education were to become identical, with permission for them to use Turkish or Greek languages – in collaboration with a British ethos. This illusion of an Anglo-Cypriot definition was enforced and reflected in the humanities subjects: geography become priority with focus on Cyprus and Britain, where classrooms were emptied of maps of Turkey or Greece; history was neither Ottoman nor Ancient Greek, but began with Britain; Ancient Greek and Ottoman-Turkish language and literature were replaced by English. Focussing on humanities subjects, literature in particular, was a common British practice in other colonies because they were a vehicle that shaped the 'character or the development of the aesthetic sense or discipline of ethical thinking [...] essential to the process of socio-political control' (Viswanathan, 3). Thus, this pedagogical policy forced Cypriots to think and learn everything British that had taken place outside, like the colonial subjects Memmi described; ironically, however, this policy also transformed Cyprus from being a 'nonentity' to a significant aspect of education and culture. Such policies were also enforced in publication, for example: the 1931–1932 Publication Laws with censorship of material coming from outside; and the 1954–1956 Public Information Services of Cyprus, when its new director, British author Lawrence Durrell, who was also an English teacher in Nicosia, oversaw the press release of materials with the mission to Cypriotise the people into Anglo-Cypriot loyal subjects.[20]

Many Greek-Cypriots and Turkish-Cypriots treated this imperial pedagogy with scepticism. The Greek-Cypriots refused the colonial policy by concluding it aimed to force de-Hellenisation by coercion; consequently, ethnic loyalty was heightened when they integrated fully an ethnic position into their education.[21] The Turkish-Cypriots did not oppose the policy, but, as in most situations, collaborated with the imperial office because they felt adopting Greek education shot through with enosis demands posed more of a risk to their Turkishness than did the British education. Furthermore, the Empire's pedagogical policy was modelled against Greek-Cypriots, because as a majority they had more potential to develop a disruptive anticolonial nationalist movement. Even though Greek-Cypriots and Turkish-Cypriots responded differently to the imperial policy, the Anglo-Cypriotism was nothing but an official text that could not compete against the dominant ethnic aspiration. Consequently, this imperial policy failed to prevent the growth of Cypriots' ethnic loyalty and anticolonial ethnic-nationalisms, which were determined by the Cypriots' stronghold on education.

Education shaped the anticolonial mobilisation, feeding into EOKA and TMT. The founding members of EOKA, for example, Makarios III and Georgios Grivas, were graduates of the same school renowned for inspiring a generation of anticolonial freedom-fighters. This was the 'Hellenic School' founded in 1815, which operated under the name 'Pancyprian Gymnasium' during British rule; it was governed by Konstantinos Spyridakis, an enosis devotee and pioneer in leading action against the British education policies and forces. Pancyprian Gymnasium was joined by all secondary schools with students involved in the EOKA mobilisation on 1 April 1955 and demonstrations throughout 1955–1956 school year, and when the colonial office closed these schools in 1956, 'the teachers [continued teaching] students inside the Church' (Persianis, *Church*, 142–43). Similarly, Turkish-Cypriot education was pivotal to TMT mobilisation; however, because the Turkish-Cypriots collaborated with the British, their relationship to education was a little different. Rather than mass demonstrations and recruitment from the schools, progress was based on clandestine selection: here Turkish militant officials from Turkey were sent to Cyprus with 'cover up positions [...] as teachers and school inspectors' (Ismail, 78), so to recruit *muchaits*, Turkish-Cypriot freedom-fighters, from secondary schools to be trained for the mobilisation. Thus, these pedagogical institutions in Cyprus paved the way for the anticolonial mobilisation that provided Cyprus with independence in 1960.

Postcolonial Partitioned Pedagogy: Two Positional Imperial Legacy

The imperial pedagogy was, as in most postcolonial cases, simultaneously rejected and preserved in postcolonial Cyprus[22]: pedagogical partition was sustained; it continued to be a powerful vehicle for the narration of the nation; and, most significantly, the narration was determined by contest over the ethnic and Cypriot positions, which transferred from Cypriot colonised and British coloniser to be between Cypriot officials from the same ethnic unit. In the first years of independence, both groups upheld colonial fear of de-ethnicisation so they aimed to safeguard ethnic positions by imitating Greece's and Turkey's pedagogies, whilst avoiding pedagogical action that contributed to an independent Cypriot position (Koutselini-Ioannidou, 400). After partition failures, this changed, when an intra-ethnic contest over the position commenced around 1967 for Greek-Cypriots, and after 1974-partition for Turkish-Cypriots: here some officials argued for the historically rooted Greek or Turkish position, dependent on the pedagogies of Greece or Turkey; other officials argued for the silenced, yet newly approved Cypriot position, independent of Greece and Turkey.

From 1960 to 1966 Greek-Cypriots adopted Greece's pedagogy without reservation; however, by 1967 contest over pedagogy began, which was triggered by Greece's momentary reforms: in 1964 Greece's Papandreou government 'struck Ancient Greek from the curriculum of the first three years of secondary school'; in 1965 the Papandreou government resigned, and the succeeding Greek government 'eliminated the innovations of the 1964 reform' (Koutselini-Ioannidou, 400). These pedagogical reforms resulted in a new attitude amongst Greek-Cypriots: the 1964 reform was welcomed, when they admitted they felt 'Greek education was backward but were reluctant to voice their grievances', here English teaching was also reintroduced; the 1967 reform was criticised, when they spoke 'openly against the educational affairs of Greece' (Persianis, *Independent*, 108–10) for the first time in history. Between 1967 and 1968 these attitudes filtered into government, ending in the first internal contest between the Ministry of Labour and Education over a Cypriot or Greek position. The Ministry of Labour argued for a Cypriot position with a policy that deviates from Greece's pedagogy by decreasing Ancient Greek studies because such studies were not in tune with Cyprus' economic and social needs and definition (Persianis, *Independent*, 107). The Education ministry supported an ethnic position that adopted fully Greece's pedagogy and Ancient Greek studies to maintain links with Greece and preserve the Greek definition of Cyprus. Such contests occurred at ministerial level throughout the first decades of independence but did not filter fully into the education, so total imitation of Greece's pedagogy was maintained until the 1974-partition.

After the 1974-partition, Greek-Cypriot education underwent a radical reform, when the government agreed it must promote Cyprus as an independent entity with its own national recovery detached from Greece whilst striving to unite and define Greek-Cyprus. This consensus on pedagogy was determined by various factors: first, the forceful uprooting of Greek-Cypriots from their homes and half the island generated a patriotism for the homeland, Cyprus; second the Greek-Cypriot connection towards Greece was damaged because the latter reserved support during the 1974 assault; and finally, the Greek-Cypriot application to European Union membership. The formation of this pedagogy was a gradual process from 1976 to 1990, which introduced a 'Cypriot-centred education policy' (Koutselini-Ioannidou, 405) and position that broke from yet maintained an ethnic position via Greece, ending in heightening contest between Greek and Cypriot positions. This post-1974 pedagogical reform and contest operate via various changes. First, the teaching hours allocated to Ancient Greek were reduced whilst those for Modern Greek increased in Cyprus compared to Greece; however, though this change was specific to the Greek-Cypriot national position, the Greek position was maintained because other than this difference in timetabling, Cyprus' Modern and Ancient Greek curricula were the same as Greece's.

The second change resulted from Cyprus' application to EU membership, where education was revised to satisfy policies of inclusivity.[23] Here Greek-Cypriots deviated further from Greece's pedagogy, reflected especially in the 1987 change to the Modern Greek curriculum that introduced literatures by Greek-Cypriot authors. This was also reflected in the governmental publications of numerous 'Cypriot' anthologies of Greek-Cypriot writings. This was the first time a Cypriot voice, consciousness and position specific to Cyprus were officially approved in the literature curriculum and canon; however, the Cypriot position figured and competed against the ethnic position. Thus, this Modern Greek curriculum imitated Greece's, whilst including a section distinct to Cyprus, and it is this curriculum that continues to be taught in the Republic of Cyprus, providing an ethnically exclusive official Greek-Cypriotist definition for Cyprus.

The Turkish-Cypriot education underwent a similar process, which started to be enforced three decades after 1974 because of north Cyprus' governance. From 1974 to 2004, north Cyprus was governed by the right-wing party, UBP, and leaders President Rauf Raif Denktash and Prime Minister Dervis Eroglu, with an ideology devoted to the Turkish position and that defined Turkey as protector and provider of national, economic and political sources they needed to exist, which is reflected in TRNC's education that imitated Turkey's. After decades of international isolation without recognition, Turkish-Cypriot feelings changed when an independent united Cypriot entity critical of dependence on and union with Turkey emerged; this feeling was first adopted by CTP in the late 1970s, yet these sentiments were a marginalised covert energy in political rallies and amongst the people which did not compete against UBP until 2004 when CTP and the leader Mehmet Ali Talat came into power. However, this Cypriot independence failed to figure in the national definition, first because TRNC depended on Turkey, ending in CTP filtering out many Cypriot-centred policies; second CTP was succeeded by UBP in 2010, whereby the Cypriot-centric policies were eliminated. Even though CTP failed to implement this 'structure of feeling' (Williams, *Marx*, 128–35) into the national and official definition, the political contest between CTP and UBP gave way for north Cyprus to transform from a Turkish to Turkish-Cypriot definition, and CTP was successful in applying the Cypriot 'structure of feeling' into the entire pedagogy.

Education underwent a radical reform when a Cypriot position was implemented into all humanities subjects. Particularly significant was the Turkish-Cypriot Literature subject introduced in 2006 and that is still in use in TRNC; Turkish-Cypriot Literature is separate from the Turkish Studies curriculum of Turkey, which suggests the first official traces of an independent Turkish-Cypriot literary definition. This was also reflected in publication through an outpouring of 'Cypriot' anthologies of Turkish-Cypriot writing. Here the Turkish-Cypriots were more successful and advanced – for the first time in Cyprus' history – than Greek-Cypriots in creating a complete literature curriculum. A study of the Turkish-Cypriot Literature curriculum, however, shows that, like the Greek-Cypriots', it is determined by an ethnic position dependent on Turkey alongside a Cypriot position. Consequently, when UBP resumed power they did not eliminate Turkish-Cypriot Literature, as they had done with the other subjects introduced by CTP, because it successfully documented/s the official ethnically exclusive Turkish-Cypriotist identification of Cyprus.

Thus, the pedagogical imperialism of Ottoman and British regimes determined and has been immortalised in colonial, postcolonial and partitioned Cyprus. Confirming that even though the Cypriots have always been pedagogically partitioned, they have shared the same pedagogical stages and contest to generate a definition for themselves. During the colonial moments, the Cypriots made Greece or Ottoman-Turkey the authors of their pedagogy and consciousness; by the postcolonial and partition moment, Greece's and Turkey's pedagogical dominance with ethnic position was maintained, yet interrupted by an emergent Cyprus and Cypriot position and author. Currently, in the 2019 moment, the literature pedagogies on both sides of the divide reflect the imperial legacy, wherein they continue to be partitioned, and are a vehicle for official definition determined by a contest over the ethnic and Cypriot positions.

Literature Pedagogy Now (2009–2019): Two Positions In Dynamic Interrelations

The current literature pedagogies for secondary school on both sides of the divide mirror each other, and document the complex process and dynamic ways that national and cultural definition operate in Cyprus. Williams' cultural model in 'Dominant, Residual and Emergent' (*Marx*, 121–28) provides an understanding of this.

Both literature pedagogies are separated into two subjects: Ancient Greek and Modern Greek for the Greek-Cypriots, and Turkish Studies and Turkish-Cypriot Literature for the Turkish-Cypriots. The Modern Greek and Turkish-Cypriot Literature curricula[24] will be my primary focus, although Ancient Greek and Turkish Studies will be referred to, to show how the overall literary framework for pedagogy evidences my argument on official identification. The literature pedagogies document the official identification – Turkish-Cypriotism or Greek-Cypriotism – related to the two positions, which are determined by geographies across the hyphen conceived as a perfectly balanced dynamic interrelation in union, yet are also an illusionary concoction overwhelmed with unbalanced dynamic interrelation in contest. The literature pedagogies show this complex process between the positions through providing a platform for the emergent voices of Cyprus alongside dominant voices of Greece and Turkey, where the emergent voices compete to exist. These pedagogies confirm that the Turkish-Cypriots and Greek-Cypriots are paralysed in the decolonial moment. Together they have failed to recover from the fear of ethnic dispossession and cleansing experienced in (de)colonial Cyprus, because the traumas, disorder and uncertainties continue vehemently to reign in postcolonial partitioned Cyprus. This has prohibited the Cypriots from forming an independent national and cultural definition for themselves and the island. In fear, they willingly deprived themselves of developing fully a Cypriot consciousness, and submitted themselves to be dispossessed of a literary history, canon and voice. In fear, they turned to a mature ethnic consciousness, a historically tried and tested canon and voice, that can provide national and cultural certainty and security. The Cypriots believe they must adopt Greece's Greekness or Turkey's Turkishness because they do not know who they are without this position, what is a Cypriot or Cypriot position, and how else can they possibly define and deal with such a young nation, a fractured territory, a broken people? The process simultaneously shows attempts of recovery with a struggle to answer these questions through including a Cypriot position detached from Greece's and Turkey's ethnic one. The Cypriots struggle to capture this Cypriot position, especially the literary feeling, consciousness and voice, because, though it was shaped during British colonialism they eliminated it throughout history and only recently accepted it, so it is in the active process of becoming; there is not a Cypriot literature in a canonical sense; there is no scholar, research collective or university department on Cypriot literature; and the teachers who teach these literatures are graduates of Turkish or Greek literature programmes. Consequently, the literature pedagogies confirm that the Cypriot position does not and cannot exist in its own terms, and must collaborate and exist in fusion with Greece's Greekness or Turkey's Turkishness, which generates an official Greek-Cypriot or Turkish-Cypriot identification that is complex, dynamic and processual.

Clearly the literature pedagogies document the way national and cultural definition operate in Cyprus, understood through Williams' model that enables us to analyse these complex processes and dynamic interrelations via what he terms the 'dominant', 'residual' and 'emergent'. The 'dominant' is the perspective followed by the majority, so in Cyprus the Greek and Turkish positions are the dominant poles of address by which people lay claim to a fixed meaning. Williams shows, however, that whilst a particular perspective is dominant, other perspectives, an older residual and a newer emergent, compete for meaning, which shows that the dominant position is neither fixed nor stable, and is not the sole pole of address for cultural and national definition. The residual perspective has been formed in the past, but is still active in the cultural process, not as an element of the past, but as an effective element of the present; here a version of this past is incorporated, yet must undergo a process of dilution, in order for the dominant culture to make sense. In Cyprus, the Greek-Cypriots incorporate a residual element by drawing on Ancient Greek and Byzantine narratives, whilst the Turkish-Cypriots focus on Ottoman values and meanings, both of which are revised to provide a definition fitting to the dominant Greek and Turkish perspective of Cyprus.

The emergent perspective usually starts at the margins of society and is a result of changes and interactions in that society, whereby 'new meanings and values, new practices, new relationship and kinds of relationships are continually being created' (Williams, *Marx*, 122–23), which offer an alternative and opposition to the dominant perspective. In Cyprus, the Cypriot position is the emergent perspective that was politically and socially marginalised until independence and partition, when it was partially approved but continues to compete against the dominant Greek and Turkish position. The complex and dynamic interrelation between the older residual position, the dominant Greek and Turkish position, and the emergent Cypriot position shows how cultural and national identification operates in Cyprus. This operation between the dominant ethnic and the emergent Cypriot position in particular is embodied in the literature pedagogies, which attempt to deviate from Greece's or Turkey's ethnic dominance to enable the emergent Cypriot position to have equal standing, so to generate a definition with both positions in perfect balanced union; however, in both literatures the ethnic position always dominates, whilst the emergent Cypriot position competes for meaning.

The Greek-Cypriots' Ancient Greek and Modern Greek curricula for secondary school (gymnasium and lyceum)[25] show this dynamic interrelation between the positions. In Cyprus the timetabling for these subjects deviates from Greece's by maintaining the 1976–1990 reforms,[26] yet these curricula are still modelled on Greece's – thus confirming a Greek position dominates. The content also shows this: Modern Greek consists of six syllabi, one for each year of secondary school,[27] each made up of three literatures that include Greek Literature, World Literature and Cypriot Literature. The Greek and World Literature sections imitate Greece's curriculum, whereby 70% of the teaching hours and texts focus on Greek authors with a scattering of 10% world authors; the Cypriot Literature section or position with Greek-Cypriot authors[28] covers 20% of the curriculum. The literature materials used for Modern Greek consist of roughly 138 texts that are divided between 13 textbooks plus a prose text.[29] Ten textbooks are used for the Greek literature section, divided between Greek literary texts and history; these are published and prepared for and by the Greek citizens in Greece, but shipped over to and for Cyprus. The remaining three textbooks – *Cypriot Literature Anthology Gymnasium; Cypriot Literature Anthology Lyceum*

1; Cypriot Literature Anthology Lyceum 2 – are used for the Cypriot section, with Greek-Cypriot authors and texts, which have been prepared and published by and for the Greek-Cypriots. This Modern Greek curriculum structuring into a Greek section that imitates Greece, and a Cypriot section distinct to Cyprus, shows Greek-Cypriot failure to generate that perfect balance, ending in the unbalanced processual contest between the two positions; this is demonstrated through the literature pedagogy as a whole and a further analysis of the curriculum.

The Turkish-Cypriots' literature pedagogy for secondary school (orta okul and lise)[30] has a very similar structure to the Greek-Cypriots', yet documents this in a different way. The Turkish-Cypriot pedagogy focusses mainly on modern literary studies, and the contest between the positions operates via two curricula subjects: Turkish Studies with Turkish language and literature, which imitates Turkey's pedagogy; and Turkish-Cypriot Literature with only Turkish-Cypriot literary texts, which is distinct to the TRNC. Here the unbalanced contest between the two positions is evident when comparing the timetabling and resources between the two subjects. Turkish-Cypriot Literature is taught in upper school (lise 1 and 2) for one hour a week in each year; there is not a syllabus, but instead the subject is taught through reading 148 texts in 2 textbooks– *Turkish Cypriot Literature I* and *Turkish Cypriot Literature II*[31] – prepared and published by and for Turkish-Cypriots. Turkish Studies is taught throughout secondary school, consisting of around five hours a week for each year, with mass of texts distributed between a total of 17 textbooks written by and for the Turkish citizens, but imported to Cyprus and processed as the Turkish-Cypriots' own. This structural overview of Turkish-Cypriot Literature and Turkish Studies shows that the ethnic position dominates over the emergent Cypriot position, meaning that the curriculum objectives to define Cyprus independent of Turkey, as introduced by CTP, struggle to exist.

This framing of the literature pedagogies across the divide shows that the two positions are in a dynamic contest: whilst Cypriot Literatures finally have some standing to teach the students a Cypriot consciousness, they also struggle to exist against Greece's and Turkey's literatures that teach the students a Greek or Turkish consciousness for Cyprus. This dynamic interrelation is documented further within the Modern Greek and Turkish-Cypriot Literature curricula, which will be analysed fully in the remaining sections: first I focus on the Turkish and Greek positions, and then the Cypriot position. Here I investigate how the syllabus structure and content aid and encourage students to receive the literary texts in specific ways. The analysed texts have been selected and read via certain criteria, including the school year, the authors that dominate, order of texts, headings with specific thematic or school of thought, introductory commentary, the questions after each text, the comments by the inspectors of literature during two interviews, and the narrative consciousness depicted. Parts of my analysis focus on diasporic writers because they dominate the curricula, and, though the curricula do not address these texts in such terms and I will not elaborate this fully here, I will highlight the diasporic narratives because they evidence my definition of literary Cyprus as (post)colonial and partition diasporic writings shaped by place, space and displacement.

Modern Greek and Turkish-Cypriot Literature: Dominant Ethnic Position

The Greek literature section in Cyprus' Modern Greek curriculum mirrors Greece's, imitating fully the literary chronology, thematics and history. In gymnasium 1 and 2, the curriculum programme is divided thematically into different units, which include mostly spatial and social themes: nature, journey, migration and displacement, civilisation, family, religion, national struggle and life. In gymnasium 3 and lyceum 1 the programme is divided chronologically into Greek schools of thought and movements, which include the units: Folk Literature, Cretan Literature, Modern Greek Enlightenment, Heptanesian School (Seven Island), School of Phanariot Greeks and Athenian Romantics (1830–1880), and School of Athens (1880–1922). In lyceum 2 and 3 the focus is on the 1930s Generation divided generically into Greek poetry and prose. All the writers are Greeks from Greece, various Greek islands and the diaspora, without any reference to Greek-Cypriots. In light of this, the Greek-Cypriots become passive 'readers' of these Greek literary narratives, without being active participants or subjects of the consciousness and definitions this canon creates, yet these definitions are acknowledged as the Cypriots' own. I will analyse five texts from the Greek Literature section of the programmes[32] that demonstrate ways in which Greek-Cypriots adopt Greek themes and Schools so to generate successfully a Greek position for Cyprus. Here all texts are unintentionally –in terms of both the educational board's and my own selection – by the Greek diaspora, especially Constantine Cavafy; this is very telling in demonstrating the diasporic and Cavafy's dominance across the Modern Greek curriculum that Greek-Cypriots find relevant for themselves, and that defines the Greek position[33] for Cyprus.

In gymnasium 1, the unit 'religion' is explored through Cavafy's poem 'Prayer', which emphasises maintaining a distinct spirit via a mother praying for her missing son:

> A sailor drowned in the sea's depths.
> Unaware, his mother goes and lights
> a tall candle before the icon of our Lady,
> praying that he'll come back quickly, that the weather may

be good –
her ear cocked always to the wind.
While she prays and supplicates,
the icon listens, solemn, sad,
knowing the son she waits for never will come back (Cavafy, *Collected*, 6).

Here is a response to an un-recovered loss that shows contrast between 'the world of men and the gods/nature' (Politis, 188), whilst the mother 'unaware' turns to religion and nature for her son's return, religion/nature are 'all knowing' of the son's unfortunate circumstance. It is this religious/natural essence that answers the mother's prayers, and provides spirit and strength to deal with the loss and indefinitely wait. Critics have defined 'Prayer' as a 'historical poem' (Politis, 188), suggesting Greek losses during wars – independence (1821–1832) and the Greco-Turkish war (1897) – against Ottoman rule. Similarly, the Greek-Cypriot students are encouraged to read this poem within a historical context, so as to deal with their history of imperial coercion and loss: 'missing sons', 'praying mothers', 'awaiting return', 'Greek spirit' and 'wind' are frozen symbols for Ottoman-Cyprus, and more specifically for 1974-partition Cyprus, when thousands went missing and are 'regard[ed] as having suffered an unknown fate – *agnoumenoi* – as not-(yet)-recovered, as living [so] cannot be presumed to be dead unless their bodies are recovered'[34] (Cassai, 195). Through this poem the Greek-Cypriots students learn that like the Greek mothers of Greece, the Greek-Cypriots, mainly mourning mothers and wives, are 'unaware' of their missing son or husband, yet they have the Greek spirit and strength indefinitely to pray for recovery, deal with the loss and wait for justice. This gendered depiction in 'Prayer' is also associated with enosis, where Mother Greece prays for her son Cyprus' return. In both interpretations the Greek-Cypriots respond to the maternal depictions of Greece and Greeks to generate an Orthodox Greek consciousness, faith and spirit for themselves.

In gymnasium 2, Cavafy's 'Thermopylae' is selected for the unit 'Life Struggle – Man's Combative Spirit'. This is a 'historical-mythical' poem about the Ancient Greek battle between the Spartans and Persians, where Cavafy uses Greek mythical allusion to explore the 'philosophical principle of the Universal Balance which exists everywhere, and when that balance is disturbed by the actions of one man another person needs to reestablish it' (Cavafy, *Poems*, 17). Cavafy states: 'Honour to those who in the life they lead/ define and guard a Thermopylae/ Never betraying what is right,/ consistent and just in all they do' (Cavafy, *Collected*, 12). Here Cavafy uses 'a Thermopylae' to suggest all those nations that have, like Thermopylae, been at risk of being destroyed and emptied of definition, and he honours all who, like Spartans, have taken responsibility and done what is 'right' to guard the pre-existing balance and definitions in a country. Cavafy also honours fighters who acknowledge defeat: 'And even more honour is due to them/when they foresee (and many do foresee)/that Ephialtis will turn up in the end,/that the Medes will break through after all' (Cavafy, *Collected*, 12). Here Cavafy suggests that those who disturb the pre-existing balance in a country are like 'Ephialtis', and those that 'foresee' are leaders, like the Spartan King, Leonidas, who though aware of defeat continue to struggle to re-establish the balance by self-sacrifice. Cavafy's 'Thermopylae' addresses this Universal Balance without a specific context; however, it is suggestive Greek-Cypriots read it within an Ancient Greek context to show they inherited the spirit to guard the balance in Cyprus. The Greek-Cypriots, like the Spartans, guarded 'a Thermopylae', against all those, 'Ephialtis', who disturbed the Greek-Cyprus and enosis, including: the Ottoman Empire and the Turkish settlers disturbing Cyprus' Greek population; the British Empire's attempts to remove Cyprus' Greekness and prevent enosis; Turkey's 1974-partition; and the Turks in Cyprus, the main Ephialtis, guided Turkey to invade. The Greek-Cypriots read the poem to show that, like the Spartans, they saw the traitors and acknowledged defeat, yet sacrificed themselves to re-establish Greek-Cyprus.

In lyceum 1, Cavafy's 'Waiting for the Barbarians' represents the Modern School of Athens, and it also teaches the students about their Greek spiritual inheritance so to struggle against imperial coercion. The poem is about civilised city dwellers waiting for the arrival of barbarians, through which everything will change; however, the barbarians do not come but in anticipation of their arrival the city dwellers change everything:

> What are we waiting for, assembled in the forum? [...]
> Why isn't anything going on in the senate?
> Why are the senators sitting there without legislating?
> [...]
> Why did our emperor get up so early,
> [...]
> Why have our two consuls and praetors come out today
> wearing their embroidered, their scarlet togas?
> [...]
> Why don't our distinguished orators turn up as usual (Cavafy,
> *Collected*, 14)

Thus, the city is reproduced 'because the barbarians are coming today' which suggests that people, nation and/or society are formed through waiting for the arrival of a foreign other. Through this, Cavafy disrupts the historical narrative of the 'barbarian' as the external other that society eliminates, and instead locates them as a presence critical to form society. The poem's last lines emphasise this, when the city dwellers state 'Now what's going to happen to us without barbarians?/Those people were a kind of solution' (Cavafy, *Collected*, 15), here confirming the barbarian's presence justified and confirmed the city dwellers' civilised existence.

This poem can be read ahistorically, as a comment on the universal condition of self and other, because neither city dweller nor barbarian is defined; here again, however, Greek-Cypriot students read the poem within a historical context that revises the Orientalist binary – colonised eastern 'barbarian' and coloniser western civilised. In the poem, the colonised city dwellers – 'senate', 'emperor', 'consul and praetor' in 'scarlet togas' – reflect the civilised west, particularly the cities Constantinople and Alexandria of the Byzantium Empire because Cavafy's parents were born in the former and he in the latter; whilst the colonisers who are arriving have the characteristics associated with the east, a backward people, embracing luxury, excess and opposed to the western logos, which suggests the Ottoman Empire who did arrive and conquer Constantinople (1453) and Alexandria (1458) from the Byzantine Empire. Here seeming to confirm the Ottoman Empire forced the civilised Greeks to regress to a barbaric state. In the poem the city dwellers willingly de-civilise themselves because they assume the barbarian conquerors prefer it: the senate are 'sitting there without legislating'; the orators are silenced because barbarians get 'bored by rhetoric and public speaking'; the consul and the praetor covered in 'bracelets with so many amethysts,/ rings sparkling with magnificent emeralds [...]canes/ beautifully worked with silver and gold' because 'things like that dazzle the barbarians' (Cavafy, *Collected*, 15).

The students are encouraged to see parallels between the fall of Byzantine Greek and Cypriot Greek history within an imperial framing, especially suggestive through the subsequent poems studied. For example, they read Vasilis Michalides' national epic poem '9 July' about the 1821 executions of Archbishop Kyprionos and many other men by Ottoman Turks. Thus, the fall of the city dwellers points to the common fate between glorious Byzantine Greeks and Greek-Cypriots, where they also fell into the hands of the barbaric Ottoman Empire in 1571, when it was forced to transform from civilised 'Greek' to barbaric Ottoman-Cyprus. The poem also shows that Ottoman arrival in Greece and Cyprus was 'a solution', where through opposing and comparing themselves to the barbaric Ottomans, the Greek united into a stronger civilised nation. The poem might be read as reassuring the Greek-Cypriots that the arrival of 'barbaric' Ottomans in 1571 and then Turkey in 1974 has made them stronger, more civilised and more Greek. Further to this, the poem can be read as commentary on British imperialism in Cyprus, which reverses the common binary between the civilised western coloniser and backward colonised, akin to Cesaire's point in *Discourse on Colonialism* on the 'decivilised', 'dehumanised', 'animal-like' barbaric characteristics of the colonial west, which '*brutalize* him [...] degrade him, to awaken him to buried instincts, to covetousness, violence' (Cesaire, 13). Here the Greek-Cypriots point to British barbarianism that attempted to de-Hellenise and de-civilise Cyprus through prohibiting the enosis; yet, this made the Greek-Cypriots more civilised and more Hellenic.

In lyceum 2 'Helen' by George Seferis represents the 1930 generation, one of the few examples amongst the Greek literature texts in the curriculum to focus on Cyprus. For Greek-Cypriots this suggests Cyprus is part of Greek literary consciousness because Seferis, a Greek Nobel Laureate, is inspired by Cyprus' history for his powerful Greek mythology and Hellenic worldview; thus, Seferis is central to the curriculum, and his poetics have influenced Greek-Cypriot poets. Seferis visited Cyprus in November 1953 and in 1955, when he wrote the collection *Logbook III* first published with the title *Cyprus, where it was ordained for me*, considered Seferis' classic collections that consists of 'Helen' and numerous other poems inspired by the Ancient and Modern Hellene history of Cyprus. The poem depicts the Ancient Greek civilisation of Cyprus through the mythological character, Teucer, son of King Telamon of the Greek island Salamis. Legend has it that Teucer and his half-brother Ajax fought together in the Trojan war, which resulted in Ajax's death and Teucer being exiled to Cyprus by his father; whilst in Cyprus, overcome by nostalgia for his homeland he re-built a mini Salamis for himself. As Seferis writes: 'Teucer:... in sea-girt Cyprus, where it was decreed/ by Apollo that I should live, giving the city/ the name of Salamis in memory of my island home' (Seferis, 120). This myth has some standing because there is a city in north Cyprus and a Greek Island called Salamis; confirming to Greek-Cypriots that even though Salamis is occupied, it always has been and will be Greek. The poem also points to parallel fates between the legendary founder Teucer and the Greek-Cypriot offspring: in 1974 the Cypriots, like Teucer, were uprooted from their homeland, and like their ancestor they long for their lost homeland.

In lyceum 3 Cavafy's 'The God Abandons Antony' is linked to the 1930 generation. The poem is about Mark Antony losing Alexandria, as depicted by the ancient writer Plutarch in 'The life of Antony' in *Parallel Lives*. Plutarch writes of the night before the city falls when Anthony hears a procession, which symbolises his end in Alexandria is imminent and that his god – 'Bacchus' – is abandoning him. Cavafy focusses on this moment – 'an invisible procession going by/with exquisite music, voices' – to advise great leaders on what they should not do: 'Don't mourn your luck that's failing now[...] don't fool yourself, don't say /it was a dream, your eyes deceived you:/ don't degrade yourself with empty hopes like these'. Instead of 'whining' for what has been lost, one should:

> As one long prepared, and full of courage
> [...]
> go firmly to the window
> And listen with deep emotion,

> [...]
> listen – your final pleasure – to the voices,
> to the exquisite music of that strange procession,
> and say goodbye to her, to the Alexandria you are losing.
> (Cavafy, *Collected*, 27)

Here, as with all poems analysed in this section, the students are encouraged via the accompanying questions, comments and the texts that proceed and follow the poem, to see parallel lives between the Byzantine/ Ancient Greek history and Cypriot history. This poem, for example, is sandwiched between Seferis' 'Salamis in Cyprus' and George Pierides 'Orange Grove', both referring to loss and longing for the island via the displaced son. The Greek-Cypriot moment of loss – 'goodbye' – has hereby been immortalised. Following Cavafy's advice, they too went to their windows and balconies, fully prepared with courage to relish the sounds of their last moments before Ottoman-Cyprus, British-Cyprus and 1974 Cyprus, and to say goodbye to the Cyprus they were losing.

This analysis of Greek Literature in the Modern Greek curriculum demonstrates that a Greek position and consciousness has been encouraged for and adopted fully by the students, through narratives confirming an immortal Greek spirit has been inherited by Greek-Cypriots from their Ancient ancestors and Modern fathers. As glorious Greeks, the Greek-Cypriots will indefinitely pray, wait and struggle for justice, and like them, they will be victorious over all losses, subjugation and traumas because they have the immortal Greek spirit, strength and courage.

The Turkish-Cypriots adopt a Turkish position and consciousness in a less direct way. The Turkish-Cypriot Literature curriculum consists of only Turkish-Cypriot texts, which is determined by and imitates Turkey's canon. The content in the curriculum is divided into Folk Literature taught in lise 1 through the textbook, *Turkish Cypriot Literature I*, and Modern Literature taught in lise 2 through *Turkish Cypriot Literature II*,[35] which follow the same structure as Turkey's literature curriculum. Turkish-Cypriot Literature begins with Folk Literature and genres divided into four units, each with two to five sections. Unit one is on Oral Syllabic poems, including Lullaby, Riddles and Folk songs; unit two is on Folk Prose, divided into Fables, Legends, Folk Stories, Thought Provoking Prose, Proverbs and Folk Theatre; unit three is Folk Poetry and Prose, which include Eulogies and Epics; unit four is on *Asik* [Romantic] Literature with focus on epic poems. The second year of the curriculum continues with Modern Literatures that are divided chronologically into Turkish movements, including: Ottoman Literature; Tanzimat Literature; National Literature; Traditionalist/ Syllabist Poetry; First New Movement-Garip Group; Second New Movement; Socialist Realist.

The Turkish-Cypriot Literature curriculum only takes form and becomes a minor literature through imitating the literary history and curriculum of Turkey. This is a separate curriculum that includes only

Turkish-Cypriot authors, yet these authors have standing because they belong to a particular Turkish literary period. This is not, however, an active literary membership, but an imitation of the Turkish movements with a two to three-decade delay. The Turkish-Cypriot Literature curriculum presents a literature that is constantly running behind and trying, without any success, to catch up with Turkish Literature, and, as in the Greek-Cypriot curriculum, the poets and students become readers that copy and adopt what is depicted as the original literary essence. The literary essence is the Turkish canon and curriculum; yet, because all the writers are Turkish-Cypriot, a Turkish consciousness is not depicted through direct narratives, as in the Greek-Cypriot curriculum, but instead a Turkish kinship is represented by imitating Turkey's literary canon/curriculum within a Turkish-Cypriot context.

Each of the five units in the Folk textbook has an introductory section on the history and characteristics of Turkish folk literatures, and then commentary on its influence on Cypriot folk literature, followed by examples by Turkish-Cypriots. Consequently, throughout the Folk textbook there are multiple examples when Turkish and Cypriot folk texts are parallel. In unit 2, for example, the 'Folk Theatre' section is on 'shadow plays', which involve two-dimensional puppets made of camel skin, reflected on a white screen and controlled by a person. The most well-known shadow play is 'Hacivat and Karagoz': Hacivat is a *Medrese* graduate, an elite institution of the Ottoman period, or that is what he claims, and as a result he represents himself as part of the Ottoman elite class through speaking in an intellectual language, that his companion Karagoz cannot understand. Karagoz is an illiterate blacksmith, yet smart and cunning; he has a laid-back expression and does not withhold his words, which are at times very rude. The fact that Karagoz and Hacivat are opposite, especially with regard to language, leads to misunderstandings and sets the comical tone of all the shadow plays. The Turkish-Cypriot shadow play in the curriculum is also on 'Hacivat and Karagoz', where other than minor changes in setting and scenarios because the puppeteer is Cypriot, the same two puppets, their characteristics, their misunderstandings, and the Turkish dialect are imitated. This imitation of Turkey's Folk Literature is maintained in the textbook, thus suggesting that Cypriot Folk Literature is dependent on Turkey's.

Similarly, in the Modern Turkish Literature textbook, the Turkish literary movements are divided into units with introductory section on the Turkish move and its influence on the Turkish-Cypriot, followed by five examples by Turkish-Cypriot authors. Below is one example from the First New Garip Group:

> In 1930, [Nazim Hikmet] Orhan Veli, Oktay Rifat and Melih Cevdet Anday introduced early examples of free-verse poetry [...] [that developed]into a movement. [...] In 1941 they called themselves

> Garip [*Strange*] with a manifesto confirming they rejected poetic rhyme, size, dependence on beautiful verse, and tools such as simile and metaphors. [...] Focusing on colloquial expression in daily life, the Garip ones rejected the forms of Traditionalist poetry [...]
> The Garip movement in Turkey influenced [...] Turkish-Cypriot poets, but with a ten-year delay. [...] [Those influenced, include:] [...] Pembe Marmara, Macit Selin [...] Mustafa Izzet Adiloglu, Osman Turkay [...] Taner F. Baybar. (*TCLII*, 66–67)

In the light of this overview students read poems by Turkish-Cypriots who adopt the Garip characteristics. The whole textbook consists of this 'Turkish literary movement– Cypriot literary follower' format, confirming Turkish-Cypriots can only be a part of the curriculum if they parallel a Turkish movement, through which the Turkish writers are replaced by the Cypriot writers.

The Turkish-Cypriot Literature curriculum's imitation of Turkey's curriculum may suggest that the Turkish-Cypriots sought a consciousness and history identical to Turkey's; however, this was not the proposed aim of the CTP government who designed it. Consequently, the Turkish-Cypriot curriculum documents the intense struggle to generate a Cypriot definition detached from Turkey's, which it partially achieves because not only is it distinct to Cyprus, but a content analysis shows that hidden between the lines of imitation there is a powerful political voice with the curriculum objective –Cypriot nation independent of Turkey.

A notable example is seen in the above-mentioned First New Garip Group section: here all the Cypriot poets are from generation diaspora who migrated to Turkey and/or Britain, and Taner Baybars' poem 'Kyrenia Pier' is about the Cypriot's desire to be part of the Turkish literary scene, to be recognised in cultural centre Istanbul, and how to deal with rejection – Cypriots must reject them. This poem belongs to a collection that was Baybars' first and last in Turkish; thereafter he abandoned the Turkish language and publishing by writing in English, translating Hikmet and others into English, all published in England. A further example is in the Folk Song unit, when the introduction provides background of the Turkish folk song with commentary on how the Cypriot folk song differs:

> Our folk songs do not follow the classical folk songs. The major difference between our folk songs and the Anatolian one is that our folk songs do not have a chorus and the syllabic forms are different. (*TCLI*, 35)

Through this commentary on the difference with the usage and repetition of 'our' folk song, the literature curriculum is documenting a political point – 'the' Turkish folk song is different and is not like 'our'

Cypriot one. This detachment is emphasised in the 'Folk Song Preparatory Work' section, a task the student completes before each unit; here students respond to the role of folk songs for a culture through this anecdote:

> Under the patronage of the Roman Empire there was one big and one small country. The big country wanted the small country to join it, and so they requested Caesar's judgement. After the request, Caesar withdrew to think about this possible unity, and sent inspectors to both the big and small country to study their folk songs. The inspectors found that the languages of the two countries were very similar; however, every aspect of the countries' folk song was different, so Caesar refused the countries' request. (*TCLI*, 37)

This is an explicit political and national comparison: the big country is Turkey and the small Cyprus, they share the same language but because they have different folk songs, as evidenced in the textbook's introduction, these countries cannot unite. This is one example of many from the textbooks that make powerful statements against the Turkish position and the historical aspiration of Turkey-Cyprus; however, such statements struggle to be understood because the Turkish literary imitation overpowers the textbooks and literary definition for Cyprus.

The investigation has thus shown that even though the Greek-Cypriot and Turkish-Cypriot literature curricula use different approaches, both show Greece's and Turkey's literature curricula and positions as dominant. Whilst the Greek-Cypriots' literature is more direct with Greek texts that provide a forceful Greek consciousness, the Turkish-Cypriots' literature is indirect whereby they copy Turkey's literary canon via Cypriot texts that attempt, though with little success, to provide an independence from Turkish consciousness. Both Cypriot communities submit to the literatures of Turkey and Greece as a means to generate a fixed Turkish or Greek definition, and to be a part of something that would give them literary existence and recognition. Consequently, however, the Cypriots submit to being followers and imitators without agency; here failing to receive any kind of literary recognition from Greece, Turkey or the international domain, and failing to be active participants and creators of Greek or Turkish literature. Even though Greece's and Turkey's literary canon has authorship and agency, both curricula detach from the Turkish or Greek position to formulate a literary moment for the Cypriot self with a Cypriot position and consciousness for Cyprus.

Modern Greek and Turkish-Cypriot Literature: Emergent Cypriot Position

The literature curricula across the divide generate a Cypriot position, and though the trajectories taken for this are different and separate, they open ground for dialogue with a collective theme, consciousness and definition specific to Cyprus. Here the curricula include a selection of Cypriot texts, predominantly poems, by Cypriot authors with a distinctive Cypriot literary history, culture and politics. By adopting a Cypriot position, both curricula evidence the operation of two positions in the official identification, Turkish-Cypriotism and Greek-Cypriotism, in different ways. First, as shown, in the general structure, the curricula are divided between ethnic texts and positions that imitate Greece's or Turkey's literature, alongside Cypriot texts and positions distinct to Cyprus. Second, an analysis of the Cypriot texts shows they are divided into ethnic-motherland nationalist narratives and Cypriot-centric patriotic narratives.

The Modern Greek literature curriculum has a separate Cypriot literature section for each secondary school year that sporadically distributes around three to six Cypriot texts (totalling 23 texts), none of which are introduced through a generic, historical or thematic grouping. The Turkish-Cypriot Literature curriculum introduces an independent Cypriot position in lise 2, consisting of 23 texts, which are grouped into two units titled: 'Nationalist Poetry' and 'Post-74 Poetry' with an introductory section detailing the historical-political developments that inspired the Cypriots without any reference to Turkey's movements. Even though the Greek-Cypriot 2009–2010 curriculum does not group the Cypriot texts, a generational grouping identical to the Turkish-Cypriot curriculum figures in the 2017–2018 updated curriculum. This literary grouping has been officially standardised in the emergent Cypriot literary curriculum and canon on both sides, where various studies, such as Kika Olymbiou's on Greek-Cypriot poetry, propose generations – i.e. '1930–1955, 1955–1974, 1974–1990' (Olymbiou, 34) – that respond to specific historical moments in Cyprus. The curricula on both sides prioritise two generations that respond to major historical periods of nationalisation, which relentlessly transformed and were detrimental to the identification of Cyprus – I name them 'Ethnic-Motherland Nationalists' who respond to the 1950–1974 decolonial period, and the 'Post-1964/74 Cypriotists' who record the partition periods.

The 'Ethnic-Motherland Nationalist' generation is a gendered ethnic-nationalism that responds to the 1950s colonial, 1955 anticolonial, and 1960s independence consciousness specific to Cyprus. The nationalist literatures in both curricula represent these moments via narratives dominated by Cypriots' spirit of resistance and struggle for ethnic preservation and unification with the respective 'motherlands' Greece or Turkey, for a Greece or Turkey Cyprus; ironically however, the narratives generate a literary consciousness specific to Cyprus without literary kinship to Greece or Turkey. The writers of this generation would reject such a detachment from literary Greece or Turkey, yet, taken out of the authors' control, the historical events of this period are so powerful, and inspired them to such an extent that they unconsciously develop a collective ethnic-motherland nationalist literary identification and Cyprus.

The 'Post-1964/74 Cypriotist' has an island patriotic flavour that responds to partitioned Cyprus, and this generation adopt two different narratives: one is the unofficial often marginalised Cypriotist definition that is ethnically inclusive of all Cypriots, struggling for a united Cyprus; the other is the official ethnic-Cypriotist definition that dismisses the Cypriot across the divide and prioritises an ethnically exclusive Cypriot consciousness for Cyprus. The Greek-Cypriot curriculum includes the ethnic-Cypriotist writers by sporadically including poems that record Greek-Cypriot feelings, rage, grief and longing for the homeland 'villages and houses from which they were forcibly ejected by the Turkish invaders' (Olymbiou, 43). In stark contrast the Turkish-Cypriot curriculum includes non-ethnic Cypriotism via the 'Post-74 Poetry' unit with Turkish-Cypriot poets from the '74 Generation: Rejection Front'. Established in 1978, the '74 Generation' is the first radical literary movement with a manifesto, which focussed on 'identity depression' (*TCLII*, 125) experienced by all Cypriots, and overtly promoted a single Cypriotist identity against Turkey, against their literary predecessors who imitated Turkish literature, and against all moves, like 'Ethnic-Motherland Nationalist' and the 1974-partition, that support ethnic separation of Cypriots. The '74 Generation', however, failed to materialise this collective Cypriotisation with united values, first because the move consisted of only Turkish-Cypriot members; secondly because it was marginalised without readership as it did not fit TRNC's official definition. The move gained some pedagogical standing in 2006 because of CTP's governance that supported non-ethnic Cypriotism, and they now figure in the curriculum as a radical idea that cannot have dominant national and political standing. Even though the curriculum on each side of the divide prioritises a different consciousness, the texts are in dialogue generating a shared 'Post-1964/74 Cypriotist' response to the partition of Cyprus.

These literary responses of the 'Ethnic-Motherland Nationalist' and 'Post-1964/74 Cypriotist Generation' demonstrate a collective consciousness and identification for colonial, postcolonial and partition Cyprus. This Cypriot consciousness operates with and through diasporic displacement, where the curricula consist of Cypriot diaspora writers and more significantly consist of diasporic themes, which parallel those of the foremost dispersed people of our generation – the Palestinian diaspora poets of resistance against Israeli occupation.[36] The Cypriot writers do not explicitly compare themselves to the Palestinians; however, the narrative practices used by the poets are comparable. This comparison provides a distinct approach to introduce the first examples of Cypriot literature that are, as I argue, all diasporic writings, and also to put literary Cyprus on the postcolonial partitioned map. The diasporic definitions and consciousness of Palestinian resistance poetry that are internationally acknowledged and recognised will be a vehicle throughout the rest of this chapter to aid an understanding of the unacknowledged and unrecognised definitions of Cyprus. Hence, one sees Cyprus' relevance to a key case, like Palestine, which has shaped postcolonial partition discourse, whilst also seeing Cyprus as a distinct case that offers new ways of reading Palestine and postcolonial partition discourse.

Like the Palestinian diaspora, the Cypriots have lived the pain of partition, uprooting and displacement. The Palestinian poets of resistance, particularly those of the 1970s, wrote because they needed 'poets to record and immortalize the Palestinian case and to speak on behalf of the people's refusal to be defeated or broken' by Israeli occupation (Ashrawi, 90). Similarly, the Cypriot curricula show that the poets of the nationalist and Cypriotist generations speak on behalf of the Cypriots; they 'record' and 'immortalise' the 1950s, 1960s and 1974s moments that put Cypriots at risk of being defeated and broken, and these literary narratives are a vehicle that guides the masses to resist, remain and rebel. The Cypriot poets of the 'Ethnic-Motherland Nationalist' generation are a powerful force because they can be compared with the Palestinian 'nationalist, committed, and politically aware poets, who view poetry primarily as a vehicle to move the masses [...] raise generations and signal resistance' particularly by being 'poet-rebels', 'poet-politicians' and 'poet-martyrs' who record the moment (Ashrawi, 84–87). Like the Palestinians, the Cypriot poets are national figures: they were freedom-fighters who served in the EOKA and TMT anticolonial struggle; some become martyrs during the decolonial and independence moments; and many were politicians who dealt with the postcolonial partition failures. However, the Cypriot poets are also distinct from the Palestinians, in that all of them were poet-educators, committed to raising the younger generations' state of resistance. Thus, the 'Ethnic-Motherland Nationalist Generation' are powerful representatives of the time because through their words, actions and professions they immortalised the moments, moved the masses and trained the future generation to resist and be steadfast in the Cypriot struggle ethnically to exist, remain and unite.

The 'Post-1964/74 Cypriotist Generation' are forceful representatives of partition; however, because of the different consciousness these poets represent, the Turkish-Cypriots and Greek-Cypriots do not share the same political and national standing. The Greek-Cypriot poets, like the nationalist poets, are poet-politicians, poet-rebels and poet-educators because they represent the official dominant consciousness. The Turkish-Cypriot writers, however, do not have much standing in government because first they support a united Cypriotism that opposes official ethnically exclusive consciousness; second, they reject official positions because, as CTP's legacy shows, it results in dependence on Turkey, which distort definitions of an independent Cypriotism. Though the 'Post-1964/74 Cypriotist Generation' of poets are different, they respond to partition in ways parallel to the Palestinian resistance poets: the literary narratives immortalise and deal with the pain of partition, they capture the living historical process between longing and belonging to overcome the alienation resulting from dislocation, dispersion and oppression (Elmessiri, 78). The literary narratives aid them to build a metaphoric homeland full of truths and concrete realities.

Ethnic Motherland Nationalist Generation

Many Cypriot poems by the 'Ethnic-Motherland Nationalist Generation' record the last decades of British colonial rule; immortalise the EOKA and TMT struggles to replace British colonialism with an enosis or taksim liberation; and document the independent moment overwhelmed by postcolonial failures. I will analyse six poems from the curricula[37] to show how they speak to each other about these colonial, anticolonial and postcolonial moments to generate an ethnic-motherland nationalist identification specific to Cyprus. 'Cyprus Agreement' by Greek-Cypriot diaspora Theodosis Pierides[38] and 'Shepherd' by Turkish-Cypriot Suleyman Ulucamgil record the last few decades of British colonial rule; 'A Song For Our Older Brother' by Greek-Cypriot Costas Montis and 'The Heroes won't be Forgotten' by Turkish-Cypriot Bener Hakki Hakeri immortalise the anticolonial liberation struggle of EOKA and TMT; 'The Letter and the Road' by Greek-Cypriot diaspora Yiannis Papadopoulos[39] and 'Punching a Knife' by Turkish-Cypriot Orbay Deliceirmak record the last stages of colonial rule and document the failures of postcolonial Cyprus. All of these poets were ethnic-motherland nationalists, committed and politically aware: Pierides, Montis, Papadopoulos and Ulucamgil served in the EOKA/TMT liberation struggles, whereby the latter is a poet-martyr; Ulucamgil, Montis, Hakeri, Deliceirmak and Papadopoulos were teachers and politicians. These poets are national figures of Cyprus whose poetry had and continues to have great force in mobilising and creating a definition for the Cypriot masses.

'Cyprus Agreement' by Pierides and 'Shepherd' by Ulucamgil are records of and resistance poetry against colonial coercion the Cypriots experienced in the last few years, particularly 1955–1958, of British rule. Here they respond to the moment when the British proclaimed a State of Emergency against the anticolonial ethnic-nationalist aspirations:

> Pierides, 'Cyprus Agreement':
> We didn't have eyes to see how they grew
> The oranges in their green cribs [...]
> We didn't have ears to listen to the drops
> the honey drops in the figs.
> We didn't have hands to harvest – and they rotted.
> In pain the spikes in our fields

and like candles melted and burnt out.
We have no heart [...]
[...]
[...] no one had an aim.
[...] everything was abroad, went afar
We were without (Pierides, *CLALII*, 21–26)

Ulucamgil, 'Shepherd':
These bullet-hearted shepherds'
Joyful stories
Are missing
You stole it (Ulucamgil, *TCLII*, 93)

Both poems express that the British attempt to eliminate the ethnic-motherland national aspiration is equivalent to emptying the Cypriots of their natural essence, senses and organic relation with the land. Pierides compares losing enosis and Greekness to losing all bodily senses, 'eyes, ears, hands and heart', through which they are unable to protect their 'harvest', 'figs' and 'oranges'. Figs and oranges are common frozen poetic symbols, like those used by Palestinian poets for Palestine,[40] to routinely mean Cyprus, and through this Pierides shows the Cypriots are unable to protect, and lose their organic connection with Cyprus. Thus, Pierides shows losing enosis results in the destruction of Greek-Cypriot and Cyprus essence, where they are left bodiless, landless, aimless and soulless. Ulucamgil also suggests that losing the ethnic aspiration is equivalent to losing the natural essence through the shepherd. The shepherd symbolises peaceful, free and communitarian nature of Cyprus, as well as the Cypriots' organic link to the territory, the 'antithesis to the corrupting, expansionist and oppressive way of life that [...] the local agent of "the West" represents' (Swedenburg, 25) – the way of life the British Imperialists represent in Cyprus. Ulucamgil shows, however, that, 'you', the British Empire, destroyed the shepherd's natural existence first by stealing his joyful stories of village life, which relates to the Turkish-Cypriots being emptied of ethnic meaning, and second by forcing the shepherds to replace their peaceful life with violent – 'bullet-hearted' – death for ethnic freedom. The poem relates to the textbook commentary that: 'shepherds [...] often have a rural village lifestyle disconnected from world problems such as colonisation and politics [however] our shepherds are sensitive to the universal problem of colonisation and they turn their vision towards the liberation struggle' (*TCLII*, 95). Thus, Ulucamgil's poem and the textbook show that shepherds, as in Palestinian resistance poetry,[41] are a pivotal vehicle that signify natural national essence of the Turkish-Cypriots, an immoveable presence on the land, and are active agents of the liberation struggle. Both poets also record the organic relationship between the ethnic national aspiration, the land and the Cypriots that grow through each other, and show how this State of Natural Peace is destroyed. This parallels the Palestinian resistance poetics, as in 'In the Deserts of Exile' by Jabra Ibrahim Jabra: 'Our Palestine; green land of ours [...] from your hills that the angels sang to the shepherds/Of peace on earth and goodwill among men?' (Jabra, 225–29), is now forcefully replaced by State of Catastrophe. In Cyprus the State of Peace is replaced with a State of Emergency by British forces:

> Pierides, 'Cyprus Agreement':
> I watched the steamships
> The immoveable cannons they loaded and counted
> we were watching at airports and
> we were counting the immoveable bodies (Pierides, *CLALII*, 21–26)
>
> Ulucamgil, 'Shepherd':
> You bring suffering
> And you're deaf (Ulucamgil, *TCLII*, 93)

Both poets show that the British brought tools of violence and silence: Pierides refers to war weapons that arrived from seaport to airport to silence Cypriot resistance, ending in a relentless armed struggle between the British and EOKA with many deaths; Ulucamgil confirms the British brought suffering because they are 'deaf' to Turkish-Cypriot ethnonational needs. Though coerced by the State of Emergency, both poems conclude by refusing defeat through violent victory howls that move the Cypriot masses to seize the ethnic aspiration, and confirm the anticolonial struggle will continue until the British are forced to leave:

> Pierides 'Cyprus Agreement':
> Enlightenment has come
> and kissed us on the mouth –
> Freedom
> We didn't lose it this summer.
>
> [...]
> Your soldier's medals, your judge's wigs
> Your jails, your laws, your narrow trees,
> And your big ships and your big names
> And your small unimportant heroism –
> You will take them all and you will leave. (Pierides, *CLALII*, 21–26)
>
> Ulucamgil 'Shepherd':
> You were hit by bottles and stones
> The day twenty-seventh January... (Ulucamgil, *TCLII*, 94)

Pierides shows that the enosis aspiration is a form of Enlightenment that they intimately connect with. This enlightened spirit enables the Cypriot to un-invent everything the British cartographically 'named' and enforced to know and control Cyprus, and instead howl to the British coloniser: 'you will take them all and you will leave'. Listing vehicles of coercion and then demanding for them to leave is a poetic practice used by the Palestinian poets of resistance: in 'Those Who Pass between Fleeting Words' Mahmoud Darwish lists Israeli weapons of occupation – 'names, swords, tear gas, tanks' – in the West Bank and Gaza and demands for them to 'be gone'. Ulucamgil also confirms that the British will be gone by referring to the 'day twenty-seventh January [1958]' when the Turkish-Cypriots, Ulucamgil included, attacked them with the limited war resources, 'bottles and stones', they had. The date and ellipsis at the end of the poem suggest the struggle is/will not be complete until the British leave and Turkish-Cypriots have their Turkish freedom. Thus, Pierides and Ulucamgil manifest shared poetic styles and attitudes to the British State of Emergency: they equate the ethno-national feeling to the Cypriots natural essence, which transforms from a state of colonial coercion, paralysis and loss, to a state of anticolonial mobilisation that the Cypriots will maintain until the British leave.

The poems 'A Song for our Older Brother' by Montis and 'The Heroes won't be Forgotten' by Hakeri record further the anticolonial mobilisation by freedom-fighters who forced the British to leave. Both poems honour and immortalise the anticolonial freedom-fighters, who sacrificed themselves for the independence and freedom of Cyprus.

In 'A Song for Our Older Brother', Montis praises the EOKA brothers' spirit to die for liberation with the following demands for its immortalisation:

> let us receive a drop of your blood
> to color our own
> so that it can never again
> be faded by fear.
>
> Let us receive your final gaze
> to watch over us lest we sway
> let us receive your final breath
> […]
> let us receive your last words
> so we can endlessly sing
> military marches to freedom… (Montis, *EOKA*, 64)

Here Montis lists the martyr's attributes that make-up the Greek spirit, which Greek-Cypriots must 'receive' so to maintain the liberation struggle for enosis: the blood prevent the risks of – 'fading' – de-hellenisation; the eyes – 'gaze' – enable a vision so not to 'sway' from the journey to ethnic freedom; the 'breath' keeps alive 'forevermore' this Greek struggle; words provide a song to sing during the journey to freedom. Of these martyr attributes, the song is considered the most powerful vehicle, which resonates with the Palestinian resistance poem of Salem Jubran: 'The songs,/ Among the comrades, will take my place/ And fight for me' (Ashrawi, 89). Montis' poem, 'A Song for Our Older Brother', is a powerful freedom song that immortalises the martyrs' spirit, and that will fight in place of the martyred brothers for liberation. Through this dissection, Montis also refers to the actual body of the martyrs: 'And, no, this grave/ is not for reflecting the sun,/the sun is for reflecting the suns of this grave' (Montis, *EOKA*, 64). Thus, confirming the EOKA martyrs' graves are suns that provide Greek-Cypriots with the immortal spirit to live and fight for enosis freedom.

Hakeri's 'Can the Heroes be Forgotten?' also praises and immortalises the martyrs:

> "They will not be martyrs in this attack"
> Let the martyrs voice be heard: to mothers
> to fathers
> To friends to foe to homeland
> [...]
> Even if they prevent your voice from being heard my hero
> Your eyes will not be left behind. (Hakeri, *TCLII*, 98)

In stating the 'martyrs' will not be 'martyrs', Hakeri suggests their words and songs – 'voice' – of strength will live in the homeland, amongst everyone within and outside the Turkish-Cypriot community. Here Hakeri's conceptualisation of the 'eye' differs from Montis': whilst Montis wanted the martyrs' 'gaze' to be left behind so the vision of liberation is maintained without going astray; Hakeri states that the martyr's heroic 'eyes' can rest without the need to be left behind because the Turkish-Cypriots will continue this fight for liberation until they too must die.

The poets immortalise the martyrs for the Cypriot communities with demands they identify with them to maintain the liberation. This compares with the Palestinian martyr poetics,[42] which show that the 'complete form [of resistance] does not come when man expresses his vision through the medium of words; it results when man becomes his own words, that is, becomes a martyr' (Elmessiri, 84). Like the Palestinian poems, the Cypriot poems call the Cypriots to adopt not only the eyes and words but the 'complete form' of resistance, to become martyrs for the liberation.

'The Letter and the Road' by Papadopoulos and 'Punching a Knife' by Deliceirmak show the Cypriots' willingness to become the complete form of the martyrs; here the poets speak as martyrs recording their experience, becoming and willingness to submit to death and danger. These poets adopt the persona of EOKA and TMT martyrs from anticolonial Cyprus, to respond to the decolonising moment in 1958–1960 when independence plans were on the agenda, and 1960–1973 when independence resulted in total failure.

In 'The Letter and the Road' Papadopoulos speaks as a freedom-fighter who sends a message to the Greek-Cypriot people to recognise that the proposal for independence has not resulted in freedom or liberation:

> We enclosed our small lives in an envelope
> [...]we wrote the address:
> Honourable Greek-Cypriot People,
> Road of Death or Freedom,
> Villages and Towns
> Cyprus.
>
> We sent it without the stamp with the foreign queen
> (Papadopoulos, 'Letter', 74)

Here the EOKA martyr sends a letter to Greek-Cypriot people that details the struggle – 'we' – experienced throughout the anticolonial period for enosis freedom, which has not been achieved and must be maintained in this decolonial moment. Here pointing to moments before and after 1960 when the Greek-Cypriots refused the official 'stamps' of the colonial office, as well as refusing the independence agreement that offered neither enosis nor freedom. Consequently, the address on the envelope – 'Death or Freedom' – invites Greek-Cypriots to maintain and die with martyrs in this liberation struggle. The envelope and its message become a vehicle that mobilises the Greek-Cypriots

> It belongs to our illiterate villagers and workers
> who opened it, who moistened it with tears and said:
> – Come in, children [...]
> On the floor we will sleep: you rest awhile
> Hide so that you are not killed, so that you are not tortured.
> We want to walk with you
> On the road of Freedom or Death (Papadopoulos, 'Letter', 74)

The illiterates receive and understand the message because it has been written in a simple language for the people as a whole to understand. This resonates with the Palestinian resistance poetry such as 'The Other Face' by Ya'quob Hijazi: 'Because I write poems for the human being,/ Peasant, oppressed, worker/ My letters I shall always make known' (Ashrawi, 88); and 'Concerning Poetry' by Mahmoud Darwish that confirms, 'And if the "simple" cannot understand our poems/ Better for us to shed them /And resort to silence' (Ashrawi, 87). Papadopoulos supports this popular address by using a simple prose-like style and showing that the illiterate people respond to the message so that the martyrs come to life – 'come in children' – and the villagers mobilise – 'we want to walk with you' –with them. This mobilisation points again, as in Ulucamgil's 'Shepherd', to the villagers as agents in the struggle because of their immoveable presence, rootedness and closeness to the land. Furthermore, the villagers confirm that this ethno-national liberation 'relies entirely on a semblance of classlessness: equality in spirit, belief, blood' (Nairn, 286) because it transforms Cypriots of all social backgrounds to have the same hopes and slogan – to Death or Freedom.

In 'Punching a Knife', Deliceirmak also adopts a martyr's persona to send a message that moves the people:

> we have grown, we are freedom-fighters...
> Bread troubles, freedom troubles
> I remember a teacher at school
> He would say, learn to punch a knife
> [...]
> We punch a knife...
> Standing against
> [...]
> The captivity that comes towards us with a tank
> It comes from the love for freedom
> This courage. (Deliceirmak, *TCLII*, 90)

The poet points to the moment 'we' freedom-fighters willingly submitted to death against the British colonial and EOKA enslavers, symbolised as knifes; here suggesting 1955–1959 during British colonial coercion, and 1964 independence when inter-communal bloodshed overwhelmed Cyprus. This courage to fight the enemy – 'punch a knife' – till death was taught to the poet at school, which illuminates the role of education to build a generation of nationalists, both Greek-Cypriot and Turkish-Cypriot, to be 'knife punchers' and martyrs for enosis or taksim. The poem also becomes a vehicle to awaken new ethno-nationalist sentiment because the same narratives that mobilised the poet-martyr are now delivered to the Turkish-Cypriot students in this failing moment of independence.

Both Papadopoulos and Deliceirmak adopt the persona of a freedom-fighter that confirms they died and killed in vain, which are a powerful tool that moves the Cypriot people to maintain the struggle and road to an ethnic-motherland national freedom in this independent moment.

The analysis of the 'Ethnic-Motherland Nationalist Generation' in the curricula has shown that, even though Greek-Cypriot and Turkish-Cypriot narratives are oppositional, separately aspiring to unite with 'motherland' Greece or Turkey, together they speak to each other so to document a collective ethnic narrative with a Cypriot position specific to colonial and postcolonial Cyprus. Pierides and Ulucamgil record colonial Cyprus when a state of natural ethnic peace was replaced by a British state of ethnic coercion that the Cypriots started to resist; Montis and Hakeri immortalise and praise the anticolonial resistance of the freedom-fighter martyrs; Deliceirmak and Papadopculos write as martyrs in response to the independence failures, who call forth the Cypriots to maintain the struggle and die for freedom. This Generation is pivotal to the curricula because it immortalised and was politically committed to these moments; it is a powerful vehicle that moved the masses against these moments; and it continues to be a supreme force that aid the Cypriots to preserve this struggle for the ethnic liberation, or rather, ethnic exclusivity of the land and people in Cyprus.

Post-1964/74 Cypriotist Generation

The 'Post-1964/74 Generation' poetry in the curricula shows a collective Cypriot consciousness for postcolonial partitioned Cyprus, which narrates a Cypriot-centric patriotism and love for the homeland, Cyprus. I will analyse eight poems from the curricula[43] to show they work together to represent and deal with the experience of partitioned Cyprus, so to generate a metaphoric homeland. Greek-Cypriot Claire Angelides'[44] 'Last Words' and Turkish-Cypriot Feriha Altiok's 'I Went Out and Sat on the Balcony' use a poetics of memory that shift between historical times and places, in an attempt to escape traumatic realities so to imagine a coherent closed place; Greek-Cypriot Nikos Kranidiotis' 'Kyrenia Memory'[45] and Turkish-Cypriot Mehmet Yashin's[46] 'Departing a Shelter' confront the hellish ruptured realities of present home to show the impossibility of an imaginary closed place; Greek-Cypriot Kyriakos Charalambides' 'I Saw it'[47] and Turkish-Cypriot Filiz Naldoven's 'Live' confirm that an imagined dream-like fantasy space without fixed times and place must exist; Greek Cypriot Pantelis Mechanikos' 'Onesilus', Lefkios Zaphiriou's 'Pentadactylos'[48] and Turkish-Cypriot Nice Denizoglu's 'Olive Branch' show that specific times, places and spaces must coexist in an organic relation for the definition of homeland.

Angelides' 'Last Words' and Altiok's 'I Went Out and Sat on a Balcony' compulsively remember and forget different home narratives to invent place, so an illusionary coherence, fixity and belonging within the homeland. This invention is determined by home past in fusion with or exclusion without home present, combined with an acceptance or refusal to a mythical return – a *nesto* – to the home past in home future. Such fusion, exclusion, juxtaposition and confusion of 'home here' and 'home there' results in a fragmentation, whereby the poets are concemned to struggle against home 'no-where' and 'be-longing'. Both poets show they struggle between fragmented home narratives so to create a fixed homeland for their fixed selves, which determine their fragmented identities. Angelides depicts her birthplace Ammohostos,[49] which has been under occupation and beyond her vision since 1974, as her past and future home, here inventing a future-perfect via a mythical return to a past-perfect that helps her escape the present home in partitioned Nicosia. Altiok depicts her birthplace Nicosia within all different historical moments to show that a poetics of forgetting over remembrance is needed to deal with the present trauma of partition.

Both poems depict the past-perfect pre-1974 home they were forced to leave after partition:

> Angelides 'Last Words':
> I double locked the front door
> [...]
> You will see the garden and walnut tree
> I watered...
> The vineyard will without a doubt have borne fruit...
> (Angelides, *CLAG*, 100)

> Altiok, 'I Went Out and Sat on a Balcony':
> that one was so beautiful
> one side sapling
> the other side a school
> when you sat outside
> the birds would fly on the Green Line
> to the Greek side
> to the Turkish side
> [...]
> The sound of a motorbike [...]
> Recognisable faces would pass from our place. (Altiok, *TCLII*, 132)

Angelides recalls the moment when she left and double locked the doors of her past home, to suggest that both the home and her memories of it are safely locked from the present outsiders/invaders on the other side of the divide. The imagery of the plants that she 'watered' and that have now 'borne fruit' simultaneously suggests a perfect memory of her past home, and that the relationship between the home, its garden and the owner is unbreakable and grows with the years. This represents the common Cypriot poetics, as in Palestinian resistance poetry,[50] that affiliate the past home with flora or fauna so to depict their organic relationship to a past-perfect homeland. Altiok generates a past-perfect home through the balcony, which has the same poetic value as Darwish's balcony in 'I See my Ghost Coming from Afar' because through it 'Like a balcony, I gaze upon whatever I desire' (Darwish, *Paradise*, 55). Altiok, like Darwish, sits on her present balcony to gaze at and listen to the beautiful scenes from her past-perfect: recreating scenes when Cypriots freely moved around Nicosia without partition borders and the 'Green Line'; gazing upon the moment when she was located between 'sapling' and a 'school'. Both poets recite the past using symbols that are growing and moving – 'plants', 'birds' and 'children' – to suggest the past was not only a time of blossoming freedom and hope, but also a time that moves the present moment. As Altiok suggests, the poets turn to recognisable past-perfect faces and places that is 'our' home, as an attempt to make this the present-imperfect space less strange and foreign.

The perfect memory of home past becomes a device for forgetfulness of home present, through which they can generate a fixed place; however, both poets struggle to hold this past-perfect home because the narrative is determined by random fragments of present moments. Consequently, the poets fight against or unwillingly submit to the horrors of present time:

> Angelides, 'Last Words':
> Hide the key. It's the house's.
> [...]
> definitely hide it somewhere
> from time to time clean it
> it shouldn't rust
> [...]
> Be careful with the key
> [...]
> Just hide the key well. (Angelides, *CLAG*, 100)
>
> Altiok, 'I Went Out and Sat on the Balcony':
> I went out and sat on the balcony
> one side a hospital
> the other side an asylum
> [...]
> a motorbike sound
> [...]
> not one hand
> not one eye is searched
> [...]
> like a busy bee the florist in front
> [...]
> children sounds are pierced
> by the sticky filthy stream (Altiok, *TCLII*, 132)

Angelides attempts to escape the present moment through a dialogue about the pre-1974 house 'key': here suggesting the speaker is the parent in possession of the key, speaking to the child who should inherit the house; however, the only thing the child is inheriting for now is the house key. The poet is simultaneously speaking to all Greek-Cypriots, advising them to hold on to their house keys till the moment of return. The pre-1974 house key has immense value for the Greek-Cypriots, generating a kind of 'key fetish', like the Palestinians observed in Robert Fisk's *Pity the Nation*, who, assuming their uprooting was brief, 'locked their front doors when they left' and stubbornly cherished their keys as years went by because they are a 'promise of return' (Fisk, 18–19). The house key is the only tangible possession that provides definition of a homeland: it is a metonym of fixity and wholeness of the past home, evidence of ownership and belonging, and myth or promise of return that will unlock the doors of occupation. The poet is advising the inheritors or key-keepers to take care, hide and clean this key, which suggests cleansing the disappointment that the years will bring, in order to keep the tangibility and ownership of home, and the myth of return and freedom clear and safe. Angelides' advice captures the dominant Greek-Cypriot consciousnesses, which is to never submit to the present experience and home but instead wait, escape and replace it by the promised powers of the past key. Angelides supports fully this rejection of the present by refusing to depict the present home. Alternatively, Altiok depicts the present home releasing herself from the forces of the past, which is reflective of the dominant Turkish-Cypriot consciousness to accept the present moment and home. For Altiok, this present home is sandwiched between 'hospital' and 'asylum' – pain and insanity – because she hears similar things – 'sound of the motorbike' – but is surrounded by everything strange, not recognising the bodies, eyes and hands that pass. Without youthful hope of the natural sapling and school of past home, there is now commerce with a florist selling artificial flowers and a filthy stream that pierces the hopeful sounds of the children. In both poems the actual horrors of present home disrupt the idealised past home: whilst Altiok depicts home past and home present in contest; Angelides attempts to escape the present home through compensating it with the myth of return, yet the key illuminates the broken promises and shattered dreams of the present moment.

The poets simultaneously struggle against present traumas by responding to a future home:

Angelides 'Last Words':
You can return
As soon as this is said, it should be ready...
[...]

You must push it,
Don't forget
I won't be returning, as I calculated

[...]
When you go bring Minas to prune the vineyard [...]
If you lose it do you know the difficulties you will face?
When you return to the city
Where will you find a locksmith to change the locks?
(Angelides, *CLAG*, 100)

Altiok 'I Went Out and Sat on A Balcony':
In short if it briefly abuses me
this place before and after
[...]
it will pass and be forgotten
and we walk
down roads we think we know (Altiok, *TCLII*, 132)

Angelides depicts that future call when the key-keeper or owner will return to the past home. Here showing she has spent a life time recreating this *nesto* with immense details – i.e. this 'key' un-locks the door, don't 'lose' it because you will not find a 'locksmith', and when you get there 'push' the door with force because it is an 'old Cypriot door' now a little cranky. Oh, and make sure you bring 'Minas to prune the vineyard' – to the extent that it becomes a narrative of insanity. This is insanity because Angelides believes that the image – house, door, locks and plants – she departed from four decades ago, and which has been occupied by someone else is, as in Palestinian narratives,[51] 'steadfast' and immoveable. The poet does not become an actor in this myth of return, which suggests that she, like many people who left their houses and half the country behind, is dying and now giving her 'last words' to her child or the children of Cyprus. These last words suggest that the Cypriots must indefinitely remember the past, and wait for the future promise, which is Angelides' metaphoric homeland. Altiok also attempts to create a future home for herself, where, tortured between 'brief' fragments of 'before' and 'after', her imaginary homeland is a space that forgets the idealised past, the strange present and the future promise, by replacing it with a future moment of fabricated identification that people would 'think' they know.

Both poets shift between a poetics of remembrance and/or forgetfulness in an attempt to escape the inevitability that Cypriots are to be-longing between fragments without a stable home. Angelides' line 'I double locked the door' (Angelides, *CLAG*, 100) supports this indefinite homelessness, wherein both poets are 'locked out' narrating home from the 'outside' garden or balcony, and never depicting the 'inside' of a home. These poems represent a collective Cypriot consciousness, which strives for definition against the reality that they are 'locked out', and can never depict a stable home for themselves because they will always belong to someone. Upon the 1974-partition, many Turkish-Cypriots moved into and have adopted homes that were and are officially owned by the departed Greek-Cypriots: whilst Angelides represents the Greek-Cypriot's motto 'We will not forget' marked on all school books as motivation to remember the past, which will enable a promised return in the future to these lost pre-1974 home; Altiok draws attention to the Turkish-Cypriots' drive of forgetting the past, and eliminating a promise of return because such moments will result in Turkish-Cypriots losing these homes they have accepted since 1974. In both poems the poets struggle between remembrance and forgetfulness against these realities to forge a coherent fixed homeland for themselves.

Yashin's 'Departing the Shelter' and Kranidiotis' 'Kyrenia Memory' confirm that such imaginary escapism and coherence between remembrance, forgetfulness and times in closed place cannot offer a future homecoming. Instead, they expose the reality that the homeland is this traumatic ruptured present, where responding to the hellish ghostly present – the aftermath of 1974 with homes Turkish-Cypriots feel they belong to, and to which Greek-Cypriots long to return – they conclude that in this horror, whereby everything is strange and changed, the past-perfect and myth of return are products of illusion that cannot exist. Whilst Kranidiotis records a past-perfect homeland that once was but now is a fantasy gone; Yashin details, without escaping to the past-perfect, the change and estrangement of the present moment:

> Kranidiotis 'Kyrenia Memory':
> I'm thinking of the past years,
> the small city,
> touches the sea, shines in the sun,
> Eleni grandma,
> goes down to God's house
> [...]
> between the cracks of the closed windows
> the light smiles and stretches on its red lace
> [...]
> And after the mobile vendors are heard announcing their
>   furniture
> the farm birds sing
> [...]
> Everything was really beautiful:
> [...]
> the wind that filled the small houses with its sea notes,
> the green olives that covered the quiet field with silver,
> the insects that glided through the days golden air,
> the young girls' eyes that dived into sky blue fantasies,
> [...]
> the boats that leave the small harbour,
> [....]
> like the summer fantasy that comes and goes, it has all passed.

Now there is nothing left but the night (Kranidiotis, *CLAG*, 96)

Yashin, 'Departing a Shelter':
When exiting the shelter, we couldn't recognise the country
They changed the colours, the sounds
The villages, the roads, their names one by one.
"Now how will we find our homes?"
[...]
We set out to search with signs,
The school was in the corner... near Atlantis bar...
[...]
Atlantis must have been a fantasy
as there is no sign of it. (Yashin, *TCLII*, 127)

Kranidiotis begins by recording an idealised image of his pre-1974 home in Kyrenia city – its nature, concrete locations, people, colours, sounds – with all its details. Kranidiotis is remembering Kyrenia without physically being there, because it is on the other, north side of the divide; yet, he assumes the nostalgic image of Kyrenia that once existed is a 'fantasy' now gone, 'passed' and changed. Yashin, on the other hand, is physically in the north side, and he is supporting fully Kranidiotis' assumption of his post-1974 Kyrenia. Yashin shows Turkish-Cypriots departing the 'shelters' they lived in, which points to the refugee status and temporary housing they were given during the 1964/1974 transfer, until they were assigned to new post-1974 homes. Yashin shows that, upon departing the shelters, Turkish-Cypriots found the country to be un-invented, where, not recognising anything, they come to the insane conclusion that remembrance of things past are just an imaginary 'fantasy' that never existed.

Both poets show the past-perfect and future promise are a fantasy, because the present realities overpower all possibilities of such an escapist coherent homeland. They confirm the homeland is this present ghostly wasteland:

Kranidiotis, 'Kyrenia Memory':
black night,
[...] in big death
a sunset will later rise Godless (Kranidiotis, *CLAG*, 96)

Yashin, 'Departing a Shelter':
We were given new houses with corpses
We were like bears that found caves for winter sleep
[...]
in my hand is the house's phone that was disowned in the war
– no one is calling, is everyone dead? –
is it only me left living under the ruins... (Yashin, *TCLII*, 127)

Kranidiotis shows that the homeland is now dark, full of death and without faith or hope. Yashin explores further this hellish present through focussing on the post-1974 homes that Turkish-Cypriots adopted, which belonged to a Greek-Cypriot prior to the transfer, and that prepared the way for all Cypriots to be in a permanent state of uncertainty. Yashin shows, unlike Angelides' imaginings, the experience and ease of entering and settling into the house of the departed. Yashin states that the houses were dark, like the 'caves' of a hibernating 'bear', to suggests that the house was a place of refuge for the Turkish-Cypriots to disappear, not functioning like humans. They are unable to function because they have been condemned to live in a ghostly house with the – 'corpse'– possessions and traces of the departed, through which Yashin is pointing to the 1974 moment immortalised in every Cypriot consciousness in Cyprus; that moment when all Cypriots departed, leaving all their possession behind, whilst new occupants arrived to be in contact with the lifeless ghostly traces of the previous inhabitants.[52] Furthermore, Yashin's reference to Turkish-Cypriots as dysfunctional non-humans points to their reality, as TRNC residents they are internationally unrecognised, isolated and stateless. The 'phone' draws attention to these inhumane realities the Turkish-Cypriots are condemned to in different ways: firstly, it suggests the actual phone that belonged to the Greek-Cypriot owner, symbolic of Turkish-Cypriots living amongst the ghostly communication; second it suggests the national telecommunication lines in the TRNC, where lacking independence and international recognition the Turkish-Cypriot's can only speak via – dialling code +90 – Turkey. Both Yashin and Kranidiotis characterise the homeland as a wasteland, to confirm that the island left behind by all those key-keepers is now a ghostly past, changed and gone.

Both poets confront present realities so to claim an alternative future that the Cypriots must remap, ending their poems with hopeful notes: Kranidiotis concludes with a 'sunset that will Godless later rise', suggesting that though people have lost faith, a hope for the future will rise; Yashin concludes that though Cypriots and Cyprus have lost all sense of themselves, 'we search for ourselves, my native shore searches its passport', the 'Cypriots are not wiped out yet', and they will struggle for a future to the 'door of the world' (*TCLII*, 128). Both poets confirm that Cypriots can only have future promise to enter the 'door of the world' with a 'sunrise' by moving beyond past-perfect and myths of return, and confronting the present wasteland. This a future promise, however, that the poets cannot yet map.

Naldoven's and Charalambides' narratives respond to Kranidiotis and Yashin by showing that the past-perfect, present trauma and a future promise can only be dealt with through entering a different fantasy that moves beyond specific historical moments; and towards perceptions and dialogue between place, space, time and energies that maps a surreal, free and timeless future promise that overcomes the aftermath of 1964/74 past and present Cyprus. In 'Live', Naldoven invites Cypriots to live a surreal freedom, and in 'I Saw It', Charalambides shows the process of living it, which transform Cyprus into a free timeless space:

> Naldoven, 'Live':
> To Live,
> To Live, at a rattling pace
> My lips must come from the place I have forgotten
> My thoughts galloping...
> [...]
> To Live, like volcanoes, live
> [...]
> The lava is opening tunnels in my pupils...
> To Live! (Naldoven, *TCLII*, 134)
>
> Charalambides, 'I Saw It':
> I saw my city, it was walking on roof tiles
> [...]
> I saw it either in my sleep or in your awakening,
> and apart from its black piece, it was a big girl.
> [...]
> It was calmly sleeping and I thought I'd sit beside it
> because its eyes were stamped, frozen
> and this a piece of the diamond found there.
>
> The strange plant of sleep's fantasy!
> [...]
> A road that eyes can't touch
> because without a doubt I was disappearing with death's stamp.
>
> Such a big risk, how will I make this slip
> I thought I'd wait[...]
> and we will see later. And what did I see?
>
> A light, an awoken eye, wait there
> [...]
> I decided I will try,
> I will run away next to it as fast as lightening
> [...]
> I saw my city sleeping on the shore
> [...]
> And it was as beautiful as the olive groves' daughter (Charalambides, *CLAG*, 98)

Naldoven fuses together volcanic-equestrian imagery to invite Cypriots to live freely, where they map a country and people with an uncontainable sight – 'lava in my pupils' – that explodes volcano-like, and 'thoughts' that gallop at a horse-like pace. Here destroying every restriction and taking every risk, to go freely to places or spaces that have been forgotten, never imagined and possibly never mapped or written. Naldoven's poetic summons, as confirmed in the textbook, are inspired by Nazim Hikmet's poem 'Invitation' that uses equestrian imagery to map his country: the geographical borderlines move 'galloping' from the Far East to the Mediterranean expanding into the shape of a 'mare's head', which suggests that a country and its people must, like a horse, live and gallop freely. Through this, Hikmet invites a nation: 'To live free and single like a tree/And in brotherhood' (Hikmet, 612). Following Hikmet, Naldoven invites Cypriots to live Cyprus as a free galloping horse that erupts like a volcano in total sisterhood/brotherhood. Charalambides captures this explosive and galloping imagination that maps a dream-like city that appears in his sleep or 'your awakening'; the city is a woman with frozen diamond eyes that he loves and longs for, who sleeps calmly, walks on the rooftops, and strolls into the bed of the poet luring him. Similarly, many Palestinian poets construct their city via such surreal gendered imagery; for example, in 'A Poem on a Closed Summer' Walid al-Hallees writes: 'Tonight I was visited by Khanyounes [...] In the robes of a hungry woman, Gaza came to me /Rested her tired head on my arm' (Ashrawi, 93–94). In these poems, the arrival of these women causes the poets much pain: al-Hallees' Khanyounes and Gaza are women he loves and desires, but whose presence, in their condition under Israeli occupation and in defeat, is painful (Ashrawi, 93); Charalambides' city is his woman, who is – 'stamped frozen' – occupied by Turkey. Consequently, Charalambides is confronted with the realities and restrictions on his city that 'eyes can't touch', and the risks – 'disappearing with death's stamp' – if he crosses the border. In light of such risks Charalambides considers 'waiting', however, decides neither to halt his imagination nor accept his woman, his city, has been defeated; thus, he is lured to gallop at the speed of 'lightening' across the border to free himself and his captured lover, his occupied city, which is now mapped as the olive tree's liberated daughter resting by the shore.

Both poets record the experience of living in partition Cyprus, where they refuse defeat by inviting Cypriots to map a free island for the free self. Whilst Naldoven invites the Cypriots, following Hikmet, to live and perceive country and self as a free galloping horse exploding volcano-like; Charalambides shows his self and country being set free. Both poems record an imaginary ahistorical fast-paced explosive route taken to overcome partition failures with future promise.

Zaphiriou's 'Pentadactylos', Pantelis' 'Osesilus' and Denizoglu's 'Olive Branch' record a metaphorical homeland through claiming the need for a historical and geographical sense, where they map myths in the present landscape; here constructing Cyprus by shifting between the past and present with focus on the poets' organic relationship to them for a future promise.

In 'Pentadactylos', Zaphiriou records legends of the Byzantine hero Digenis Akritas, in 'Onesilus' Pantelis writes about the ancient city of Salamis, whilst in 'Olive Branch' Denizoglu draws on the historical olives:

Zaphiriou, 'Pentadactylos':
Pentadactylos breathes
to my rhythm
attuned to my pulse
assimilated inside me
and you cannot tell Pentadactylos and me apart
his blood from my blood.
And so together we pace and coexist: (Zaphiriou, 88)

Pantelis' 'Osesilus'
Straight out of history and legends
Alive and breathing (Pen, 44)

Denizoglu, 'Olive Branch':
a broken
a sorrowful
a bent neck
olive branch I am
I will go from the Mediterranean
to those who don't understand my tongue
to explain this broken, this leafless
this oliveless branch of mine (Denizoglu, *TCLII*, 139)

Zaphiriou focusses on the Pentadactylos mountains in north Cyprus, which are the most widely used Greek-Cypriot literary symbol to signify Cyprus; they are often personified as a man, especially Digenis Akritas, a folkloric mythic frontiersman in the Byzantine state. Legend has it that to free Cyprus from the Saracen invaders, with one hand Digenis gripped onto part of a mountain and with the other he threw a gigantic rock: here leaving an immortal handprint on the mountain named 'Pentadactylos', meaning five-fingers that is also reflected in its shape; and an everlasting sea stack named the 'Rock of the Greek' (*Petra tou Romiou*) in Paphos, considered both the rock Digenis threw and Aphrodite's' birth location. Many more legends have formed around the Digenis struggles that have developed a cycle of Akritic folk songs or tragoudia, which Greek-Cypriots have successfully preserved through oral tradition (Politis, 22; xvii). Zaphiriou maps the mountain with these historical songs to show that, like Digenis, the occupied homeland struggles, has courage and will achieve freedom against the invaders. Zaphiriou simultaneously defines himself as the land and Digenis, whereby they give breath to the poet's 'rhythm', are 'attuned' to his pulse, they exchange blood[53] and 'they live and coexist as one', to suggest his organic union with the land and its legendary history, and his courage to struggle for freedom. Furthermore, Zaphiriou suggests that the ancient Akritic songs inspired him to write this poem, such that the poem becomes Zaphiriou's modern immortal Akritic folk song, which sings of the heroic struggles of Cyprus and its people. The necessity to sing an immortal song to the homeland is a common trope in both Cypriot and Palestinian poetry; the West Bank poet Mahmoud Awad Abbas 'expresses the need for a truthful song to be sung to the "olive," to the "peasants" and (in pain) to the "beloved land"' (Ashrawi, 88). In fusing the Pentadactylos landscape, the ancient heroic legends, and his own existence, Zaphiriou creates an immortal truthful song to the homeland and Cypriots that unite in struggle for future freedom.

Pentellis engages with the ancient city of Salamis via the living pulse of legendary Onesilus, which is another popular symbol that defines liberating Cyprus. Denizoglu engages with the Mediterranean olive, which is commonly used by contemporary Cypriot poets as in the frozen symbol that forms Palestinian poetry to 'automatically mean [...] the land and the will of the people to remain' (Ashrawi, 91). To enhance an understanding of this contemporary consciousness, Denizoglu addresses the olive branch via a historical symbol of peace and holiness spanning from Ancient Greek mythology to Qur'anic scripts. Here the broken olive branch is Cyprus and the Cypriot self to suggest that the organic relationship between the island, its people and its historical values has been destroyed. As a result, the poet and island struggle to fulfil their historical role as olive branches, which shed peace and holiness; therefore, the poet decides to 'go from the Mediterranean' so as to explain in a universal language the world will understand that the olive – her Cyprus and Cypriots – historically and globally cherished as symbol of peace, has been devoured. Denizoglu shows she must explain – like the Palestinian poet, Samih al-Qassem, 'I speak to the world... tell it/ About a house whose lantern they broke' (Ashrawi, 90) – so as to immortalise and internationalise that peace has been broken in the homeland.

The poets engage with Pentadactylos, Salamis and the Mediterranean olive so as to write an immortal international song to the world about the historical struggle for freedom and peace, which is undefeated because it lives in the broken bones, blood and veins of the Island, the poets and the Cypriot people; and it is this that provides future promise.

The 'Post-1964/74 Cypriotist Generation' in the curricula together generate a collective Cypriot consciousness that write partitioned Cyprus. Together they build a metaphoric homeland for the Cypriot-selves: layering and fixing immortal walls with bricks of past-perfect, present-pain and future promise, and raising windows and balconies that gaze towards a historically and geographically conscious galloping and explosive freedom and peace that sings to the world.

The literary analysis of the curricula document the ethnic and Cypriot positions within the official identification, Turkish-Cypriotism and Greek-Cypriotism, in two different ways: first the 'Ethnic-Motherland Nationalist Generation' are motivated by the ethnic position, whilst the 'Post-1964/74 Cypriotist Generation' are driven by a Cypriot-centric patriotism; second the Cypriot literatures of both Generations generate a Cypriot position, which contest and are separate from Greece's and Turkey's literatures that generate a Greek or Turkish position. Together the curricula produce a distinct Cypriot position for Cyprus that builds, immortalises and sings of a struggle for freedom, peace and love for the homeland; this is an immoveable homeland that responds to and shelters them from the failures of colonial, postcolonial and partition.

Official Identity: Condemned to Shift and Achieve a Processual Form

The chapter has captured the actual production of the pedagogical 'sector' (*espace*), particularly literature education, that has been and continues to be a pivotal vehicle in dividing, defining and documenting colonial, postcolonial and partitioned Cyprus. It has been demonstrated that pedagogical imperialism set the foundations for postcolonial pedagogy in Cyprus: establishing pedagogical partition; paving the way for literature education to be a vehicle for official definitions; and setting the stage for the dynamic contest over pedagogical/official formation. Consequently, Turkish-Cypriots and Greek-Cypriots have undergone and shared mainly the same pedagogical trajectory; they have gradually detached from only adopting the dominant Turkish or Greek position determined by Turkey or Greece, to introducing the historically silenced and emergent Cypriot position determined by Cyprus. These two positions shape the official national identification that is determined by place, which Loizides rightly coins: 'Turkish-Cypriotism and Greek-Cypriotism'.

The analysis of the current literature curricula has demonstrated the ways they document this official identification: whilst the ethnic position is dominant, providing a fixed Greek or Turkish definition, the Cypriot position is emergent, new and processual. Even though both curricula have always prioritised Greece's Greek or Turkey's Turkish literary position, whilst extensively silencing the Cypriot literary position, this contrast between the positions shows that neither has the original essence. The curricula show that the Cypriot authorities strive but fail to produce a stable ethno-national identification with both positions in perfect balance. The curricula confirm that the official identification – Turkish-Cypriotism and Greek-Cypriotism – is unstable without balance, condemned to shift ambiguously between the positions across the hyphen and to be in the process of becoming, which is always determined by place and space.

The remaining chapters in this book will separately explore and expand upon these literary positions introduced in the curricula, to clarify how the official identification has achieved such a processual form via spatiality. This exploration will only cover mainly Cypriot literatures, and it will not be limited to the curricula because they – these documents of the pedagogical 'sector' – have been politically and ideologically filtered by the authorities on both sides of the divide to read and construct an official ethnically exclusive Cyprus. Both curricula have silenced Cypriot literatures in various ways: voices from across the divide muted; the 'Post-1964/74 Cypriotist Generation' filtered; the Cypriot diasporic realities forbidden. The rest of this book refuses to silence the literatures of Cyprus, and will freely explore Cypriot voices as widely as possible to un-mute the literary dialogue and dialectics from across the divide, which have collectively recorded and immortalised a narrative for colonial, postcolonial and partitioned Cyprus that is always determined by place and space. Henceforth, I will examine the actual process and production of Cyprus, which serves as a tool of thought, action, control and domination – the most powerful force in postcolonial partitioned cases. The next chapter, 'Ethnic-Motherland Nationalist: Mothers' Bloody Spiritual Place', will listen attentively to the dominant and loud ethnic literary position to expose the reading and construction of place by the Ethnic-Motherland Nationalist Generation, which the curricula respond and adopt fully. Chapter 4 will un-filter the Cypriot literary position to capture the reading and construction of place and space by the 'Post-1964/74 Cypriotist Generation', which has only been partially adopted in the curricula. Chapter 5 will un-silence the marginalised literary positions, to examine and join forces in the actual process and production of place and space by the Cypriot diaspora, which the curricula erase and forbid in full force. Though secreted the chapter has shown and the book will show that diasporic traces haunt the curricula and emergent canon, because displacement and dispersion are an inescapable Cypriot experience and positionality that make-up the transnational literatures of Cyprus, which ultimately define postcolonial partitioned cases.

Notes

1 The standardised name Turkish-Cypriot and Greek-Cypriot will be used because the investigation is based on the official identification and Cyprus. On name games, see Ch. 1.

2 See also Bryant 'Education'; Bryant and Papadakis. On Greek-Cypriot education, particularly curriculum as political text hindering resolution, see Varnava & Philippou; on history textbooks hindering cultural diversity, see Varnava 'Minorities'.

3 On Greek-Cypriot literary debates, see Papaleontiou, Zaphiriou, Constantinides in Papaleontiou; Kechagioglou.
4 On Turkish-Cypriot literary debates, see Yashin 'Cypriot', *Stepmother*, 'Three'.
5 See Yashin *Stepmother*; Kappler.
6 This was a gift from Alexandrian Greeks, which introduced the first newspaper.
7 Magazines: in Greek, *Philogiki Kypros; Pnevmatiki Kypros*. In Turkish *Cardak, Cig, Ilk Demet, Yasemin.*
8 In English, see Decavalles; Montis and Christophides; Kouvialis *27 Centuries Cypriot, and Contemporary Cypriot*; Sophocleous *Cypriot*; Spanos *22 Contemporary Cypriot,* and *Cypriot Prose*. Many of these English publications are part of the Cyprus PEN Centre founded in 1979, when from 1981 to 1993 they released 5 Anthologies, and the Cyprus PEN Review Vol. 1, 2, 3 and 4. Since 1993, they released a series of 'Literary Profiles', which are mini-monographs of 48–60 pages long on the author's work, selected criticism and sample texts. Starting with Costas Montis they now have over 51 profiles, including profiles for all Greek-Cypriot authors writing in Greek discussed in this book. For a full list of profiles see bibliography. Since 2003, Pen have also released the *In focus* magazine with around 40 issues. In Greek, see Gritsi-Milliex; Ioannides *Short Story*; Pernaris Cypriot; Panayiotunis; Krandiotis *Cypriot Poetry*, and *National*. Magazines: *Themata Kritikis; Kypriaka Chronika, Nea Epochi.*
9 See Altay; Ersavas; *Kibris Turk; Kuzey Kibris Turk Milli; Kuzey Kibris Turk Cumhuriyet*; Yashin *Kibrisliturk*.In English: Canit; Yashin *Series*. Magazines in Turkish: *Sanat Postasi, Kultur, Birinci, Karanfil.*
10 See Ch. 4; Korkmazel_*Cypriotgreek*; Moleskis *Contemporary Turkish*; Hadjipieris. Magazines in Turkish: *Sanat Emegi, Isirgan; Ucsuz. In Greek, Haravgi, Nea Epochi.*
11 See Ch. 5; On magazines, in English see *Cadences*; *In Focus*; *The Cyprus Dossier*. Anthologies in English, see Adamidou; Stephanides *Culture/Memory, Cypriana*; Collette; Costello; Yashin *Stepmother*. Notable local publishers that release English or translated material, include Moufflon and Armida.
12 This includes Armida, Isik Kitap Evi, Free Birds, Kochlias, Khora, Galeri Kultur Yayinlar, Barangas Moufflon, PEN, Rustem.
13 On Greek-Cypriot pedagogy commissioned by the Church see, Persianis, *Church*.
14 On Greece's education, see Kazamias.
15 On Vakf, see Gazioglu *The Turks*; Yildiz.
16 In Turkey the pedagogical reforms during the *Tanzimat* period were influenced by France's system, hence the grading of schools as Lise, drawn from the French lycées. Similarly, Greece's education was heavily influenced by France's and Germany's education, where they used lyceum and gymnasium. See Kazamais.
17 On education from 1878 to 1915, see Varnava Ch. 6 in *Imperialism*.
18 On British pedagogical policy, see Weir; Spyridakis; Persianis' 'Lending'; Heraclidou.
19 On implanting Palestine model to Cyprus, see Persianis 'lending'.
20 See Ch. 4.
21 See Heraclidou.
22 On imperial pedagogy in various postcolonial cases, see Altbach; Kazamias and Epstein; King.
23 Suggests an educational neo-colonialism, wherein foreign educational models from an advanced western nation/association replace the education of a less developed area. See Altbach. This also relates to ways Cyprus appropriates Greece' and Turkey' pedagogical systems, who, in turn, adopted Germany's and France's pedagogical systems.

24 The fieldwork for this chapter, mainly interviews and translations, was undertaken in 2009–2010; therefore, the literature curricula investigated are from the 2009 to 2010 academic year. In the TRNC the current curriculum for Turkish-Cypriot Literature was introduced in 2006, and no changes have been introduced since. In the Republic, the Modern Greek curriculum was introduced in 1987, and no major change has been introduced since; however, every two to three years the curriculum undergoes some minor changes, and the curriculum analysed here was overviewed in 2007. It was subsequently overviewed three more times, with the last being in 2017–2018, where the decade has shown only minor changes.

25 Greek-Cypriot secondary school is made up of six years graded into lower gymnasium 1, 2, 3 then upper lyceum, 1, 2, 3. This grading mirrors Greece's, and is influenced by pedagogical system of Germany's Gymnasien and France's lycée – thus pointing towards an educational neo-colonialism.

26 In Cyprus Modern Greek is taught throughout secondary school, for four to five hours a week in each year; Ancient Greek is taught in the first five years consisting of three hours a week in gymnasium and lyceum 1, and one hour a week in lyceum 2. In Greece, Ancient Greek and Modern Greek are taught throughout secondary school, where the former is allocated more teaching hours.

27 The 2009–2010 Modern Greek curriculum was provided by Lambros Lambros, Inspector of Literature at the Ministry of Education, during an interview in May 2009. It was discussed further with Lambros Lambros and Stylianos Charalambous, Inspectors of Literature, in August 2010. The Modern Greek curriculum can be found on the official website: www.schools.ac.cy. I am indebted to Pembe Ozocak, who translated all Modern Greek materials to English.

28 There are no texts by Turkish-Cypriots. In the World Literature selection, which will not be explored here, there is a Turkish poem by Nazim Hikmet, whose poetic legacies are accepted by Greek-Cypriots because: first, he criticised Turkey's Imperialist attitude; Hikmet supported EOKA, calling Turkish-Cypriots to join it; finally the poem in the curriculum 'Lullaby to My Son' fits Greek-Cypriot narratives on the martyred or missing sons. On missing sons, see Cavafy and '1950s Ethnic-Motherland Nationalist' section in this chapter, and Ch. 3. Hikmet's poem has been removed from 2017 to 2018 curriculum.

29 See 'Official Governmental Publications: Print' in Bibliography for full list of material. In lyceum 3 the core prose text is Dimitrios Hatzis' novel *The Double Book*; in other years, the teacher selects one text from three to four options, where of 19 prose texts there are 14 Greek texts, two Cypriot texts and three world texts.

30 Turkish-Cypriot secondary school education consists of seven years, divided into lower (orta okul 1, 2, 3) and upper (lise 1, 2, 3, 4); this mirrors Turkey's system. The main focus here is on the lise curriculum.

31 I have translated all the Turkish-Cypriot Literature curriculum materials to English.

32 Each programme includes compulsory authors with a recommended text related to the unit: here the teachers can select an alternative text listed in the textbook; however, most teachers in Cyprus use the texts recommended by Greece, which have been analysed in this chapter. These texts are internationally renowned, and therefore available in English translation.

33 An analysis of the other Greek authors – for example, Galetea Saranti; Nikos Alexis Aslanoglu; Dionysios Solomos; Dido Sotiriou; Corfiot Lorentzos Mavilis; Yiannis Ritsos; Odysseas Elytis; Angelos Sikelianos; Ninet Zotz Sari;

Vincenzo Cornaro; Angelos Sikelianos; Kotsis Palamas; Kostas Karyotakis; Maria Polydouri; Alexandros Papadiamantis; Konstantinos Theotokis and George Ioannou – in the curriculum would generate similar effect in terms of the Greek position.

34 On missing people, see Uludag.

35 All Turkish-Cypriot literary texts are from *Turkish Cypriot Literature I* and *Turkish Cypriot Literature II*; I have undertaken all translations from the textbook.

36 On Palestinian poets of resistance, see Ashrawi; Elmessiri; Pitcher.

37 All Turkish-Cypriot poems are taught in lise 2 from the textbook *Turkish Cypriot Literature II* (*TCLII*) and have been translated by me; the Greek-Cypriot poems are taught throughout secondary school, are from *Cypriot Literature Anthology for Gymnasium (CLAG); Cypriot Literature Anthology for Lyceum, Part I* and *Part II (CLALI and CLALII)*, and have been read in translations. The teachers on both sides can choose alternative poems; however, they teach only those recommended in the curricula, which are the poems I analyse here.

38 'Cyprus Agreement' is introduced in lyceum 2, is from the textbook *CLALII*, and Pembe Ozocak has translated the poem to English.

39 'A Song for Our Older Brother' is introduced in gymnasium 3 and 'The Letter and the Road' in gymnasium 1, both introduced in *CLAG*. In this analysis I use Irene Joannides' translation in Michalis Maratheftis and Roula Ioannidiou-Stravrou edited collection.

40 On frozen symbols, see Ashrawi.

41 On shepherds, villagers and peasants in Palestinian poetry, see Swedenburg.

42 On Palestinian poet-martyrs, see Elmessiri; Pitcher.

43 All Turkish-Cypriot poems from the post-1964/74 generation are taught in lise 2 from *TCLII*; the Greek-Cypriot poems are taught in different years throughout secondary school.

44 Claire Angelides' 'Last Words' is introduced in gymnasium 3, is from the textbook *CLAG* and was translated by Pembe Ozocak. Literary critics have included Angelides in the '1974–1990 Generation'; however, I believe her poetic legacy and national commitment are pivotal to understand the consciousness for both the nationalist and Cypriotist Generation. Angelides wrote and served throughout these periods: she was a head teacher at secondary school during colonialism, fought in the anticolonial EOKA liberation and was Member of Parliament and Minister of Education during independence and partition. Many of Angelides' poems are motivated by and generate a nationalist position; consequently, in Chapter 3, I focus on Angelides within the ethnic-motherland nationalist framework. In this section, however, I will analyse a poem by Angelides that adopts the consciousness of the 'Post-1964/74 Generation' as related to a Greek-Cypriotism.

45 'Kyrenia Memory' is introduced in gymnasium 2, is from the textbook *CLAG* and was translated by Pembe Ozocak. Literary critics have included Kranidiotis in the '1930–1955 Generation'; however, I believe that his poetic legacy and national commitment are pivotal to understanding all three – 1930–1955, 1955–1974, 1974–1990 – literary periods. Kranidiotis wrote and officially served throughout these periods: he was a teacher during colonialism; he served in EOKA and was exiled by the British during anticolonialism; he served as Ambassador of Cyprus during independence. In this section, I analyse a poem by Kranidiotis that adopts fully and is pivotal for an understanding of the consciousness and definitions of 'Post-1964/74 Generation' as related to a Greek-Cypriotism.

46 Yashin is a founding member of the '74 Generation: Rejection Front'.

47 I Saw It' is introduced in gymnasium 2, is from the *CLAG* and has been translated by Pembe Ozocak. Charalambides belongs to the '1974–1990 Generation'; he is a committed national poet who served as a secondary school teacher and as Head of Radio for Cyprus Broadcasting Co-operation.

48 'Onesilus' is introduced in lyceum 1 from textbook *CLALI*, and 'Pentadactylos' is introduced in gymnasium 1 from the textbook *CLAG*. In this analysis I use Nicos Orphanides translation of 'Onesilus' in the *Literary Profile*, and I use Irene Joannides' translation of 'Pentadaktylos' in Michalis Maratheftis and Roula Ioannidiou-Stravrou edited collection. Mechanikos belongs to the '1955–1974 Generation', he is a committed national poet and served in the customs department. Zaphiriou belongs to the '1974–1990 Generation', is a committed national poet who served as a secondary school teacher and since partition has been teaching Greek-Cypriots at a school in Rizokarpaso/Karpas in north Cyprus, who chose to remain.

49 Places names in Cyprus are important, often operating in threes: the city is Ammohostos in Greek, Gazimagusa in Turkish and Famagusta in English. On name games, see Ch. 1.

50 On organic symbols, see Ashrawi.

51 On Palestinian steadfast, see Elmessiri.

52 This partition moment of possessions has a physical presence when entering Cypriot homes. An example is that of my paternal grandmother who transferred from her home Kofinou/Kofunye in the south to Lefkoniko/Gecitkale in the north into a Greek-Cypriot home. When departing from her home my grandmother left everything behind, and upon entering the new home she was in contact with the Greek-Cypriot's possessions, or corpses as Yashin suggests. Many Turkish-Cypriots threw away the lifeless possessions of the past occupant; my grandmother, distinct from the majority, packed away the possession and kept some –especially the pictures – in their place. In 2003, after the opening of the border, the owners of the house returned to visit their home; here my grandmother gave them their possessions, and when attempting to give them the picture they said: "you can keep it, let us not have an empty space on our wall". In my grandmother's narrative the possessions were given a new life; however, this is not a common narrative because most possessions were thrown away or lost without a trace.

53 Digenis was of mixed Greek and Arab birth, so a hybrid diasporic hero policing and disrupting identity, yet this is not addressed in this Greek-Cypriot poem or curriculum.

3 Ethnic-Motherland Nationalists

Mothers' Blood and Spiritual Place

> Some over systematic thinkers [...] make society into the 'object' of a systemisation which must be 'closed' to be complete; they thus bestow a cohesiveness it utterly lacks upon a totality which is in fact open – so open, indeed, that it must rely on violence to endure. (Lefebvre, *Production*, 11)

> Power – which is to say violence – divides, then keeps what it has divided in a state of separation; inversely, it re-unites – yet keeps whatever it wants in a state of confusion. (Lefebvre, *Production*, 358)

A territory is carved up during the processes of transforming, in Paul Carter's terms, from an empty space into a national place by the readings and constructions of both the coloniser and the colonised. The coloniser reads the colonised territory as an empty primitive space, and embarks on a project, considered as a civilising project, that un-invents the colonised subjects' inscription and meaning to re-invent it into a place that the coloniser can know and control. For the colonised subjects, however, it is not, as the coloniser reads it, an empty space but a place that has been ethnically and historically inscribed, and so they struggle to maintain and recover the territory by un-inventing the coloniser space, and transforming it into a cohesive national place. During these colonial and postcolonial processes of transformation and invention, both the colonised and the coloniser carve up the territory, whilst also masking, resisting and violating the open palimpsestic possibility, to produce a closed cohesive united place. In Cyprus, the Greek-cypriots and Turkish-cypriots[1] separately produce a national place for themselves; they read and construct an island that is ethnically measurable, complete, closed and united through carving up the body and masking the spatial palimpsestic possibility of Cyprus. This Cypriot process of reading and constructing place determines the formation and agency of the ethnic-motherland nationalist identification, which dominated throughout the last decades of British colonial and into postcolonial Cyprus.

Little has been written on Cyprus and its people within a comparative nationalist framework; however, there have been various initiatives towards such understanding. Most studies on nationalism in Cyprus are from a historical or political perspective with limited comparative approaches. In recent years there has been an anthropological turn, focussing predominantly on majority Greek or Turkish ethnic-nationalism with some comparatives.[2] To a lesser extent, there has been a literary turn with few edited collections and chapters on nationalism,[3] yet without a comprehensive comparative. A common theme within and between these initiatives is place and space, especially gendered spatiality, yet this has not been addressed directly. This chapter draws from, adds to and is shaped by this emerging body of work, so as to initiate a comparative ethnic-nationalist literary examination within a gendered spatial framework.

In this chapter,[4] I will examine the Greek-cypriot and Turkish-cypriot ethnic-motherland nationalist literatures, with emphasis on the ways the writers actively write, read and construct the dominant production of Cyprus that shapes the ethnic selves. Here showing that this production is a 'tool of thought and of action [...] of domination, of power' (Lefebvre, *Production*, 26) and most importantly a tool of colonial liberation and decolonial competition and solidarity. The chapter will show that even though the Greek-cypriots' and Turkish-cypriots' writings are based on deeply 'competing narratives', they have used the same processes and practices to produce a Greece-cyprus or Turkey-cyprus for their ethnic selves. This spatial competition and solidarity will be examined through the spatial model, illuminating the decolonial partitioned invention of gendered nationalism by using Tuan's perspectives on experiencing national place, coupled with Lefebvre's spatiology as related to the abstract nation. Here illuminating new ways of understanding the ethnic-motherland nationalist production of Cyprus, whilst offering new insights, particularly in relation to gendered nationalism, into these spatial considerations.

This literary production is based on the 1955–1974 decolonial moment of national recovery, and in support of Lefebvre and Tuan the ethnic-motherland nationalists reclaim their rights actively to experience, read and construct a Cyprus for themselves, which can be considered social because it is the people, particularly Cypriot authors and their literatures, actively producing. Lefebvre and Tuan refer to literary spatial constructions as a space of the imagination associated with social conditions, by which for Lefebvre such spatial imagining captures the directly lived spaces, and for Tuan it is a directly felt freedom and openness. The ethnic-motherland nationalist practices, however, manipulate these conditions associated with the space of imagination, to create an illusion that deceives the user or reader to assume the construction offers such social agency and freedom. This construction, which is determined by political and nationalist formations, is based on prohibition that eliminates social agency by replacing the openness of concrete experience with a closed mental abstraction. This chapter will focus primarily on this ethnic-motherland nationalist concrete-abstract gendered production, so to show the specific processes and practices that made this nationalist identification and Cyprus the most dominant. Here, as the epigraph shows, the nationalists mak[e] space and society into an 'object' which must be 'closed' to be complete, and that presents a cohesiveness and a totality; this space and society relies on violence that divides, then keeps what it has divided in a state of separation, inversely, it re-unites – yet keeps whatever it wants in a state of confusion (Lefebvre, *Production*, 358). In this process the 'truth of space' will partially be illuminated, revealing the confusions, deceptions and problems in the dominant production, which aggressively oppose the 'right to difference' and country, so as to conceive an ethnically homogeneous mental place that is closed.

The main focus is to show this decolonial production, whereby the ethnic-motherland nationalists 'invent', experience and conceive an ethnically homogeneous mental place through gendered mappings, which are projected as concrete and complete. Such abstract processes of gendering are the key tool that construct place, shaped the ethnic-motherland nationalist identification, and mobilised the Cypriots willingly to die and violently to kill for such production. In short, this abstract production of place is the most powerful vehicle in the Cypriot national project. As is apparent, this production is determined by more than one geographical territory – duality of spatial reference[5] – that refers to Turkey or Greece and Cyprus; therefore, the first half of the chapter will focus on the former, and the second half on the latter production of place.

Greek-cypriot and Turkish-cypriot Writers: Montis, Angelides, Yasin and Ulucamgil

The decolonial moment resulted in a deeply divided yet parallel literary turn amongst the Greek-cypriots and Turkish-cypriots. There was an outpouring of ethnic-nationalist literary activities, including state-sponsored publications with competitions and anthologies[6] – i.e. *A Poetry and Prose Anthology of the 1955–1958 EOKA Liberation Struggle; National Poetry from the Turkish Republic of Northern Cyprus* – literary magazines and zines – *Cardak, Cig, Ilk & Ikinci Demet, Yasemin, Philogiki Kypros, Pnevmatiki Kypros,* and *Themata Kritikis* – prose and especially poetry books, all shaped by pioneering authors – Greek-cypriot: Kypros Chrysanthis, Niki Ladaki-Philippou, Costas Montis, Claire Anelides, Christodoulos Papchrysostomou, Nikos Kranidiotis, Andis Pernaris. Turkish-cypriot: Orbay Delicermak, Pembe Marmara, Oktay Oksuzoglu, Suleyman Ulucamgil, Ozker Yasin, Bener Hakki Hakkeri and Oguz Kusetoglu. Soo much activity created the most significant literary turn, where Cypriot writers and works developed a strong political, social and national consciousness distinct to Cyprus that was well received by the people. Throughout this chapter several Greek-cypriot and Turkish-cypriot writers will be explored; however, the primary focus will be on works by the Greek-cypriot writers Costas Montis and Claire Angelides, and the Turkish-cypriot writers Ozker Yasin and Suleyman Ulucamgil. Montis and Angelides wrote in Greek, and the analysed texts have been read in English translation and glossed through interviews.[7] Yasin and Ulucamgil wrote in Turkish, and the analysed texts have been read in Turkish and translated into English by me.[8] All four writers represent the ethnic-motherland nationalist production of place by writing during and about the anticolonial struggle in 1955–1960, the independence failures in the 1960s, and the results of geographical partition in 1974. These writers are considered amongst the national writers of Cyprus because of their influential contribution and commitment to the literature and politics of Cyprus; they not only record and immortalise these nationalising moments and struggles, but they also served and some died in these moments by being committed members of the anticolonial liberation movements – 'National Organisation of Cypriot Fighters' (Ethnik Organosis Kiprion Agoniston – EOKA), or the 'Turkish Resistance Association' (Turk Mukavemet Teskilati – TMT) – and/or had official governmental positions after independence and the 1974-partition.

Costas Montis was born in 1914 in Famagusta, and is considered the national writer of Cyprus by Greek-cypriots. Montis is a poet, playwright and novelist, and has over 50 publications that span from 1934 to 2008; Montis' work records the historical and political developments of Cyprus throughout these periods. The works that will be analysed include selections from the poetry collection *Moments* ([1958]1965) and various poems in translated anthologies. The novella, *Closed Doors: An Answer to Bitter Lemons by Lawrence Durrell* ([1964] 2004), will be a primary source throughout the chapter. During the anticolonial movement, Montis served in the struggle as a political guide to EOKA members in Nicosia, and upon independence Montis was appointed the Minister of Tourism.

Claire Angelides was born in 1938 in Famagusta, and has published mostly poetry and some prose works from 1967 to 2011. Angelides' work records the EOKA struggle, the failing moments of independence and the traumatic experiences of the 1974-partition. Angelides is considered the pioneer of the Greek-cypriots' '1974–1990 Generation'; however, I believe her narratives also resonate with the characteristics of the '1955–1974 Generation'. The works that will be analysed are a selection from the poetry collection *Venerable Lady the Sea* ([1995–1997] 2000), *Pentadaktylos My Son* ([1991]1994), *The Mirror of the Soul* ([1998]2010) and a selection from her prose work *Streets* (2003). Angelides served in the liberation struggle as the EOKA leader of all women's groups in the Karpasia district; after independence Angelides was appointed Minister of Education.

Ozker Yasin was born in Nicosia in 1932. He is considered the pioneer of the 'Nationalist Poetry' movement, and the leading national writer of Cyprus by Turkish-cypriots. Yasin has over 20 publications that span from 1952 to 2010, which record the events of these times; these mostly consist of poetry collections with some prose collections, plays and novels. A selection of Yasin's poetry from the compilation, *Cyprus My Homeland: Collected Poems I* and *First the Birds Wake Up: Collected Poems II*,[9] and the play, *Song of the Bayraktar*, will be explored. Yasin served in the TMT struggle, particularly through his work at the first Turkish-cypriot radio station, Bayrak (Flag), and after independence he was a founding member of political parties.

Suleyman Ulucamgil was born in 1944 in Phota and died in 1964. Ulucamgil is the poet-martyr of Turkish-cypriot literature, and both his biography and poetry have been immortalised and embedded in the Turkish-cypriot narratives. Ulucamgil was killed whilst serving in the TMT movement in the Dillirga area at the Bozdag village. Throughout his service, particularly from 1960 to 1964, he wrote poems that were serialised in the newspapers *Nacak* and *Hursov*. Shortly after Ulucamgil's death, the poet Orbay Deliceirmak published a selection of Ulucamgil's poetry in *The Call of a Martyr*, *Dillirga* and *Rebel*, and in 1989, he edited and published *Suleyman Ulucamgil Collected Works*, which includes all of Ulucamgil's poetry. Ulucamgil's poetry represents anticolonial resistance and records the ethnic-conflict during independence.

Competing Narratives In Spatial Solidarity

The ethnic-motherland nationalist identification, which dominated throughout the last decades of British colonial and into postcolonial partitioned Cyprus, is built on the foundation of deeply competing narratives, yet its formation has been shared by the Greek-cypriots and Turkish-cypriots. The identification is determined by 'perceptions of common origin and history with Turkey or Greece' (Loizides, 'Adapt', 173–74); it is determined by spatiality.

The Greek-cypriot and Turkish-cypriot nationalist writers employ the same processes and practices from the spatial model. In this decolonial moment of nationalising, they have been dislocated and lost command of their historical homeland; however, this is also a moment where they reclaim a relationship with the territory by resisting the imperial and Other ethnic contaminative forces. In these early stages of resistance and recovery, the nationalists negotiate with the postcolonial and partition 'invention',[10] selecting only those decolonial partition processes that conceal the 'open zones'[11] and reveal the 'closed zones'. These processes imitate and personalise the modes of colonial categorisation, by which they invent through a revised Manichean partitioning of territory that systematically 'divide[s] into compartments' (Fanon, *Wretched*, 29) with an uncompromised binary: an 'ethnic compartment' that is good, consisting of inscriptions that re-invent and pre-invent the territory to its ethno-religious glory; a 'contaminated compartment' that is evil, consisting of colonial and Other ethnic inscriptions, which must be cleansed and un-invented from the ill land. This is a nationalist 'invention'– un-inventing by emptying the colonial world and ethnically cleansing the Others' world so as to pre-invent ethno-religious origins and re-invent an ethnically complete body – operating through gendered symbols and substances. In this process they construct a homogenised cohesive place, which gives them total knowledge and command against the danger and frailty that they see everywhere.

Through this struggle, the nationalists do not employ Tuan's balance between experiencing place and space that provides a healthy relationship with the environment; instead they replace the experience of 'space', which is openness, freedom and danger that brings about frailty, chance and flux, with 'place' that is closed, secure, permanent and complete. They attempt to create 'place' through gendered and familial symbols that provide intimate attachments, deep kinship, awareness and knowledge of the environment, which are, however, problematic, given that Tuan's place, which operates through intimacy, kinship, awareness and knowledge, is based on directly lived and felt concrete experience that the nationalists do not appropriate. Instead, they manipulate and order these social experiences into objects of systemisation conceived through abstractions, which appear concrete. This experience of 'place' can be understood further through Lefebvre's spatiology, where the writers adopt the tripling-triad to master and manipulate the 'regressive-progressive' approach[12] in and for the concrete-abstraction of the nation. Here they adopt the 'representation of space' with its idealistic 'mental space' that uses archaic and arcane gendered symbols and substances to 'conceive', 'order' and compartmentalise. In using these gendered symbols, they manipulate 'representational space', transforming 'social space' that is directly 'lived' and concrete into an ethnic abstraction, now with pre-colonial archaic inhabitants and users wherein space is not dominated and passively experienced, but dominates and is actively recovered. This recovery simultaneously manipulates 'spatial practice', where, dominating over 'physical space', they perceive archaic ethnic journeys and routines, which ensure continuity, cohesion and competence that has no association with concrete daily reality and routine in decolonial Cyprus.

To understand this complex spatial production, we must begin with the dialectics of enslavement and liberation that are central themes in the ethnic-motherland nationalist literatures, and a starting point in postcolonial – particularly decolonial and anticolonial – considerations. Both Tuan and Lefebvre negotiate with the processes between being enslaved with prohibitions or liberated with rights to experience, read and construct place and space. The ethnic-motherland nationalist literatures are driven by ethnic enslavement and the struggle towards ethnic liberation for the construction of place, which represent the dominant practices during decolonial Cyprus. Greek-cypriots and Turkish-cypriots represent British colonialism as a significant force in Cyprus' enslavement, and both literatures immortalise the EOKA or TMT anticolonial[13] movements that struggled to un-invent British contamination and to pre-invent and reinvent liberated Cyprus. These nationalists also have separate accounts of what contributes to their enslavement, with different struggles towards liberation, resulting in a competing narrative whereby liberated Cyprus for one ethnic community is the enslavement for the other community. The Greek-cypriots write Ottoman rule, taksim, the 1974-partition, and Turkish presence as major factors in Cyprus' ethnic enslavement; un-inventing the island of such inscriptions, and pre-inventing it with Ancient Greek and Modern Greek origins to reinvent enosis is their liberated Cyprus. These Turkish factors are emphasised by the Turkish-cypriots, whilst the Greek-cypriot ethnic inscriptions that contribute to Turkish-cypriot enslavement are emptied from their liberated Cyprus. Liberation for the ethnic-motherland nationalists means an ethnically homogeneous Greek or Turkish place, which not only focusses on Cyprus but more specifically maps Greece or Turkey within the construction of the nations. Not only did the ethnic-motherland nationalists record this dominant narrative of enslaved-liberated place, but they also served them by re-mapping the ethnic borders of Cyprus through gendered abstractions. This process resonates with Tuan's and Lefebvre's points on nations being mental and symbolic processes that blur the social, political and historical for the construction of a closed place.

Nations and Nationalisms are gendered constructions, and numerous studies on postcolonial cases[14] have confirmed this as a point of departure. Many studies focus on gender roles in nationalism and national formation: Anne McClintock's 'No Longer in a Future Heaven: Gender, Race and Nationalism' elaborates on the active role of men as the 'progressive agent of national modernity', and the passive subjective role of women as the 'atavist [...] and the authentic body of national tradition' (McClintock, 'Longer', 92). Other studies explore depictions of men and women in the national place: Sumathi Ramaswamy's 'Maps and Mother Goddess in Modern India' explores the feminisation of India as figured through the scientific map of India; Lyn Innes' 'Virgin Territories and Motherlands: Colonial and Nationalist Representations of Africa and Ireland' shows the feminised depictions of Africa and Ireland. A few studies, for example, Rebecca Bryant's anthropological study 'The

Purity of Spirit and Power of Blood', explore both types of gendered nationalism in Cyprus. McClintock's, Ramaswamy's, Innes' and Bryant's gendered studies will be a point of reference in this chapter.

The ethnic-nationalisms of Cyprus are dominated by narratives with gendered depictions, particularly maternal and familial mappings inscribed on the territory, rather than gender roles. Whilst Greece and Turkey are represented within a fixed immoveable maternal frame that dominates official narratives, Cyprus does not conform to a fixed gendered narrative, but instead is in a constant shift, when in some contexts Cyprus is female – a mother, a sister or a daughter – and in others is inscribed with masculine characteristics. Though there is this difference between depictions of Cyprus and the ethnic centres, in both cases the abstract nation appears concrete through gendered symbols operating with blood or spiritual ethnic substances in the island.

Reading the nation through gendered blood or spirit has a foundation in numerous studies on Cyprus, which have been covered thoroughly in Bryant's 'The Purity of Spirit and the Power of Blood',[15] a study I am indebted to. Bryant's study is the only one that analyses both Greek-cypriot and Turkish-cypriot substances, so as to demonstrate the dual processes by which a specific kinship between land and the Cypriot people comes into being for the construction of the nation. Bryant confirms that the 'gendering of the nation', and kinship in particular, is possible only through 'some idea of a shared substance' (Bryant, 192) invested in the land: whilst the Greek-cypriots represent their kinship through the 'substance' of the Ancient Greek spirit attributed with purity, the Turkish-cypriots show their kinship through the substance of Ottoman-Turkish blood associated with power. Bryant argues that the 'naturalisation' of these substances in the land is based on the way the Cypriots narrate and 'prove' the spiritual or blood substances as 'historical' and 'biological facts', which make concrete the abstraction of the nation.

This relates to Tuan's and Lefebvre's definitions of nation as a mental place, which manipulates concrete social and historical time and space, so as to make the abstract political and national space appear a concrete place. This is an ethnically homogenised 'mental space whose dual function is to reduce "real" space [i.e. social, lived and historical space] to the abstract and to induce minimal difference' (Lefebvre, *Production*, 398), experienced as a Tuanian place through attachments, kinship, awareness and knowledge. The nation is a process – which is, in Tuan's words, determined by 'symbolic means to make the large national state seem a concrete place – not just a political idea – toward which a people could feel deep attachment [...] based on direct experience and intimate knowledge' (Tuan, 111–12); and, as Lefebvre defines, a sort of natural substance matured within historical and social time, or an ideological imagining projected onto historical and social time (Lefebvre, *Production*, 176–77) – that creates the illusion of a concrete bodily place. Even though Tuan and Lefebvre do not extensively engage with gendered nations, the gender principle is significant to understanding the nation as mental place: Tuan explores gendering as a symbolic means that captures deep kinship between people and their environment to create concrete 'place'; Lefebvre explores space as carved into male or female bodies to secrete a peoples' agency and/or mental abstractions in the actual production of the nation.

Combining Lefebvre's and Tuan's studies of concrete-abstract nation with Bryant's discussion of blood and spiritual gendering, this chapter will analyse how these symbols and substances are narrated and 'proved' as 'historical' and 'biological facts' for the concrete construction of the abstract nation. For this I will depart from Bryant's cultural anthropological approach based on participant-observations, interviews and direct questions to the Cypriots; instead my readings will be determined by the Cypriots' own observations, interrogations, expressions and experiences with the symbols and substances, as narrated in the ethnic-motherland nationalist literatures for production of the nation.

Thus, in making use of these spatial approaches, this chapter will expand upon the ways these competing narratives pave solidarity, revealing the shared ways the ethnic-motherland nationalists invent, experience and conceive an ethnically homogeneous closed mental place through various gendered processes that make the abstract nation appear concrete.

Mother Greece and Mother Turkey

The ethnic-motherland nationalists' narratives construct a closed mental place through a 'pre-invention' – a return to a past primordial condition – that manipulates spatial and social practices based on deep kinship, intimate attachments and knowledge of the environment. The starting point for this reading and construction of place is the mother; in the ethnic-motherland nationalist discourse, Greece and Turkey are the Mothers, and the narratives attempt to prove this maternal kinship as biological fact through elaborating on the deep attachment between Mother Greece or Mother Turkey and Child Cyprus. This is developed further through narratives about the process by which the Mothers gave ethnic birth to Cyprus; here showing knowledge of the Mothers' Ancestral Journey to Cyprus, which is conceived through organising historical, social and spatial practices into fetish spectacles and objects operating/invested with a blood or spiritual substance. These processes and practices are represented as Gifts from the Mothers to the Children of Cyprus, which paves the way for the absolute blood or spiritual ethnic Gift from the Mothers that is the Child Cyprus.

Mother and Child

The literary depictions of Mother Greece and Mother Turkey give way to narratives of the Cyprus Child, and this maternal principle is often introduced within the context of the EOKA or TMT anticolonial campaign. Costas Montis' *Closed Doors* is a recording of the EOKA liberation struggle, which writes back to Lawrence Durrell, a British writer and officer who served in British-Cyprus from 1954 to 1956, and who wrote about the EOKA struggle in *Bitter Lemons*. In *Closed Doors*, Montis immortalises the anticolonial case of Cyprus from a Greek-cypriot perspective through his protagonist, a young Greek-cypriot schoolboy, who narrates the EOKA campaign as experienced in Nicosia. In the opening of the novella the narrator states:

> the long-standing struggle of the island to shake off the foreign yoke, an unbroken effort that had taken many forms, all peaceful [...] we children [...] accepted the mild level of protest as customary, traditional even. It had been closely interwoven into our lives since birth. Until that fateful (fateful?) January. (Montis, *Closed*, 3)

The passage claims that throughout colonial rule – British and others – the Greek-cypriots had been mild and weak in protesting against colonial enslavement. The narrator's emphasis that 'we children' were born into this mildness, and accepted this as 'tradition', suggests that the Greek children of Cyprus were losing sense of the meaning of ethnic tradition and heritage by accepting weakness and enslavement as their traditional or habitual state. The narrator shows, however, that the mobilisation of EOKA in January 1955[16] changed the history of enslavement, and provoked the Greek-cypriots to rid the island of British rule and fight for liberation. The narrator clearly states the term that defined this liberation, which suggests that 'we children' simultaneously refers to the actual Greek Cypriot child and the island:

> 'Enosis,' a demand for liberation that echoed from time to time as the ultimate aspiration of every Greek territory outside of the borders of the free motherland. (Montis, *Closed*, 4)

'Enosis' – Union with Greece – was liberation. Greece is the 'motherland', and Cyprus is represented as a Greek territory that is geographically separate, but with aspirations to unify with free Mother Greece; this suggests that Cyprus, like all Greek Islands, is the child of Mother Greece. Such maternal representations of Mother Greece and her baby Cyprus were frequently used in literary and political representation, and throughout the resistance EOKA recited it in hymns. Christodoulos Papachrysostomou's poem 'EOKA Hymn' is a momentous example of this gendered kinship, because it was an inspirational poem sung by the EOKA freedom-fighters during their imprisonment in colonial detention camps: 'Onward, onward, EOKA calls/ and may the earth thunder beneath your feet, [...] mother Hellas waits to crown /all her children with laurel wreaths' (Papachrysostomou, 71).

Similarly, in Turkish-cypriot narratives, Turkey is the motherland and Cyprus the 'babyland'. In his poetry collection *Letter of Cyprus*, Yasin attempts to immortalise the first Turkish-cypriot anticolonial struggle on 27–28 January 1958 towards a taksim – Partition to Unite with Turkey – liberation, which is a milestone recorded in Turkish-cypriot resistance narratives. Yasin's is a particularly good example of the gendered associations related to this significant struggle. *Letter of Cyprus* is a narrative between two friends communicating by letter, which is also reflected in the poem's form. The first section is written in letter form, dated '29 January 1958' and addressed to a Cypriot from a Turkish citizen. In this poetic letter the Turkish citizen questions his Cypriot friend on the anticolonial events of '27 January 1958', which he read about in the Turkish newspapers. The remaining sections of the *Letter of Cyprus* are divided into seven poems, all of which are a Turkish-cypriot reply to the letter from the Turkish friend. Here the first section is symbolic of Turkey, and suggests a letter from the mother who confirms awareness of the Turkish-cypriot struggles, which Yasin elaborates on in the reply poem 'II':

> ...we would say that in the motherland
> The officials sat around a table
> We heard that our future would be a subject.
> We knew victory was ours
> We knew our Turkey
> We knew our mother eagle
> Would not leave its orphaned baby on its own. (Yasin,
> *Collected I*, 106)

Cyprus is defined as the 'orphaned baby' because it has been separated from its Mother Turkey, and has been lacking the freedom to fly; this maternal separation resonates with the dominant narratives regarding the events of 1914 when the Ottoman-British agreement lapsed, and more so after 1924 when Cyprus was officially named a British crown colony.

Montis, Papachrysostomou and Yasin are just three examples of the numerous nationalist writers who represent Greece or Turkey as the Mother, and Cyprus as her child, whereby the anticolonial struggle against British rule is simultaneously a struggle that seeks to re-unite Cyprus, the vulnerable baby, with its Mother. The ethnic-motherland nationalist gendered configurations relate to numerous postcolonial cases, where the nationalist representations of place are commonly gendered through female figures: Ramaswamy explores India as 'Mother India' or 'Mother Tamil' through 'bodyscapes' on the scientific map (Ramaswamy, 98); Innes explores various representations of Mother

Africa and Mother Ireland. McClintock states, 'nations are frequently figured through the iconography of familial and domestic space' (McClintock, 'Longer', 90), through figures such as 'mothers' to emphasise that, like a family, the nation is an organic unity and a natural construction. Similarly, in the ethnic-motherland nationalist narratives, Greece and Turkey are figured as the Mother, and Cyprus and its people as her child, to show that together they form an organic family unit. Through such maternal associations, the nationalists expand further the experiential dimension of natural or maternal unity for the construction of national 'place'. This resonates with Tuan's place as developed through the child's actual experience with the environment: 'place as a focus of value, nurture and support' which makes 'the mother [...] the child's primary place' (Tuan, 29). The writers suggest that the people of a nation experience the national territory, like a child experiencing its mother, as the centre of intimate attachment and deep kinship that is a secure safe place. Tuan engages with actual maternal and familial experience to define place, and it is clear that these concrete social experiences are manipulated for the ethnic-motherland nationalist definition of the nation. The maternal dimension is manipulated and transformed from being the centre of social practice and active reproduction to being the centre of political abstraction and passive action, by which the abstract nation is made concrete. For example, in the nationalist narratives the EOKA or TMT anticolonial liberation campaign is determined by a process that replaces the social, particularly the lived relationship between mother and child, with a political notion of enosis or taksim for the mental conception of a united concrete nation. Reading these maternal configurations of the nation through Lefebvre clarifies further the emptying of social experiences. Lefebvre states that for society to enter the process of creating appropriated social space, 'the principle of fertility (the Mother) undergoes renewal', and the foundation of social space is 'prohibition [...] dislocation of most immediate relationships (such as the child's with its mother) [...] prohibition, which separates the child from its mother' (Lefebvre, *Production*, 34–35). The ethnic-motherland nationalists and postcolonial nations generally refuse or struggle against these necessities, in that the reading and construction of the nation as a fruitful reproductive mother is steadfast, and this production is determined by uniting the mother and child. Such representations of the nation through the mother and child not only empty the social condition, they also reflect, as McClintock argues, the national hierarchy, whereby the females are figured to have the subjugated roles within the nation. In the gendered depictions of Turkey and Greece, however, there are some differences. Mother Greece and Mother Turkey are both represented as all-powerful, free and untouchable forces that control, provide and protect the children, both male and female, of Cyprus, with supremacy to liberate and unify with Cyprus. Mother Greece and Mother Turkey are not subjugated women, like the weak women symbolising colonised national cases as in McClintock and Innes. However, it is the sons of Cyprus and of the motherlands that are the 'active agents' who struggle and sacrifice themselves for the family, Mother and Child to re-unite.[17]

Even though there are some similarities in the gendered nationalism between Cyprus and other postcolonial nations, unlike most postcolonial cases, the Turkish-cypriot and Greek-cypriot nationalists rarely define their own home, Cyprus, as the motherland, but instead as the child, whilst Greece and Turkey are always mapped as the mothers of the nation. The Cypriot identification with an alternative territory as motherland can be compared to the case of Ireland, whereby the Ulster unionists defined the British Empire as the motherland, which gave birth to and protects the Irish nation. Similarly, in the case of Cyprus, Greece and Turkey are the mothers, creators and protectors of the Greekness and Turkishness in Cyprus, which is emphasised through representations of Mother Greece's and Mother Turkey's 'Ancestral Journey' and gifts into Cyprus. The nationalist literatures are dominated by pre-inventing the 'Ancestral Journey', which is used as a tool to prove that Mother Greece or Turkey gave ethnic – Greek or Turkish – birth to baby Cyprus. The ancestors are the Ancient Greek people from Greece who arrived and invested a pure spirit in Cyprus; or the Ottoman-Turkish soldiers from the conquest whose powerful martyred blood inseminated and married Cyprus.[18]

The Gift: Fetish Objects and Spectacles

Both Greek-cypriot and Turkish-cypriot narratives claim that the ancestors, mostly sons, of Mother Greece and Mother Ottoman-Turkey produced Cyprus. The writers create this production through demonstrating knowledge and systematically ordering spatial and social practices into objects or spectacles imbued with blood or spiritual value, which gives way for Cyprus to be a blood or spiritual object or spectacle. Cyprus is thus a product of worship from the ancestors; it is the 'gift' of a Greek or Turkish place.

This nationalist production of Cyprus supports McClintock's definition that 'Nationalism inhabits the realm of fetishism'; it operates through organising 'fetish objects' (ships, flags, architecture) and 'collective fetish spectacles' (Ancient Greek or Ottoman journeys and military display) (McClintock, 'Longer', 102). This nation is created through organising social and spatial practices – matrimony, procreation, language, journeys – into blood or spiritual fetish spectacles or objects, thus revealing the ways in which social space is transformed into abstract symbols and arcane substances, which are personified and projected onto the impassioned object and spectacle. In this way the nationalist writers manipulate and master concrete social practices, constructs and relations to transform Cyprus into a fetish spectacle and object.

McClintock's theory of fetishism for nationalism can be illuminated through Lefebvre's appropriation of Marx's 'commodity fetishism'[19] for spatial production. Marx explores commodity fetishism through associating it with religious practices of object worship, whereby the object of commodity is personified to the extent that it dictates the social relations that produced them. Lefebvre adapts Marx's commodity fetishism to space: spaces are defined as objects of worship or fetish objects that manipulate and master the social practices and relations that produced them. Lefebvre's definition of space as a commodity fetish provides an understanding of the ethnic-motherland nationalists' production of Cyprus. At first glance, it may be suggestive that the nationalists reveal the social relations, particularly the ancestral spatial practices coupled with the familial and maternal relations, which produced Cyprus. It is clear, however, that this process is based on manipulating and mastering the actual social relations and directly lived experiences of the people and former inhabitants who created the island, wherein the concept of production – Who produces? How? Why? For whom? – does not become fully concrete but remains purely and powerfully abstract (Lefebvre, *Production*, 69), thus enabling the unanswerable and unquestionable production of Cyprus as an ethnically pure or powerful complete object.

This production of Cyprus as a complete object is further enhanced through Tuan's exploration of place: 'Objects and places are centres of value [...] [place, like an object,] achieves concrete reality when our experience of it is total' (Tuan, 71). Tuan focusses on the child's experience with place as a type of object, where the child's primary place, which is simultaneously referred to as the first enduring object, is the mother, and as the child grows, they become attached to other places – family members, toys or a specific location like the naughty step – experienced as objects of value because they are considered gifts from the mother. This childhood experience speaks directly to the ethnic-motherland nationalist production, by which the writers manipulate and master actual childhood experiences and relations within and for the creation of place. The nationalists depict Cyprus and its people as the child, whose initial place or object of worship is Mother Greece or Turkey. Subsequently, Cyprus and the child are attached to an array of objects – flags, ships, tombs, etc. – that define and are defined as places or objects of worship because they are gifts from the Mothers. This process gives way for Cyprus to be depicted and experienced as the object or gift from Mother Turkey or Mother Greece to the people, who will perpetually be babies of this baby nation.

The ethnic-motherland nationalist literatures are loaded with such practices, readings and constructions, which attempt to prove the production of an ethnically closed concrete place or gift, and the chapter has thus analysed this in relation to Turkey and Greece. The maternal abstractions capture Turkey and Greece as the fixed Mother, and Cyprus as the child; the ancestral journey and arrival, which operate with the blood or spiritual objects and spectacles, evidence the Mothers as agents who gave birth to Baby Cyprus, who created Cyprus as Gift.

In this first section 'Mother Greece and Mother Turkey', the chapter has partially shown the competing narratives in spatial solidarity, where the nationalist identification is determined by this production that operates via contradictions. The nationalist writers attempt to create a 'place' through capturing intimate attachments and detailed knowledge of maternal and ancestral spatial and social practices, yet these practices are based on manipulating directly lived and perceived experiences through the conceived; thus, there is a dialectic between concrete reality and mental abstractions, where the latter masters, secretes and appropriates the former, particularly through a gendered process of production. This gendered process of production makes and breaks the national project. It is a crucial device to make fact the deep familial kinship between the ethnic centres and Cyprus, biologically and historically proving the Mothers gave birth to Baby Cyprus, and validating the Turkish-cypriots or Greek-cypriots as the offspring who must protect the ethnic Gift. It is a device that filters who is 'included' and 'excluded' from the national project, and that confirms Cyprus was not an empty space open to British imperial or Other ethnic contamination, but an ethnically cleansed, complete and closed place. This national device moved the masses and mobilised the anticolonial campaign to be dictated by, to kill and to die for the mental construction and preservation of this Baby Gift. The examination has partially revealed that this gendered process of production simultaneously breaks this national project, exposing not only the spatial solidarity between the ethnically divided people of Cyprus, but also exposing Cyprus not as a complete closed place but as a shifting ground, represented as a baby, heroic son and luring woman. These shifting representations are especially revealed as a result of colonial and postcolonial failures, which will be shown in the remaining section 'Cyprus Our Enslaved Liberated Woe-Man'.

Cyprus Our Enslaved Liberated Woe-man

> [T]he ways in which space is thus carved up are reminiscent of the ways in which the body is cut into pieces in images (especially the female body, which is not only cut up but deemed to be 'without organs'!). (Lefebvre, *Production*, 355)

The colonial and postcolonial failures – particularly the anticolonial struggles of 1955–1960, the brief period of 1960 independence, the civil war of 1960–1970s, and the 1974-partition – have meant that Cyprus, the Mothers' Gift, has been enslaved, endangered and carved up into pieces. Consequently, the Turkish-cypriot and Greek-cypriot nationalists, endowed with the responsibility to preserve and protect the Gift, compete against not only these colonial and postcolonial legacies but also each other, which contributes further to carving up the body of the island. This is the ethnic-motherland nationalist construction of Cyprus, which differs to the construction thus shown, because here the people of Cyprus, rather than the ancestors, are the agents that actively construct place; this construction is based on a struggle against the dangerous openness and strangeness of a space to construct a secure closed ethnic place. In this construction gendering through the blood or spiritual substance continues to figure as a device for the national project; however, in this gendered construction, the process of invention – un-invention that wipes out and puts an end to existing construction, pre-invention that returns to a past primordial construction, re-invention that is to start anew for future construction – coupled with the dynamic of ethnic enslavement and liberation, is the most powerful national vehicle, such that it gives way to inconsistent shifts in the gendered production of Cyprus. Moreover, this narrative construction represents the actual Cypriot people, events, nature and landscape; however, in the process of territorial reconstruction these experiences are emptied of directly lived and physical value and are transformed into mental symbols and abstractions. Consequently, Cyprus is 'invented' and carved up into an enslaved-liberated actual-imaginary woman-man in the ethnic-motherland nationalist struggle that attempts to reconstruct and restore the Gift to its former ethnic glory, to a complete closed secure place.

Gendered Enslavement: Our Enslaved Woman

The colonial and postcolonial failures of Cyprus are frequently represented through gendered enslavement. Cyprus, the ancestral gift, is depicted as a woeful woman enslaved to symbolise the ethnicity that has been emptied from the island, and it is the duty of the men of the nation to restore it to its ethnic glory and beauty.

In Angelides' *Venerable Lady the Sea*, the poems in the 'Ammohostos' section represent the enslavement of Ammohostos, which is the city that often figures in Angelides' writing because it is her birthplace and place of inhabitancy up until the population transfer of 1974. Ammohostos[20] is represented as an enslaved woman, and the encounters that caused this point to readings within Ottoman, British and especially the 1974-partitioned contexts: whilst Ottoman and British rule incarcerated the Greekness by implanting their imperial cultures, the 1974-partition emptied it by uprooting all Greek-cypriots, and transferring Turks into Ammohostos. Ammohostos is host to the ruins of Salamis depicted via the Greek spirit of heroic Teucer in Angelides' poem, 'Fate, Myth and Pain' in the 'Cyprus' section; however, in the 'Ammohostos' section the ethnic spirit is incarcerated so the city is not depicted as heroic Teucer but instead as an enslaved anguished woman.

'Ammohostos is my sister', Angelides confirmed in an interview,[21] and the two poems 'Beautiful Bride-Like Ammohostos' and 'I Sing' are read through this sibling association. In 'Beautiful Bride-Like Ammohostos' the city is compared to a bride:

> Clotho weaves
> her threads around us.
> But you rise erect, Beautiful
> though the legs of the horses
> of your thoughts
> are injured from wandering
> Beautiful, bride-like Ammohostos. (Angelides, *Venerable*, 58)

The passage demonstrates the common representation of the nation through gendered dichotomy; the territory is an enslaved woman, and the sons of the nation are the active agents that can save and protect the land. Ammohostos is feminised into a bride to suggest both the purity of Greekness in the land, and to show that Ammohostos is a fragile innocent chaste virgin. The thoughts of Ammohostos, the bride, are 'wandering' in search of and longing for her missing groom, son of the nation, because the Greekness of the land has been harmed and rendered unsafe. Through this, Angelides at once points to the Greek-cypriot men that were killed and went missing during 1974, and the EOKA freedom-fighters tortured and imprisoned in British detention camps. These Greek-cypriot men are symbolised through the 'injured horses', here suggesting the loss of virility and manhood, particularly the loss of war and power of these men who failed in their duty to wed and protect Ammohostos and her Greekness. Both Ammohostos and the Greek-cypriot men are injured because of this separation, and Angelides suggests that victory would be achieved upon the unification of bride Ammohostos and Greek/Greek-cypriot groom(s), who can recover and protect the purity of Greekness in Ammohostos.

Even though the men of the nation are injured and missing, Ammohostos waits 'erect and beautiful' in hope that she will be saved and wed by her groom. Here Angelides employs what Bryant calls the 'politics of waiting', which is 'the politics in which the body is compelled to kneel but the soul remains intact and erect' (Bryant, *Imagining*, 196), practised by the Greek-cypriots leading up to independence and through to partition. For Angelides, the body of Ammohostos is enslaved and corrupted but the Greek soul and spirit remains pure, free and erect.

Even though Angelides represents the hopelessness and ill fate of Ammohostos' body, the poem suggests that Ammohostos' fate will change because the land is immortally inscribed with the Ancient Greek spirit of 'Clotho'. Clotho is one of the three mythical fates responsible for spinning the thread of human existence to make decisions of birth, life and death, which suggests that the ancestor 'Clotho' will spin the thread to make a different decision for Ammohostos' current existence, by which the city will recover its Greekness. Through 'Clotho', the bride Ammohostos will re-unite with her groom who will protect Ammohostos' body from total destruction. In 'I Sing' Angelides elaborates on this destruction:

firmly holding your lily – white fingers
Ammohostos.
Now night engulfs you
pirates have violated your body.
Your soul erect, Ammohostos. (Angelides, *Venerable*, 75)

Angelides points to the violation of the bride, Ammohostos, who was wandering alone in the previous poem. The pirates suggest the British colonisers and the Turkish occupiers who abducted and harassed Ammohostos' feminine body. The 'white lily' suggest both the pirates' brutal sexual abuse as related to the Ancient Greek symbol of the masculine eroticism and sexuality, as well as Ammohostos' chaste virginity as in Christian lily symbol of feminine innocence, purity and piety. Through this symbolism of the white lily, Angelides confirms that although Ammohostos' body has been sexually violated by the besieging pirates, Ammohostos' Greek spirit stands pure and cannot be destroyed.

In both 'Beautiful Bride-Like Ammohostos' and 'I Sing', Ammohostos is a signification of Cyprus, figured as an innocent chaste virgin whose 'Greek body' has been violated by the 1974 occupation and British colonisation but whose Greek spirit stand erect. There are many writers that use such gendered imagery to represent Cyprus, and in 'Song for Stalo', Montis associates Cyprus with his daughter Stalo: 'your presence compiles Cyprus/compiles Nicosia, Kyrenia, Famagusta' (Montis, *Moments*, 49). Here, Montis does not represent the violation of Cyprus, his daughter, but uses such an association to suggest innocent purity and his deep kinship to Cyprus.

Such gendered links are also used by Turkish-cypriots. In Oguz Kusetoglu's 'Cyprus My ill-fated Daughter', Cyprus is defined within the context of British colonialism and the EOKA campaign:

Cyprus, my gazelle, oh my ill-fated daughter
Spoilt children have put their sinister eyes on you
My scarlet veiled, bright wired and ill-fated daughter
Do not mourn, you will reach the homeland. [...]
Why are your hopes broken? Why are you pale? (Kusetoglu, *TCLII*, 98)

Here Kusetoglu feminises Cyprus into his daughter, a bride and a 'gazelle', who is ill-fated, weak, 'pale' and 'broken' because of the EOKA and British colonial forces – 'eyes' – that are on her; these are depicted as eyes of 'spoilt children' because they do not have the adult male power to abduct his daughter. Kusetoglu's Cyprus is a bride – symbolised through 'scarlet veil' and 'bright wire', both worn by Turkish-cypriot brides in old traditional weddings – who 'mourns' because she too is separated from her groom; here the groom is the masculine Turkish blood that needs to pour into feminine soil of Cyprus to release it from its paleness, thus colouring and marrying the Cyprus bride with its groom Turkey. Kusetoglu ends the poem with confirmation that the Cyprus daughter will reach the homeland, Cyprus will marry Turkey.

In both nationalist representations, Cyprus is figured as the virginal bride, which can be compared to the imperial British gendered representation of 'Ireland or Hibernia [...] as a virginal young maiden, fair-haired and helpless, besieged by a group of bestial, apelike Irish men' (Innes, 6). Cyprus is also the helpless young bride, yet the beastly men that besiege her are not, as in the Irish context, from the same ethnic group, but those who have a different ethnic background. Both Cypriots represent British forces as a danger that abducts Cyprus; additionally, the Greek-cypriots' Cyprus-bride is in danger from the Turkish forces, and the Turkish-cypriots' Cyprus needs to be protected from the Greeks. Innes also analyses a visual image of Ireland and England from a nineteenth-century journal to suggest that Ireland is '"the Intended"; she is the virginal young woman awaiting Union, her role is to be wed to John Bull or England, and thus to be saved from defilement by the bestial men of Ireland' (Innes, 8). Similarly, Cyprus is also the 'Intended', awaiting Union with the sons of Mother Greece and Turkey, as well as to be wed with the Cypriot sons of the same ethnicity, which will save Cyprus from bestial men of the Empire and other ethnicity.

The Greek-cypriots and Turkish-cypriots also represent gendered enslavement without directly associating the woman and land, but instead through women characters. In Cyprus, as in the literary cases of Africa and Ireland explored by Innes, there is an 'overloading of central women characters so that they become in some sense signifiers of the nation' (Innes, 11). In Greek-cypriot representations there is a flood of women characters – mothers, wives, sisters and daughters – always weeping in danger: in Bryant's 'Purity of Spirit and the Power of Blood', and Floya Anthias' 'Woman and Nationalism in Cyprus', it is suggested that since 1974, Cyprus is frequently represented as a mourning mother in black (Bryant, *Imagining*, 199; Anthias, 155). Even though weeping mothers and women did become more dominant after 1974, such depictions can also be evidenced in pre-1974 narratives. *Closed Doors* concludes with a weeping mother from newly independent Cyprus:

> Mother is alone in the house wandering about. She grips the walls, she fumbles about Niko's bed, father's desk and armchair, and Stalo's purse and books. Mother does not hear the noise of the

> crowds, she has no contact with the festivities at all. She has no place on this day since no one will knock on the closed doors of the house. The prisons and detention camps will not send anyone home to her, neither father (I haven't told you that he won't be coming back) nor Stalo (I haven't told you that she won't be coming back either). [...]
>
> And don't tell her that I will not return, don't let her know that I am gone as well. Don't let her grope at my books or my school cap. In her mind, at least let her have me. Let me be with her, let her hold me in her arms, so we can listen to the sounds of bells together. I will trick her into thinking we are waiting for the others. "Do you hear, my son?" "Yes". (Montis, *Closed*, 117)

As a result of the EOKA struggle, the narrator confirms that the family – himself, his sister Stalo, his brother Nikos, and his father – have all died, leaving the mother alone longing for her family to return. This represents the actual missing family members consequent upon the EOKA struggle, as well as the displacement of the Cypriot national family – Mother Greece and her child Cyprus – during the decolonial period. During the anticolonial struggle, the EOKA fought to unite the displaced actual and national family; however, they were prevented by harsh British military repression that employed curfews and imprisoned the freedom-fighters in detention camps. Consequently, like the mother in the passage, the EOKA and Cypriots were held behind closed doors or bars weeping for the displaced actual and national family. The concluding passage indicates that Cyprus gained its independence with 'crowds celebrating'; however, the mother is mourning behind closed doors because her family members will not return. Here the mother is a signification of independent Cyprus, which suggests that though Cyprus became independent the actual and national family continued to be separated because many Greek-cypriots were killed, and Cyprus was prohibited from unifying with Mother Greece, which meant Cypriots, like the mother, continued to long for the family.

The above passage indicates that the narrator is dead, informing the reader, here in this concluding paragraph, that it was his spirit that hauntingly narrated the novella, *Closed Doors*. Not wanting his mother to know of the entire family's death, the narrator's solution is for the mother to imagine he is there and continue believing the family will re-unite. Similarly, upon independence the Cypriots could not accept the impossibility of re-uniting the actual and national family; therefore, like the mother, they too imagined and waited steadfastly for the unification of the Greek family.

Montis also depicts anticolonial Cyprus as a mother and wife suffering familial displacement. During the anticolonial struggle the EOKA fighters were imprisoned and tortured in British detention camps, whilst their families were unaware of their whereabouts. Montis records several of these stories; one example is the experience of Antonis' wife:

> At first his wife had no idea where they had taken him or what had happened to him. She nearly went out of her mind. Every day in tears she left her children (she had a whole nest of them) with neighbours so that she could run to police and military. They sent her from one department to another, from one interrogation center to another from one city to another
>
> [...]
>
> she came back drained in the evening (pale and strained, hardly human in appearance and gathered her children from the neighbours.) [...] She did not walk, she did not run, she flew with the children chirping behind her.
>
> [...]
>
> But she was not flying when she returned that evening, she drooped, her once wavy hair stuck to her head all askew, her once fluttering arms now stuck to her sides like she was an archaic statue. And behind her the children despondently dragged themselves along. (Montis, *Closed*, 43–44)

The wife, like the mother, is weeping over the destruction of her family; in this case the woman is left longing without her husband, Antonis. The wife, animal-like, wanders the whole of Cyprus in search of her Antonis, going from one door to the next, each of which is closed. Antonis' absence leaves the wife pale and weak with a family falling apart; the wife goes off searching whilst the children are left, orphan-like, to the neighbours. Once informed of Antonis' whereabouts the family are compared to birds, the wife 'flies' and the children 'chirp' towards him, showing that re-uniting the family, both the actual and national family, is freedom. When returning from Antonis, the bird-like characteristics disappear, and instead the family 'drag' themselves back home, because though alive, Antonis had been tortured so badly that he was no longer recognised as the father or husband they knew – the family now wingless, enslaved and incomplete. Montis chooses not to give Antonis' wife or children a name to suggest they exist through him, and now without him they no longer exist.

During the colonial and independent period, the literature of Cyprus frequently deployed such gendered imagery: the destruction of the actual and national family through weeping females who simultaneously signified actual Cypriot women who lost family members, and Cyprus being ripped away from Mother Greece. As of 1974, such gendering overwhelmed the island; Cyprus was dominated by images of weeping women, particularly mourning mothers, representing actual mothers who lost family members, particularly sons, and the Cypriot nation who lost their land – this time both Mother Greece and Cyprus. In these images the mourning mother often holds a photo of her missing son to symbolise Cyprus as both an anguished mother and the missing son.[22] The mother usually has the same appearance: 'after 1974 posters appeared everywhere in the south of the island depicting an anguished black clothed woman, her face tormented, and her clothes ragged' (Anthias and Yuval-Davis, 155). Cyprus overflowed with this image through various mediums, and the literature of Cyprus also participated in this gendering: in *Pentadaktylos My Son*, Angelides' narrator is a mother mourning the loss of her son and the land: 'A mother hangs over a photograph' (Angelides, *Pentadaktylos*, 5). In 'Black Garbed Mother' Zitsea Chrysanthi writes: 'Mothers of Cyprus/with robust souls/and black kerchiefs around your heads' (Chrysanthi, 126).

Like the Greek-cypriots', the Turkish-cypriots' literary production of colonial and postcolonial Cyprus is dominated by gendered imagery of weeping women characters in danger. In the play *Song of Bayraktar*, Yasin represents the enslavement and danger that Emine, the daughter of the family, is confronted with as a result of EOKA and British forces. The play is based around a family: mother, uncle, two daughters Zehra and Emine, the son Ahmet, and the son's Turkish friend Ozdemir. The family are at home sleeping, whilst outside the Turkish-cypriots are protesting against the killing of their men in the Paphos/Baf area by British and/or EOKA forces. Consequent upon the loud protest, the sleeping family are woken, and after some time discussing the situation, Emine suggests they return to sleep because, 'Tomorrow we will be prisoners in the house... You can speak lots' (Yasin, *Song*, 35). Here, Emine confirms that the family, as well as the whole of Cyprus, will be condemned to a day of British curfew, when they will be locked up behind closed doors because of this protest. Once returning to bed, it becomes apparent that the family's subject of thought turns to Emine. The death of the Turkish-cypriots, the curfew, the enslavement the Cypriots will face, and the mobilisation for freedom are all replaced by thoughts of Emine: whilst the mother dreams of Emine, Ozdemir spends the night writing love poetry for Emine, the intended. The next morning, which is the day of the curfew, Emine is the central topic, the mother shares her dream:

> MOTHER: The EOKA kidnapped Emine...
> The filthy murderers tied my daughter's hands,
> My baby was crying, asking God for help
> But her tears dried in her eyes...
> Where she was tied a huge bird descended,
> Chirping it untied the ropes from her hands,
> Like a white crane Emine and the bird
> Flew to Turkey... What is the signification of my dream? (Yasin, *Song*, 57)

In the dream, Emine, the innocent chaste virgin, is kidnapped, which represents the Turkish-cypriot fear of actual 'kidnapping' of their girls by Greek-cypriots, and a signification of the kidnapping and harassment of Cyprus by the EOKA. Bryant discusses the discourse of 'kidnapping', where Turkish-cypriots believed that, as propaganda, the Greek-cypriots sought to seduce and marry, 'kidnap', the Turkish-cypriot girls. Consequently the '1950 family law [...] prohibition of marriage between a Muslim woman and a non-Muslim man' (Bryant, *Imagining*, 201) was a means to overcome this 'kidnapping'. In the dream, Emine is set free by a bird and together they fly to safety, 'Turkey'. On the day of the curfew, the meaning of the dream is un-coded, and it partially comes true, impelling the uncle to state: 'The signification of the dream is proven, Emine's mother will be setting her free to fly, my dear sister, there is a suitor for Emine' (Yasin, *Song*, 58). Ozdemir, who is from Turkey, proposes to Emine, suggesting that Ozdemir is the Turkish 'bird' that arrives to protect Cypriot Emine from the kidnapping of EOKA by making her a Turkish bride. Again, this represents actual marriages between Turkish-cypriot girls and Turkish men that most Turkish-cypriots desired at the time; it also represents the marriage between Cyprus and Turkey, where the Turkish army, 'bird', will free and wed the 'intended' Cyprus – symbolic of the geographical unification of Turkey-cyprus, and the masculine Turkish blood inseminating the feminine Cyprus soil.

In the *Song of the Bayraktar*, Cyprus' gendered enslavement is represented through implicit associations and symbolisms of dreams and matrimony; however, Yasin's poem 'Girls on Ropes' in *Bloody Cyprus* is an explicit representation of women being sexually abused:

> More than twenty women, young girls and children
> In the rooms
> Distraught, layered upon each other
> All doors of hope closed
> [...]
> Like greedy wolves they went into their homes
> Collected the women and children in a house
> And killed the men...
> [...]
> "Hey crazy Turks
> Aren't you hungry?
> If you have a mind
> You won't fight against our wishes
>
> If your girls have sex with us
> Plenty to eat for you..."

And the girls in the room
Killed themselves one by one
With the rope they hung on the ceiling. (Yasin, *Collected I*, 197–98)

Here captured by the EOKA 'wolves', the women are hopeless because most of the men who can save them have been 'killed'. These women represent the actual experiences women had at the time, and Cyprus being abused and tortured by EOKA. In the poem, the EOKA members state that if the surviving Turkish-cypriot men accept the enosis 'wishes', and the Turkish-cypriot girls have sex with them, then they will be given life – 'plenty to eat'; here suggesting that accepting enosis is equivalent to allowing men to devour the body of their women. When the women are confronted with the fact that they will be devoured they hang themselves, which suggests that the Turkish-cypriots would prefer to see the death of their women and Cyprus rather than seeing them as a Greek wife or island. The death of the women also suggests that the EOKA's enosis demand is killing Turkish Cyprus.

Yasin also represents this enslavement through the mother in the poem 'Son, Don't Go':

Son return to me,
In your strong hands green my fertility
Bring enlightenment
Bring freedom to my veins,
I am so in need of you. (Yasin, *Collected I*, 29)

Cyprus is depicted through a mother weeping over her son's departure from the island. Here Yasin is pointing to the many Turkish-cypriots, like his own son, who fled to the United Kingdom or Turkey in order to escape the trauma in the anticolonial and independence period, so as to signal that Cyprus, the anguished fragile mother, needs the return, support and mobilisation of these Turkish-cypriot sons in order to recover her 'freedom'.

These depictions of Cyprus as the mother should not be mistaken for a representation of Cyprus as the Motherland, but only as a signification of the shared experience between that of a mourning mother (and multiple other mourning women) and Cyprus, because Greece or Turkey are the sole Mothers in the ethnic-motherland nationalist narratives.

The Greek-cypriot and Turkish-cypriot gender narratives represent Cyprus as enslaved weeping women, which resonates with McClintock's commentary on gendered representations of the Anglo-Boer war: 'In 1913 [...] the Vrouemonument (Women's Monument) was erected in homage to the female victims of war. The monument took the form of a circular domestic enclosure, where women stand weeping with their children'.

McClintock states that such gendered representation of the nation masks the actualities of the national liberation:

> by portraying the Afrikaner *nation* symbolically as a weeping woman, the mighty male embarrassment of military defeat could be overlooked [...] in images of feminine tears and maternal loss. (McClintock, 'Longer,' 104–105)

McClintock's analysis speaks to the Cypriot narratives, which are overloaded with imagery of weeping women to mask the endless failures of the Cypriot men. The men of Cyprus failed to protect the nation from the British colonial and the postcolonial enslavement, defeated without re-uniting the national family (Mothers and Cyprus), incapable of preventing the 1974-partition and/or illegal isolation (TRNC) of the island. Whilst McClintock's interpretations provide an understanding of the processes by which these male failures were/have been replaced by imagery of the feminine tears and maternal loss, it is also apparent that such gendered imagery was a major contributing factor that enhanced the mobilisation of the Cypriot men.

In 'Maps and Mother Goddesses in Modern India' Ramaswamy explores gendered depictions that figure on the map of India to respond to Anderson's question of 'what enables the nation to become an entity that causes so many millions of people "not so much to kill, as willingly to die for such limited imaginings"' (Ramaswamy, 109). Ramaswamy writes that 'bodyscapes', which portray the map of India as the body of the mother and goddess, are one such visual tool because 'they invite the citizen-subject who gazes upon them to relate to the nation not as some abstract, dead geographical space, but as a near-and-dear person, his personal goddess, his vulnerable mother, even a beloved lover' (Ramaswamy, 110). Similarly, the gendered depictions of Cyprus – as a captured sister, a weeping mother, a beloved daughter, a raped lover – also generate a familial and emotive attachment to the land that the Cypriot citizens are willing to kill and die for. The Cypriots die to free Cyprus not only because it is an enslaved family member, but also because that enslavement causes the ethnic ancestors an immense amount of torture: in her *Anthology* Niki Laddaki Philippou points to the Greek 'Ancestral screams' (Philippou, 179); in *Letter of Cyprus*, Yasin shows how the ancestors' 'Bones ache-shake' (Yasin, *Collected I*, 115). The ancestors from Mother Greece and Mother Ottoman-Turkey ethnically inscribed and gave Cyprus to the Cypriots as a gift; however, the ancestors or Mother Greece and Mother Turkey – if we consider the mothers in the above passages as also symbolic of Mother Greece or Mother Turkey mourning for the loss and displacement of her child Cyprus – are in anguish, enslaved and suffering, because the Cypriot offspring are losing and failing to preserve the ancestral heritage in Cyprus. Such gendered depictions of Cyprus, through familial and ancestral enslavement, are a forceful device that mobilised the ethnic-motherland nationalists willingly to sacrifice themselves for the liberation of Cyprus.

These gendered narratives show the process by which the ethnic-motherland nationalists construct Cyprus as an enslaved woman to signify the loss of ethnicity, the danger, unfamiliarity and openness, which resonate with Tuan's 'space'; however, they struggle against this condition by depicting Cyprus as family members with actual experiences to signify ethnic kinship and attachment, security, familiarity, closure and containment, which is the condition of Tuan's 'place'. In this process the nationalists manipulate the social dimensions, particularly directly lived experiences of Cypriot people, to transform the strangeness and difference in the feminised 'space' into a familiar familial feminised 'place' that they can know and control. Such a process gives way for Cyprus, which is depicted via a mental abstraction to generate the illusion of a concrete humanised social 'place'; this is understood via the dynamics of Lefebvre's 'mental space' and 'social space' by which the mental space that is conceived is a force that manipulates, secretes and dominates the social space that is lived.

It is the experience of 'place' that defines the liberation of Cyprus, and the ethnic-motherland nationalist literatures serve in this attempt to liberate Cyprus through various narrative processes that un-invent enslaved and endangered Cyprus to pre-invent or re-invent ethnically familiar and safe Cyprus. The next part of the chapter will analyse three of these processes that attempt to free enslaved Cyprus, all of which result in the sons of Cyprus willingly dying for the cause. This will lead to the final sections of the chapter, which will explore the narratives about these sons of Cyprus, who not only sacrificed themselves for liberation but who re-gendered Cyprus into a masculine martyr.

Free Our Enslaved Woman: 1,2,3

Free Our Enslaved Woman 1: Un-invent the 'Others' Inscription

The enslavement of familial and ancestral Cyprus is a result of the imperialist and other ethnic victories, and so in this ethnic production of Cyprus the writers set out to un-invent the island of these contaminating palimpsestic forces.

Greek-cypriot Demetris Chamboulides writes: 'The time has come for the Last Supper/ of the Enslaved of Cyprus' (Chamboulides, 17), and in *Closed Doors*, Montis asserts that this 'time' has come via

EOKA freedom-fighters who emptied Cyprus of British and Turkish contamination:

> THERE WAS ALSO A WAR against the English language – against English road signs, English street names, stores with English names. The war was to completely eliminate their language from our daily life, to eliminate anything that reminded us of the English, to uncover our language just as we uncovered the mosaic in saint Mary Aggeloktisi at Kition under the whitewash painted over it by the Turks. (Montis, *Closed*, 36)

This passage demonstrates that there was a war against colonial 'investment of culture in the construction of place' (Ashcroft et al, *Reader*, 391), and supports Carter's notion, in *The Road to Botany Bay*, that the colonisers were '"namers" [with the] intention to characterise a space' (Carter, 46), to turn empty space into place. Montis shows that the British read Cyprus as an empty space that they named and anglicised in order to make a –'road, a street, a store' – a place for themselves, which they know and control. This dynamic of naming is a colonising process that captures Cyprus in a language the British understand, but which the Cypriots cannot; a process that impels Ashcroft et al to confirm that the colonised is confronted with a 'lack of fit' between the place named by the imperial namers and the place that they actually experience. Consequently, Cyprus is made foreign to the Cypriots, causing a sense of dislocation from their historical homeland, which makes Cyprus an enslaved, unsafe and unhomely space. In light of this, Montis confirms that this is a war to un-invent the word and world created by the British by removing all these false names and burning away British history in Cyprus. Montis confirms that the war is against all palimpsestic inscriptions and languages, the British as well as the 'Turks', which will pave the way to free enslaved Cyprus by uncovering 'our Greek language' and inscriptions.

Similarly, in the poem '27–28 January 1958', Ulucamgil focusses on the two-day Turkish-cypriot anticolonial resistance that sought to free enslaved Cyprus by un-inventing British investments: 'The black curtain was whitening / Here since 1878 / The person that ripped this curtain/Was returning the poisonous knife /Bringing freedom' (Ulucamgil, *Complete*, 115). Ulucamgil defines British colonialism as a 'black curtain', which suggests the British did not civilise and enlighten the Cypriots but covered them with darkness, implying it subjected them to a dangerous space, where they were left in the dark unable to understand, see and move. The resistance sheds light on, 'whitens', Cyprus because it 'ripped' and emptied Cyprus of British 'poison' that was killing Turkishness, and restored its Turkish 'freedom' that Turkish-cypriots could command and understand.

Both Montis and Ulucamgil attempt to free enslaved Cyprus through a process that un-invents strange and dangerous British-Cyprus, which gives way for them to restore Cyprus into an ethnic place that they can know and control. The Cypriots set out to recover an ethnic place, different to the imperialist's by returning to an old language and civilisation that is familiar; this is a return to the former battles and heroes, that is to say returning to the 'fetish spectacle and object' as mentioned in earlier sections, where Greek-cypriots return to Ancient Greek, and the Turkish-cypriots to Ottoman journeys, battles and heroes.[23] In this liberation process there is some difference: the Cypriots simultaneously return to pre-colonial Ottoman/Ancient Greece, as well Modern Greece/ Turkey battles and heroes, through which they do not just *represent* the spectacle, but they bring them to life to the extent that Cyprus and the Cypriots become battles and heroes from the motherlands. So one can say that in this process they pre-invent themselves into pre-colonial ethnic existence, they pre-invent themselves into the fetish spectacle and object.

Free Our Enslaved Woman 2: Pre-invent Battles and Heroes

The nationalist narratives free enslaved Cyprus through re-enacting old and modern moments related to motherlands Greece or Turkey, through which the freedom-fighters pre-invent themselves and the land into heroes and battles from the ancestral and modern journeys – some of which have no association with the island. In becoming these heroic sons in battle from the motherland, they are not only considered eternal guides towards victory and liberation, but they reconfirm that the Cypriots are the offspring who inherited this glorious ethnic history. Through this pre-invention the ethnic-motherland nationalists simultaneously represent the kinship between Cypriots and the forefathers, and the Cypriots as the forefathers who pre-invent Cyprus into an ethnically enclosed mental place.

In *Closed Doors*, Montis focusses on the EOKA fighters, considered the national heroes of Cyprus, who imitated heroes of Ancient and Modern Greece along with the Byzantine Greeks. Montis focusses on the EOKA leader and renowned national hero, Georgios Theodoros Grivas, who pre-invented himself into the mythical warrior and legendary frontiersman, Digenis Akritas[24] by making his nom de guerre Digenis:

> Dighenis? [...] But really, who could have dared to take the name of the greatest hero [...]
>
> How could we have known, or even guessed, that for four years this EOKA and the leader Dighenis would capture not only our young minds, but the imagination of millions of people throughout the world? [...] who would ever have believed, that even our new Dighenis would also wrestle with Death and win? (Montis, *Closed*, 17)

Questioning the signature on the first EOKA leaflet, 'EOKA the leader, Dighenis', the narrator is trying to comprehend how anyone dare appropriate the name of one of the greatest Ancient heroes, whose legends of power – especially via the popular Akritic cycle of folk-songs – overwhelm Cyprus. Montis shows that the EOKA, and the leader Grivas in particular, proved worthy of this name because, like Digenis Akritas, he fought to rid the island of the foreign invaders. Montis confirms that Grivas is not only the off-spring who has inherited these characteristics of the greatest warrior, but he *is* the modern Digenis whose heroism is immortally inscribed all over Cyprus.

Montis shows that it is not only particular legendary heroes, but also Ancient battles that are pre-invented by the EOKA. The Battle of Thermopylae[25] is appropriated through the resistance of the EOKA fighter, Gregoris Afxentiou:

> Gregoris Afxentiou, already wounded, held off an entire English regiment for ten hours. The soldiers were puzzled and embarrassed. They were not prepared for Thermopylae [...]
>
> No one had told them how to handle a Thermopylae. (Montis, *Closed*, 94)

> There were 300 at Thermopylae, but Afxentiou was all alone. (Montis, *Closed*, 37)

The passage is referring to Afxentiou's (an EOKA hero ranked second to Grivas) heroism against British forces. In 1955, after vigorously attacking the British forces, Afxentiou was on the British wanted list with a reward of £5,000. Consequently, Afxentiou went into hiding in the Pentadaktylos and Trodos mountain range where he continued to serve and train the EOKA forces. On the 3 March 1957, the British were informed of Afxentiou's hideout near the Machairas Monastery, and they surrounded him, with orders that he surrender his arms; in reply to the British forces, Afxentiou quoted, the King of Sparta, Leonidas' words from the Battle of 'Thermopylae': 'come and take them' (*Molon Labe*). Afxentiou was able to defy the British forces for a long period of time, which resulted in the British burning Afxentiou to death whilst he hid in a cave. The narrator suggests that Afxentiou successfully pre-invents the Battle of Thermopylae, because, like the Spartans, Afxentiou was able to block the entire enemy; again, this confirms that Cypriots have not only inherited such heroic qualities from the ancestral glory days, but they are the warriors of those days. Afxentiou is the new modern Leonidas; however, here Montis shows that EOKA's heroism surpasses even those of immortal warriors because Afxentiou fought against the regiment all alone, whilst Leonidas had an army of 300.

This and other passages throughout *Closed Doors* show that the EOKA also pre-invent the Ancient Greek civilisation through habitually quoting Ancient Greek phrases, which is a vehicle to recover an archaic language that replaces the foreign tongue. This is a device to confirm that the false British or Turkish mappings cannot compete or un-map the almighty Greekness of Cyprus.

Closed Doors evidences that the EOKA simultaneously became modern Greek heroes:

> The Captain of caique, Koutalianos, occupied the largest part of our thoughts [...] because he shared (think of the coincidence) his name with a legendary hero [...] now it was Koutalianos who ripped up an entire tree. (Montis, *Closed*, 8–9)

The EOKA fighter Evangelos Koutalianos is compared to the modern Greek hero Panais Koutalianos. Evangelos was the captain of the small vessel, *Saint George*, that carried military supplies to the EOKA, and on 25 January 1955 the British authorities seized all supplies, arresting Evangelos and his crew. Panais Koutalianos (1847–1916) was a Greek hero, who also worked on a ship, and was considered to have immense power. Unlike Grivas, Evangelos did not appropriate the hero's name but was given the name upon birth, and the narrator emphasises this coincidence between Evangelos and Panais to confirm that they, like brothers, had the same surname, occupation and immortal heroism.

The Turkish-cypriot narratives also pre-invent former battles, and in 'My Heart's Country', Ulucamgil recreates the Ottoman conquest. Whilst Ulucamgil was a student in Turkey, he was called to serve in the resistance against the British and EOKA, and in the poem Ulucamgil defines his modern journey from Turkey to Cyprus as a 'legend' and 'freedom song', which is identical to the Ottomans' legendary journey of 1570 that the Cypriots sing with 'dehydrated lips' (Ulucamgil, *Complete*, 122). Ulucamgil suggests the Cypriots and Cyprus are dehydrating because they have been singing of this same journey since 1570, and because the Ottomans' blood that watered the island is being eliminated. Ulucamgil's poem confirms that he is not just the Ottoman offspring who has inherited their heroism, but he is the new Ottoman repeating the journey that will provide a refreshed freedom song to revive the dehydrated lands with the Turkish blood.

Ulucamgil also has numerous poems that pre-invent Modern Turkey's battles. In 'Response', Cyprus' struggle is depicted through the Battle of Izmir, when Ulucamgil writes: 'The waves of cracked land/Were in our eyes/Are in our eyes', and 'Kemal Pasha in/ Our eyes' (Ulucamgil, *Complete*, 179), to confirm that Turkish-cypriot freedom-fighters have become the Turkish army as well as the leader, Mustafa Kemal Ataturk, from the Izmir battle who cracked the land with their almighty march and eyes. In the poem 'Ataturk' (Ulucamgil, *Complete*, 99), Ulucamgil shows that the Turkish-cypriot resistance on 28 January 1958 is identical to the Turkish Battle of Canakkale. Consequently, Ulucamgil states that the land is no longer 'barren' and 'enslaved' because the new Ottoman, Canakkale and 'new Izmir warriors' will shed their blood (Ulucamgil, *Complete*, 179).

The Greek-cypriots and Turkish-cypriots pre-invent the Ancient and modern battles and heroes of the ethnic glory days to mould their own liberation struggle; this 'fetish spectacle' confirms that they have inherited the qualities of, and they *are*, the spiritual and powerful heroic ethnic figures that can resist the contaminative forces to free Cyprus. Here again the concrete lived experiences and specific details of the freedom-fighter are replaced by mythical and archaic abstractions – 'spectacles' – from a former time. Here, in line with McClintock's and Lefebvre's spatial considerations on fetish practices understood through Marx, the fetish spectacle is anthropomorphosised to the extent that it dominates over the actual freedom-fighters who fought and created liberated Cyprus. This ethnic-motherland nationalist process of construction, which replaces progressive social practices with a regressive mental practice, is the ethno-national device that is proposed to transform Cyprus from an enslaved dangerous foreign space into a liberated secure ethnic place. To enable fully the restoration and preservation of this Greek or Turkish Cyprus, the ethnic-motherland nationalists point to a process of re-invention that introduces a re-vision of the 'fetish spectacle and object' for the reconstruction of free Cyprus.

Free Our Enslaved Woman 3: Re-invent Nature for Mothers' Journey via a Balcony

The ethnic-motherland nationalists construct liberated Cyprus by re-inventing a new 'fetish spectacle' based on a journey from Greece or Turkey to Cyprus; the creation of this 'fetish spectacle' is determined by calling and accommodating the Modern Mothers to come free Cyprus. In the poetry collection *Moments*, Montis writes the Cypriots are calling and 'waiting for Athens' (Montis, *Moments*, 44); Ulucamgil and Yasin have numerous poems that wait and call upon Turkey. To create and accommodate the Modern Mothers' new journey, the writers re-invent the natural landscape and environment, particularly the sea, mountains and wind, into blood or spiritual fetish objects that are symbols of an opening or boundary within the route for the motherlands' new arrival into Cyprus. Though the Greek-cypriots and Turkish-cypriots respond very differently to these natural symbols, through them they remap Cyprus to re-invent a new modern journey and arrival from Greece or Turkey to Cyprus.

The Greek-cypriots define and associate the sea with freedom and unity, particularly an opening for Greece to arrive; the Turkish-cypriots associate the sea with imprisonment, a boundary that prevents Turkey from arriving. In many Greek-cypriot narratives, the sea is represented as the enabling device that brought the ancestors, and one that will bring Modern Greece to Cyprus. Angelides' historical poem 'Kyrenia Ship' shows that the sea is the device that enabled the ancestral journey from Rhodes to Cyprus, which evidences Ancient Greek inscription, and proves that this arrival can be repeated. Throughout *Venerable Lady the Sea*, Angelides confirms that the sea is an enabling force because it is imbued with an Ancient Greek spirit that generates a Greek network to open routes for Modern Greece. Angelides' poetry is overloaded with this Greek spirit in the sea[26]: the sea God Amphitrite, the Nereid sisters, and the Nymphs – Calypso, Aegle, Thetis, Panope and Doris – unite, spreading across the sea freely to dance and sing on the shores of Cyprus; Ancient Greek writers, Sappho and Alcaeus, swim and walk hand in hand with Aphrodite. Angelides confirms that as long as there is the sea, there will be freedom because Greece, the Greek islands and Cyprus are 'balconies' of the sea that unite through an immortal Greek network. The Cypriots can watch from the 'balcony', whilst the Greek spirit directs the Greek ships and missing ships to return to Cyprus. Angelides shows that it is mostly women that gaze from this 'balcony' and wait by the sea, expecting the return of sons who are at once the new heroes of the Modern Greece and the Cypriot freedom-fighters who have been missing. She confirms that through this Greek network and spirit the Greek heroes, like rivers, will pour into the sea to bring enosis and Greece to Cyprus.

Angelides' attitude to the sea resonates with the classical idea of the Mediterranean Sea as a connective and unitarian medium. In *The Corrupting Sea*, Peregrine Horden and Nicholas Purcell explore Mediterranean unity as figured in studies from antiquity by the Greek historians, and the element of its continuity into twentieth-century Mediterranean historiography. Horden and Purcell state that:

> The Greek historians of fifth century B.C. had already conceived of the past as a sequence of 'sea-powers' or thalassocracies, with the secret of imperial success residing in control of the connecting medium. The prime example was Athens in fifth century, binding together many dozens of scattered settlements across the Aegean Archipelago and on the inaccessible coasts of that sea, by virtue of being [...] 'the Power that rules the Sea'[...] What was ruled [...] was a network of communications. (Horden and Purcell, 24)

The passage shows that for the Ancient Greeks imperial success was determined by Mediterranean unity, achieved through having control of 'the connecting medium' and the communicative network between the surrounding islands in the sea. The Ancient Greeks believed that in the fifth century Athens ruled and had power over this Mediterranean unity and network.

Horden and Purcell demonstrate that the Ancient Greek conceptions of Mediterranean unity are maintained, which expand into twentieth-century readings of the Mediterranean through works by Mikhail Rostovtzeff, Henri Pirenne, Slomo Dov Goitein and Fernand Braudel. Horden and Purcell discuss these four influential writers with focus on their 'interactionist' approach that enlarges the Romantic idea of the Mediterranean. An 'interactionist' approach focusses on the cultural processes that produce the Mediterranean, with emphasis on the communication between people and politics to enable 'the unifying effect of shipping lanes' (Horden and Purcell, 37) that generate, as in antiquity, a grand 'network of "channels"' (Horden and Purcell, 32). The four writers argue that it is not only this network that is preserved from antiquity, but certain distinct characteristics, a 'Mediterranean type', also show an element of continuity from antiquity. This draws upon the idea of a Romantic Mediterranean, which reached its climax during the era of the Grand Tour in the eighteenth century, when elites travelling to the Mediterranean constructed romantic images of the Mediterranean as always positive and peaceful, with inhabitants that were 'peculiar natural people – lovers of open air, happy, hospitable, unreflective, their society simple and harmonious[...] refreshingly classless [. .]passionate' (Horden and Purcell, 29).

Angelides' poetics of the sea mould together both Ancient Greek and twentieth-century historiography on Mediterranean unity. In 'Kyrenia Ship', Angelides refers to the Ancient Greek network between Rhodes and Cyprus to point to the actual unitary network between the islands that gave the Ancient Greeks ultimate 'sea-power'. Similarly, through the narrative on the sea spirit, Angelides shows that there was an Ancient Greek connective and communicative medium between the islands or 'balconies' – Cyprus, the Greek islands and Greece – in the sea. Consequently, Angelides suggests that there is a network, unity and spirit in the Mediterranean Sea that the Greeks continue to rule over. Angelides proves this through the interactionist approach with a Romantic ideal: in 'Kyrenia Ship' Angelides elaborates on the shipping lanes and trade network between 'Rhodes' and Cyprus, pointing towards the sea network Greece had during the eighteenth and nineteenth centuries, with 'naval units manned by Greeks [that] virtually controlled the Aegean sea [...] [with] commercial [networks] between Greece and Germany, Venice.[...] Greek merchant marines became the commercial carriers of most shipping in the Eastern Mediterranean and Black sea' (Kazamias, 10). In other poems the sea is defined through the communication between the sea creatures characterised as harmonious, peaceful and hospitable, which resonates with the Mediterranean type drawn from the Romantic Mediterranean. Angelides' poems demonstrate that Mediterranean unity is a model preserved from antiquity, which not only proves the connection between Ancient Greeks and modern Cypriots, but confirms an immortal and unbreakable network between the 'balconies' – Cyprus, the Greek islands and Greece – that unite as the super Greek spirit and power in the sea.

The Greek-cypriots welcome the Mediterranean Sea with narratives dominated by this 'balcony metaphor' because it confirms Greek unity, power and the possibility of a new journey and arrival. In contrast, the Turkish-cypriots' narratives reject the sea and represent it as a barrier that blocks the route and arrival of Turkey. Consequently, many Turkish-cypriots eliminate the sea between Turkey and Cyprus so they can geographically unite: as Ulucamgil confirms in 'For Ataturk', many Turkish-cypriots have 'Told the sea to fuck off numerous times/From the middle' (Ulucamgil, *Complete*, 104). They seek to destroy the sea: 'I see that freedom will destroy the salty water' (Ulucamgil, *Complete*, 106); or as Yasin writes, they re-invent nature: 'I become a rainbow and set up a bridge/From Cyprus to Ankara' (Yasin, *Collected I*, 90) to create a path that will accommodate Turkey's arrival. The Turkish-cypriots' negative attitude to the sea can also be compared to a former moment and its subsequent traditions, which has relevance and connects them to their primordial or early modern history and genesis; this moment is the pre-Islamic and Islamic as well as the Ottoman relationship to the sea. In *The [European] Other in Medieval Arabic Literature and Culture: Ninth-Twelfth Century AD (New Middle Ages)*, Nizar Hermes points to the negative attitude depicted in pre-Islamic and classical Arabic literature, which 'emphasises the Arabic leitmotif of *al-khawf min-al-bahr* (the fear of the sea) quite common in classical Arabic and *jahilli* (pre-Islamic) poetry' (Hermes, 101). In a footnote to this section Hermes states:

> in pre-Islamic poetry, the sea was [...] a metaphor of fear, uncertainty, separation, and sorrow. Despite numerous Quranic injunctions to take to the sea, in several aspects, the pre-Islamic fear of the sea did not vanish in classical Arabic literature. (Hermes, 199)

This attitude towards the sea is not only depicted in literary text but also in Arabic traditions – as Horden and Purcell confirm 'The Arab tradition portrayed the sea as poor, alien and uninviting' (Hurden and Purcell, 12) – as well as in Islamic practices and texts, which are explored by Xavier de Planhol in *Islam and the Sea: the Mosque and the Sailor 7th–20th Century.*[27] Planhol states that 'Islamic history reveals a profound inaptitude and revulsion for the sea' and 'Islam was hostile to the sea' (Conrad, 125–26). Planhol shows evidence of this attitude by citing *hadiths*: 'The sea, the prophet is supposed to have said, "is hell, and Satan reigns over its waters"' (Planhol, *Islam*, 144), which confirm that 'for Muslims the sea was the "throne of Satan"' (Conrad, 126). Planhol argues that this attitude is because maritime culture gives way to practices and behaviour –'pragmatic, erratic, non-normative ill-defined, poorly structured and weakly integrated, and susceptible to rapid adaptation; [...] it is ambiguous, excessive ostentatious and prodigal, competitive, adventurous, and irregular' – that are not fitting or compatible with Islam, which is 'a faith stressing submission, and Islamic society is a staid society of law and precise regulation of personal conduct that rejects excess and the wanton pursuit of personal adventure' (Conrad, 125–26). In light of this incompatibility between maritime culture and Islam, Planhol states that it is not possible to be a good Muslim on the sea, and because of this, 'Never has a Muslim power been able to establish an enduring presence on the seas. Never has Muslim society been able to familiarize itself intimately with the sea' (Conrad, 126). Planhol claims that of all the Muslim societies it was only the Ottoman Empire that had great opportunities to be a force at sea, but they failed to capitalise on them (Conrad, 126). This commentary points out and suggests that the maritime weakness of the late Ottoman Empire in comparison to the maritime power of Europe, particularly during the European colonial venture, is one of the reasons for the fall of the Ottoman Empire, by which it became the 'sick man of Europe' who lost financial control and a lot of territory.

In light of this history of aversion to the sea, it can be argued that the Turkish-cypriot ethnic-motherland nationalists loathe the sea not only because of their relationship to pre-Islamic, Islamic or Arabic practices, but more so because they agree the sea aggravates the weakness of the Ottoman Empire, and it is the sea that enabled the British Empire to gain control and rule over Cyprus – thus resulting in the end of Ottoman-Cyprus connection and kinship.

The Turkish-cypriots reject the sea; however, like the Greek-cypriots, they engage with a 'balcony metaphor' for the Modern Mother's arrival. The Turkish-cypriots' 'balcony metaphor' engages with mountains to signify arrival, freedom and union, whilst Greek-cypriots associate the mountain with imprisonment. In 'These Mountains' Angelides writes:

These mountains obstruct my view of the horizon.
These mountains of Asia Minor
Constrict
[...]
wherever I turn, block
the way to my Dreams.
They diminish my world.
They diminish my joy.
They block the approaches.
They block the exits.
[...]

torture me
[…]
How can I fly kites of hope
[…]
These mountains encircle my native lands. (Angelides, *Venerable*, 27)

Angelides is referring to the Taurus mountains in Turkey that can be seen from Cyprus, as imprisonment – 'constrict', 'block', 'diminish' and 'torture' – because they represent Turkey and the Turks, confirming the closeness that enabled the Ottoman and 1974 conquests. Through the Taurus, the dream and joy of having a free Greek Cyprus and the arrival of Greece is diminished because they, both the mountains and Turks, block the route and have 'invaded' the island.

The Turkish-cypriot narratives, most of which were written before 1974, are dominated by representations of the mountains to symbolise Turkey's closeness and potential arrival; they are a symbol of freedom whose appearance they joyously welcome and praise from their balconies. In *Letter of Cyprus*, poem 'III' and 'IV' Yasin writes:

With happiness your eyes shine
The Toros[28] Mountain opposite, right opposite,
The land of warriors and martyrs:
Our Great Motherland, dearest Anatolia…

With you we watched them my friend,
[…]
When my eyes filled with tears
And I explained my dream:
[…]
Tomorrow the Turkish army is coming… (Yasin, *Collected I*, 108–109)

Yasin is recording a moment when the appearance of the Toros mountains brought both happiness because they evidence that the 'Great Motherland' is 'right opposite' and can arrive to free enslaved Cyprus within seconds; and tears because they evidence the physical reality that the 'motherland' is absent and Cyprus continues to be enslaved. Even though the reality at the time was that Turkey was not present in Cyprus, Yasin's reference to Toros and his dream confirm the longing will come to an end and the Turks will arrive.

In the poem 'The Roads to My Homeland' Urkiye Mine Balman writes, 'Explain my homeland to me/ Explain the roads to my homeland', and shows that Toros' appearance from her balcony, 'Dawn in Toros/ I see from my window' (Balman, 72), is the road to the homeland, to Turkey. In referring to 'Dawn in Toros', Balman points to the clear vision and closeness of Turkey seen from Cyprus, which is enhanced further in 'I saw the Toros':

> Straight like marble
> [...]
> In front of us, the distance has shortened [...]
> Goosebumps [...]
> Like waves, my soul overjoyed. (Balman, 49–50)

Balman defines Toros's texture, 'like-marble', to suggest she is touching the mountains; here confirming that the distance between Cyprus and Turkey is so short they can touch each other, and the longing for geographical unification and Turkish arrival is practically a reality. Both Yasin and Balman engage with the Toros mountains seen from their balconies to map the route from Turkey to Cyprus as open, short, clear, easy and close to being a reality.

Similarly, the wind is also symbolised as Turkey: for the Greek-cypriots the wind is a destructive force and barrier, for the Turkish-cypriots it is freedom and arrival. In the poem 'Ammohostos Buried in Sand' Angelides writes that we Greek-cypriots 'bolted our houses and/ Our hearts/ To keep out the high winds' (Angelides, *Mirror*, 52), suggesting their struggle to keep the Ottomans and 1974 Turks out of Cyprus. Unfortunately, the Turks arrived, and in the poem 'The Fate of Men', Angelides confirms 'the north wind blew/ bringing total devastation' (Angelides, *Venerable*, 63). Consequently, in the prose *Streets*, Angelides shows that their homes and '[t]heir doors and windows are battered by the wind in Winter and cry endlessly' (Angelides, *Streets*, 55).

The Turkish-cypriot writers engage with the wind within pre-1974 contexts to symbolise the open route for the Turkish arrival. In 'From Cyprus to Ataturk' Yasin states:

> He is now like the faithful wind
> Secretly quietly blowing to all four sides
> And when a piece of this wind
> Reaches the babyland
> I inhale to my lungs
> And become drunk. (Yasin, *Collected I*, 90)

The passage shows that through the wind, Ataturk, the father of the Turks, and Turkishness arrives in the 'babyland' Cyprus, which provides Cypriots a life force. In 'Flag Ceremony in Lefkosa' Yasin states that 'Ataturk is waiting for a wind/To secretly quietly blow from Anatolia' (Yasin, *Collected I*, 100) to suggest Ataturk expects Turkey to arrive in and free Cyprus.

Both the Greek-cypriots and Turkish-cypriots engage with the natural environment and landscape of Cyprus, which suggests spatial awareness for the construction of place. In this process, however, rather than depicting the physical and social space, so the sensual or directly lived experiences and concrete practices with nature, they depict nature as a mental space conceived, contained and organised into objects that will accommodate the journey and arrival of the Modern Mother. They re-invent the sea, mountain and wind into a mode of transportation, particularly an ethnically ordered network, bridge or barrier, which gives way for the island to be constructed into a concrete 'balcony' that looks towards the open route for the journey and arrival of the Mother into Cyprus. In this way, the ethnic-motherland nationalists re-produce familiar spatial practices with routes that resonate with the 'ancestral journey', thus enabling the re-invention of the journey, arrival and unification between Mother Greece or Mother Turkey and her Baby Cyprus. The arrival and unification are frequently instantiated through a magnificent entry or eruption of new masculine warriors from Greece and Turkey into Cyprus, resulting in Cyprus being signified as male.

In *Closed Doors*, Montis elaborates on the arrival of the Greek warriors:

> We saw before us once again the Greek revolution, no longer in lifeless print with beautiful, colored pictures but alive, raw, and fierce–thundering with the force of the eyebrows of General Kolokotronis [...] thundering with the power of the broken sword of the warrior Dhiakos[...] Inn of Gravia, Missolonghi, and Maniaki[...] horse whinnied[...] the air filled with battle cries [...] the most breathtaking repetition of history. (Montis, *Closed*, 6)

Montis points to heroic figures – Greek General Theodosis Kolokotronis (1770–1843) and commander Athanasios Dhialos – and battles – 'Inn of Gravia (1821), Missolonghi (1826), and Maniaki' (1825) – from the Greek War of Independence against the Ottoman Empire (1821–1828), here confirming that these earlier heroic leaders, which dominated every Greek-cypriot child's imagination, coupled with new warriors and powerful horses, arrive and join forces with the Greek-cypriots to map a free Greek Cyprus.

In 'From Cyprus to Ataturk', Yasin also exhibits the arrival of Turkey, when after his call Cyprus pulsates with Turkish war heroes:

> Echoes of my voice
> I notice the sound from the Toros Mountains
>
> The Mountains respond to my call
> A radiant light touches the darkness
> [...]

Soldiers with naked swords pass the sky.
Warriors pass, martyrs pass

Bayraktar passes, Cambolat passes
[...]
A star-like dawn opens in the horizon
Rearing up its Arabian horse to gallop fully
Majestic like the mountain, strong like the mountain
With all the victories he won
Ataturk passes smiling. (Yasin, *Collected I*, 91)

As the narrator watches the ghastly sea, he calls Ataturk, after which the Toros Mountains repeat his call and the Turks wake up and arrive. The Turkish military, 'soldiers, warriors and martyrs', Ottoman heroes, 'Bayraktar and Cambolat', and Ataturk arrive and are inscribed in the sky and landscape. In 'Our Father Left Us Orphaned', Yasin remaps Cyprus into Ataturk by stating: 'You're on our mountain our plain/ You're in our city our village [...] You are the flag [...] the soil [...] the homeland' (Yasin, *Collected II*, 206).

The three processes to free enslaved Cyprus – un-inventing Others' inscriptions, pre-inventing the spectacle of warriors and battles and re-inventing a new journey and arrival – provide for the successful recovery, liberation and production of an ethnically closed and complete mental Cyprus. In this process the narratives point specifically to the powerful men who willingly sacrifice themselves, such that Cyprus figures as a newly masculinised warrior from the motherlands. This masculinisation of Cyprus is enhanced fully and further through the discourse on the Cypriot martyred son, which gives way to the ultimate recovery of the gift Cyprus that was given to the Cypriots from the Mothers. Cyprus is fully restored to its former ethnic glory; the island is restored to be the Greek or Turkish martyred son of Mother Greece and Mother Turkey.

Well Done Our 'Martyred' Son!

The ethnic-motherland nationalist literatures are dominated by narratives of the EOKA and TMT soldiers, which serve to immortalise the freedom-fighters and martyrs in relation to the land. These narratives are distinct in that the actual EOKA and TMT soldiers and the island, particularly the freedom-fighters' lived struggles and the physical landscape, are immortalised. The writings confirm that the fighters must be immortalised because they were the central figures, at the frontline, who struggled and died to recover the ancestral gift, Cyprus, to its original ethnic glory, emptied Cyprus of all palimpsestic spatial history, freed enslaved – ancestral, mother, sister, daughter – Cyprus to unite the actual and enosis or taksim national family. These narratives show that the freedom-fighters were able, as in the case of Ireland, to 'affirm their manhood in the process of redeeming the mothercountry, and restoring her to her youthful beauty' (Innes, 10). Whilst Ireland is often gendered as the mothercountry, Cyprus, as shown, is depicted as different women as well as male warriors from Greece and Ottoman-Turkey; however, like the Irish sons, the Cypriot sons are the agents who restore Cyprus. Through the EOKA and TMT sons, Cyprus is produced as an ethnically liberated place, and to make sure that they are not forgotten the literature immortalises a martyr discourse that results in the production of Cyprus as 'our martyred son'.

The martyred Cypriot sons imbue the land, and through them the whole of Cyprus is renamed and changed. Throughout the literary texts, knowing and naming the EOKA and TMT martyr soldiers are pivotal for the national project, which, as pointed out by Bryant, contrasts with Anderson's claims regarding the necessity for the 'Unknown Soldier' to remain undiscovered. In the narratives of the TMT and more so of the EOKA (Bryant does not mention the EOKA in her study), there is a forceful shift into naming and identifying the 'known martyred Soldiers', who are often associated with place names or land. In this process of naming and knowing the 'soldiers', and associating them with place names, there is a difference between the Cypriot narratives: whilst the Turkish-cypriots assert that knowing *all* TMT martyrs and representing their blood in the whole land is crucial, the Greek-cypriot narratives, like the Turkish-cypriots' Ottoman narratives,[29] are overloaded and dominated by naming specific soldiers and associating them with particular place names.

In the Greek-cypriot's *A Poetry and Prose Anthology of the 1955–1958 EOKA Liberation Struggle*, Andreas Angelopoulos' foreword confirms that the 'heroism, death-defiance and self-sacrifice of its freedom-fighters brought moral grandeur to the cause, placing it among the most noble and selfless struggles ever fought in the name of freedom' (Angelopoulos, 11). Consequently, the EOKA were a source of inspiration for the Cypriot writers and there is an overload of literary works on the EOKA martyr: a selection from this and other Anthologies will show the literary process by which Cyprus is imbued and re-mapped as these EOKA martyrs.

Angelides' epic poem *Pentadaktylos My Son* is narrated through a mother who is mourning and honouring her martyred sons. During the anticolonial and the 1974-partition struggle, many EOKA fighters served, hid and died on or around the Pentadaktylos mountain range, and as a result Angelides confirms that the EOKA martyrs have been inscribed, and are now the Pentadaktylos:

> Five peaks, five hearts.
> And Digenis and Zedros
> [...]

And Matsis and my gallant son.
[...]
Mount Pentadaktylos changes its covering
But not its heart.
[...] And my son standing upright. (Angelides, *Pentadaktylos*, 35–37)

The Pentadaktylos [Five-Finger] mountain range has five sharp peaks, like a hand, and Angelides inscribes each peak with the name of an EOKA martyr to show that together they re-map the mountain. Two of the peaks, possibly peak four and one, are mapped with Digenis, the Ancient Byzantine warrior, whose legends give the mountain its name, and more so Georgios Grivas, the founder and highest-ranking official of the EOKA. The second peak is Zedros, the code name for Gregory Afxentiou, because he was ranked the second EOKA official. Angelides also maps Afxentiou into his birthplace and village 'Lysi' (Angelides, *Pentadaktylos*, 25), and immortalises him as the 'Golden Eagle of Kalorka' (Angelides, *Pentadaktylos*, 5), a village near Pentadaktylos where he trained the EOKA whilst in hiding from the British. The third peak is mapped with the first EOKA member, Kyriakis Matsis, who was imprisoned by the British in 1956, but escaped and continued fighting on the Pentadaktylos mountains. Angelides also inscribes Matsis into the town 'Dikoma', where he was killed by the British in 1958. The fifth and final peak is mapped with the narrator's gallant son, symbolic of all the Greek-cypriot EOKA sons that died for Cyprus. Even though all the gallant sons are of significance, it is Grivas, Afxentiou and Matsis that are a major symbol in Greek-cypriot literature; one, if not all, of these EOKA heroes is mapped onto the landscape of Cyprus.

Angelides confirms that even though the Pentadaktylos mountain 'changes its covering', the five sons 'stand upright' strong and unchanged because their heroic hearts and spirits are forever mapped in the mountains. The 'coverings' here are the inscriptions of the Turks, which torture Pentadaktylos' body:

How he suffered when the invaders
Desecrated him with their emblem. (Angelides, *Pentadaktylos*, 5)

Do you see how they have nailed the crescent symbol
Upon Mount Pentadaktylos? (Angelides, *Pentadaktylos*, 23)

This passage affirms that the son, 'Pentadaktylos', suffered when the Turkish 'Invaders' inscribed emblems onto it, and in an endnote to this section Angelides writes, 'trees were cut down to open space for these emblems, and this is the desecration of Pentadaktylos'. Angelides is referring to Turkey's national slogan 'How Happy are those who say "I am a Turk"' that was carved on the slope of Pentadaktylos in 1984.

This slogan represents the Kemalist ideology for the Republic of Turkey promoted against the Ottoman slogans 'long live the sultans, caliph or Sheikh', which Ataturk first used on 29 October 1933 (Republic Day) in his speech for the tenth Anniversary of the Republic, and in 1972, the Republic added this motto to the existing 'student pledge'. This national slogan is repeated by every Turkish and Turkish-cypriot student on a daily basis, and is inscribed all over Turkey and Cyprus, and, as Angelides states, an 'emblem' that figures on the mountains in Cyprus. Another Turkish 'covering' that Angelides refers to is the flag of Turkey and the TRNC, the 'crescent symbol', which has been physically mapped onto and thus 'desecrated' the 'son' Pentadaktylos.[30] Angelides repeats the lines 'my son stands upright' and 'Pentadaktylos changes its covering/but not the heart' to emphasise that the Turkish inscription may destroy the body, but it cannot destroy the EOKA son and their spirit immortally mapped in and that are the Pentadaktylos and Cyprus.

Numerous Greek-cypriot poems map the EOKA heroes onto Pentadaktylos; however, the Trodos mountains are also frequently associated with the EOKA sons. In the poem 'Grigoris Afxendiou'[31] Montis inscribes Afxentiou onto both the Pentadaktylos and Trodos mountains: 'That Morning/one man was destined to change the name of the mountains' (Montis, *Faces*, 17), suggesting his heroism has re-mapped and renamed both mountains to 'Afxentiou'. In the EOKA Anthology, like Montis' poem, numerous poems share titles with the names of EOKA heroes. As example 'Gregoris Afxentiou' by Nikos Kranidiotis depicts the EOKA martyr beyond just the landscape, and inscribes him everywhere in Cyprus. He is the air the Cypriots inhale and sky they see, because, 'inscrib[ed] with burning letters across the skies/of glory – your name, Afxentiou'; the energy that gives life – 'You've become one with the Sun'; the water – 'morning dew' – that replenishes the fertility of the land; he is the 'earthly soil' and the 'burning bush of the land of Machairas'. Kranidiotis consistently returns to images of fire to confirm that it did not bring death to Afxentiou, but instead created an immortal powerful flame: 'you've become one with the fire' (Kranidiotis, *EOKA*, 39–40).

The Turkish-cypriot narratives also immortalise the freedom-fighters through 'knowing' and mapping them onto Cyprus; however, they do not have a shared master narrative of particular hero names and place names[32]– there is not a Turkish-cypriot equivalent to the Greek-cypriots' 'Afxentiou, Matsis or Digenis'. Instead, the Turkish-cypriots record and immortalise the case of *all* the martyrs: there is an overload of different Turkish names to suggest that knowing *all* the fighters is important, and the 'known' fighters' blood pours into and maps the whole of Cyprus. The narratives prioritise blood because, like the Ottomans', it not only joins the land in matrimony, but it unites with the Ottoman blood to produce Cyprus as the masculine Turkish land of martyrs.

In most poems, the blood of the Ottoman, TMT and 1974 martyrs unites in the land, and the anthology *National Poetry from the TRNC* is dominated by such blood narratives. The anthology is a collection of poems selected for the 'National Anthem and March' competition,[33] and Mehmet Levent's 'Freedom and Peace Anthem', Oktay Oksuzoglu's 'Republic', and Mukadder Uckan's 'My Flag' are examples that map Cyprus with this united blood:

> Hail to you Mucahit, Mehmets Hail!
> Hail to the martyrs' blood that gushes from this land. (Levent, 'Freedom', 1)
>
> In this homeland kneaded by the blood of the martyrs. (Oksuzoglu, 'Republic', 2)
>
> With their blood the martyrs have given you colour. (Uckan, 'My Flag', 41)

These passages assert that it is the blood of every single martyr that 'gushes' and is 'kneaded' all over the landscape: the 'Mucahit' is the blood of the TMT Turkish-cypriot freedom-fighters, the 'Mehmet' is the blood of the 1974 Turkish soldiers, and the martyrs' blood suggests all martyrs including the Ottoman ancestors' blood. Many of the poems 'knead' the TMT with the Turkish and Ottoman blood, to confirm that TMT are as honourable and have united with the ethnic fathers and brothers who poured their blood for Turkishness. In numerous Turkish-cypriot poems, as shown in Uckan's poem, this union of the martyrs' blood is associated with the Turkish flag, whereby the outpouring of blood gives the Turkish flag greater red 'colour' – together the blood refreshes Turkishness imbued in the flag and Cyprus.

There are numerous poems that focus on the new, particularly TMT, blood that is mapped in the land, and this emphasis often begins with the bloodshed during '27–28 January 1958' when the British forces killed seven Turkish-cypriots. In Ulucamgil's 'A Wish' and Yasin 's *Letter of Cyprus*, both writers record the heroism of these seven martyrs. Ulucamgil states that 'Since 27th January' the freedom-fighters have 'By dying/Maybe to be water with the honourable field/Being blood under the raining sky' (Ulucamgil, *Complete*, 116). Here confirming that the seven martyrs were the first to shed fresh blood onto the fields of Cyprus since the Ottoman martyrs of 1570, so as to suggest that their blood 'waters' and 'refreshes' these honourable fields full of Ottoman martyrs, and inspired all the other freedom-fighters to shed blood and die for Cyprus. In *Letter of Cyprus* (Yasin, *Collected I*, 104–25), Yasin also writes about the 'Day 27 January' by giving more details of the seven martyrs and those that followed, through the schema of naming and mapping. Yasin writes the names 'Ahmet and Hasan', and refers to the place names 'Magusa and Lefkosa', which suggests the 27 January martyrs Hasan Bondigo and Ibrahim Ahmet or Mustafa Ahmet who were killed in Magusa and Lefkosa. Yasin also lists other Turkish names,

'Ismail, Ulus, Kubilay', and places, 'Limassol, Girne' that are listed besides the seven martyrs. This dynamic of naming demonstrates that the seven martyrs, 'Hasan', 'Mustafa Ahmet', 'Ibrahim Ahmet' and the four other martyrs who died in either 'Lefkosa' or 'Magusa', directed the rest, 'Ismail, Ulus, Kubilay...' who died and mapped the whole of Cyprus.

Both the Greek-cypriots and the Turkish-cypriots show the significance of immortalising the freedom-fighters for the national project: whilst the Greek-cypriots commemorate a few EOKA fighters and inscribe their spirit into particular places and landscapes, the Turkish-cypriots record *all* the names of TMT fighters and inscribe their blood into the whole land. Even though the Greek-cypriots and Turkish-cypriots employ different narrative processes of mapping the freedom-fighters into Cyprus, both read and reconstruct Cyprus into the martyred sons. These narratives capture the actual struggles of the EOKA and TMT heroes coupled with the concrete landscape of Cyprus to show intimate attachment and deep kinship between freedom-fighters and the land for the construction of a place. In this process, however, the concrete practices and land are still determined by mental abstractions, by which the Cypriot males' Turkish blood or Greek spirit construct Cyprus, transforming it from an endangered enslaved woman to an ethnically secure martyred son. The ethnic-motherland nationalists demonstrate that the freedom-fighters have taken responsibility to restore, protect and preserve Cyprus, the ancestral gift, to its ethnic glory; they have successfully restored Cyprus to be the Greek or Turkish child of Mother Greece or Turkey. In this process of production, however, the ethnic-motherland nationalists have in fact emptied the Cypriot males of power and agency by depicting Cyprus as dependent child controlled by the Mothers' order and praise.

The Greek-cypriot and Turkish-cypriot narratives are overloaded with national honour and praise for the martyrs who sacrificed themselves for liberation; this is frequently signified through the actual mothers of the martyred sons and Mother Greece and Turkey. In 'Today as I Laid Eyes on You', Antonou Afxentiou, the actual mother of Gregoris Afxentiou, writes about her martyred son, and in 'Mother of Cyprus' Andis Pernaris writes about a Greek-cypriot mother who loses both her sons in the EOKA struggle:

> It is shameful for the mother of a hero such as this to cry,
> her tears will take away from her son the glory he should enjoy
> the Homeland is worth the life of my son [...]
> [...]
> And I shall stand a mother like all Greek mothers. (Afxentiou, 135)

> Full of pride, her voice she raises:
> "You are worth it, Homeland, even if they are my children,

> and not because there are only two, even if there were forty.
> [...]
> The Homeland needs bravery; Freedom needs animals for slaughter
> You must not let foreigners see your eyes in tears.' (Pernaris, 'Mother', 95)

Antonou is honoured by her son's actual sacrifice, where she stands, like every Greek mother should, with pride not tears. Similarly, the mother in Pernaris' narrative is honoured by the sacrifice of her two sons, and refusing to weep she proudly calls out that she willed the sacrifice, and would give up more sons if she had them. The mothers are neither enslaved nor tortured, but instead are proud and strong, guiding all the Greek mothers of Cyprus to offer their sons for the freedom of Cyprus. The mothers in both poems are also symbolic of Mother Greece, who praises the EOKA sons for sacrificing themselves for the freedom of Cyprus. Mother Greece's praise of the EOKA sons is also directly referred to in many narratives; in the 'EOKA Hymn' Papachrysostomou writes, 'mother Hellas waits to crown/ all her children' (Papachrysostomou, 71) – the EOKA martyrs are the sons of the Greek ancestors, who sacrificed their lives for Greekness in Cyprus, and for this they will be crowned the heroes of the Greek race.

The Turkish-cypriots also represent this praise and honour of the Mother. In Yasin's 'Red Coronation' (Yasin, *Completed I*, 134–39) a proud mother stands by the grave of her martyred son, and recounts the heroic biography and journey that made him and other Cypriot sons honourable Turks. The narrator records the first words that her son, and all heroic sons write: 'TURKEY' and 'TURKEY IS MY HOMELAND' and 'THE CRESCENT-STAR IS MY FLAG' (135); here, Yasin shows that identification and communication of Turkishness is the foundation of all Turkish-cypriot heroic becoming. The mother then narrates how proud she was when her son went to Turkey to continue his education: this refers to the vast number of Turkish-cypriots who study in Turkey, and all those who aspired to send their children to be educated and moulded in Turkey, so they could, like the son in the poem, fall in love with the motherland and die for Turkishness. Finally, the mother in 'Red Carnation' records the return of her son by emphasising the 'call to service' – the 1950s–1960s call when all Turkish-cypriot men abroad had to return to serve in the ethnic war against the British and Greek-cypriots – and his moment of death. The mother confirms that she willed her son's sacrifice for the freedom of enslaved Cyprus, and states, 'I believe your blood did not pour for nothing/How beautiful you stand in your grave my martyred baby/With white almonds red carnation/ Like a piece of the Turkish flag' (139). The mother honours his sacrifice because through it he is mapped as one with the Turkish nation and flag, and has inscribed this Turkishness into 'almond trees' and 'carnations' – he has mapped and become Turkish-cyprus.

Mother Turkey also frequently honours the martyrs, voiced through the almighty representative of Turks and motherland, Ataturk. In Yasin's 'Mustafa Kemal Says', Ataturk says:

> Welcome my sons,
> Welcome to my soil
> With your blood
> You have given colour to my flag
> Now with hope I look to tomorrow. (Yasin, *Collected II*, 230)

Here the martyred fighters join the land of the Turks, where they become the sons of Father Ataturk and Mother Turkey. Yasin suggests that through the TMT martyrs, Ataturk has been made proud and has hope for the future of the Turkish nation in both Cyprus and Turkey.

Both narratives seek to show that gendering and mapping Cyprus as the martyred son frees the enslavement of the actual mother/women, or the motherlands' ancestral inscription in Cyprus. Through the martyrs' sacrifice and insemination in Cyprus, the mothers or women are no longer enslaved, weeping, screaming, but are proud, free and strong because the ancestral gift, the island's ethnic glory is restored; the ethnic child has been restored. The narratives indicate that the role of women, the Cypriot mothers in particular, is to nurture and rear such heroic martyrs for the ethnic re-production of Cyprus. This discourse of the Cypriot martyred sons was one of the most powerful devices that encouraged the mobilisation because it not only promised to free enslaved Cyprus, but also showed that almighty Mother Greece and Mother Turkey, or their representatives – Ataturk – were made proud, and the Cypriots, particularly the ethnic-motherland nationalists, would take any measure to hear the Almighty Ethnic One say, *Well done My Son*!

Conclusion: Cyprus as Hermaphrodite

The ethnic-motherland nationalist identification is determined by the production of Greece-cyprus and Turkey-cyprus, which is built on the foundation of deeply competing narratives in spatial solidarity.

This chapter has outlined the literary process by which the ethnic-motherland nationalists produce a 'place' for themselves. The analysis has demonstrated that even though the Cypriots have separately and competitively invented, experienced, read and constructed, in the process of production they have followed a parallel quest and used very similar, if not identical practices to systematically organise and build this enslaved-liberated place. In this process they are extremely selective, using only those practices that can produce an ethnically homogeneous place. Throughout this decolonial moment of nationalising, the nationalists reclaim their agency to struggle against the imperial and Other ethnic mappings, through a process of compartmentalised 'invention' that gives them a 'closed zone' with total knowledge, command and control. This is a Tuanian closed complete 'place' determined by symbols and substances that capture 'spatial awareness and knowledge', 'intimate attachment' and 'deep kinship' to provide 'permanence and security' to the Cypriots who see and struggle against the condition of space. In this process they read and construct, in Lefebvre's terms, an abstract 'mental space' that is only conceived and idealistic, without concrete 'physical space' that can be touched, or a 'social space' that is or can be actually lived and felt. Here the writers create a place through capturing intimate attachments and detailed knowledge of spatial and social practices, which are based on manipulating socially lived and physically perceived experiences through the mentally conceived; thus, a dialectic between concrete reality and mental abstractions, where the latter masters, reduces, secretes and appropriates the former, particularly through a gendered process of production. This escapist mental and gendered production of place makes and breaks the national project. It was and often is the dominant pole of address that moves the Cypriot masses to fabricate and to be fabricated by an ethnically exclusive national place. It is apparent, however, that in this national building project, the nationalists cannot control the complexity of the 'spatial production' that gives way to truth, particularly Lefebvre's 'truth of space' (*Production*, 297–400), wherein secreted processes are alive with a pulse, which put the whole ethnic-motherland nationalist project of a closed fixed 'place' in immense danger of being contradicted and exposed.

This national project has been exposed as a gendered production shared by Greek-cypriots and Turkish-cypriots, through which the case of Cyprus is distinctly modelled on a multiplicity of spatial references and genders. Here the chapter showed gendering as the most powerful symbol and practice because through it the ethnic-motherland nationalists produce a place that escapes the colonial and postcolonial actualities of Cyprus: the national struggles gave the Cypriots an independent country, but did not concretise the ethno-national place they desired; however, in both literatures, gendering with arcane and archaic blood or spiritual substances has enabled the Cypriots to conceive Mother Turkey or Mother Greece in union with child Cyprus. The nationalist Cypriots 'prove' and 'factualise' – attempt to render fantasy as fact – this ethnically organic national family into a fixed enclosed place; however, in this process, it is only Mother Greece and Mother Turkey who remain sexually steadfast, and, unfortunately, for the ethnic-motherland nationalists, Cyprus is neither fixed nor bounded but undergoes multiple sex changes – implying that Cyprus is intersexed. Cyprus is inescapably a Hermaphrodite, possibly as 'biological-historical fact' when considering that the term derives from Hermaphroditos, the son of Hermes and Aphrodite, the former of whom was born in the Ancient lands of what is now Modern Turkey, and the latter an Ancient Greek Goddess who was born and is an icon in Cyprus. Cyprus' Hermaphrodite condition enables it to be a Greek or Turkish gift from the ancestors in union with Greece or Turkey; here confirming that Cyprus was never an empty space waiting for imperial inscription, but an ethnically inscribed Hermaphrodite place – a Hermaphrodite Cyprus that the children of Cyprus and this world must protect and preserve.

In this process of production, it is clear that Cyprus is inescapably chopped up, supporting Lefebvre's point: '[t]he ways in which space is thus carved up are reminiscent of the ways in which the body is cut into pieces in images (especially the female body, which is not only cut up but deemed to be "without organs"!).' However, this carved up Hermaphrodite condition and production of Cyprus is not the model the ethnic-motherland nationalists propose; this condition is the unconscious process of production that is secreted, repressed and masked by the ethnic-motherland nationalist model that consciously proposes a place that is enclosed and united with an ethnically rooted, fixed, 'Gifted' identification, which provides the dominant meaning of Cyprus. In support of the epigraph to this chapter, this ethnic-motherland nationalist production 'divides, then keeps what it has divided in a state of separation; inversely, it re-unites – yet keeps whatever it wants in a state of confusion' (Lefebvre, *Production*, 355–58). Chapter 3 has partially highlighted the conscious and unconscious dynamics in the nationalist process of production; however, the chapter has predominantly examined the competing spatial solidarity between the Turkish-cypriot and Greek-cypriots, especially via the separate nationalist victories based on a conscious construction of a closed place, without fully elaborating or exposing the unconscious forces that destabilise and challenge such censored constructions of Cyprus. The remaining parts of the book will examine alternative readings and constructions of Cyprus, which consciously re-write and reproduce via a truth of space that expose, contradict and problematise the ethnic-motherland nationalist production.

Notes

1 In Chapter 3 it would be most fitting to use the ethnic names, Greek and Turkish, for the Cypriots; however, in parts of the chapter, I will refer to the citizens of Turkey and Greece, and so, for clarification purposes, I will use Greek-cypriot and Turkish-cypriot. The name 'cypriot' is lower case because for the ethnic-motherland nationalists this identification is one of insignificance and does not need to exist. On name games, see Ch. 1.

2 On majority and comparative nationalism, see Attalides; Bryant *Imagining*; Loizides *Majority*; Papadakis and Peristianis.

3 See Calotychos *Cyprus*; Killorian, 'Nationalist', 'Space'; Layoun; Yashin *Stepmother*.

4 A version of Chapter 3 has appeared as 'Writing Gifted Baby Cyprus: Anti-colonial Ethnic-Motherland Nationalist Literatures,' *Interventions International Journal of Postcolonial Studies* 19.18 (2017): 1088–1111.

5 Revising Huggan's point on colonies, particularly settler colonies, which have a multiplicity of spatial reference. See Introduction.

6 On anthologies in English, see Decavalles; Montis and Christophides; Ioannides *Faces*; Korfioti; Kouyialis *27 Centuries of Cypriot*; Spanos *22 Contemporary Cypriot*. In Greek, see Pernaris *Cypriot Letter*; Panayiotunis; Krandiotis *Cypriot Poetry, National Character*; Ioannides P. *Anthology EOKA*. In Turkish, see Altay; Ersavas; *Kibris Turk Edebiyati; Kuzey Kibris Turk Milli*; Yilmaz.

7 The analysed texts by Montis and Angelides have been published in English translation; unfortunately, numerous others published in Greek have not been explored fully because of my limited Greek. To compensate for this, I interviewed Stalo Montis, who manages Costas Montis archives since his passing in 2004, and Angelides on their works and biographical information.

8 Ulucamgil and Yasın do not have any translated collections. I have translated all the texts analysed here.

9 *Cyprus My Homeland: Collected Poems I* is a compilation consisting of eight books, namely: *The Epic of the Bayraktar* (1953); *From Cyprus to Ataturk* (1953); *Flag in Cyprus* (1953); *Letter of Cyprus* (1958); *Namik Kemal in Cyprus* (1960); *Mehmet In Cyprus* (1960); *Bloody Cyprus* (1964) and *A Letter to My Son Savas* (1965). *First the Birds Wake Up: Collected Poems II* consists of five books, namely: *Die People* (1952); *A Ship at the Harbour* (1956); *Babel is Still Far* (1963); *Respect to Ataturk* (1963) and *Last* (1986).

10 On 'invention' in colonial, postcolonial and partition discourse, see Introduction.

11 'open zones' is a term I use for the colonial and postcolonial processes of inventing place, or in Tuan's terms the openness and freedom of 'space'. Such processes offer the possibility of understanding the territory through, for example: Fanon's 'zone of occult instability', Huggan's 'rhizomatic (open) or shifting ground', Carter's palimpsestic notion of 'spatial history', Bhabha's hybridity and difference, Spivak's representation in/of the world when speaking from marginal spaces, Appadurai's 'disjuncture' and 'number games' in the postcolonial global world and Pandey's layers of partition. See Introduction.

12 A modus operandi proposed by Marx (Grundrisse), which informed Lefebvre's work and who argued it should be used by all researchers and people; it informs my work and provides an understanding of nationalist production of Cyprus. The approach comprises a movement starting from the present to the past, then retracing its steps to the yet-to-be, acting retroactively upon the past, making it appear in a different light. The past becomes the present, which also takes on another aspect (Lefebvre, 65–67).

13 On the anticolonial movements, see Introduction. Some scholars may claim TMT is not an anticolonial movement because it was not founded to remove British rule; Turkish-cypriots preferred British colonialism over EOKA's enosis, considered Greek colonialism; British and Turkish-cypriots, as claimed by Greek-cypriot nationalists, collaborated. Though the anti-Greek sentiment dominated over the anti-British one, TMT's plan was always to remove the British because they prevented Turkey's involvement, leaving Turkish-cypriots without taksim and at the mercy of the British, who treated them like second-class citizens (Tansu, 19).

14 See Blom et al, eds.; Chatterjee; Anthias and Yuval-Davis; Innes; Richard Kearney; McClintock; McClintock et al.; Nasta; Parker; Ramaswamy; Wilford and Miller.

15 Including: Killoran's study of blood in the Turkish-cypriot literary narratives; Paul Santa Cassia's findings that document the Greek-cypriot virtues and spirit of Hellenism.

16 EOKA officially mobilised on 1 April 1955 – intentionally on April Fools' Day; Montis is acknowledging the date EOKA was founded.

17 The subjugated woman and active male agents of the nation have been explored in latter sections.

18 For more on the 'Ancestral Journey' in relation to blood and spirit, which is a poetic trope and foundation of ethnic-motherland nationalist definitions, see Kemal's 'Writing Gifted Baby Cyprus'.

19 See Marx *Capital.*

20 Places names in Cyprus are important for nationalist. Places in Cyprus often operate between three names: the city is Ammohostos in Greek, Gazimagusa in Turkish and Famagusta in English. On name games, see Ch. 1.

21 Angelides, Personal Interview, 18 April 2011.

22 Masculinised Cyprus will be explored in 'Well Done Our Martyred Son' section of this chapter.

23 For more on the returning to Ancient Greek and Ottoman Ancestral Journeys, battles and heroes, which is a poetic trope and foundation of ethnic-motherland nationalist definitions, see Kemal's 'Writing Gifted Baby Cyprus'.

24 In *Closed Doors*, the name has been translated as 'Dighenis'; I will use Digenis in this analysis. Digenis is a Byzantine Akrite, frontiersman and hero, who is associated with Cyprus via myth of Pentadactylos mountains and 'Rock of the Greek', as well as the Akritic cycle of folk-songs, where Cyprus has been noted for preserving them. Digenis is of mixed – Greek and Arab – birth, wherein he polices and disrupts ideas of pure ethnic identity; however, this is dismissed in such poetic about him. On Digenis, see also Ch. 2.

25 Addressed in Diodorus Siculus' and Herodotus' *Histories*; Homer's *Iliad*; and Sophocles *Ajax*.

26 Most poems in *Venerable Lady the Sea* are associated with the sea: the sea spirits are seen in 'Amphitrite' (13), 'Nereids' (37), and 'White Sea' (21); sea as hope and freedom in 'As Long as there is the Sea' (14); sea as related to balcony in 'Patmos' (32); the arrival is expected in 'Venerable lady, the sea' (9); the Greek ships and Greek men arrive in 'Return' (73), 'My Seas' (67), and 'Sea Magic' (10).

27 Planhol's L 'Islam et la mer: la mosquée et le matelot, vi-xx siècle' is in French and has not been translated. My understanding has been drawn from Planhol's article 'Islam and the Sea: The Causes of Failures' in Hastings Donnan (ed.), *Interpreting Islam*; the review essays, 'Islam and the sea: paradigms and problematics' by Lawrence I. Conrad that provides an illuminating account with a wide selection of passages translated into English, and 'L'Islam et la mer: La mosquée et le matelot, VIIe–XXe siècle by Xavier de Planhol Review' by James Howard-Johnston.

28 Taurus mountains in English. In light of the importance of naming, when addressing Turkish-cypriot narratives I will use the title 'Toros'.

29 For more on the Ottoman martyred narrative as related to shedding their blood in specific places, see Kemal 'Writing Gifted Baby Cyprus'.

30 The map carving started in 1984 and was completed in 2006 on 20 July (anniversary of peace operation/invasion). The flags are 500 × 240 metres and visible from south Cyprus. The interview (April 2011) with Angelides was conducted in her home, where from her balcony you can see the

Pentadaktylos mountain range with the mapping of Turkey and TRNC flags and motto. As we watched the Pentadaktylos, Angelides said 'I have three sons, and I watch one of them (pointing to Pentadaktylos) being tortured everyday'.

31 Translated as Gregoris Afxentiou or Grigoris Afxendiou: I refer to him as Gregoris Afxentiou; however, when quoting directly from the text I use the same translation as in the published material.

32 In Turkish-cypriot narratives, associating specific places to people is dominant in representations of Ottoman conquest – Bayraktar in Lefkosa and Cambolat in Mağusa. See Kemal's 'Writing Gifted Baby Cyprus'.

33 The competition was titled 'National Anthem/March Song' (*Ulusal Mars Gufte Yarısmas*); *Mars* means both Anthem and March. The purpose of the competition was to select a poem to be the TRNC's national Anthem/March song. Fifty of the submitted poems were published in the Anthology, and the winning poem was Mehmet Levent's 'Freedom and Peace Anthem'.

4 Colonialist, Communist, Post-1964/74 Partition Moments

UnHyphenated DeEthnicised UnOfficial Cypriotists

A turning point in the colonial world was the 1920s, when the rise of the Soviet Union sent shockwaves across the globe with its vibration rhythmically hitting the Mediterranean island of Cyprus; this can be understood through Cypriotism. Cypriotism or the Cypriotist identification has a three 'moment'[1] formation, each of which separately developed from the colonial to the partitioned period. I have named the three moments of Cypriotism: Colonialist-Cypriotism, Communist-Cypriotism and post-1964/74 Partition Cypriotism. The founders, supporters and objectives within each Cypriotist moment were very different: the former moment, Colonialist-Cypriotism, was a British imperial construction from around the last three decades of British rule (1930–1960); simultaneously the Cypriot subjects developed Communist-Cypriotism that was a left-wing political feeling active from the colonial to the postcolonial period (1926–1974); and the Cypriots developed the final moment, post-1964/74 Partition Cypriotism, a largely literary, cultural and social formation and feeling adopted in the post-partition periods (1964–1990s). Even though each moment is different, all three shared the same Cypriotist goal and definition for Cyprus, ultimately to replace the dominance of the ethnic-motherland nationalist production of place with a localised Cypriot-centric formation, which would unite and define the Cypriots and Cyprus. In all three moments, the nationalist production that masked the palimpsestic spatial history, and diminished the local physical and social identification of Cyprus, is recovered. The ethnic-motherland nationalist production was the most dominant and official throughout the British colonial period, which filtered into the postcolonial period; however, the British Colonial-Cypriotists, the Cypriot Communist-Cypriotist and post-1964/74 Partition Cypriotist narratives always hampered and impinged upon its dominance. This three-moment Cypriotism is the key to understanding social and cultural politics of the left in this postcolonial and partitioned east Mediterranean island, yet it has been marginalised in scholarly studies.

Most studies of Cypriotism are by scholars in the social sciences, with ample focus on the left-wing or Communist-Cypriotism in opposition to ethnic-nationalisms.[2] Although there are no studies on Cypriotism in relation to Colonialism and post-1964/74 Partition Cypriotism, some works – on education by Persianis; works on Lawrence Durrell's or Ivi Meleagrou's writing of 1964 by Calotychos – have contributed to these concepts and names. Similarly, there are no studies on Cypriotism which focus on literature and spatiality. Nevertheless, these ideas subtly resonate in previously mentioned works – for example: Mavratsas' Cypriotism forms a Cypriot nation through 'political-territorial category'; Loizides mentions the poet Nese Yashin's definition of Cypriots as 'the land, a geographical place'; Calotychos reads Meleagrou's Nicosia in relation to personal-public space and reproduction of social and political. This chapter will provide a detailed exploration of this three-moment Cypriotism, emphasising spatial literary Cypriotism as a powerful force in producing postcolonial partitioned Mediterranean cases, like Cyprus.

The chapter will focus on the Cypriotist case for Cyprus, through demonstrating the individual development of the three – Colonial, Communist and Post-1964/74 Partition – Cypriotist narratives struggling for a reading and construction of Cyprus. I create a dialogue between the three different Cypriotist approaches that have attempted to displace the ethnic-motherland nationalist production, and have shaped colonial, postcolonial and partition policies, politics and cultures in the process. The main focus will be on the post-1964/74 Partition Cypriotists because this is the most effective and consistent narrative, which successfully wrote back to and re-defined the ethnic-motherland nationalist, the imperial, and the partitioned readings and constructions of Cyprus. However, before delving into a thorough analysis of post-1964/74 Partition Cypriotist writings, readings and constructions of Cyprus, I will explain the development and definitions of the first two moments of Cypriotism, with brief focus on relevant writers – Lawrence Durrell for Colonial-Cypriotism, and Tefkos Anthias for Communist-Cypriotism. This will help demonstrate how post-1964/74 Partition Cypriotism splintered out of and rewrote the terms of the former Cypriotist formations, which resulted in it being the most effective in producing a Cypriotist Cyprus.

Spatial Literary and Artistic Post-1964/74 Partition Cypriotism: Lefebvre, Tuan, Boym

Post-1964/74 Partition Cypriotism will be explored through a broad selection of literary and artistic activities with focus on pioneering movements and a diverse group of authors – particularly George Moleskis and Fikret Demirag alongside others, such as Ivi Mealegrou, Elli Peonidou, Nese Yashin and Mehmet Yashin – that respond to postcolonial failures, especially the 1963–64 partition and/or 1974-partition.

In this postcolonial moment of failure, the authors adopt 'open zones' by inventing the territory in ways best described by means of Carter's 'spatial history', Huggan's 'rhizomatic shifting ground' and Fanon's 'zone of occult instability'. These 'open zones' are, however, disrupted because the Cypriotists adopt the 'closed zone' by compartmentalising, which is not based on an ethnic binary and homogenising, but a Cypriotised sectioning of historical, natural and social investments, thus enabling them to produce a Cyprus that gives them total knowledge and control, as a means to overcome the risk of losing their united Cyprus in this moment of failure. For this reading and construction, the Cypriotist authors who identify with Marxist sentiments use fully those aspects of Lefebvre's spatiology that draw on Karl Marx, including: the 'regressive-progressive' approach that comprises movement between present and past, making both appear different (Lefebvre, *Production*, 65–67); and spatial adaption of 'concrete-abstraction', which builds on Marx's concept of commodity, to reveal the force of human and social practices in spatial production. The chapter will show how the Cypriotists use the 'regressive-progressive' approach to capture the 'concrete-abstraction' within and for the production of Cyprus: here they capture an abstract 'mental space' that is idealistically 'conceived' in the mind, and a 'physical space' 'perceived' through the body, which gains concreteness through 'social space' that is directly lived, dynamically alive and experienced by the Cypriot within Cyprus. To show the force of spatial and social practices, the Cypriotists play with the three Lefebvrean 'representations of the relations of production': they disrupt the 'representation of space' by adopting the persona of specialists, particularly archaeologists and historians, to unearth and 'order' Cyprus – they must take on this persona to seize control from the most powerful agents of production because 'they can represent Cyprus, it must not be represented'.[3] They reclaim, with full capacity, the 'representational space', which gives agency to the 'passively experienced' and 'dominated' social spaces of the Cypriot people, through a process that embodies 'complex symbolisms' (Lefebvre, *Production*, 33) to appropriate the 'time (or times), rhythm (or rhythms)' of 'everyday activities of the users [that] has an origin, and that origin is childhood' (Lefebvre, *Production*, 356–62). They restore 'spatial practice' in Cyprus, through interactions and journeys that represent Cypriot daily routines with a 'guaranteed level of *competence* and a specific level of *performance*' (Lefebvre, *Production*, 33). In this process of production, the Cypriotists employ what Lefebvre terms 'rhythmanalysis', which is a way to analyse 'rhythms' – repetition, cycles, moments, movements and interaction between a place, a time and an expenditure of energy – in everyday life. Thus the Cypriotists create an island that is more open and inclusive of social and spatial practices and difference, yet they only read and construct through Cypriot-centric practices and 'rhythms' that produce a unified place; they experience Cyprus as a Tuanian place with Cypriotised 'knowledge' and 'attachments' that assure a closed secure permanence they can control.

The Cypriotists produce a 'place' with a Cypriot-centric wholeness, oneness – in short 'Cypriotness' – that is anti-partition, against any kind of ethnic exclusivity. This production is framed around an actual and idealistic quest for united peace, and the chapter will illustrate how the authors habitually wander and border-cross, struggling against and re-writing ethnic-motherland nationalist and partitioned spatial blockades via a Hikmetian style communist-romanticism and an attitude akin to Svetlana Boym's nostalgia, to re-produce a pre-partitioned, borderless, inclusive homeland. It will be shown that the foundation and success of this Cypriotist construction is determined by two interrelated dynamic narrative cycles, 'Birth Cycle' and 'Journey Cycle', which elaborate on past-present moments with rhythms that capture the 'concrete-abstraction' of *only Cyprus*. In the 'Birth Cycle' the writers reclaim the linear-cyclical rhythmic roots and routes of, and maternal connection to 'Mother Cyprus'. In the 'Journey Cycle' they capture a spatial and local wandering around Mother Cyprus through appropriating three narrative codes or gifts: the 'spatial palimpsestic archaeology: linear rhythm'; 'material romantic cyclical rhythm of nature' and 'social-domestic linear-cyclical rhythm'. Each of these codes/gifts captures either a historical, natural or social abstraction in Cyprus, which are made concrete through the writers' focus on communal interactive practices.

In explicating the post-1964/74 Partition Cypriotist literary production, Svetlana Boym's claims in *Future of Nostalgia* will be a point of reference. The shift between the past and present, and concrete and abstract is synonymous with Boym's concept of nostalgia that shifts between the actual and imagined return to, as in restorative nostalgia, or a more self-consciously critical longing for, as in reflective nostalgia, a united homeland. The Cypriotists unconsciously shift between the various practices of homecoming, whereby they enter a process that confuses them, often prioritising the imagined coherent abstraction, or what Boym calls restorative nostalgia. Through this confusion and unconscious shift, the Cypriotists, as in Boym's restorative nostalgia, 'reconstruct' and submit to an idyllic place, not the actual way it was, but the way it could have been in the light of an un-partitioned idealistic future; this reconstruction of home is considered an 'absolute truth', but it is a 'place' that does not, and possibly never did exist. Consequently, the Cypriotist reading and construction of Cyprus continue to be exclusionary because they only engage with enclosed Cypriot-centric imagined rhythms located within the island borders, which points to a new type of nationalism – island patriotism. In this chapter as we wander with the Cypriotists, both spatially and locally around Cyprus, their Cypriot-centric practices will be illuminated; however, the main focus will not be on the Cypriotist closures and exclusions, but on how they critically respond to the ethnic-motherland nationalist productions, to form a more open, inclusive and united Cypriotist Cyprus.

Colonialist-Cypriotism (1930–1960): Lawrence Durrell

Colonialist-Cypriotism was a British attempt at forming and giving the Cypriots an identification against the dominance of the anticolonial ethnic-motherland nationalisms, which was putting the Empire at risk of losing control. This was a colonial fallacy framed around an artificial Cypriotist identity that filtered out ethnicity, and built on the illusion of a united collaborative Anglo-Cypriot identity. During the last three decades of colonial rule (1930–1960), there were two different British investments that attempted to Cypriotise the Cypriots through Cypriot-centred pro-British constructions. The first British investment in Cypriotism was within the context of education policy as discussed in Chapter 2; the second was a literary focus that was materialised by the services of Lawrence Durrell's editorial and imperial input into the journal *Cyprus Review*.[4]

The British education policy made Cypriotism an official voice; however, the Cypriots did not make it a dominant voice or aspiration, and as a result anticolonial ethnic-motherland nationalism flourished. In July 1954 the British made a literary attempt to disrupt the development of ethnic-motherland nationalism, through employing the writer Lawrence Durrell as Director of the Public Information Service of Cyprus in charge of the government press releases. Durrell's official role and publications – particularly his editorial input, from 1954 to 1956, in the *Cyprus Review* – evidence imperial politics and propaganda, whereby he attempted to create a Colonial-Cypriotist Cyprus. Durrell's comment on his objective for the *Cyprus Review* is as follows:

> I am planning to give the government a really good Middle Eastern Review. It really does need something to project Cyprus and to give some standing to the British culture generally. (Durrell, *SP*, 127)

For Durrell 'to project Cyprus' meant to replace the ethnic-motherland nationalist identity with a Colonialist-Cypriotist one, which would Cypriotise the Cypriots whilst creating a British cultural influence and ethos.[5]

Durrell attempted to Cypriotise the Cypriots by 'foster[ing] Cypriot pride and identity through thoughtful – and non-political – articles' (MacNiven, 418). This attempt to do away with politics is also foregrounded in his autobiographical work, *Bitter Lemons,* which opens with the line: 'This is not a political book' (Durrell, *Bitter*, 11). However, both texts were rooted and overflowing with imperial politics and propaganda.

Durrell's *Cyprus Review* filtered out the island's ethnic-motherland nationalist political voices dominant at the time: erasing the reality of the strong ethnic identification; ignoring the ascendance of anti-British tension and excluding the upsurge of divided enosis and taksim tensions. Instead, the *Cyprus Review* built on the illusion of a collective consciousness for all Cypriots by publishing articles on an imagined Cypriotness that mapped a Cypriot-centric history, geography and culture through focus on folklore, food, forestry and so on. Durrell also attempted to project this collective Cypriotness by promoting inclusivity, wherein Cypriots from both communities were urged to contribute. This was further crystallised in the priority given to the Cypriotturks[6]: the *Cyprus Review* was in the English language, but in 1956 a Turkish edition was published and there is evidence that Durrell 'pleaded with Freya [Stark] to write on a Turkish-Cypriot subject' (MacNiven, 418). Durrell attempted to provide the Cypriotturkish minority a stage upon which to be represented as equal to the Cypriotgreek majority; this projected an illusionary Cypriot collaboration, and, as argued by Calotychos, reflected the political collaboration the British sought to have with the Cypriotturks against the Cypriotgreek's EOKA dominance and its pro-enosis, anti-British force (Calotychos, *Modern*, 255).

Durrell's *Cyprus Review* also attempted to create the illusion of collaboration between the British and Cypriots, particularly Cypriotgreeks; it promoted a 'British ethos' (Roessel, 43; Herbrechter, 361–62) with Cypriot distinctiveness. Well-known British writers were pivotal to this British-Cypriot identity building project, shown in Durrell's letter to Freya Stark: 'Important people coming here and bothering to write about it will make life seem all the more worth living for us Cypriots' (Durrell, SP, 127). Here, as reiterated by Roessel and MacNiven, Durrell claimed that the island needed 'important people', meaning established British writers, to write up an 'identity' and thereby to foster a culture for 'us Cypriots' identity with a strong Britishness (MacNiven, 418). Durrell crystallised this British-Cypriot unification in the *Cyprus Review* by including British contributions alongside Cypriot ones. This British-Cypriot idea is also suggested in the phrase – 'us Cypriots' – by which Durrell defines himself as Cypriot to imply that he himself is the perfect model for the new Cypriot identification – through him British-Cypriotism is born. This British-Cypriotness clearly shows Durrell's attempt to replace the anti-British pro-ethnic sentiment of Cypriots, mainly Cypriotgreeks, with a pro-British flavour (Roessel, 44); Durrell tried to 'promote a sense of Cyprus as an independent cultural entity, with Britain as a friendly godparent [...] to convince Greek Cypriots to accept the perpetuation of a benevolent British mandate, rather than to press for Enosis' (MacNiven, 418).

Beyond British and Cypriot contributions, Durrell attempted to include and gain support by authors from Greece (Roessel, 44–45); he asked George Seferis, the Greek poet who subsequently became Greek ambassador to London (1957–1962), as well as other Greek writers, who were influential writers and his close friends, to contribute. Durrell's aim here was clearly tactical, he planned to use these influential Greek friends as a device, which would not only result in mass Cypriotgreek readership, but that would lead to the Cypriots' full support of this new Cypriot identity. This part of Durrell's project was a tactical blunder, whereby all of Durrell's Greek friends refused to participate and, as warned by Maurice Cardiff when he was assigned to the colonial office, he lost many Greek friends. The Greek friends' opinion of Durrell can be summarised through statements drawn from a letter Seferis sent to G.P Savvides:

> when I see intellectual institutions – quite artfully, I agree – placed in the service of these gentlemen, I tend to become suspicious. And when I see intellectuals and friends (e.g. Durrell) become propagandists for these gentlemen and use the friendship they had in Greece in order to infiltrate and enslave conscience, then I become absolutely suspicious. (MacNiven, 419; Roessel 45)

Seferis and other Greek writers recognised Durrell's actions as imperialist propaganda, where he attempted to use them as a tool to replace the Cypriots' ethnic identification with a British-Cypriotness. Durrell's Greek friends were very hurt by his tactics to 'use' his friendship for the benefit of the gentlemen of the British Empire, concluding that 'genuine artists prostituted themselves to compromised goals and masters' (MacNiven, 419).

Even though some Cypriotgreeks and Cypriotturks supported the *Cyprus Review*, most Cypriots, particularly established Cypriotgreek writers such as Costas Montis, held the same opinion as Seferis and stood firmly against Durrell's identity building project. The *Cyprus Review* only succeeded in representing the 'idea' of imperialist identity politics – to replace Greekness and Turkishness with British-Cypriotness – but failed to materialise this concoction beyond the 32 issues of the *Cyprus Review*. The *Cyprus Review* was not a reflection of the identification the Cypriot majority embraced, and it was far from creating an alternative voice that could overpower the ethnic-motherland nationalists.

The British education policy and Durrell's literary activities demonstrate Colonial-Cypriotism, which was the imperial attempt to un-invent ethnic-motherland nationalist formations into a non-ethnic collective British-Cypriotism. This Colonial-Cypriotism failed fully because it was an imperial concoction that did not appeal to the Cypriots; Communist-Cypriotism, however, had more appeal because it was authored by the Cypriots themselves.

Communist-Cypriotism (1920–1974): Tefkos Anthias

Communist-Cypriotism is reflected in the historical development and mobilisation of the communist political parties in Cyprus, whereby their principles aimed towards a united Cypriot-centric identification within a communist framework. The periods between the 1920s and the 1970s show the development of communism in Cyprus through two interrelated political parties, the Communist Party of Cyprus (CPC) rebranded into Progressive Party of Working People (AKEL). This communism was conceptualised in Cyprus around 1924 by Cypriotgreeks, who subsequently established the first non-ruling communist party, CPC, in 1926, which was outlawed by the colonial office in 1931; by 1941, the CPC members resurfaced to found AKEL.[7] This development will be addressed through the poet Tefkros Anthias, because, as recently stated by Andros Kyprianou, the General Secretary of AKEL, at a conference to mark 50 years since Anthias death, he was a leading member of CPC and AKEL at the forefront of the battle for the workers movement of Cyprus.

CPC set the stage for the Communist-Cypriotist principles and trends towards independence, which continued throughout communist history. A new kind of unification was key: globally they represented a unification influenced by the principles and politics of Vladimir Lenin, they aspired to a communist network with the Soviet Union and other communist states, so as to create a united Middle Eastern communist power against the west and NATO countries. Locally they struggled to re-define the ethnic-motherland nationalist constructions from an ethnically divided Greece-Cyprus or Turkey-Cyprus unification, to an all-inclusive Cypriot-centred unification – a Communist-Cypriotist patriotism. The communist Cypriot goal was to create a patriotic front with all Cypriots, towards an independence that provided union, equality and self-determination for the people of Cyprus. CPC was the first Cypriot group to trigger anticolonial tendencies into a movement; however, Cyprus's anticolonialism is mostly associated with the ethnic-motherland nationalists – EOKA and TMT – movements (1955–1960). CPC was also the first Cypriot group that strictly contested the terms of ethno-religious, class and social exclusivity, through which they envisaged an independence different from the ethnic-motherland nationalists. For CPC, independent Cyprus was not a struggle for ethnic revival and unification with Greece or Turkey, with slogans 'Cyprus is Greek or Turkish'; but was instead a Cypriot-centred revival and unification, with supporting slogans 'Cyprus is and belongs to all its Cypriot people'. CPC independence meant reclaiming the agency of *all* Cypriots – particularly the proletariat who sold their labour and the farmers who toiled on the land – and an emptying of those powers – imperialists, capitalist local rulers, dominant ideologies – that diminished unity, equality and self-determination in Cyprus. CPC struggled to recover the rights, voice and land to the people of Cyprus who they defined as the original owners, the sole rulers and the almighty mother; Cyprus is *our* people, *our* land, *our* country. Throughout Cyprus's communist history the supporters struggled to maintain this Communist-Cypriotist independence through a resistance, peaceful and non-violent, founded and mobilised by and for the Cypriots in Cyprus.

The communists had a specific strategy, set up by the CPC, to form this all-inclusive Cypriot-based communism. First, they founded or joined trade unions and labour groups shaping many mobilisations to improve working conditions for the people of Cyprus. Second, they travelled around Cyprus, particularly to rural communities, to communicate their principles and gain membership from all Cypriots. This resonates with Anthias' poetic practices during his youth, before he was a communist, when he travelled from his own village to others in the Famagusta district, reciting his Greek poems to Cypriotgreeks. This points to the question of party membership, where, even though the goal was to unite all Cypriots, the communists failed to get support from the non-Greek, particularly Cypriotturkish, population because of various ethnic barriers: Cypriotgreeks were the founders and core members of the communist party, thus limiting appeal to Cypriotturks in the first instance. In subsequent years, after the late 1930s, some Cypriotturks supported communism by joining labour unions and strikes[8]; however, most Cypriotturks distrusted communism mainly because of the Cypriotgreeks' increased enosis sentiments and the communists' inconsistent policies in relation to it. This relates to a further barrier – the Cypriot communist members, particularly activists that fought for a united bi-communalism, were under threat and/or murdered by the ethnic-motherland nationalists who considered them agents of British or the other ethnic side.[9] Thus bi-communal communism was suppressed by the nationalists of both communities, whereby the Cypriotgreeks and Cypriotturks helped each other to eliminate any such Communist-Cypriotist mobilisations that may have threatened their enosis or taksim.

CPC was somewhat consistent in its anti-enosis pro-self-government appeal; however, upon CPC's termination and AKEL's advent, the inconsistencies towards enosis began. CPC was outlawed by the colonial office in 1931, when the Cypriotgreek ethnic-motherland nationalists mobilised against the British. Even though the nationalists formed the mobilisation, CPC participated in it, overtly claiming it was for their principles and slogan – 'Cyprus belongs to its people' – of independent Cyprus, and definitely not in support of the enosis slogan – 'union with Greece'. Consequent upon the 1931 uprising, CPC was deemed illegal and its members imprisoned and/or exiled by the colonial government, which was supported by the Church's anti-communist agenda, ending in communist politics going underground for the next decade. By 1941 the former CPC members and labour leaders had returned and founded AKEL. Anthias provides an illuminating reflection of this communist development as related to Church and State: In May 1931, the Church excommunicated Anthias because of his poetry *The Second Coming*, which suggested people would judge God for societies' tribulations. Subsequently, Anthias wrote *Purgatory* and become a CPC member, where he helped shape the 1931 uprising, and was consistently imprisoned, under persecution and surveillance.[10] After CPC went underground, Anthias served as teacher and editor, whilst continuing to write with strengthened Marxist-Leninist feelings, when he published 14 works of poetry, prose and plays, including *Our Son,* considered Cyprus' first children's play. In 1941 Anthias was at the forefront of AKEL's formation, including serving on the Central Committee and composing the party anthem, whilst publishing around ten poetry and play collections until 1955.

Since the founding of AKEL, particularly from 1942 to 1955, the communist legacy regarding enosis was established, where there was a frequent shift between a pro-enosis to self-government attitude; this was a tactical policy that depended on which would benefit the party whilst being in line with their communist principles.[11] AKEL's momentary enosis support was because the Cypriotgreek majority wanted enosis, which was detrimental to the party gaining political power. AKEL's enosis support simultaneously resulted in un-adjustable losses, including the lack of trust from the non-Cypriotgreek population; the party putting the communist principles of an all-inclusive independence at risk of becoming an exclusive ethno-national communism; a detachment from principles that were in line with both the Soviet Union and its international communist networks. Consequently, AKEL would replace enosis support with a united inclusive Cypriot self-determination. AKEL's history is framed around such 'shifting tactics [...] from *enosis* to self-government and back to *enosis*' (Adams, 34) that resulted in moments of great success; however, by 1955 such tactics caused AKEL to reach its, and Cyprus communism's, lowest point in history.

In 1955, EOKA successfully mobilised against the British, but AKEL refused to join the campaign for several reasons.[12] First, AKEL dreaded any alliance with the founder of EOKA, Colonel Georgios Grivas, who was a fanatic against communists. Grivas stated his duty in the campaign was 'to fight three enemies, the British, the communists and the Turks' (Adams 46; Foley, *Grivas*, 104).[13] Second, AKEL claimed that the campaign did not provide for the rights of the Cypriotturkish community, stating that: 'the liberation of the people of Cyprus can only be realistic if it provides for the liberation of the Turks as well'.[14] Third, AKEL supported peaceful tactics and they argued EOKA was violent. Finally, AKEL claim they stayed out of the campaign because EOKA told them to. AKEL's refusal to join EOKA was a failure, resulting in AKEL members splitting into opposing factions – supporters versus non-supporters of EOKA – and the party losing many Cypriotgreek supporters. Even though AKEL's opposition to EOKA could have served British interests, particularly the Colonialist-Cypriotist ideas, during the British Emergency period (1956–1959) AKEL was outlawed, the offices of the party ransacked, all official documents seized and party members were sent to detention camps. Anthias was one of 135 AKEL members kept at Dhekelia detention camp. After his heart attack there and subsequent public protest, he was put under house arrest; he then departed for London in 1957. The British responded to AKEL in such terms because they were aware that AKEL – though anti-ethnic and Cypriot-centric, also anti-British – was a threat to the imperial hold on Cyprus. AKEL's practices during the EOKA campaign cost them greatly, a tactical blunder that was to haunt the party for the rest of its history; however, AKEL was able to regain political significance in independent Cyprus. By 1959 AKEL gained legal status and after independence it developed to be the most organised political party in Cyprus.

AKEL supported the independent government of Cyprus by being in alliance with the first president, Makarios III, for the benefit of the party. AKEL's alliance with Makarios was a tactic to help them gain support from the Cypriotgreek majority who supported Makarios. Furthermore, AKEL believed Makorios III prioritised an independent government over enosis, where they agreed that the independence agreement did not provide complete self-determination; however, they focussed on different points of the constitution. AKEL disagreed with the stationing of non-Cypriot authorities – Greek and Turkish troops and the British bases – in Cyprus; they disagreed with the organisation of government framed around a coalition that partitioned the two ethnic communities; and they attended to the rights of Cypriotturks.[15]

At first glance AKEL's developments suggest continued support of Communist-Cypriotism with slogans 'Cyprus is and belongs to its Cypriot people'; however, this is not the case. Though there were some Cypriotturks who supported AKEL, with numerous Cypriotturkish students in Turkey and elsewhere who identified with communism, AKEL failed in recruitment because of ethnic tensions at the time. First, AKEL failed to respond to the widespread inter-communal conflict between the Cypriotturks and pro-enosis Cypriotgreeks, because they did not want any friction against the pro-enosis faction; this meant Cypriotturks who were pro-communism and united Cyprus were unable to align themselves with AKEL. Moreover, even if AKEL openly struggled for its united principles, it would not have appealed to the Cypriotturkish majority, who were suffering greatly from the ethnic-conflict, most were TMT and taksim supporters, and those who were not were under threat or murdered.[16] AKEL failed to materialise its slogan, and stood back whilst the slogan became 'Cyprus belongs to its Greek-Cypriot people', when in 1963 the government remained solely in the hands of the Cypriotgreeks.

AKEL's policies resulted in them disassociating from the Communist-Cypriotist principle: with only local ethno-national interests, they failed to execute inclusive politics of 'all working Cypriots' and did not pursue the collective Cypriot communist, global communist or Leninist terms. The Makarios and AKEL alliance was not in line with Lenin's principles; Makarios's supporters were bourgeois, and AKEL's were working class and proletariats; this broke away from the Lenin-Bolshevik – worker-peasant alliance – and was in line with Menshevik principles –working-class-liberal bourgeoisie alliance. AKEL was aware that their developments after independence had moved them far from their Communist-Cypriotist principles; however, this alignment with Makarios seemed AKEL's only option to regain the political support lost during 1955–1959. Furthermore, opposing Makarios's leadership could have put them at risk of being outlawed by the Republic, and this would have been the end of the party. AKEL's tactics could suggest Lenin's famous approach of 'buying time', whereby the communists wait for certain 'events' to take shape before they take action; however, 'buying time' put them at total risk of losing the Communist-Cypriotist definitions.

Makarios, who was neither a communist nor a supporter of AKEL's principles, was also being tactical by tolerating AKEL for his vision of independence. Makarios's alignment with AKEL was firstly, on an international level, a means to put pressure on the western powers to notice that Cyprus could be a threat if their demands for a reformed independent agreement were not met. Makarios frequently sought arms and support from the Soviet Union, whereby he even offered them a military base in Cyprus; this made the west – the Americans and their British allies – feel anxious that communism was developing in the Mediterranean, which could result in another Cuban style crisis. Similarly, Turkey became concerned that it might be geographically sandwiched between two communist – Cyprus and the Soviet Union – governments. Second, on a national level, the alignment was a means to tame national tension, whereby Makarios recognised the importance of Cypriotgreeks uniting against the TMT Cypriotturks. Here Makarios also used the communists' anti-enosis attitude to play off the pro-enosis extremist faction of the Cypriots.[17] By the 1970s Makarios' united Cypriotgreek independence failed to materialise, and instead the Republic of Cyprus was drowning in civil war and bloodshed based on intra-communal and inter-communal conflicts. Because the conflict was used as an excuse to secrete the real western concern over the relationship between the Cyprus Republic and the Soviet Union, Turkey intervened, with the consent of America and Britain, and partitioned Cyprus.

Since partition AKEL has continued its political legacy, successfully winning the governmental elections in 2008, when they eliminated the Communist-Cypriotist identification for a Greek-Cypriotist one. It seems the act of 'buying time', ended in CPC's/ AKEL's communism, Cypriotism and Leninist principle being replaced by an ethnic-based western capitalism in alliance with the European Union.

The analysis of Colonial-Cypriotism and Communist-Cypriotism has demonstrated two different attempts to re-define the ethnic-motherland nationalisms of Cyprus by Cypriotising the Cypriots. Both were successful in conceptualising the idea of Cypriotism; however, neither was successful in constructing fully this Cypriotism, or gaining mass Cypriot support for a movement against ethnic-motherland nationalism. Consequently, Cypriotism never became the dominant and/or official identification of Cyprus. It can be argued, however, that both Cypriotist moments challenged the ethnic-motherland nationalisms, and thus were instrumental in the transition from the ethnic-nationalist to the post-partition Cypriot identifications and Cypruses.

Post-1964/74 Partition Cypriotism: Literature through Places, Spaces and Times

Post-1964/74 Partition Cypriotism is a term I have coined for a largely cultural rather than political movement of those Cypriot voices on a literary and lived quest to re-define and reproduce partitioned Cyprus in favour of a unified Cyprus. Post-1964/74 Partition Cypriotism simultaneously extends and refutes the terms of Colonialist-Cypriotism and Communist-Cypriotism: it extends the Cypriot-centric definition for the island, being in line with CPC/AKEL's failed and defeated patriotic slogan 'Cyprus belongs to its Cypriot people'; and it refuses to be an ideology with a strategic postcolonial policy forced upon the Cypriots or a political principle entailing tactical blunders and power struggles. Post-1964/74 Partition Cypriotism is a literary and artistic moment, not battling for leadership and control, but instead engaging with the actual and active readings and constructions of Cyprus, capturing Cypriot-centred identification, social and lived experiences, and shared practices, authored by and for all the people of Cyprus. Post-1964/74 Partition Cypriotism has not become an official narrative and is not as yet a canonised literary movement; however, since the independence failures, especially the 1964 and 1974-partitions when Cypriot identification was at risk of elimination, authors from both communities have consistently reacted to the risks by engaging with Cypriotist formations, which flourished and gained prominence within Cyprus's unofficial literary scene. The post-1964/74 Partition Cypriotist authors successfully, yet often unconsciously, unite as one with common literary and lived practices: centred on reacting to risks resulting from partition, they focus on 'Cypriot identification' in relation to place, a Cypriotness via an island turn. They mobilise in a writerly quest towards a rebirth that replaces the ethnically bounded production with a Cypriot-centric reading and construction that is fully inclusive of Cypriots, and the whole culture, history and nature of Cyprus. Post-1964/74 Partition Cypriotism has developed through various interrelated literary and artistic activities: with an increase in authors came an outpour of writings, movements, publications and translations defining the 'Cypriot' within a Cypriotist framework determined by a united Cyprus.

Since partition numerous anthologies, newspapers and magazines edited by Cypriots and published in Cyprus have claimed the name 'Cypriot' operating via translation, a significant trait in post-1964/74 Partition Cypriotism. From 1965 to 1986, the name 'Cypriot literature' gained prominence, where both sides of the divide released collections with Cypriot writings in either Greek or Turkish as well as English translation.[18] From around 1978, 'Cypriot literature' also emerged as ethno-linguistically inclusive, through magazines, zines and newspapers – i.e. *Sanat Emegi* (1978–1980), *Haravgi* (1978) – alongside anthologies with Cypriot writings in Greek and Turkish translated across languages and communities, here enhancing a significant bi-communalism/lingualism in Cyprus.[19] Since 2000 there has been an outpouring of works by all Cypriots in English translation, enhanced via collaboration between Cypriotist and diaspora authors.[20]

Parallel to this there has been an increase in literary movements and organisations. This includes the more official canonised moves, wherein local literary critics and officials separately design curricula and anthologies for their ethnic Cypriot-selves, which divide the Cypriotgreeks and Cypriotturks into a distinct '1974–1990 Generation'[21]; it also includes unofficial moves, wherein the Cypriots mobilise to claim a generation, movement and/or organisation for all selves, collectively towards a united Cypriotness. Early examples of organisations for 'Cypriot' writers include: 'The Union of Cyprus Writers' (UCW) founded for Cypriotgreeks in 1978, and 'The Turkish[22] Cypriot Union of Writers and Artists (CUAW) for Cypriotturks in 1989; here the 'Cypriot' is mainly ethno-linguistically divided, yet with recent developments towards inclusivity via collaborative events and competitions. Other more unofficial moves include the '74 Generation: Rejection Front' and 'Poetz4Peace'. '74 Generation' was shaped by Cypriotturkish poets around 1978; it focussed on 'Cypriot identity' depression, promoted Cypriotness and was against ethnic divisions created by the 'Ethnic-Motherland Nationalist' and the 1974-partition. This links to 'Poetz4Peace', the first bi-communal poetic-musical movement initiated by Cypriot poets and musicians in 1990s, which introduced the fundamental themes – peace and political poetry – towards united Cyprus.

Since 2003, the poets and writers from across the divide have increased collaboration through co-organising events towards peace; a notable example is the 'Yes' poem, when 15 poets together wrote a poem for reunification and peace. Such moves were largely marginalised and lack mass Cypriot following; however, they demonstrate core Cypriotists traits with authors who are peace activists in a writerly quest for a Cypriotness in united Cyprus, that became a popular address in more recent times.

This increase in literary publications and movements is a result of a definitive rise in authors who adopted distinct traits and practices, which shaped post-1964/74 Partition Cypriotism. These Cypriot authors are central to this literary Cypriotism, here listed in chronological order of published or performative output: Tefkos Anthias (1933) Ivi Mealegrou (1950), Achilleas Pyliotis (1955), Taner Baybars (1955), Fikret Demirag (1959), Mehmet Kansu (1959) Sener Levent (1962), George Moleskis (1967), Elli Peonidou (1970), Zeki Ali (1970) Tamer Oncul (1974), Hakki Yucel (1978) Nese Yashin (1978), Mehmet Yashin (1978) and Hadji Mike (1980). Each shaped post-1964/74 Partition Cypriotism in different ways, which will be addressed; however, I will focus on Moleskis and Demirag for two interrelated reasons. Firstly, they are Cypriotist pioneers whose deep collaborations that captured common grounds unconsciously began in 1974; by capturing the Cypriotist identification and feelings in all its moments and forms, they demonstrate the core literary and lived practices, narratives and experiences commonly adopted by the post-1964/74 Partition Cypriotist authors. Second, their practices have influenced the more official and dominant formations, enabling popular address and support. These literary-lived practices include mainly their reaction to both partitions via core themes, which are 'Cypriot identity', place/space and time: Cypriotness through an island, homeland or land turn towards united Cyprus; the focus on journey and birth cycles, which replace ethnic dominance with a Cypriot-centric emergence, inclusive of all Cypriots, their whole culture, history and nature. They identify also with communism meeting displacement and exile, especially via the romantic-communist peace poet, Nazim Hikmet,[23] central to post-1964/74 Cypriotism. For example, Hikmet influenced Peonidou, Baybars,[24] Kansu, Levent and the Yashins, and appeared in *Sanat Emegi.*[25] Such practices also include Moleskis and Demirag's commitment to shaping Cypriotist literary and cultural scenes, especially through their writing, official civil service and participation in literary organisations/movements.

Moleskis was born in 1946 in Lysi. He works as a senior cultural officer at the Ministry of Education and Culture in Cyprus, served as president of The Union of Cyprus Writers (2013–2017), and shaped literary activities that hosted Cypriots of all backgrounds. His first publication was in 1967 and since then he published 13 poetry collections and a novel in Greek.[26] The three poetry collections *Poems, Selected Poems* and *Yiorgos Moleskis,* which are selected translations from Moleskis's poetic legacy, are the primary texts I will explore.[27] Moleskis completed his studies at Moscow State University, with a BA in Philology, an MA in Russian, and a PhD in Philology. In 1989 he translated the anthology, *One Hundred Years of Russian Poetry,* and in 2002 he translated Vladimir Mayakofski's *A Cloud in Trousers* from Russian to Greek. As UCW president, he changed its vision so as to include members and commission translations by Cypriots of all background.

Fikret Demirag was born in 1940 in Lefke. He was a secondary school teacher, served as president for 'The Turkish-Cypriot Union of Writers and Artists', and founded and edited magazines, anthologies and cultural newspaper columns. Between 1959 and 2011 Demirag published 25 poetry collections, a memoir and a novel in Turkish.[28] The primary texts that will be explored are the first three volumes of Demirag's poetic tetralogy (1992–1994): *From Limnidi's*[29] *Fire until Today* (Volume 1.); *Mother Grief* (Volume 2) and *The Rootmirror*[30] *Whose Secrets Are Exposed* (Volume 3).[31]

Other important figures include Ivi Meleagrou who demonstrates the earliest examples of Cypriotist practices related to 1950–1970s. Meleagrou worked as a teacher and for radio, shaped leading Cypriot literary journals including *Kypriaka Chronika (Cypriot Chonicles)*, and published short stories and novels. Her debut novel *East Mediterranean* (1966) is about independence failures as related to the first partition during the troublesome nationalisms in 1963–1964, which traces Cypriotist identification through Nicosia.

Mehmet and Nese Yashin are very well-known Cypriotturkish poets, who contributed greatly to defining Cypriotism after the 1974-partition. However, their literary-lived practices problematise the primary principles of collective Cypriotism or Cypriotness in solidarity, without concrete materialisation of what it means in terms I shall claim most useful. Nevertheless the Yashin siblings are significant figures who will appear in parts of this chapter: they initiated the '74 Generation: Rejection Front' and introduced core traits that shaped post-1964/74 Partition Cypriotism, including: 'Cypriot identity' and 'Cypriotness' in poetry, writing back to the ethnic-nationalist, and bi-communal activities between Cypriotgreeks and Cypriotturks. This is mostly captured in their work from 1978 to 1997, starting with contributions to *Sanat Emegi's* special issue on 'peace poetry'; here they co-wrote an article considered the manifesto of the '74 Generation: Rejection Front', and collaborated, through translation, with poets from the other ethnic community.

M. Yashin, is a poet, novelist and scholar. He contributed to the Cypriotist literary scene through his commitment to defining Cypriot identification and defying Cyprus' borders in various ways, which includes: anthologising Cypriot literatures;[32] in his own writings, especially his early works such as *My Love the Dead Soldier,* where, for example, the poem 'Flowers for Peonidou' is for a poet from the other side.

N. Yashin is a poet, novelist and activist, who questioned 'Cypriot identity' through illicit border-crossing and a bi-communalism for a united Cyprus. Defying borders, N. Yashin moved, lives and works in the south, where she teaches Cypriot literature at the University of Cyprus, and has been involved in multiple literary moves towards peace. All of her writings disturb divisions; her debut novel *The Secret History of Sad Girls* (2002) focusses on Cypriotgreek and Cypriotturkish romance across the divide, and her debut poetry collection *Sumbul ile Nergis* (1978) includes her most famous anti-partition poem entitled 'Which Half':

> They Say we must love our country
> That's what my father tells me – often
> My Country has been split in two,
> which of the two parts must I love. (*Sanat Emegi*)

This poem is defined as the unofficial anthem of divided Cyprus by Peonidou, the poet who translated and promoted it in 1979. The poem triggered a bi-communal literary turn in partitioned Cyprus, where N. Yashin, the Cypriotturk in the north, gained recognition and started to work with the Cypriotgreek community in the south. Collaborations, like Peonidou and N. Yashin, extended to include, for example, Cypriotgreek musician Marios Tokas who composed a song of the poem, which they shared at the Camden Cypriot Festival in 1991. Such practices gave way to moves like Poetz4Peace founded by Ali and Mike in 1998.[33]

Peonidou, who contributed fully to such bi-communal movements, is a translator, poet and activist. She served as a teacher, then a journalist and published over 30 volumes of poetry – including *The Soil of Cyprus* (1971), *The Circle of Accusation* (1977), *Songs of Lost Mint* (1979), *Hours* (1983), *Hourglass* (1987) and *Journeys* (1997) – and has joined numerous projects vital to shaping Cypriotism. Most significantly she translated and published the Yashin siblings' poetry along with numerous other Cypriotturkish literary works from Turkish to Greek for Cypriotgreek readership, especially in *Haravgi* (1978); this is relayed in *Sanat Emegi* (1978) and then again in her essay 'Illicit Lovers: Border Crossing'. Thus, these collaborations, especially poets uniting for peace via translation between languages, communities and creative forms, set the foundation for Cypriotism.

The Cypriotists translate or experiment between form and style in various ways. Most outputs are poetry and then prose, yet with crossings into art, music and/or history. For example, art or music meets poetry or prose in Tokas', Ali's and Mike's musical poetry; Peonidou's *The Circle* uses her poetry with drawings by George Skoteinos; Meleagrou's prose narrative meets actual colour– brown for Cyprus' soil and mauve for Cypriot feelings – printed on the page. There is also a fusion of narrative styles, where, for example, Demirag's tetralogy consists of historical poetry in frames, tables, different fonts and sizes, so as to mirror the physical archival research of historian or archaeologist; some of Peonidou and the Yashins' poetry are fairy tale narratives for children. In this way the Cypriotists successfully write Cyprus and the Cypriot through adopting different personas and professions for different audiences, where, like poets, painters, archaeologist, and historians, for example, they unearth the sites, sights, sounds, scents, feelings of Cyprus – landscape, cityscape and countryside – and its people.

These post-1964/74 Partition Cypriotists successfully write, read and construct the 'Cypriot-selves' into and through Cyprus, by engaging with identification as determined by a homeland turn, which starts with nostalgia. Boym states that '[t]o unearth the fragments of nostalgia one needs a dual archaeology of memory and of place, and a dual history of illusionary and of actual practices'. Boym confirms nostalgia is: 'a yearning for a different time – the time of our childhood, the slower rhythms of our dreams' that are at once past-present and imagined-actual practices. Such a return to childhood is dangerous because 'it tends to confuse the actual home and the imaginary one' (Boym, xv-xviii), resulting in a fantasy homeland people would die for, because the individual is 'nostalgic not for the past the way it was, but for the past the way it could have been' (Boym, 351) – a homeland that 'no longer exists or has never existed' (Boym, xiii). To show the processes of these dual practices, and to offer a recipe that can be conscious of it, Boym interrogates and divides nostalgia into its component parts, 'nosta' and 'algia': 'nosta' is 'returning home', which Boym defines as 'restorative nostalgia', whilst 'algia' is longing, which points towards a 'reflective nostalgia'. Restorative nostalgia is a bounded nationalistic nostalgia, which focusses on returning home, national memory and a single plot for national formation, with two main destinations, that are return to origins and religious revivals. This return of restorative nostalgia does not see itself as nostalgic, but instead sees itself as absolute truth and tradition, and this is imagined through a transhistorical reconstruction of the lost home – this nostalgia is the dangerous kind that refuses to acknowledge the dual practices, and confuses the actual and imaginary home. Reflective nostalgia, on the other hand, thrives in longing itself and delays the homecoming, whereby it engages with social memory and a collective framework that explores ways of inhabiting many places/spaces and different time zones at once (Boym, xviii). This nostalgia doubts absolute truth and acknowledges the dual practices of homecoming; therefore, Boym prioritises this reflective nostalgia.

The post-1964/74 Cypriotists inconsistently employ both restorative and reflective nostalgia to perform ambiguously between actual and imagined practices in Cyprus. To understand these nostalgic practices in the Cypriotist production, it is helpful to read them through Tuan's concept of closed place-open space together with Lefebvre's space as a 'concrete-abstraction', which involves mental abstraction and a material physicality that gains concreteness via social practices – this is possible through what Lefebvre calls 'rhythmanalyst', so analysing rhythms – interaction between place, space, time and energies. The Cypriotists use restorative nostalgia by drawing on ethnic-nationalist spatial production, as discussed in Chapter 3: here they experience a Tuanian closed place via Lefebvre's 'mental space' and 'representation of space' as well as the 'physical space' and 'spatial practices', which reinvent a birth and journey cycle bounded by a single plot and destination that searches for 'absolute truth' of 'origins' and strives towards a united Cypriot homecoming. This is an idealistic construction that 'returns' to the slower 'rhythm' of imagined (mental) and actual (physical and social) practices, where, as in nationalism, the former condition is prioritised. Through this 'return' they reconstruct the palimpsestic abstraction of history, the romantic abstraction of physical nature and the domestic abstraction of childhood and family, to produce a 'place' of united Cypriotness that is considered an absolute 'abstract' truth. The Cypriotists also use reflective nostalgia: here they experience a Tuanian space by prioritising actual 'social/spatial practices' between multiple places, spaces and times that complicates the absolute truth; here the abstractions are made concrete.

The Cypriotists 'return' and 'long' for a 'physical' and 'mental' abstraction, experienced as a closed secure 'place' and an open free 'space', which is a Cypriot-centric inclusive homecoming. This homecoming exposes both the single and multiple narrative plots and times, which capture the national and social memories and interactions to make concrete the history, nature, and social constructs shared by the Cypriots to produce Cyprus. In this process of production, however, the Cypriotists, unlike Boym, prioritise restorative nostalgia. Here they do not fully define Cyprus the way it was with its ethnic division and bloodshed; they define it as a Tuanian united safe place through manipulating Lefebvre's 'rhythms' so that they can construct an un-partitioned future for Cyprus.

Birth and Journey Cycle

> and whatever is in it, it's an island poet's
> initiated tracks that are without a dishonest heart
> with what he knows true from the sound of water. (Demirag,
> *Limnidi*, 15)

> I was born one day in April, there
> in the shadow of an olive tree
> where my mother lay heavy with child. (Moleskis, *Profiles*, 15)

Demirag's and Moleskis's poetry is concerned with a journey, whilst drawing on and beginning with a birth: these are central post-1964/74 Partition Cypriotist themes that introduce the process by which both the production of literature and Cyprus are formed. Demirag's poetic tetralogy opens with the first passage above, which acknowledges both the production of the book and context, confirming he is an 'island poet' and 'whatever is in' the book has been collected from his honest 'tracks' around Cyprus. Demirag shows that both journey and book have been assisted by 'the sound of water', a core Cypriotist image symbolising the freedom and organic interaction the poet has with Cyprus; water symbolises the poets' spatial and local practice in Cyprus, where, like water, they unite, flow and interact with the land and people for a reading and construction of Cyprus.

Whilst Demirag's passage introduces the crucial significance of the journey for Cypriotist production, Moleskis's passage, drawn from 'My First Song', introduces birth. Birth is a pivotal narrative tool, where through it the journey begins, can continue and its success aided: it symbolises a return to Cypriots archaic cultural roots and origins, as well as the actual biological birth and imagined national birth within a maternal framework. Here through engaging with the 'olive tree', another core Cypriotist image, Moleskis draws on the birth symbolisms to show that the islander is the offspring of the archaic cultural roots and origins in Cyprus, a physical piece of Cyprus, biologically born in Cyprus – the child of Mother Cyprus.

This journey and birth is a central thematic in all Cypriotist narratives: Meleagrou's *East Mediterranean*, for example, focusses on Margarita, one of the main characters, who compulsively journeys, drives and dives, both mentally, physically and socially, through the walled city with momentary visions of the countryside, which often break through divided Nicosia. A narrative on 'birth' or 'roots' of inhabitants is developed through her focus on Cypriot histories, physical urban cityscapes or landscapes, and social familial relations. Similarly, N. Yashin's and Peonidou's poetry emphasises a journey through Cyprus via its people, especially through a deep turn to and love for the homeland that focusses on the senses, social experience, history, memories and myths, which delves into the island's and islanders' birth – a return to roots. Thus, these passages introduce the general narrative scope of Cypriotist writing; they turn to the actual land, to Cyprus, to capture the birth cycle that enables the journey cycle for the Cypriotist production of Cyprus.

This literary birth and journey of post-1964/74 Partition Cypriotism is demonstrated in the preface to Demirag's *Limnidi*:

> throughout 8 thousand years of Cyprus's history it has been those who came from 'outside' that have been a subject, while the 'local inhabitants' have been 'objects' [...] The Cypriots have now mobilised to be subjects, they are at the historical point where they can make decisions and represent themselves. (Demirag, *Limnidi*, 5)

Demirag's commentary is a communist moment that echoes Marx's renowned phrase in *Eighteenth Brumaire*: 'They cannot represent themselves, they must be represented' (Marx, 124). The idea that the Cypriots were 'objects' without 'subjectivity' suggests their lack of agency during different imperial regimes, when they were treated as possessions owned and defined. This also relates to a localised national narrative, when Cypriotists were frequently overpowered and silenced by the official and dominant ethnic-motherland nationalists. Demirag's and Moleskis's birth and journey cycles show that the Cypriotist construction of Cyprus is finally 'born' to be the sole 'subject', whereby the Cypriot inhabitants have 'mobilised' to have subjectivity, definitions, make decisions and represent themselves. The Cypriotist poets show this subjectivity through responding to history, particularly the legacy of conquests and colonisation inscribed in Cyprus, rather than erase it like the ethnic-motherland nationalists, or allowing the rulers to write this history for them, as the British attempted to do. In this process, as Melih Cevdet Anday states in the commentary on Demirag's *Limnidi,* 'the conqueror is the conquered' because their narratives are rewritten by the Cypriots who are no longer empty objects or submissive subjects. The Cypriotists rewrite history in their own terms of identification; here showing they have been moulded by these imperial moments, and are representing these histories, cultures and languages of past Cyprus. In this Cypriotist historiography all ruling regimes are represented as equal in their palimpsestic inscription, power and coercion in Cyprus. The Cypriotists also play with the subject(ivity) within local narratives, where Cyprus – its history, nature and people – is recovered to be the central subject over the ethnic-motherland nationalists' Greece/Greeks and Ottoman-Turkey/Turks for national definitions. Through these narratives, as Anday suggests via Demirag's poetics, 'a new dough, a new identity has arrived [...] "one identity": the Cypriots' (Demirag, *Limnidi*, 9–10).

Birth Cycle: Route and Root to Gifts of Mother

Demirag and Moleskis start their Cypriotist narrative by returning to the land, Cyprus, and engaging with a birth within the context of cultural roots and a maternal frame.

They reject restorative nostalgia as practised by the ethnic-motherland nationalist through using reflective nostalgia, which complicates the truth of origins by compulsively questioning where, what and how to define the Cypriot. The Cypriotists confirm that the answers can be found through returning to the land: 'How much of our roots are with you, how much of it is in a far uncertain space?' (Demirag, *Limnidi*, 30). Thus, Demirag sets the stage for the Cypriotist literary quest, which is to read Cyprus through unearthing origins and roots – historical, cultural and social – in *only* Cyprus. These Cypriot roots are in an 'uncertain space' because they have a palimpsestic existence with complex layering, which has been erased throughout Cyprus' ethno-national and imperial constructions. Demirag frequently refers to and questions the Cypriot origins through this layering and erasure:

> Stop and ask: After shovels and shovels of soil were thrown
> on top of all those hopes
> **WHO** are you now? From where do you start your journey which
> [...] layered **alluvial** are you?
> [...]
> O time, with what kind of dough did you complete me? (Demirag, *Limnidi*, 78)

Demirag confirms that the answers to Cypriot origins and 'who is the Cypriot now' are determined by asking land and time, the culprits that provide 'uncertainty' and definition. They provide explanation of the layered experiences and cultures – 'hopes', 'journeys', 'roots' – inscribed by past and present inhabitants, particularly of the nationalist and imperialist inventions that emptied the land of its historical meaning to cover it with a new language they can control.

In 'Roots' Moleskis also turns to the land and time to engage with origins:

> A flower,
> which scattered as a petiole and has blossomed,
> turns towards the earth,
> afflicted by the burden
> of its own existence.
> It wants to touch its roots,
> to be assured...
>
> But where
> can it find the roots,
> which are buried in such depth,
> which have scattered to so many directions
>
> And yet it knows,
> it is its roots which nourish it. (Moleskis, *Selected*, 18)

Moleskis uses the flower-root as metaphor to show that the individuals, like the flower, turn towards the land – 'roots' – to find meaning in their 'existence'. He suggests the roots are primordial and cultural codes in the land – ancient architectures, ruins, tombs, dead bodies – that not only nourish and attach the person to the land and their heritage, but provide a substance for cultural and national growth. In this way Moleskis shows that answers to the Cypriot beginnings are provided solely by the 'roots' in Cyprus, determined by palimpsestic layers falling into all 'directions' without a single ethnic narrative plot of absolute truth and 'certainty'. Cypriots are firmly located, nourished and survive by the variability, interconnectivity and unification of multiple histories invested in the land of Cyprus.

Similarly, in *Soil of Cyprus* Peonidou turns to the land, where looking deep into the soil or source she experiences multiple histories, social relations and nature that capture the union between the Cypriots and Cyprus: 'Myrtle of Cyprus / sound of Cyprus / snakes, birds and heartbeats have found / in your roots brotherly shelter' (*Profile*, 10). Meleagrou also turns to the soil via words printed on the page in a brown colour, which describe the cultural, political and historical layers of Cyprus.

These writers show that their reading and construction of Cyprus is determined by a journey, which starts by turning physically to the island with questions on the Cypriots' origins or birth, rather than to Greece or Turkey as advocated by the ethnic-motherland nationalists.[34] They develop further this questioning by turning to Cyprus within a maternal framework, where, refusing to associate Greece or Turkey as Mothers, they map Cyprus as Mother and Cypriots as her children, they reclaim a new birth for the Cypriots. The Cypriotists mappings resonate with numerous postcolonial studies on gendered nations, especially those by Lyn Innes and Anne McClintock. The Cypriotists use gender to materialise an organically united Cypriot family in Cyprus, against nationalists' ethnic family in the ethnic centres. Unlike the nationalists', the Cypriotists' Cyprus is within a fixed gendered frame, in that the nation is always represented as the 'Mother' and the Cypriot her child; Cyprus is stably united, both geographically and consciously, as 'the Mother' for all Cypriots. Through this kinship the Cypriotists can answer 'who is the Cypriot?' – the Cypriot is the child of Mother Cyprus.

The Cypriotists engage with Mother Cyprus through narratives on actual maternal relations – as in N. Yahsin's poems on 'mother and baby' in *Tears of War* when the child speaks to its widowed mother about ruins of war – as well as in narratives that gender Cyprus, as in Demirag's *Limnidi*:

> Cypri!* is it not a few that notice, that our seeds are planted in you;
> 'a wind' left us in your soil, and as it transpired
> here we greened! [...]
> [...] here we were pruned, fertilised with your soil's divine hymn
> [...] there are not a few who ask directions to another country,
>   Maaaaaany ask for directions,
> But is it not that our roots are in you, and wherever we go
> Our roots will carry a grain from your soil,
> So they can ask the plant spikes about us
>   Ask the green and amber grains –
> [...]
> [...] there is no need for an Ithaca

[...]
Think: didn't this mother soil, in its womb,
also feed you – to germinate –
bring you up? (Demirag, *Limnidi*, 25–26)
* The name of Cyprus on the maps produced by the Roman Empire.

The passage depicts the relationship between Cyprus and Cypriots through maternal botanical imagery. Cyprus is the 'mother soil' and the Cypriot is defined via its birth, from being a 'seed planted' in the soil – 'womb' – of Cyprus to being and becoming – 'fertilised', 'pruned' and 'germinated' – a plant. They reject nationalist spatial practices – asking directions to another country through an Odysseus-like journey – towards Greece or Turkey. They reject the ethno-historical chronological narrative of Mother Turkey or Greece who gave birth to Baby Cyprus/Cypriot with Turkey as the 'wind'; instead the maternal relationship is – the 'wind left us in the soil' – a random accident of nature. Here Demirag further disrupts this ethno-national fixity by defining Cypriots not as Greek or Turkish 'sons of the nation', but as all of 'you' born in Cyprus. Thus, he affirms that all Cypriots are an organic, yet accidental, piece of Cyprus intimately and naturally bound to the land, like a child to its mother.

In 'A Letter to Gregory Afxentiou', Moleskis responds to the ethnic-motherland nationalists by engaging with Afxentiou, the EOKA freedom-fighter:

...the Motherland is the earth amongst the sea
with the mountains, the forests and the people's houses.
Above all it is the people who inhabit it,
who sow and harvest...

When something is lost the motherland becomes deficient and starts to deteriorate
and if the people are lost everything is lost.
You do not find the Motherland on another soil, nor on another star.
It is on the earth and the stones
which were watered with your first tears. (Moleskis, *Selected*, 38)

Here Moleskis rejects the 'Mother-Baby' and 'Martyred-Son' nationalist narrative by referring to Greece not as motherland but as 'another soil', and Cyprus not as the ethno-heroic son Afxentiou but as the Motherland. Moleskis confirms the 'Motherland' is the place Afxentiou was – 'first tears' – born, Cyprus. The motherland is the place a person was born and 'inhabits', which is mapped with and belongs to all the people in it; it is the farmers who work – 'sow and harvest' – the land, as well as the physical landscape – 'earth, mountains, forest, houses and stones' – with their mappings. Here recovering the Communist-Cypriotists' slogan 'Cyprus belongs to and is its people', Moleskis shows that the 'almighty Mother' is Cyprus and its people, and shows that to refuse this ethno-inclusive definition, as the nationalists do, is to diminish the Motherland. Moleskis concludes by confirming that though the new Cypriot generation – 'children' – are 'in danger of repeating' the journey carved by nationalist, they will find 'a road beyond'; and throughout Moleskis', and the Cypriotists', poetic quest they define this new journey and road to 'freedom' that rewrites the nationalists' 'Ancestral Journey and Gifts'.[35] Before analysing the Cypriotists' three interrelated journeys that enable them to recover new gifts of independent Mother Cyprus, I will show how they engage with overcoming road blocks that enslave Mother Cyprus and her gifts.

Enslaved Mother: Road Blocks

The Cypriotist poets revise the nationalist narratives on 'Gendered Enslavement' into a Cypriotist framework, to show partial confrontation with Cyprus the way it actually was in the past and is in the present. They show the Cypriotist journey and wanderers are subject to road blocks, which result in the mother's journeys and gifts being devoured, because of the ethnic-motherland nationalists and the actualities of partition. The nationalists devour spatial palimpsestic history, nature and social-domestic formations because they only include archaic inscriptions from Greece and Turkey; Cyprus' partitions devour the spatial and local journey because the borders prevent Cypriots from freely wandering and interacting with their island. The Cypriotists show that erasing history, nature and social-domestic inscriptions, or creating borders in these journeys enslaves Mother Cyprus.

In 'Our Homeland is Small', Moleskis responds to the nationalist narratives responsible for enslaving Cyprus:

> Frightened we look more back to the past than to the future,
> unearthing forgotten saints and heroes.
>
> The homeland diminishes and the heroes multiply,
> [...]
> The heroes have become armies killing the man inside us (Moleskis, *Poems*, 28)

Moleskis criticises the nationalists who read Cyprus by returning to past – 'saints and heroes' – ethnic codes and abstractions. These abstractions 'kill' Cypriots and Cyprus because they block actual spatial history, physical nature and social-domestic rhythms, thus, making the homeland 'dangerously smaller' because these gifts determining Cypriot formations and a united un-partitioned present-future are compromised. Similarly in *Hourglass*, Peonidou writes 'when I open my mouth / may my voice be my own / not the voice of my forbears [...] Our country, a small nail on the map / Lend a hand to keep it there/ For if it falls with it we will be lost' (Literary, 16–17).

The Cypriotists frequently depict this 'dangerously smaller' demolished Mother Cyprus who falls victim to the ethnic and 1964/74 partition narratives, as in Moleskis 'Portrait of My Mother':

> Mother, your face
> a rocky land burned by the sun,
> a land that's never had her fill of water
> but which continuously bears fruit
> the wheat, the wine and the herd.
> Your face, mother
> a land of torment
> soil cracked by drought
> burned by the sun.
> And when the bombs fell,
> a thousand craters opened
> a thousand graves
> a land of scorched forests
> and lonely scorched trees. (Moleskis, *Profile,* 16)

Here Moleskis shows that Mother Cyprus has been tormented, bombed and scorched without 'water' by weapons of the competing nationalist mobilisation and the 1964/74 partitions. As in all Cypriotists poetics, 'water' is the source that enables the poets to read, have an organic connection with and construct Cyprus; water is the layers of history, nature and social domesticity that cultivate Cyprus. Moleskis has numerous other poems, in *The Water of Memory* for example, that refer to water as the social memory and nature of the island. Similarly Demirag's poetic tetralogy confirms his narrative has been aided by the 'sound of water'; Peonidou writes about the 'thirsty land' gone months without rain (*Mint*, 31), yet with hope: 'do not insist that the sources have dried up; have your fingers forgotten how to dig' (*Hourglass*, 18). In his poem, Moleskis shows the water exists, so the three gifts exist because the land 'bears fruit', yet they are being emptied from Mother Cyprus. Like Moleskis' Mother, Demirag's collection *Mother Grief* is about 1964/74 partitions as narrated by enslaved Mother Cyprus mourning borders that imprison her spatial and local gifts. Peonidou's *The Circle of Accusation* and N. Yashins' *Tears of War* respond to Mother Cyprus enslaved after 1974.

Even though the Cypriotist poets show Mother Cyprus is devoured, they also show Mother Cyprus' strength with the immortality of her gifts. In *Limnidi*, Demirag states:

> My homeland, beautiful mother, how many ashes of pain does it hide
> your always forced prostituted, unmarried and widowed soil?
>
> This woman who was raped throughout Mediterranean history;
> with every age how the human-grasshoppers swept and wiped the beautiful crops
> [...]
> till I die it is my duty to sing your song,
> the plundered hopes of the community in every age. (Demirag, *Limnidi*, 54)

Cyprus is depicted as a rape victim because of spatial history – multiple rulers and inhabitants – that injected something into it, confirming the impossibility of historical erasure and of attaining an ethnically purified Mother Cyprus. Mother Cyprus is an impure woman whose 'pain and rape' have been 'wiped away' by the nationalists and new rulers that replaced these historical inscriptions with their own. Demirag shows, however, that erasing these inscriptions does not diminish the spatial history or fact that Cyprus is a rape victim because the children born, 'beautiful crops', are a result of these sexual encounters. The rulers inseminated their cultural inscriptions in Mother Cyprus but then departed, leaving her to procreate a fatherless nation

Both Demirag's and Moleskis's gendered Cyprus responds to the common depictions seen in most postcolonial gendered nationalism, wherein nations figure as females to symbolise inner traditions and passivity of the nation, which is rendered unsafe and in danger of being exploited. Such depictions suggest it is the duty of the male agents of the nation and/or the colonial empire to save and restore the inner beauty of the feminised homeland. As McClintock states, the feminised land is symbolic of 'the passive atavist of the nation', whilst the men are symbolic of the 'active agents' of liberation ('longer', 92). In these gendered narratives the ultimate goal is to make an honest woman out of the feminised nation, to protect her chastity and/or cleanse her, through being wedded and uniting with either the sons of the homeland or the colonial empire.

In gendering Cyprus, the Cypriotists reject these claims of 'atavism', 'evolutionary throwback' and 'purification' of the nation. They do not return to atavism in an attempt, as with the nationalists, to revert Cyprus to the ways of thinking and living within a single former ethnic time and ancestral type; instead they shift between multiple times and ancestral types, whilst engaging with historical, natural and social layers. The Cypriotists refuse to make Mother Cyprus the purified submissive intended: it does not conform to the traditional role of a nurturing and pure mother figure; instead Mother Cyprus – prostituted, unmarried, widowed – is honoured for being comparatively unconventional and sexually free. As Demirag shows, it is the Cypriotists' 'duty to sing' and praise the layers of spatial and local inscriptions the land has independently endured and the 'beautiful crops', the fatherless children born out of each era. The narratives suggest that exposing Mother Cyprus as an impure woman subject to multiple harassments actually frees rather than enslaves her; she is freed from the gender roles of being the passive 'intended' wife or weak widow in need of male authority. Unlike feminine symbols in other postcolonial figurations, this Mother Cyprus does not need to be purified, protected or saved by the male agents as she survived and reproduced without them. In fact, the men of the nation do not figure or have a significant national role in any of the Cypriotist narratives; instead, the freedom of Mother Cyprus is determined by acknowledging these spatial and local layers through which all Cypriot people are the active agents of the national building project.

Free Mother Cyprus with Nazim Hikmet's Help

For the Cypriotists, to liberate enslaved Cyprus is to wander spatially and locally around the island, unearthing the palimpsestic spatial history, physical nature and social gifts of Mother Cyprus. In this way they re-define the nationalist narratives characterised as 'Free Enslaved Cyprus 1, 2, 3' and 'Our Martyred Son',[36] showing how these processes enslaved Mother Cyprus.

In 'Our Homeland is Small' Moleskis states: 'freedom, freedom/ from where will you come to liberate us' (Moleskis, *Poem*, 28) to show Cypriots need a different source to the nationalists' one. Moleskis' and Demirag's struggle for liberation is a peaceful mobilisation against nationalist and partition binary militant mappings of Cyprus, where they 'call' forth the local Cypriots to unite and join hands, as shown through Mother Cyprus who shouts:

> GET UP AND LET'S GO PLOUGH OUR SMALL FIELD
> (IT IS TIME TO LIFT THE ASHES). (Demirag, *Mother*, 241)

This is a mobilisation within a post-1964/74 Partition Cypriotist frame, whereby all Cypriots are called to 'plough' and reap the land. The Cypriots, particularly villagers that work the land, are reclaimed as pivotal in this liberation struggle because through them the social life, daily routine, physical nature and history of Cyprus are recovered and made free. The passage is a 'call' for all Cypriots to imitate these local villagers as opposed to ethnic warriors, because they are not only the majority in Cyprus, but it is they who fully interact, unite with and bring the actualities of the land to life. Through them, not through ethnic warriors, Mother Cyprus will be liberated. This call is a communist image, whereby the Cypriot people unite with their tools – pitchfork, spades, sickles, hammers – to help free and unite the island. Here it is time that as villagers, the Cypriots prioritise nature that is mapped with – 'ashes' – past and present social life, where they 'plough', recover and free these historical, natural and social gifts so they can read the layers that define them. In this passage all Cypriots are called to become one as villagers, united in the struggle to free and bring Mother Cyprus and these gifts to life.

In 'The Sun is Hot' Moleskis also reaches out: 'To this I call you./ Come/Brothers, come/ Come quickly' so they can 'build new moulds/ within which to reshape' and free enslaved Mother Cyprus. In this poem, Moleskis 'calls' forth all Cypriots and a 'brother' who is not Cypriot: this 'brother' is a pivotal figure that most Cypriotists engage with in their narratives on liberation; this 'brother' is a pioneer of peace who has the ability to support the Cypriots to liberate Mother Cyprus. Moleskis 'calls' and dedicates the poem to 'Nazim Hikmet' (Moleskis, *Profile*, 12) – a worldly romantic-communist poet, who dedicated his literary, lived and bodily existence to his ideals. Hikmet spent most of his life in prison and exile for his writings and beliefs; he was not only a communist activist committed to revolution, protesting against injustice and struggling for peace, but also a romantic committed to and in love with his country and his people. Moleskis, like many Cypriotists, calls Hikmet to help free Cyprus from enslavement because he has the experience and knowledge, having spent most of his life struggling against imprisonment; Hikmet[37] affirms this struggle in the poem, 'Since I have Been Inside': 'Since I've been inside/ the world has turned around the sun ten times./And again I repeat with the same passion,/ what I wrote for them/the year I came inside' (Hikmet, 899). Moleskis' call suggests that Hikmet's undefeatable political commitment against the dominant narratives, and his dedication to world peace, can help the Cypriots unite and mobilise against the injustice and war the island and islanders have suffered. Similarly, Hikmet's romanticism can help accommodate the interaction between the land and people, whereby the Cypriots can follow Hikmet's wise actions shown in 'Today is Sunday': 'Then with respect I sat on the soil/ [...] at this moment neither fighting, nor freedom nor my wife / The soil, the sun and me/I'm fortunate...' (Hikmet, 668); and words from 'Advice to Our Children': 'Only recognise the soil/believe the soil./ Do not separate it from your mother/ your mother soil./Love the soil/as much as your mother...' (Hikmet, 233).

The Cypriotist feel that Hikmet's communist-romantic legacy can help liberate their spatially and locally enslaved Mother Cyprus. Whilst Moleskis directly calls Hikmet in his poetry, Demirag's calling for Hikmet is different, in that he aligns himself with a literary movement, the socialist realist generation, pioneered by Hikmet. Similarly Peonidou,

Levent and Baybars engaged with Hikmet and/or communist-romantic approaches in their works; many Cypriotist magazines, especially *Sanat Emegi* consists of works by or related to Hikmet. Through appropriating Hikmet's romantic-communism, the poets show that in this Cypriotist liberation struggle all Cypriots have a duty to free Mother Cyprus.

They reject national narratives of martydom, as advocated by the ethnic-motherland nationalists' 'Our Martyred Son' and 'Well Done My Son', by following Hikmet's words: 'There's an unfavourable side to our national anthem,/Don't know how to explain it,/[...] But I do not believe/ all of what he [Mehmet Akif Ersoy, author of Turkish anthem] believes./Is the ecstasy of martyrdom the thing that holds me here/I don't think so' (Hikmet, 608). They endorse Hikmet's attitude to martyrdom, 'don't want my child killed at twenty/ if a boy at the front-line/ if a girl in the shelters in the middle of the night' (Hikmet, 949). Like Hikmet, the Cypriotists do not believe in advocating death: 'We are the ones that create and destroy [...] this liveable world./Our footprints are bloody on the roads we left behind, [...] Is it our bloody footprints that stand before us on our road?' (Hikmet, 1830). In light of this, the Cypriotist poets continue Hikmet's legacy of poetic-political criticism to question constantly those national agents, most often men, who enslave the land: 'Gentlemen, how could you harm this homeland?' *[Beyler bu vatana nasil kiydiniz]* (Hikmet, 1688).

Even though the Cypriotist narratives reject martyrdom, they do have a Hikmetian calling, 'Call [...] people I am calling you' (Hikmet, 1833), towards a united peace and liberation, which wills two kinds of symbolic sacrifice. Firstly the call for a symbolic sacrifice of ethnic ideas, when they state: 'don't ask where your roots are' (Demirag, *Limnidi*, 87) because the 'roots [...] have scattered to so many directions' (Moleskis, *Profile*, 31) and 'You do not find the Motherland on another soil' (Moleskis, *Select,* 38). Secondly, they commend a symbolic sacrifice of the self, which is like Hikmet's; Hikmet willingly sacrificed his life for peace and freedom, resulting in him being a political prisoner and exile, with a life sentence from his birthland that defined him as treasonous. In 'Traitor', he writes: 'Nazim Hikmet is still continuing to be a homeland traitor [...] If homeland is your farms/ if it's what's in your safes and cheque books / If dying of starvation in the middle of the highway, is homeland / If it's drinking our scarlet blood in your factories / [...] if it's your payments and salaries/ If homeland is not escaping from our stinking darkness / then, I am traitor' (Hikmet, 1826). The Cypriotists were willing to be labelled traitors by the dominant nationalists for their literary-lived quests that struggled for a de-ethnicised united Cyprus. Moleskis has numerous poems that engage with this sacrifice, where he dedicates his mind and body to share a united inclusive Cyprus:

> 'I am a Candle':
> I am a candle

[...]
I burn and shed light (Moleskis, *Poems*, 27).

'Returning':
gathering and spreading the light
[...]
like the mountains, the sky,
the sun and the rock,
and like this more secret fountain
which grew enlightening me
and which will grow still claiming me (Moleskis, *Selected*, 20).

'Light I will become':
I will become logos
and as logos I will be given to the people.
And when I am no longer myself
I will be logos
from which the people will draw light. (Moleskis, *Profile*,
11–12)

'Turn the Wheel':
Cut me into pieces
[...]
annihilate this body. (Moleskis, *Profile*, 32)

Here Moleskis defines himself as 'light', which is the knowledge he collects when wandering around Cyprus, and which he returns to the Cypriots to 'draw' from by willingly sacrificing– 'cut me into pieces [...] annihilate' – his body. This body symbolises Moleskis' literary texts that provide Cypriots with knowledge of Mother Cyprus' enslaved gifts – layers of spatial history, a connection with nature, and recovery of social Cyprus – so that they can help free them.

Thus, the Cypriotist poets show that their sacrifice is a symbolic one, whereby ethnic abstractions of Cyprus are killed without ceremony or immortalisation, and replaced with divine immortal knowledge of Mother Cyprus and the gifts she offers. Through imitating Hikmet's legacy the poets and Cyprus are freed: freely they wander into and perform a spatial and local journey around Cyprus without a trace of ethnic-motherland nationalist or partition blockades.

Journey Cycle to Three Gifts: Palimpsestic Archaeology, Nature, Social-domestic

In this journey the Cypriotists analyse Cyprus, as it were via Lefebvre's concrete-abstraction: they conceive a mental abstraction and perceive a physical materiality of the history, nature and people of Cyprus, which are made concrete through the poets' and Cypriots' lived and daily interactions, experiences and social practices. Throughout this journey the mental, physical and particularly the social, conceived, perceived and particularly lived conditions of Cyprus are recovered, and they blur into each other to expose the active and actual production of Cyprus. Here they experience Cyprus through Tuan's closed place that is controlled and open space of freedom. In this process the closed place combined with the idealistic mental, physical and social abstractions is prioritised, because through it the Cypriotists construct Cyprus not the actual way it was but the way it could have been in the interest of an un-partitioned united future. This process, particularly the recovery of the three gifts, is central to Cypriotist writings, which now bring us deep into the journey cycles. The remaining three parts will demonstrate the recovery of these gifts through trailing our wandering poets, who grasp fully the 'rhythms' – like Lefebvrean rhythmanalysts – for the production of Cyprus.

Spatial Palimpsestic Archaeology: Linear Rhythm

The Cypriotists perform a spatial journey through unearthing the palimpsestic possibility of Cyprus. Here the wandering poets free and recover the spatial history[38] through an inclusive recording of all cultural inscriptions in linear rhythmic form, from primordial and tribal groups, old and new inhabitants, to the foreign and imperial rulers. They show that these spatial palimpsestic inscriptions, like all historical constructions, are inescapably abstractions that must be unearthed and made concrete through readings and interactions, because they not only expose the truth of secreted Cyprus, but are also a primary force in the production of Cyprus.

Demirag's *Limnidi* will be the primary focus here because it is concerned with wandering and recovering the chronological history invested in Cyprus, doing justice to the Cypriotists' legacy with spatial palimpsestic archaeology. Demirag starts the spatial journey by confronting the difficulty of reading and writing a coherent history, resulting from the nationalist and partition blockades meeting multiple histories entangled in 'uncertain spaces', which he deals with by responding to time:

> Time has eroded my rock of life, and
> I still don't know, oh my homeland mother;
>
> explain to your old, ignorant son
> where is the place of this stone in our lives? (Demirag, *Limnidi*, 27)
>
> its court case still open, its top crossed (Demirag, *Limnidi*, 50)
>
> the stones have no tongue, and most of the witnesses
> have spread and mixed in soil a long time ago. (Demirag, *Limnidi*, 55)

> Tell me my homeland, on which distant love traces am I
> stepping on now,
> walking on a desolate shore! On which mysteries of far
> cruelty, near
> cruelty and wisdom! Which pit is your soil covering.
> (Demirag *Limnidi*, 74)

Here and throughout *Limnidi*, Demirag defines nature – rocks, stones, land – as witnesses to an entire cultural past, which can provide an understanding of spatial history to construct Cyprus. Demirag reveals however that he struggles to read and recover this history because it is shaped by man-made and natural erosions, particularly a repetitive cycle of erasures and replacements, where histories' witnesses – nature and people – are either dying or being silenced by different regimes. This results in Demirag persistently asking Mother Cyprus for a coherent spatial history, which enables him to un-silence and gather the witnesses via physical, natural and social evidence that brings justice to the 'open court case' of Cyprus history.

Demirag states that to recover and read the spatial palimpsestic history of Cyprus: 'We need a human archaeologist; maybe we should be our own archaeologist' (Demirag, *Limnidi*, 30), confirming that *Limnidi* is an archaeological project. Through this Demirag adopts the persona of a spatial specialist to be the expert witness – an archaeologist with skills and methods to collect and study materials that bear the remains of past human life. He uses his own 'unorthodox' methods, drawn from archaeologists alongside psychoanalysts, musicologists, historians, sociologists, a poet – thus becoming a Lefebvrean rhythmanalyst who successfully unearths, gathers, grasps all materials of the past as 'rhythms' for a coherent chronological history. In the opening of *Limnidi,* Demirag shows his unorthodox process of spatial analysis via rhythmanalysis, where he states: 'I am trying to read from the mysterious face […] Read yourself to me!' (Demirag, *Limnidi*, 37). The materials he collects are grasped as Lefebvrean rhythms – movement between places, spaces, times and energies – via all senses; they are mental and physical abstractions of the inhabitants' and rulers' 'face' from past cultures, with which Demirag has a conceptual relationship because he can read them, yet he also has a spiritual and intimate relationship with them because he can actually see, feel, taste and experience them. When Demirag struggles to read past inscriptions he socially interacts and speaks to them ('read yourself to me') through which the historical abstraction is made concrete – they come to life. Throughout Demirag's quest he collects these material witnesses, the bundles of rhythms, from the natural landscape and environment – stone, water, soil, wind, trees and living beings – showing that though they do not always speak, he has the social and spatial skills of a rhythmanalyst to read, grasp and bring them to life.

'Water' and soil are core source witnesses the Cypriotists interact with to read spatial history:

> what you hear is all the sounds of Life from the soils scent
> [...]
> your homeland, a whole geography that embraces Life.
> (Demirag, *Limnidi*, 78)
>
> The lines have been collected one by one
> from times dust
> [...]
> Under the soil – still –
> from those whose blood screams
> from the ashes of remembrance. (Demirag, *Limnidi*, 122)

Demirag shows the whole geography is inscribed with past-present Life, and through sensory and communicative powers – 'smell' and 'hear' – he can recover this history – 'times dust' and 'ashes' – from the soil. He elaborates on life in the soil through referring to 'blood scream' and 'blood types' (Demirag, *Limnidi*, 55), which suggests the soil is imbued with many groups within an archaic biological (abstract arcane ancestors' blood) and a temporal biological (actual blood) context. Contaminating the ethnic-nationalists' narratives of pure ethnic blood, Demirag suggests the Cypriots are hybrids with mixed blood from multiple geographies. Similarly, the 'wind' is also a witness re-defined: 'If we listen to the wind/it could bring us/ an antique grandfather's bones' (Demirag, *Limnidi*, 75), where, unlike the nationalists' wind as Ottomans, it symbolises all past colonisers, conquerors and inhabitants of Cyprus. Trees, especially 'Olive Trees', are the wisest and all-knowing witness, because 'Other than the old olive trees no one remembers' the multiple histories (Demirag, *Limnidi*, 50).

Demirag also collects witnesses via living beings, mainly animals who speak history: 'It's a mythological sound that comes down to the field/ With the thin goat rattles of the evening'. Also Cypriot people who have inherited physical and social characteristics from former cultures also carry histories:

> On how many faces is there a little mixture of the Dor face?
> (Demirag, 45)
>
> Wait! It is maybe a Dor's whisper
> that you hear in my voice!.
> [...]
> is a poetic spell that drops from the voice
> of Dionysus while vacillating the streets!
> Day time, your Lusignan aunt's meaty lips
> are being kissed by the youth of your neighbours' son.
> (Demirag, *Limnidi*, 77)

Demirag has gathered the 'rhythms', the material witnesses from the natural landscape and living beings, and developed the rhythmanalytical social skills to read, interact and make concrete the abstraction of history. He can now record a scrupulous and inclusive chronology for the Cypriotist case, a spatial history that has a guaranteed level of coherence with some performance. Using restorative nostalgia, he captures an idealistic national history through a 'transhistorical reconstruction of the lost homeland' (Boym, x) that has a single chronological 'linear rhythm' with a coherent plot, which starts with Cypriot origins and ends with Cypriots today. Demirag also uses reflective nostalgic practices of historical appropriation, where he performs between multiple time-zones and cultures. Unlike the reflective nostalgic, however, Demirag does not inhabit rhythms in different geographies, but inhabits and reads rhythms located solely within the island's geographical borders.

Demirag records both ancient mythology and historical moments inscribed in Cyprus.[39] The classical Greek phase is recovered through mythical figures, especially Aphrodite – 'coquettish, mind bender Aphrodite [...] came out to your shores from the waves of the antique and wise Mediterranean' (Demirag, *Limnidi*, 28) – who, born from the Paphos rock in the sea, shaped the life of multiple mythical figures. Here he confirms Cyprus is Aphrodite's homeland, and 'Is the Homeland of imaginary Pygmalion, Galetea, Paphos, Anaxarete, Iphis, Kinyras and his son Adonis' (Demirag, *Limnidi*, 28)' – who collectively have a relationship with the island,[40] suggesting they are his ancestors who invested a culture and belong to Cyprus. Unlike most Cypriotturkish narratives, through this gesture, Demirag identifies with the Ancient Greek phase to claim an immortal inscription in Cyprus's history, and also shows, unlike Cypriotgreek narratives, it is not the sole essence for constructing Cyprus. Demirag randomly refers to the Greek mythical phase throughout the volume; however, historical facts are documented chronologically.

Starting with the title 'From Pre-Historic to Ancient Filled Days', Demirag writes of the Neolithic period to the Christian conversion. Demirag concretises the pre-historic moment through focussing on first inhabitants and place names in Cyprus:

> a
> the first sweat was poured by the man of the Neolithic period
> with his heart he polished the first stone in Hirokitya
> weaved honeycomb houses and buried their dead in the rooms.
> The man of the Chalcolithic period used the first copper
> and poured the bronze, moulded it in old Ambeliku. (Demirag, *Limnidi*, 35)
> [...]

> c
> who shaped with their skilled hands, the ceramic
> at Enkomi and Kition? (Demirag, *Limnidi*, 39)

Here Demirag refers to actual Neolithic remains – 'polished stone', 'houses' they built and dead 'bodies in the room' – found in Hirokitya (Khirokita) south Cyprus, considered as evidence of the earliest traces (8200–3900 BCE) related to woman/man in the Middle East. The 'Chalcolithic' period (3900–2500 BCE) is associated with Ambeliku in the north, where copper remains were found. Mycenaean settlement from the late bronze age (1600–1050 BCE), and the first Phoenician settlement from the Iron age (850 BCE) is linked to 'Enkomi' in north and 'Kition' in south, where the ceramic remains were found (Hadjidemetriou 41). Demirag links these pre-historic moments though shifting between place names in north and south Cyprus not only to make concrete the abstraction, but also to show – unlike nationalist 'place-ancestor' narratives – that these non-ethnic inscriptions belong to and created the Cypriot and Cyprus. Demirag also reads powerful rulers from pre-historic moments (1450 BCE to 1200 BCE): 'Tuthmosis III's ancient Egypt?/ and the Hittite passed like the wind' (Demirag, *Limnidi*, 41); here, without prioritising the Hittite Kings of Ugarit as the Cypriotturkish nationalists do, Demirag lists rulers from pre-historic days through to rulers of the ancient period:

> (a)
> on you Assyrians heavy shadow,
> then, repeated ancient Egypt, Persian hurricane.
> [...]
> The shocks were left on your little body.
> [...]
> Macedonian's hurricane
> the young and indisputable conquerors' shadow
> also fell on you
> [...]
> Sunny Onesilos's, glorious Evagoras'
> where are your flags, your wounded flags. (Demirag,
> *Limnidi*, 53–55)

Again without prioritising 'Macedonian Hurricane, the reign of Alexander the Great and Hellenistic' period (330–58 BCE) as Cypriotgreek nationalists do, Demirag lists inscriptions by four different rulers. These rulers meet different Kings of Cyprus – Onesilos then Evagoras – who fought against the reign of the Persian Empire. In addition, he lists scholars from this period: 'My homeland! Is Zenon's Homeland. Also the wise and ignorant far-near' (Demirag, *Limnidi*, 29) – the ancient stoic philosopher, who was in Cyprus (334–262 BCE).

Demirag continues by unearthing the Roman Empire (59 BCE–295 ACE), 'my homeland, your soil started to be chewed/by their horses hoofs, the cruel bloody Romans [...] like a glass of love wine you were given to/Cleopatra' (Demirag, *Limnidi*, 56); here referring to the Roman leader, Mark Antony, the first to materialise Cyprus as a gift when he gave it to Cleopatra on their wedding. In referring to Cleopatra and her gift, Demirag suggests Cyprus has always been claimed as a gift for powerful rulers, and that these, Roman and otherwise, inscriptions make Cyprus a gift to the Cypriots. Demirag also focusses on a spiritual gift from the Roman period, which is the spread of Christianity:

> [...] reading secrets
> that echoed in old Baf's stone streets
> [...]
> oozed like a seed gently to your heart,
> and a new young tree loaded with commentary of belief
> sprouted from the soil with an unbelievable speed
> stretching its branches to Serguis Paulus. (Demirag, *Limnidi*, 63)

In 47 ACE when 'Apostle Barnabas visited Baf (Paphos), the capital of Roman Cyprus, he persuaded the Roman governor Paulus to adopt Christianity' (Demirag, *Limnidi*, glossary); here Demirag concretises Christianity onto nature, defining its spreading as a natural plant-like growth. Demirag also wanders to other religions:

> Oh You; icons and writings of *Bismillah ir-Rahman ir-Rahim* statues of Aphrodite [...] Mother Mary's and Ummu Haram's, Aysaaba's and Zoi women's, Christian saint's and Muslim saint's small country!.
> (Demirag, *Limnidi*, 29)

Ambiguously moving between pre-Christian faith when Cyprus was host to the cult of Aphrodite, Christianity and Islam – Ummu Haram is Prophet Mohammed's aunty who died falling off her horse in Larnaca around 644–806 ACE (Demirag, *Limnidi*, glossary) – Demirag shows these religions are materialised through contemporary Cypriots like 'Aysaaba',[41] a Turkish-Muslim name, and, 'Zoi', a Greek-Orthodox name.

Demirag entitles the next moment 'Navy Darkness in the Middle Ages', which recovers the inscriptions from Byzantine to Frankish Rule. Starting with 'the Byzantine clock tolled [...] And histories hand slowly/Pulled and covered the curtains of the ancients' (Demirag, *Limnidi*, 65), Demirag draws on the palimpsestic process wherein the Byzantine replaced the pre-historic and ancient cultures with their own, yet, as shown, Demirag is able to recover them. From this Byzantine time,

Demirag moves to the crusader conquest from 1191 'the heavy and glorious shadow of the English crown first fell on the soil [...] "Lion" Richard', then in 1192 it passed to Frankish rule when Guy de 'Lusignan sirs and seigniors took control of the produce!' (Demirag, *Limnidi*, 73).

The next moment three entitled 'Early Modern Pages Turned by the Wind' introduces Venetian and Ottoman-Cyprus. Venetian rule (1473–1571) is depicted through the first woman ruler of Cyprus '"secret sword" Catherine Cornaro [...] Then the "rose's" face turned to a Latin time' (Demirag, *Limnidi*, 81). Demirag also uncovers other inscriptions '...And like a light Master Leonardo pours and passes' (Demirag, *Limnidi*, 83), which refers to claims that Da Vinci visited Lefkara village in Cyprus, and used its crochet traditions in his own artwork' (Demirag, *Limnidi,* glossary). Here suggesting it is not only Cyprus and Cypriot shaped by western, Venetian or otherwise, cultures but influential westerners, like Da Vinci, were shaped by Cyprus. Demirag ends the 'Early Modern': 'With a prayer they hit your shores, making your soil shiver. [...] An Ottoman hurricane!' (Demirag, *Limnidi*, 85) – this shows the Ottoman period (1571–1878), unlike the nationalists' rendition, as just another layer on the island's palimpsestic spatial history.

Demirag titles the final moment 'The Sunrise from the Modern Age to the Space Age', which maps 1878 when 'The English crown dropped and kept its shadow in your soil a second time', to Independent Cyprus. He randomly interrupts the British mapping via lines like 'it hits your shores Rimbaud's "drunk ship!"' that refers to the period (1878–1880) when the French poet Arthur Rimbaud visited Cyprus, serving as a stone quarry foreman for the construction of the colonial palace in Trodos (Demirag, *Limnidi*, 99). Through this gesture, as is apparent throughout the volume, Demirag simultaneously shows his scrupulous recording of all cultural investments, and the random cultural mixing and palimpsest of Cyprus. This passage is an introduction to and sets the moment for the 'Space-Age', which is independent postcolonial Cyprus – unearthing and making concrete the abstract palimpsestic spatial history of 8,000 years, achieved through *Limnidi*.

Like Demirag other Cypriotists share the same sensibility in *Writing Cyprus* via spatial history. Moleskis demonstrates this in essays and interviews, when he states:

> History has a particular place [...] that influences deeply the character and conscience of the people. It is an inheritance which you take, whether you want it or not. (Moleskis, 'History', 45)

> The Cypriot cannot turn away from [...] 'Cypriot reality', [which is the] social, political and historical. [...] Futile to attempt to disengage Cypriot literary production from Cypriot history. (Moleskis, *Selected*, 10).

Literary critics of Moleskis's work also confirm this: Theoklis Kouyiallis writes, 'His contact with and reference to the world of the ancestors' (Moleskis, *Profile,* 18); Chrysanthis Zitsaia states, 'Within this poetry the "Taste of the Homeland" is intense. It makes its appearance through [...] the past, it stops at important historical moments' (Moleskis, *Profile*, 25); Sofia Xanthakou writes, 'the poet manages to stir memories of our forgotten personal past: old neighbours and ancient buildings, burnt cities, marbles and inscriptions' (Moleskis, *Profile*, 29). Thus Moleskis's poetry is overloaded with spatial history: in 'Optimism' he states, 'you dig areas [...]/ And you go back many centuries [...]/epitaphs on tombs by a human hand [...]/ and the world of wisdom from centuries old speaks to you/about things you carry inside you' (Moleskis, *Poem*, 12); in 'The Moon Used to be Great' he confirms, 'each corner loaded with memories. [...] the cypress in the middle of the yard with alluring epigraph engraved on its trunk' (*Poems*, 7); in 'Ancient Stones', 'these stones appear and recognise us'; in 'A Difficult Time' Cyprus is full 'of so many dead ancestors' (Moleskis, *Profile*, 18). Similarly Mealegrou's novel writes Nicosia via multiple endnotes detailing its history; Peonidou's poetry writes Cyprus by performing between historical moments; and M. Yashin's poetry – 'The Human Torch' (33), for example – is dominated by reinventing a spatial history of Cyprus.

Material Romantic Cyclical Rhythm of Nature

Cyprus' nature is a central theme in Cypriotist works. The poets consistently record the romantic mental conception and the physical materiality of nature, showing their own and the islanders' intimate connection and communication with it, so as to capture the power and concrete force of nature. Demirag and Moleskis show that this concrete-abstraction of nature defines Mother Cyprus and makes it a gift for the Cypriot.

The poets' recording of nature draws on nostalgia: 'yearning for a different time' (Boym, xv). In this romantic mental conception, the poets capture the idealised rhythm of nature that is indifferent and neutral to time-zones and historical chronologies; unlike in the spatial palimpsestic archaeology, this natural rhythm is not located within a Cypriot timeframe – it is a timeless moment: there is no specific moment of colonisation, ethnic-conflict, independence, or partition. This is, as Boym suggests, a nostalgia for the slower rhythm of the poets' dreams, wherein they mentally construct and 'imagine' an island not the way it was but the way it could be in an un-partitioned future. In this process, the poets also engage with the physical materiality that captures the actual rhythms of nature – that is to say, the narratives record the physical appearance of trees, the sea and the landscape, and the material cycles of day-night, seasons, plants and animals in Cyprus. Through this recovery, the poets show practices related to Lefebvre's 'representational space', which is a directly lived moment that returns to 'time (or times), rhythm (or rhythms)' (Lefebvre, *Production*, 356) of everyday experiences that Cypriot 'users' have with nature, and these experiences 'ha[ve] an origin, and that origin is childhood' (Lefebvre, *Production*, 362). In this material romantic journey, the Cypriotists capture nature through experiencing a Tuanian closed familiar place and an open free space with emphasis on the former; the poets move between the mental romantic conception and the actual physical materiality, where they capture lived perceptions, interactions and experiences with nature, which enables it to be made concrete – it comes alive as the wise one who teaches the Cypriot its neutral and actual rhythm – its places, times and power.

The Cypriotists repetitively reclaim a narrative for Cyprus's local produce – 'grapes, carobs, olives, oranges' (Demirag, *Limnidi*, 28) – to show them as primary natural resources that define Mother Nature and her power. It is mainly the olive tree the Cypriotist return to, where it comes alive, speaking, as in Demirag's *Limnidi*:

> I AM AN OLIVE TREE OF MANY THOUSANDS OF YEARS. I AM HERE. MY ARM BRANCHES, MY EYE LEAVES HAVE SEEN AND LIVED THROUGH A LOT. WHAT I HAVE LIVED HAS BEEN RECORDED WORD FOR WORD ON MY TORSO. MANY CHILDREN HAVE GROWN ON MY BRANCHES [...]
>
> I AM A HISTORY-TREE; I GET SHOT EVERY THREE TO FIVE YEARS, COVERED IN HOLES. THERE IS STILL SOOOOOOOOOOOOO MUCH I WILL SEE. I WILL RESIST. (Demirag, *Limnidi*, 121)

This passage shows immortality and endurance of the olive tree, which Demirag has an intimate connection with because he hears it speak of itself as a 'history-tree' dis/located neutrally and inclusively within all timeframes. Demirag listens to the wise one whose body – 'torso', 'eyes', 'arm-branches' – carried Cyprus's children, suggesting it not only nourished multiple cultures throughout history but through this bodily palimpsest it unites them. The children also symbolise the actual childhood relationship with nature. This interaction with the tree at once enabled Demirag's 'word for word' revisiting of spatial history, and for the tree's body and glory to be recovered and concretised – confirmed as the source in the production of Cyprus.

Like Demirag, Moleskis also engages with nature's power by showing that to be redeemed, humans must communicate with it. In 'Ancient Stones', Moleskis's intimate relationship enabled the stones to come to life, 'these stones appear and recognize us', when they remember how 'us' Cypriots, who have been in conflict and partitioned, lived harmoniously together as a united family, and when 'with my brothers I s[a]t and talk[ed]'; whilst man lacks this power because since partition the Cypriots 'cease to recognize each other, in other tongues we speak' (Moleskis, *Poems*, 10).

Moleskis and Demirag show not only their ability to communicate and make tangible nature's almighty power over man, but also their ability to have an organic and spiritual connection with nature. They claim and are claimed by Mother Nature when they unite and are inscribed within it, thus becoming an immortal piece of Mother Cyprus. Moleskis narrates this organic relationship in 'Life': 'I gather my blood from the earth /and I return it like water to the thirsty roots,/throwing it back into my veins (Moleskis, *Selected,* 19); through this playful exchange between blood in the land and water in man, Moleskis rewrites the nationalists' blood symbolism, so as to capture the organic cycle between all Cypriots and the land feeding and nourishing each other. Moleskis expands on this organic cycle between him and Cyprus by engaging with 'light', as in 'Returning':

> gathering and spreading the light
> [...]
> I shall also be an anonymous fountain
> which the world will draw from as a light
> like the mountain, the sky,
> the sun and the rock
> and like this more secret fountain
> which grew enlightening me
> and which will grow still
> claiming me. (Moleskis, *Selected*, 20)

Here Moleskis and nature enlighten each other with the knowledge of Cyprus, which he gives back to the 'world', the island, for Cypriots to draw from. In elaborating on uniting with Cyprus, Moleskis and Demirag set the stage for the actual relationship that all Cypriots should have with Cyprus. Here showing it is not only an exclusive handful of ethnic figures that have this ability, as in the nationalist narratives, but they themselves and all Cypriots are inscribed and have an organic union with Cyprus. Both poets focus on the Cypriotist relationship with nature through elaborating on childhood and women, which draw on the characteristics of purity and innocence that they define as enabling devices for the organic union between the Cypriots and nature.

In *Rootmirror* Demirag shows the union between childhood and nature:

> under an olive tree it sat (my childhood)
> [...]
> under the shadow of an orange tree it lay (my childhood)
> [...]
> The last drops from the leaves
> of a fig tree's branch is my bird-childhood
>
> •
>
> Childhood: the inscription in the soil
> from the drops of rain
>
> •
>
> Breastmountains! My roots are with you !
> [...]
> (...and still my childhood is water,
> it stops and flows beneath the shadow of far olive trees)
>
> My childhood's cool water still stops and flows
> Under the shadows of the 'fantasy olive trees'. (Demirag, *Rootmirror*, 305–14)

Demirag again claims a narrative for Cyprus's common agricultural produce by showing that his childhood is inscribed into and defined through them. Demirag's childhood is also inscribed in the 'soil' and the 'breastmountains' – 'the twin peaks opposite my childhood neighbourhood [Lefke village] were the breasts of a naked woman lying on her back' (Demirag, *Rootmirror*, 306). Water imagery suggests childhood immortality in a natural cycle and an organic relationship with the land. Through this mapping, Demirag confirms that childhood, like water, nourishes the land, and this union provides the island and islander with life – this organic union is Cyprus. The water also symbolises the freedom not only of childhood, but of Cypriotist poets, who wander without boundaries around Cyprus.

In 'Mature Summer' Moleskis meditates on children and nature: 'Run small children of the earth,/ immerse yourself in the fruit/which awaits you', showing nature waits to be nourished and to nourish the child. The children 'stroke the blossoms [...] smell them/drunk from their colour' (Moleskis, *Select,* 24–25), suggesting that their innocence and purity enable them intimately to unite with nature, and, as in Demirag, it is this union that defines Cyprus. Here Moleskis also shows that these characteristics and the connection are at risk of being devoured, and portrays himself as the wise one, who will teach children how to value and preserve this organic union with nature. In 'First Day' Moleskis elaborates on the risks and teachings:

> for the grace of your birth
> MARIA
> [...]
> And taking you from the hand
> I spoke to you
> [...]
> and bitter and joyful
> and the road long...
>
> The stone will tie your muscles
> the earth will enrich your body
> and the brine will water your soul. (Moleskis, *Selected*, 22–23)

Maria symbolises birth and becoming of all children born in Cyprus, and here Moleskis teaches these children about the spatial and local journey they will experience. The road is 'joyful' because it enables the child to unite with nature, here explaining baby Maria will become one with Cyprus: 'stones' will strengthen her 'muscles', the 'earth's' local produce will nourish her body, and the sea –'brine'– will provide her 'soul' with water. The road is 'bitter' because as the child becomes an adult this organic union is devoured. Moleskis teaches the children about the long journey to guide them on how to wander and grow into Cyprus without losing the childhood ability to unite with nature.

Moleskis also elaborates on the women uniting with nature, in 'A Woman by the Sea':

> She walks. And as the sea
> takes the sadness and loneliness
> from the starless sky
> so she too takes the bitterness and solitude
> from the sea.
>
> And there is such a resemblance between them
> that looking at them, a third party leaves hastily
> so not to spoil their companionship. (Moleskis, *Selected*, 28)

Here the woman and nature – 'sea and sky' – are in an organic cycle, exchanging emotions and experiences – 'sadness' and 'loneliness' – resulting in a strong 'companionship' that make them one.

Moleskis and Demirag emphasise the organic relationship that women and children have with nature to suggest they are not only symbolic enablers of this rhythm of nature – the spiritual and physical union – but are symbolic of Mother Cyprus' secreted private inner domain. Moleskis and Demirag also show that they, as adult men – the culprits of war – have the ability to unite with nature, suggesting all Cypriots can enter this inner spiritual and physical domain of Cyprus. Other Cypriotists also enter this inner domain, especially through uniting the childhood or feminised selves with nature: Peonidou, for example, writes nature through mixing the sense – she hears the soil's scent, sees lemon and olive trees' calling, feels the figs' white milk; N. Yashin writes children and women growing with nature; M. Yashin offers odes to nature and children, as in 'The Child and his Tree', 'Songs of Orange Blossom and Latest Tales of Heroism', 'Canticle for a Schoolteacher', 'Bitter Olive Tree' and 'Palm Trees' in *Don't Go Back to Kyrenia*. The poets capture further this inner domain through the social-domestic journey in Cyprus.

Social-domestic Journey and Rhythm

In this social-domestic journey, the Cypriotists wander into the rhythm of pre-partitioned Cyprus to prioritise the daily practices of the Cypriot families and community over those of ancestral ethnic families advocated by the nationalists.

Moleskis consistently returns to a pre-partitioned united Cyprus by reclaiming the social-domestic rhythm within houses, yards and public squares. In 'Other Times', Moleskis records a narrative of Cypriots in the home:

> The house never knew peace. It always buzzed
> and managed everything
> the clocks measuring the days and evenings,
> the years measuring winters-summers
> the harvest measuring grain in the garden
> and the harvest-gatherer weighing grapes. (Moleskis, *Profile*, 33)

The 'buzz' suggests the rhythm – place/space, time, energy – of Cypriot people, especially families and farmers in the actual and national house. Moleskis personifies the house as 'buzzing' and 'managing everything' to suggest these interactions shape both home and country, they control everything: time, the seasons, and nature's demands. Thus, Moleskis defines place/space and time into a social-domestic construction controlled by the families and farmers of Cyprus.

Moleskis develops further the Cypriots' 'management' over rhythms in 'The Sun is Our Yard', when he joins a family's communion in the yard:

> We had a sun in the yard that was ours alone
> Little children played with him,
> [...]

and when mother would take out the bread from the oven
when she would lay it out, golden across the yard
he would descend from the sky,
become bread, lay himself upon the white sheet
waiting for mother to cover him. (Moleskis, *Profile*, 20–21)

Moleskis reclaims a common Cypriot domestic scene of children playing in the yard, beside the traditional stone oven for baking bread. Here the sun becomes the bread the mother made and that the family will eat, showing both the organic union between the Cypriots and nature, and that the family, particularly the mother, manages the time, environment and life in Cyprus.

Moleskis consistently reclaims a narrative of families in houses and yards to show this is an all-inclusive Cypriot rhythm that constructs a united Cyprus. In 'A Blind Speaker at a Meeting for Peace', Moleskis develops this united Cyprus by wandering into a gathering in a village square:

A blind speaker rose to the podium
opened his manuscript
began to talk, touching words one by one
with his fingers. A Turk
speaking Greek. His words
Greek and Turkish together
flew over frontiers like birds
whose nationality cannot be determined
[...]
to fly around the hall,
searching for windows, for open doors. (Moleskis, *Profile,* 38)

The public speaker is blind to separating the community into ethno-linguistic groups, and instead simultaneously addresses the people in and as Greek and Turk beyond national fixity. Moleskis shows that this united Cypriotness flows from the square into 'windows' and 'doors' of homes in the village. Through this imagery, Moleskis captures the collective memory of Cyprus before partition, when both ethnic communities lived side by side in mixed villages, towns and cities.

In *Rootmirror* Demirag also captures the social-domestic rhythm of pre-partitioned Cyprus, where here again he questions what defines his childhood, and finds answers by randomly listing snapshot moments from colonial Lefke (1951–1960):

Its face in the waters mirror, a herd of goats and a crazy shepherd
[...]
If I search where is it now; what does it symbolise my childhood,
What symbolises it most;

A single shoe left amongst the weeds
in a long left rotted orange grove?

The stone I sat on to listen to the
sound of a frog in the bank ditch, a first poem and bird?

The crowd in the festival of the pay and settling days?
[…]

The fantasy years of the father who undressed for a new hope
when he left the mine without poetry and health?

His grieving and Hillman face that stands between
fruits-vegetables like a bard of colours?

The rare and timid happiness of the village mother of Paphos

[…]

My elder sisters-My little sisters? An orthodox bell
[…]
It sat under an olive tree (my childhood)
[…]
My father and all the things (beauties?) that are now dead and gone
they still live. (Demirag, *Rootmirror,* 301–305)

The Muslim Uncle's, Fat Havvaba's
[…]
a mother's voice, a little myrtle scent –
Desbosini Mariya, the workers who went down to strike –
[…]
In bleak darkness with my mother we pluck meadow.
(Demirag, *Rootmirror*, 311–14)

The extended passage juxtaposes actual locations and people that can be re-organised into four Cypriot-centred themes – family, workers, cultural events and mixed village – that define Demirag's childhood, whilst also capturing a collective social-cultural memory and social-domestic rhythm for the Cypriotist reading and construction of united Cyprus.

Demirag elaborates on family through recalling images of mothers, sisters and fathers in Cyprus. The image of a father returning home from his work as a 'miner' represents both his own father and the collective memory of Cypriot fathers in Lefke. The occupation draws attention to the American owned mines Cyprus Mining Corporation (CMC – 1916–1978) located in Lefke,[42] which shaped the community in several ways. First, the CMC impacted employment because a majority of the employees were males from Lefke; here Demirag reclaims a voice for these mineworkers. Second, Demirag shows that CMC united Cypriots in Lefke because its employees were Cypriots of different ethnic backgrounds who came together to celebrate and protest CMC. Finally, Demirag draws on ways CMC reconstructed the cultural foundations of Lefke, when they built it up as a company town, through which Demirag responds to the private domestic and public worldly domains of Cyprus.

Demirag's representation of the CMC's impact on the cultural domains could be understood in terms of Partha Chatterjee's claims in *Nation and its Fragments*. Chatterjee states that the colonised Indian nation divided its culture into the private inner and the public outer domain: the private domain refers to the spiritual domestic and is symbolic of the Indian woman; the public outer domain is the modern material world and symbolic of the man.[43] Demirag's narratives respond to this gendered cultural binary to show how colonial Cyprus both adopted and interrupted this divide as a consequence of, but not exclusively, the CMC framework. At first glance, Demirag's version of Cypriot colonial culture adopts this gendered binary that separates the rhythm of Cypriot men and women. As with the cultural divide in India, so also Demirag depicts the females as symbols of domestic inner private and males as the outer public domain: the wives and daughters are within the home carrying out their domestic duties and representing traditions, or working outside the home – 'pluck[ing] the meadow' – symbolising the spiritual connection they have with the land. The men, captured through the 'miner father', are agents of the outer modern industrial world, particularly in light of Demirag's reference to 'strike', which refers to the actual uprising in 1948 when all the Lefke miners mobilised against the CMC in an attempt to modernise and humanise working conditions. However, Demirag simultaneously interrupts this gendered binary. Demirag claims a site for women in the public domain, where women – 'Desbosini[44] Mariya' – joined the miners' strike to mobilise against the CMC. He also symbolises the male mineworkers with private spiritual imagery, when stating that his father's face blends between nature, 'fruits-vegetables', like a 'bard of colours', to confirm that he is a romantic poet who has a bodily and spiritual connection with the land. Here Demirag states that the 'father and all beauties are dead', suggesting the spiritual musings of his father have been killed, leaving him 'without poetry' because of his excessive 'grieving' and bad 'health' – actual physical health and healthy relationship he had with the inner domain – caused by bad working condition at CMC. Even though Demirag shows that the fathers', or male Cypriots', connections with the private domain are diminished, he simultaneously reclaims their indefinite positioning within it; here declaring the father 'undresses' himself, shedding his miner's uniform and public role, so to replace it with a 'new hope', to enter the private inner role and spiritual 'beauties [...] that still live' immortalised within him and the land. Demirag also frequently interrupts the binary between the public and private through showing that Lefke was a company town established by the – public world – CMC, but which accommodated and was driven by the – private world – domestic activities of Cypriot family and community. This blurring is shown through his reference to cultural events,[45] here focussing on the 'fair of the paying and settling' hosted by the CMC for the mineworkers and their families in celebration of them receiving their wages. Through this CMC narrative, Demirag blurs both the gendered and ethnic binaries in the interest of the social-domestic construction of Cyprus. Cyprus is mapped as a place of gender equality and ethno-religious inclusivity, which Demirag develops through snapshots of his mixed village –'Muslim uncles', Christian 'Orthodox bells', Cypriotgreek 'Desbosini Mariya' and Cypriotturkish 'Fat Havvaba' – in pre-partitioned Cyprus.

The passage analysed from *Rootmirror* is an answer to the question, 'Which one [snapshot] is my childhood?' Demirag confirms all these snapshots – family, workers, cultural events and mixed villages – are his childhood. Through this return, Demirag captures everyday life in Cyprus; he reclaims the rhythms of Cypriot families and workers within the inner spiritual and outer public domain, and, most importantly, reflects upon a collective memory and unity between all Cypriots, who worked and struggled, attended social events and peacefully lived together. Similarly, the Yashin siblings' and Peonidou's poetry frequently captures Cypriot rhythms through families in yards, Cypriots at work, cultural events, and mixed villages that blur the gendered and ethnic binaries to create a united Cyprus.

Thus the Cypriotists return to a pre-partitioned 'moment' to reclaim a social-domestic rhythm of a perfect united inclusive Cyprus. Mother Cyprus is read and constructed through this rhythm of collectivity that is inclusive of everything and everyone that the poets experience during their social-domestic journey; it is this that frees Mother Cyprus, and makes Cyprus a gift to the Cypriots. This production draws on actual collective memories of Cypriots, yet is not an exact reflection of the way Cyprus was – the pre-1974 period, particularly the 1950s–1960s the poets write about, was the moment of the ethnic-nationalist uprising when ethnic-conflict, bloodshed and massacre reigned – but instead is a production of the way Cyprus could have been in the interest of an un-partitioned Cypriotist Cyprus.

Idealistic Production

The chapter has illustrated that the post-1964/74 Partitioned Cypriotists were the most successful in *Writing Cyprus* within a Cypriotist frame because they focus on the actual rhythms – the places, spaces, times and energies, that produce Cyprus. The poetic accounts of the Cypriotists, especially Demirag and Moleskis, but also Meleagrou, the Yashin siblings and Peonidou amongst others, have successfully immortalised a Cypriotist reading, construction and experience of Cyprus because they are a lot more receptive to the spatial model: they play with the inventions, particularly the spatial palimpsest, in postcolonial partitioned understandings of place; they read and write Cyprus through spatial analysis and rhythmanalysis, particularly the concrete-abstraction that Lefebvre discusses; and they create a Cyprus that supports Tuan's notion of open space versus closed fixed united place.

Even though the post-1964/74 Cypriotists successfully re-define the ethnic-motherland nationalist and partitioned constructions to create an ethnically united, more inclusive and concrete Cyprus, these narratives to some extent continue to reproduce a closed, secure and idealistic Tuanian place. The Cypriotist productions are bounded within a Cypriot-centric framework, which is an idealistic abstraction of Cyprus, not exactly the way it was or is, but the way it could have been – ethnically and temporally inclusive and collective, yet geographically and culturally exclusive and patriotic. This Cypriotist construction restricts the possibility of capturing fully the social and cultural 'truth' of the spatially different, inclusive and immeasurable production of Cyprus, which is clearly illuminated through the Cypriot diaspora narratives that will be the focus of the next and final chapter.

Notes

1 Moments is a key motif explored in Lefebvre's 'Theory of Moments' in *Critique of Everyday Life* (634–652). 'Moments' are intense experiences of everyday, as well as instants of dramatic change and disruption of routine. They are unforeseen circumstances buried within the everyday, especially an immanent subversion; they relate to dialectical relations between society with itself, and between social life and nature. They are a theory of presence and a practice of emancipation; without duration they are lived and re-lived.

2 See Attalides; Mavratsas; Peristianis 'Left'; Loizides 'Adapt'.

3 Building on Karl Marx's comment, 'They cannot represent themselves, they must be represented' (124), in *The Eighteenth Brumaire of Louis Bonaparte (1852)*.

4 Andrekos Varnava shows there were also earlier manifestations of Colonial-Cypriotism: in 1913 when J.C.C Davidson, secretary to Lewis Harcourt, proposed the implementation of pure Cypriot ideals into a Cypriot government to bring genuine administrative peace and quality (Varnava, *Imperialism*, 262); from the 1920s, the official policy to discourage Hellenism gave way for the British to invent the Eteo-Cypriots, an indigenous population from Iron Age, in attempts to generate an authentic ethnic Cypriot that predated the Greek, the Hellenic Cyprus (Given 'Invent', 162).

5 Durrell's identity building practices are illuminated fully in MacNiven; Herbrechter; Calotychos *Modern*. These will be a point of reference.

6 In this chapter it is fitting to use the name Cypriots; however, for clarification purposes, I use Cypriotgreek and Cypriotturk: here the name 'Cypriot'

is upper case, because for the Cypriotist this identification is significant, whilst ethnic names do not need to exist. On 'name games' see Ch. 1.

7 Focus is on the CPC and AKEL because they have a long history. The Cypriotturkish left-wing party is CTP, which assumed Communist-Cypriotist principles that claimed only the toiling masses and working class in Cyprus will bring genuine peace (*Political Parties*, 39–40); however, because CTP is a more recent formation (founded in 1970, enhanced in 2004) it will not be discussed here. On CTP, see Chs. 1 and 2. There are very few works in English on CPC and AKEL: Thomas W. Adams' study is the only extensive study on the general scope, which has been the primary source here. Katsourides provides the first extensive study related to 1920s–1940s, and Alecou on 1945–1955. Katsiaounis', and Pantelis Varnavas' studies on Cypriot worker consciousness are very helpful.

8 See Pantelis Varnava.

9 From 1955 to 1968, EOKA and TMT murdered numerous communist and bi-communal supporters. See endnote 13 and 16.

10 Anthias was designated colonial police file 'Red 398'. See Katsourides; Katsiaounis.

11 On a chronological recording of AKEL's shifts, see Adams.

12 On reasons for AKEL's refusal to join EOKA, see Adams.

13 Martyrs of the left killed by EOKA from 1955 to 1959 include: Ilias Ttofaris, Michalis Petrou, Demetris Yasemis, Andreas Sakkas, Panagiotis Stylianou, Nicodemos Ioannou, Maria Charitou and Despoula Katsouri, Savvas Menikos, Neoklis Panayiotou and Euripides Nouros.

14 From an article by N. Zachariades in *Neos Democratis*, May 1, 1955.

15 On AKEL attitude to agreement, see Adams, 46.

16 Cypriotturks adopted anti-communist attitudes, for example, Fazil Kucuk, the Vice president of Cyprus, claimed: 'If a Turk becomes a communist in Cyprus, then he also becomes a Greek' (Adams, 197). Martyrs of the left killed by TMT from 1960 onwards include: Fazil Onder, Ahmet Yahya, Ahmet Ibrahim, Ayhan Hikmet, Ahmet Muzzafer Gurken, Dervis Kavazoglu and Costas Mishaulis.

17 On Makarios's alliance with communism, see Adams.

18 See Ch. 2. Examples of anthologies in English translated from Greek include Montis and Christophides; Kouyialis *27 Centuries*, *Contemporary Cypriot*; Spanos *22 Contemporary*. In Greek, Gritsi-Milliex; Pernaris *Cypriot Letter*; Panayiotunis. Anthologies in English translated from Turkish, Cahit; Yashin *Series*. In Turkish, Altay; *Kibris Turk Edebiyati*. Magazines: *Kypriaka Chronika*, *Nea Epoch*, *Sanat Postasi*, *Karanfil*.

19 More recent magazines in Turkish, include *Isirgan*; *Ucsuz*. See also Korkmazel *Cypriotgreek*; Moleskis *Contemporary Turkish*.

20 See Ch. 5. On magazines, see *Cadences*; *In Focus*; *The Cyprus Dossier*. Anthologies, see Adamidou; Stephanides' *Culture/Memory*, *Cypriana*; Yashin's *Stepmother, Cypriotturk;* Collette; Costello.

21 See Ch. 2.

22 'Turkish' was recently removed from the title.

23 Hikmet sent a message to the Cypriotturks to unite with Cypriotgreeks against British imperialism; confirming conflict between the Cypriots served only the interest of the foreign ruler. *Avgi* Athens 17 April /January 1955.

24 Baybars was childhood friends with two martyrs of the left, Ayhan Hikmet and Muzzafer Gurkan, who worked together to shape *Cardak* magazine.

25 *Sanat Emegi* also consists of works by the Greek communist Yiannis Ritsos and the Palestinian poet Mahmoud Darwish (09/1979).

26 Poetry: *Beautiful Country* (1967); *The Road* (1970); *Autobiography* (1972); *The Moon Used to Be Great* (1980); *The Trees in the North* (1982); *Transient*

Spring (1984); *Larnaca Patterns* (1987); *The Reservoir of Passions* (1987); *The House and the Time* (1990); *The Water of Memory* (1998) and *From the Minimum* (2001). Novel: *Stolen Grapes* (1985).

27 In the emergent Cypriotgreek literary canon, Moleskis is grouped into the '1974 Generation' (Moleskis, Selected, 9), without address of his literary-lived commitment to a Cypriotist communist feeling.

28 Poetry: *Life of Two* (1959); *Passion* (1960); *Esperanza* (1962); *The Orbit Flowers Blossom* (1963); *The Songs of our Love* (1965); *The short poem stop* (1968); *Don't Caw partridge, I'll Die* (1972); *Bear up my Heart* (1974); *Poems from the Era of Hope and Horror* (1978); *Listen to My Song* (1981); *Mediterranean Poems and Song Lyrics* (1984); *Wounded with its Name* (1986); *A bards songs in the wind or the long walk of the poem* (1986); *Tetralogy: From Limnidi's Fire until Today: An Experimental Text on and by a Small Sunny Mother Soil and its Injured History* (Volume 1, 1992); *Mother Grief* (Volume 2, 1992); *The Rootmirror whose Secrets are Exposed & Solitude Night Music* (Volume 3 and 4, 1994); *Selected Poems* (1994); *Psalm for Poet time* (1996); *Eros's Arrow* (1997); *Alfa and Omega* (1999); *God's Music at a Silence: Selected Poems* (2002); *At my Island's Coast* (2005). Novel: *The Rain Trees* (1963) and *These Fantastic War Years* (1985). All translations of Demirag's texts are mine. Both Demirag and Moleskis, who wrote mainly poetry, coincidently turned to prose in 1985. Given that *Stolen Grapes* has not been translated, I am unable to discuss further; however, this has potential to be further researched by scholars able to read texts in both Greek and Turkish.

29 Limnidi is a village in north-west Cyprus, close to Lefke. I will refer to volume 1 as *Limnidi*.

30 *Kokayna* is a neologism for kok ayna – *kok* is root and *ayna* is mirror – as used in Cyprus, equivalent to Tas Ayna – stone mirror – used in Turkey. This is an antique framed mirror from around the nineteenth century, when mirrors were a very valuable material and highly skilled artisans would make frames for them; these framed mirrors were heavy and fragile, so once hung they remained there for years – it would get rooted in the wall, hence the usage root. Kok Ayna ownership and craftsmanship, once very common in Cyprus, is not practised anymore. I have translated this as *Rootmirror*, and will refer to volume 3 using this term.

31 In the Cypriotturkish canon, Demirag is grouped into 'Socialist-Realist' and '2nd New' movements shaped by Hikmet, and via a Cypriotness (TCL, 100, 112; Selcuk, 76); however, here Demirag is pinned down as outdated mimic man of Turkey's literary canon, and second, the meaning of Hikmetian 'Cypriotness' is not expanded. See Ch. 2.

32 See Yashin, *Series*; Cypriotturk.

33 Mike is an Anglophone poet of the diaspora, and before Poetz4peace he founded Cypriot harmony with Ramzi, which can be considered the first bi-communal move.

34 See Ch. 3.

35 See Ch. 3; Kemal 'Writing Baby Cyprus'.

36 See Ch. 3.

37 All translations of Hikmet's poems are mine.

38 See Carter.

39 Demirag's glossary in *Limnidi* provides historical details, which has been a point of reference in this analysis.

40 Iphis, Anaxarete, Paphos, Pygmalion myths figure in Ovid's *Metamorphosis*: Kinyras figures in Homer's *Iliad*.

41 Aysa is a name, and *Aba* or *Abla* is a title used when referring to an older female member. In the Cypriot dialect Aysa *abla* is pronounced as one-word *Ayssaba*, thus Demirag draws attention to the local dialect.

42 In a footnote Demirag details CMC as related to poor working conditions and strikes in Lefke (*Rootmirror*, 306). See also David Sievert Lavender; Pantelis Varnavas.

43 This relates to McClintock claims in 'No Longer' regarding women as 'the passive atavist of the nation' symbolic of the private traditions of the family and home or the natural national homeland, and men as the 'active agents of modernity' and the world.

44 Desbosini is a Cypriotgreek title used when referring to an older female member.

45 Cultural events represent tradition and the communities' relationship to them, where Cypriots from all over Cyprus unite in celebration. Most cultural events celebrate the local produce, including the orange, olive, potato and grape festival; Demirag mostly returns to the orange festival in Lefke, famed for its Jaffa citrus from Palestine.

5 Rhythmanalysts of Post-Linobambakoi Diaspora

Transnational Whale of Space/Place in the Middle-Sea We Can All Inhabit

Like a wanderer, I hang around aimlessly
In homes that belong to others.
(Terzis)

The only 'true Cypriot', the only genuine postcolonial Cypriot, is the Linobambakoi. (Constantinou, 266)

The truth of space thus leads us back (and is reinforced) by a powerful Nietzschean sentiment: "But may the will to truth mean this to you: that everything shall be transformed into the humanly-conceivable, the humanly-evident, the humanly-palpable!". (Lefebvre, *Production*, 399)

By birth, strangers, he said, I am a Cypriot. I set off from my native land along with my son – on a great ship, and we were gulped down in the mouth of the whale. [...] my journey began when I appeared on the easternmost island in the Middle Sea. (Stephanides, 'Lips', 102)

The people of postcolonial partitioned territories are, as the cypriotmaronite poet Napoleon Terzis says, wanderers who hang around aimlessly in homes and identities that belong to others. The Cypriot diaspora demonstrate what it means to be and become these displaced people from the Mediterranean, living without a single concrete home and identity, where they transform identity into 'identification' with 'positions' determined by places, spaces and times related to their birth-country, adopted-country and global geographies beyond. In this way they capture the true being/becoming of the Cypriot and differential transnational Mediterranean island of Cyprus; in this way they show the actual positioning and production of colonialism, postcolonialism and partition that create multiple-mutable homes and identities, always missing, deferred, ambiguous and in process.

This diasporic positioning and production relate to a Derridean supplementation, whereby they consistently 'add' or 'substitute' another place, space and identity that is always deferred and in process. Through this supplementation they expose the impossibility of a single understanding of place, space and identity, because they are, as Derrida states, supplementing something – for example, concrete homely place and identity of belonging – that is 'missing', and which has 'never taken place: it is never present, here and now' (Derrida, *Of*, 314). In this process, the diaspora play with the supplement, compulsively adding and substituting places, spaces and identities, which create a 'chain of supplements' inclusive of many formations within and beyond the island, so as to celebrate multiple readings and constructions. In playing with the supplement, the diaspora show that they dwell in a place of homely belonging and a space of unhomeliness and longing between multiple identities that are in a network, yet always under negotiation; these places, spaces and identities are lived, conceived and perceived, actual and imagined, and/or absent and present, all at the same time. There is no fixed measurable definition of place, space and identity, but instead an entry into an immeasurable operation with multiple places and spaces that defer definition and transform identity into 'identification' with multiple 'positions'. Like Derrida's 'supplement', this is a haunting-maddening experience, whereby the Cypriot diaspora are indefinitely framed in-between and subject to alienation; yet, this experience enables them to claim a literary and lived dwelling and narrative that celebrates diasporic mobility for an inclusive production. In this process the diaspora enable a gateway to what I will introduce as the 'whale of space', a literary-lived site for supplementation that offers an in-between positioning so as to produce multiple Cypruses, the Mediterranean and the world in inclusive ways. By Mediterranean I mean Chambers' definition based on mutual interactions between cultures with 'overlapping territories and intertwined histories', ending in a transnational complexity where 'borders are both transitory and zones of transit' that make a mutable-multiple Mediterranean (3–5, 9–10). This chapter and book demonstrate that this Mediterranean can be understood through the island of Cyprus.

This chapter concludes my book. It demonstrates that the Cypriot diaspora, which has been largely marginalised in a national and international domain, must be assigned as the most significant figures in writing postcolonial partitioned cases, like Cyprus, for various interrelated reasons. They display my definition of the literatures of Cyprus through engaging with earlier identifications and constructions discussed in the book alongside those not yet discussed. In this process they reclaim the Ottoman Linobambakoi identification, which offers many Cypruses. The diaspora display the spatial production the book has been studying – solidarity that captures the 'truth of space' and place for a 'differential' Cyprus. Thus, the chapter and book demonstrate Cyprus' contribution to humanly-palpable experiences with places, spaces and identifications that have come to define postcolonial partition studies.

Henri Lefebvre refers to Nietzsche to strengthen his 'truth of space', which is to expose dominant 'mental space' in the interest of dominated 'social space' for a 'differential space'. To demonstrate this truth, the chapter[1] will focus on the Cypriot diaspora. Here I will introduce the colonial and postcolonial Cypriot diaspora more generally, then focus on the Anglophone postcolonial Cypriot diaspora specifically. In this way I demonstrate the broad scope within the literatures of Cyprus, especially illuminating the identifications and constructs discussed in the book through diasporic identifications, constructs and other figures. The chapter will refer to a diverse group of figures: the main focus will be on the literary-lived social/spatial practices of Stephanos Stephanides, Aydin Mehmet Ali and Alev Adil, whilst other authors – such as Taner Baybars, Andriana Ierodiaconou, Nora Nadjarian, Miranda Hoplaros, Niki Marangou, Gurgenc Korkmazel and Jenan Selcuk, amongst others – will inconsistently arrive and depart. I choose Stephanides, Ali and Adil to direct discussion because they engage fully with literary Cyprus via spatial considerations. For this they adopt what I call a post-Linobambakoi hospitality, which identifies with multiple 'positions' that carry the weight of diasporic and Cypriot experiences within the colonial, postcolonial and partitioned moments; these experiences are related to the literary-lived identifications and constructs, official and unofficial, and dominant and marginalised narratives, which capture the making and breaking of multiple Cypruses.

This positioning and production will be demonstrated through examining the ways in which Stephanides, Ali and Adil actively write, read and construct Cyprus in relation to identifications with marginalised diasporic positions between their birth-country of Cyprus and adopted-countries, as well as dominant Cypriot positions between Cyprus, Britain, Turkey and Greece within colonial, postcolonial and partition moments. In this way, they produce a Cyprus that determines their diasporic selves, Cypriot-selves and various other-selves without any exclusions. Through such positioning and production, these writers engage fully, unlike all the other identifications in this book, with the spatial model the book has proposed. They employ the empirical-theoretical spatial approaches, especially Tuan's closed 'place' and open 'space' where neither perspective is selected as prime, and Lefebvre's 'spatiology' expanded via 'rhythmanalysis' that capture the 'truth of space' for a 'differential space'. In this process the Cypriot diaspora show colonialism, postcolonialism and partition are conditions that are here to stay, which they successfully deal with via the 'whale of space' site. Here embracing and exposing earlier constructs as abstract closed mental places, which do not deal with the concrete social places and spaces. Here they experience Cyprus with its concrete-abstract actualities, as an unpredictable shifting ground between the truths of hazardous open spaces and falsity of nonsensical safe closed places. Through this site they analyse places, spaces and identifications related to many positions and Cypruses.

The chapter is divided into seven sections: the first introduces the diaspora in relation to literatures of Cyprus, Tuan's and Lefebvre's spatiality, and Derrida's, Hall's and Gilroy's critiques of identity via 'identification' with 'positions'. The second section discusses the 'whale of space' site, combining Constantinou's Linobambakoi, Lefebvre's 'rhythmanalysis' and Wilson Harris' 'womb of space' to offer insight into how the diaspora position themselves as post-Linobambakoi rhythmanalysts to create a differential Cyprus and world. The remaining five sections provide five examples of identification with positions and Cypruses. These are examples of a way the Cypriot diaspora read and write about the colonial, postcolonial and partition condition. They are in a Derridean 'chain of supplements' with an overlapping exchange, which are organic and alive with an overactive pulse, flowing and colliding in contradiction and harmony, dynamically competing, interacting and cohabiting different times; however, throughout the chapter, this chain is interrupted, and the 'position' and Cyprus separately explained. This structure of the chapter mirrors the ways identity operates as identification with shifting positions ambiguously crossing into each other, all shaped by Lefebvre's and Tuan's spatiality.

Stephanides, Ali and Adil negotiate with these positions and Cypruses in distinct ways; however, given the limits of room, I prioritise their collective similarities to demonstrate the 'global diasporic solidarity' and 'conviviality', which acknowledges mutual experiences and interaction between displaced people. These writers share literary-lived practices, where they have lived in and written from the margins, emphasising social interactions so as to draw on and disturb dominant definitions; together they negotiate with the broad scope within literary Cyprus, working with writers in Cyprus, Britain and beyond so as to shape (trans)national literary turns for a differential island, Mediterranean and world.

Defining the Literatures of the Cyprus via Cypriot Diaspora: Places, Spaces, Identities

The Cypriot diaspora negotiate with multiple identifications and constructs related to colonial, postcolonial and partitioned Cyprus, through which they provide an understanding of the literatures of Cyprus as a transnational world literature (WreC). Through them we can see how the literatures of Cyprus are writings by cypriotgreek, cypriotturkish, cypriotarmenian, cypriotmaronite,[2] as well as Greek, Turkish, British and other authors. These are (post)colonial diasporic writings operating via a system of inequality and displacement, especially in relation to literary, cultural and language centres and peripheries that are outside. These are Cypriot literatures positioned between Greek, Turkish and English literatures and languages – so multilingual, uncanonised, minor literatures between major literatures. This is writing about the cultural and political history of colonisation, partition and conflict in Cyprus operating through Britain, Greece, Turkey and beyond. It is writing across geographical boundaries, where places, spaces and identities are central themes. They show that regardless of positionality – such as language, ethnicity, class, geography – all literary identifications share the trope of writing, reading and constructing Cyprus.

Such a definition is enhanced through understanding the meaning of Cypriot diaspora in relation to the literatures of Cyprus. The Cypriot diaspora are Hellenophone, Turkophone and Anglophone writers, who identify with positions that are official and unofficial, and dominant and marginalised as related to colonial, postcolonial and partition moments. These writers engage with cultural movements, translation projects and publishing ventures, which demonstrate ethno-communal, bi-communal and/or multi-communal initiatives with national and transnational literary turns. The Cypriot diaspora refers to colonial and postcolonial migratory waves related to internal and external displacements, inclusive of people who departed from, remained in and/or returned to Cyprus. The diaspora who remained refers to all the people of Cyprus, so all the writers thus discussed in the book who experienced internal displacement during the decolonial and partition failures. The Cypriot diaspora who departed refers to people who experienced external displacement as part of various migrations, including the following groups: (1) the colonised cypriotgreek diaspora in Egypt from the late nineteenth and early twentieth centuries who are Hellenophone writers included in south Cyprus' official literature; (2) the colonised cypriotgreek and cypriotturkish writers, part of the first migration to Britain, Greece or Turkey during the troublesome 1930–1950s, who are Hellenophone and Turkophone writers also included in official literatures; (3) the postcolonial Cypriot diaspora, part of the second and largest migration to Britain during the late 1950s anticolonial, 1960s postcolonial, and 1964/74 partition moments, who are Anglophone writers excluded from official literatures. In addition, there are diasporic Anglophone writers who migrated to other colonies or colonial centres, such as Zimbabwe, Australia or France.

The Anglophone writers of the postcolonial diaspora who are part of the largest migration to Britain, especially Stephanides, Ali and Adil, capture these definitions of the Cypriot diaspora and their literatures by negotiating with the aforesaid generations, identification and constructs. For instances, Stephanides, Ali and Adil engage with writers who remained in Cyprus: they respond to the competing anticolonial ethnic-motherland nationalists from Chapter 3, who wrote back to the dominant coloniser so as to construct a Greece- or Turkey-cyprus. They worked with the post-1964/74 partition Cypriotists from Chapter 4, who wrote back to the dominant coloniser and ethnic-nationalist binaries so as to construct a unified Cypriotness beyond partition. They expose official Turkish-Cypriotists and Greek-Cypriotists constructs of hyphenated ethnic-Cyprus from Chapter 2. The diaspora writers also engage with other identifications and constructs, mainly post-1980/90s generation – including poets Marangou, Selcuk, Korkmazel – who extend Cypriotist positions beyond Cyprus' geo-national borders. Stephanides, Ali and Adil have also been inspired by the diaspora who left Cyprus: Stephanides, for example, idenitifies with cypriotgreeks in Egypt, enabling us to honour figures like Nikos Nicolaides, George Pierides and Thodosis Pierides who shaped Hellene literary scenes in Cairo and Alexandria from 1908 to the 1940s, and the first to construct Cyprus via diasporic displacement. Similarly, they connect with the colonised diaspora, especially Taner Baybars, Tefkos Anthias, Osman Turkay, Mustafa Adiloglu, the first to animate British-Cyprus. More recently they have worked with the Anglophone writers – Hoplaras from Zimbabwe, Iecorodiaconou in France and cypriotarmenian Nadjarian – who have constructed Cyprus through their displacements.

Stephanides, Ali and Adil have negotiated with these literary figures through various projects, including symposiums, anthologies and magazines/zines, mainly operating in translation between English, Greek and Turkish. For example, Ali co-organised one of the first symposiums on cypriotturkish identity with discussion by nationalist, Cypriotist and diaspora generations in 1988.[3] Ali and Adil contributed to the first bi-communal Cypriotist event in the 1980s in London, when the Yashin siblings met Peonidou as depicted in the latter's essay 'Illicit Lovers' in a collection edited by Stephanides; this and other collections by Stephanides consist of works by Moleskis, Kormazel, Selcuk and Marangou.[4] Ali and Stephanides were also involved in the 'Yes' poem. Further to this, they helped shape literary movements and magazines/zines: Stephanides was one of the first cypriotgreek members to Turkish Writers Association and Union led by Demirag; Stephanides and Ali together with Stavros Karayiannis are on the editorial board for *Cadences*; and Ali and Adil together with fifteen other women shaped Literary Agency Cyprus.

Thus, Stephanides', Ali's and Adil's negotiation with the literatures of Cyprus enable exposure of core dominant cypriotgreek and cypriotturkish ethno-linguistic binaries for the interest of peripheral marginalised multilingual/multi-cultural pluralities. Here are multiple writings, readings and constructions of Cyprus by writers identifying with multiple positions so as to create an island for themselves, ending in many Cypruses for many selves. Here confirming Cyprus and its people are always displaced in production, which blurs the dominant binary legacy of historical-political deadlock discourse, so as to capture 'solidarity' between these people all shaped by multiple-mutable Cypruses. Stephanides', Ali's and Adil's positioning as post-Linobambakoi enable them to stand between these identifications and constructs, so as to capture this 'solidarity' for the production of a differential Cyprus.

For this production and positioning they make tacit but full use of the spatial model the book has proposed,[5] especially the postcolonial partitioned inventions illuminated through Lefebvre's and Tuan's spatial approaches. These diasporic writers adopt the postcolonial partitioned inventions that are in a complex interaction between language, history and the environment; they address successfully the open-closed zones created by and between the dynamics of colonised-coloniser, native-native and native-other competition in colonial, postcolonial and partitioned moments. In this process they expose the 'closed zones' as false nonsensical compartments with uncompromising binaries that produce a homogenised nationalistic or patriotic Cyprus. This exposure enables them to capture the 'open zones' through addressing the territory as a 'zone of occult instability' and 'rhizomatic shifting ground' ruled by processes of hybridity, translation and spatial history, wherein different cultures affront and enrich each other, so as to produce a heterogeneous transnational Cyprus. They have a vigorous relationship with the environment through a Tuanian healthy balance between experiencing 'space' that is openness, freedom, movement, danger and longing, and 'place' that is a closed, secure, paused and complete belonging. They absorb Lefebvre's regressive-progressive 'spatiology', especially using the tripling-triad. Here they dance between the 'representations of the relations of production': they expose 'representation of space' as 'mental' abstractions 'conceived' by powerful agents; they capture 'representational space', actively reclaiming passively experienced and dominated literary-'lived' spaces linked to the clandestine side of social life and art; they transform 'spatial practices' related to 'perceiving' daily routines and networks between people and 'physical' spaces (*Production*, 33). In this process they blur together mental, physical and social spaces, all inconsistently conceived, perceived and lived, so as to prioritise the social-spatial practices lived with total body; thus, they actively claim and capture the 'right to difference' and 'truth of space' for the production 'differential space' (*Production*, 352–99).

Stephanides, Ali and Adil claim their own and others' rights to produce many Cypruses for many selves, which echoes Lefebvre's 'right to difference' (*Production*, 396): the right of all people to construct a city, a country and a world without discrimination and exclusion. Through this they capture the 'truth of space', which is tied to social and spatial 'practices' with the tripling-triad, so as to expose contradictions in dominant abstractions for the benefit of dominated concrete realities. Here recognising similarities and differences between the dominant abstractions – i.e. mental space conceived by the nationalists and imperialist – and dominated concrete realities – i.e. social space lived by the colonised subjects – so as to prioritise the latter severely compromised spaces related to Nietzsche's humanly-palpable 'truth' (Lefebvre, *Production*, 397–99). Through this 'truth of space' the writers produce a 'differential space', which is an '*other* space that is different, and [w]hat is different is [...] *excluded* [...] the spaces of forbidden games' and 'desires' (Lefebvre,

Production, 391, 297, 373). A differential space creates and is created by the other, like the postcolonial Cypriot diaspora, who manipulate dominant mental abstractions to privilege dominated social concrete realities, experienced as 'place-space' for a concrete-abstract differential Cyprus.

This process points to ways spatiality determines identity, where both are in production. This can be understood via extending Constantinou's idea on the postcolonial Cypriot as Linobambakoi, and linking it to Derrida, Hall, Gilroy and Said. I use post-Linobambakoi to define those people who extend the Ottoman Linobambakoi's theologically hospitable positioning and practices, from identifying with religious positions – Islam and Christianity – subject to binary opposition, to identify with multiple positions open to many oppositions beyond binaries. The post-Linobambakoi is the true postcolonial Cypriot because it is based on a diasporic hybridity and translation that refuses to identify with a single monumental history shaped by the dominant mind, and instead identifies with many histories shaped by all different minds, where they identify with multiple-mutable positions embedded in Cyprus as a consequence of colonialism, postcolonialism and partition. This true Cypriot, like the former Linobambakoi, is an unofficial marginalised Other excluded from national and political narratives of Cyprus.

The post-Linobambakoi can be understood via Derrida's 'disorder of identity' that confirms 'there is no identity, there is identification' (*Taste*, 28) that occupies 'the site of a situation that cannot be found, a site always referring to elsewhere to something other, to another language, to the other in general' (*Mono*, 29); this identification is bound up with supplementarity, a logic of adding on, making up, or replacing so that 'we are (always) (still) to be invented' ('Psyche', 61). This supplementary process of identification resonates with Hall, Gilroy and Said's usage, which – in Gilroy's words – makes a nonsense of closed, fixed and reified notions of identity (Gilroy, xi) because, as Hall states, it is a 'production that is never complete, always in process [...] producing and reproducing [itself] anew, through transformation and difference' (Hall, 392, 402). Gilroy calls identity 'an always-unpredictable mechanism of identification' (Gilroy, xi), and Hall asserts that 'identities are the names we give to different ways we position ourselves', so that we recognise different parts – such as histories, cultures, politics – of ourselves and other-selves for the creation of new, original, different subjects (Hall, 394). Such recognition also relates to Said's positioning, wherein

> Seeing the 'entire world as a foreign land' makes possible originality of vision. [...] Exiles are aware of at least two [cultures, nations] and this plurality of vision gives rise to an awareness of simultaneous dimensions, an awareness that [...] is *contrapuntal*. ('Mind', 55)

This 'identification', which is modelled on diasporas and exiles, provides an understanding of post-Linobambakoi practices used by postcolonial Cypriot diasporics who departed from Cyprus to arrive into the British imperial centre amongst other centres. They lived a life of displacement between different positions or dimensions that enabled them to combine an originality of vision with contrapuntal awareness. This identification can be localised to understand that all Cypriots are post-Linobambakoi, who have been displaced between positions within colonial, postcolonial and partitioned moments. However, unlike the postcolonial Cypriot diaspora, the Cypriot majority refuse to recognise these positions because they consider the Linobambakoi as extinct and the diasporic positionality as belonging only to those people who physically departed Cyprus, thus failing to capture the contrapuntal awareness.

Stephanides, Ali and Adil consciously capture, willingly descend into, and actively write this identification for themselves and the people in Cyprus. They voyage globally and wander locally between multiple places, spaces and identification, which accommodate their diasporic and Cypriot positions in Cyprus, Britain, Greece, Turkey and geographies beyond within colonial, postcolonial and partition moments. The 'whale of space' is my term for this site that enables supplementation, where one can occupy a situation that cannot be found, always referring to another place, space and identification, to elsewhere, to something other. The 'whale of space' is the site where the 'disorder of identity' operates, transforming identity into an identification with multiple positions determined by various places and spaces which produce multiple Cypruses.

Positioning Post-Linobambakoi Rhythmanalyst In the Womb: Middle Sea, Balcony, Whale

The 'whale of space' is a literary and lived site combining the characteristics of post-Linobambakoi developed by Constantinou, 'rhythmanalysis' coined by Lefebvre, and the 'womb of space' by Harris – all three propose new ways of positioning the self to read, write and construct the world in a more inclusive way. This section shows how the writers position themselves as post-Linobambakoi rhythmanalysts in the womb of space, particularly through the three concrete metaphors – middle sea, balcony and the whale. This forms part of the preparation for their reading and construction of Cyprus that will be explored in the subsequent five sections.

As stated, post-Linobambakoi is an identification that extends the Ottoman Linobambakoi's in-between hospitable positioning and practices, which identify with opposing positions shaped by official and unofficial and dominant and marginalised minds so as to prioritise the latter, thus enabling a cross-ethnoreligious, cross-cultural and transnational production of Cyprus. This can be enhanced through rhythmanalysis, which is concerned with an in-between positioning and practice that can turn the concept of rhythms into an interdisciplinary field of knowledge, so as to enable the analysis of rhythms; rhythms are formed by repetition, movement and interaction between a time, a place and an expenditure of energy. Rhythmanalysis is based on the actual positioning of the self, which provides the right to consciously analyse and actively experience the 'rhythms' of everyday to capture the 'truth of space' for a 'differential space'. The rhythmanalyst is a person who analyses rhythms through a distinct positioning and practice: first, a positioning and presence of the body, which feels, indulges and grasps rhythms, and conceives, perceives and lives rhythms; second, positioning in terms of disciplines, analysing the rhythms as statistician, biologist, sociologist, ethnologist, psychologist and especially as a poet (Lefebvre, *Rhythms*, 13). Lefebvre confirms that the true rhythmanalyst is the poet, and the ideal site to capture rhythms is in middle sites, especially on a balcony, where one is simultaneously inside-outside. The 'womb of space' is a literary positioning and practice that provides a gateway to the 'territory of the imagination' and 'cross-cultural reality', which is submerged. It is submerged because the authors are unaware of it, and they are unaware because 'a work of profound imagination, is [a] paradox; it is both a cloak for, and a dialogue with live "otherness" that seek to break through in a new light and tone expressive of layers of reality' (Harris, xvii–xix). Harris shows that 'awareness' of this paradox, which hides and is in 'dialogue' with different cultures – 'otherness'– is the source that enables the 'break through' with 'gateway' to the authors' submerged or subordinated psyche so as to reveal the cross-cultural 'reality' and palimpsest within different texts. Harris' primary focus is on unearthing this cross-cultural palimpsest by re-reading literatures from different parts of the world: here showing how two different cultures are in dialogue, whereby the relationship is tormenting and nightmarish with marks of 'schizophrenia', 'twinship' and/or 'doubling', yet results in exciting cross-cultural possibilities. The gateway into the territory of the imagination and particularly the cross-cultural breakthrough is what Harris coins that middle 'womb of space'.

Stephanides, Ali and Adil can be considered post-Linobambakoi rhythmanalysts in the womb of space because they adopt this positioning and practice within an in-between site, which emphasises diasporic and Cypriot positions to create multiple Cypruses. Through this positioning, as post-Linobambakoi they practise a hospitality that identifies with two or more opposing positions, and as rhythmanalysts they consciously analyse and experience multiple rhythms – places, spaces, times and energies – enabling them to extend the terms of the 'womb of space' in three interrelated ways: first, they 'consciously' break through to the submerged imagination with full cross-cultural capacity; second, they enter multiple rather than two different cultures, framed around tormenting, doubling and tripling; third, this entry operates through the author's life and literary texts, so it is based on both imaginative territory and the actual lived territory.

The diasporic writers demonstrate this positioning and practice through their literary-lived[6] practices related to the balcony, middle sea and whale. Stephanides leads the discussion here because his engagement with these three concrete metaphors in *The Wind Under my Lips*[7] is representative. It begins as follows:

> *By birth, strangers, he said, I am a Cypriot. I set off from my native land along with my son – on a great ship, and we were gulped down in the mouth of the whale. (Lucian of Samosata)*
>
> Journeys become layered with time. [...] [M]y journey began when I appeared on the easternmost island in the Middle Sea, which was when I came into the world in the Fall before the new decade that marked the middle of the century. [...] I was brand new then when the new century had become middle aged. [...] [S]huttling between them [North Sea and South Sea] sometimes I would hop and drop off into the Middle Sea, onto the island from which we all departed. ('Lips', 102)

Here Stephanides positions himself, like Cyprus, in the 'Middle Sea' or Mediterranean between the 'North Sea' and 'South Sea'. He does this by personalising it into his family saga, particularly his parents' divorce; the 'Middle Sea' refers to Cyprus, where they all departed from, 'South Sea' to Formosa where his mother lived, and 'North Sea' to Britain where his father lived. In island-hopping between the Middle, North and South Sea, Stephanides consistently names and claims the 'middle' position: born in the Middle Sea 'when the century had become middle aged', or 'apart from [being born in the middle of] family struggles, the island was in the middle of a colonial war' ('Somewhere', 127). Through this positionality, which is central to all parts of texts that shift between colonial, postcolonial and partition moments, Stephanides addresses Cyprus' position in the middle of the global north-south divide, whilst localising it to understand partition Cyprus as in the middle of the north – Turkish Republic of Northern Cyprus, and south – Republic of Cyprus. Thus, Stephanides exposes the ways he, like Cyprus, cannot be identified with either the global north or south, and does not belong to the local north or south; instead he is always in the middle speaking from and to multiple geo-political and cultural positions that disturb the dominant binary of the island and world. Ali and Adil also explore this 'middle' positionality through writing that deals with their experiences between north-south Cyprus, Cyprus-Britain and beyond.

The writers illuminate further this middle positionality through frequent allusion to the balcony. In 'The Wind Under my Lips', Stephanides mentions a 'green balcony' (105–107) from his childhood home in Trikomo, north Cyprus. In her short story 'Forbidden Zone' Ali writes about hotel balconies before and after UN-controlled buffer zones started appearing: 'wall-to wall balconies [...] The pigeons in defiance of orders fly in and out, settle anywhere they wish, shit indiscriminately, even worse dance in courtship and fuck all over the balconies, in full view of the guards' (11). In *Fragments from an Architecture of Forgetting*, Adil captures images of balconies in Cyprus' capital city, Nicosia, associated with her childhood. These balconies point to a positionality that negotiates with partition 'places' by representing scenes of occupied closures, whilst proposing pre- and post-partition 'spaces' by representing the past childhood and longed for future scenes of freed openness without division. These partition balconies also point to the ethnic-nationalist balcony discussed in Chapter 3: cypriotturkish poets, like Balman, narrate actual balcony scenes of the Taurus mountains to symbolise Turkey-cyprus; cypriotgreeks, like Angelides, narrate Greek islands and Cyprus as balconies in the sea within a Great Greek unity. Thus, Stephanides, Ali and Adil negotiate with partition and nationalist balconies to create a new balcony where they, like Ali's pigeon, defiantly experience, see, and feel what they please. In this process the balcony exposes the inescapable position of the Cypriot in middle with Cyprus as the balcony, whilst firmly positioning the writers as rhythmanalysts in the womb of space for a differential Cyprus and world.

The actual analysis and experiences of the rhythms operating within the 'womb of space' is shown through the whale; the whale is a metaphor for the ways the writers engage with – 'layered journeys' – the spatial palimpsest or spatial history (Carter, *Road*, xx–xxiii) as related to journeys between Cyprus and beyond. Stephanides provides an understanding of the whale through his epigraph drawn from Lucian of Samosata's *True Story*, which is about an Ancient Greek journey to geographies beyond. The quote is from the episode when the explorers, who are trapped in the 300-mile-long belly of a whale, communicate with a Cypriot who was 'gulped' by the whale when journeying with his son. Whilst in the whale's belly, the explorers are exposed to tormenting encounters with strange beings, and are informed by the Cypriot that the belly is a world: 'of so many nations doth this country consist [...] a thousand' (Lucian, 103). Adil also refers to it: 'Let me be the whale to carry you away from the carnage. Become an imaginary boy-swallowed-whole [...] a whale to shelter her from the drones, the bombs, for a space of becoming' ('Nights', 6).

The whale is a definitive metaphor for experiencing rhythms in the 'womb of space', where the imaginative literary texts meet actual lived diasporic and Cypriot positions and practices. First, like the 'womb of space', the whale's belly relates to the tormenting experience of displacement within strange alienating places, spaces, times and energies, which have cross-cultural capacity. For example, Stephanides narrates his own diasporic biography with focus on his childhood-adulthood wandering in Cyprus and beyond; like the Cypriot in the myth who departed with his son, he also departed from Cyprus with his father to go to the north island and found himself swallowed and inhabiting the whale: 'I had never imagined I would end up on another island inside a whale before the year would end' ('Lips', 110), and subsequently he writes: 'in the belly of the whale, and hop and leap like a flying fish' ('Somewhere', 133). Here the whale's belly at once points to global diasporic and local Cypriot displacements: globally it is the diaspora who departed from Cyprus or a homeland and entered foreign 'spaces' in new geographies; locally it is the Cypriots, who were uprooted from their homes and had to inhabit unfamiliar 'spaces' in partitioned Cyprus. In this way Stephanides suggests that these local and global wanderers are like those in the whale, they have been subject to the experience of torment, longing and dislocation in unfamiliar 'spaces'; yet through it they share experiences that result in a cultural crossing, intimacy, solidarity and conviviality between them. The whale's belly also relates to the islanders' and island's positionality, which is a permeable unbounded site that allows whatever the sea offers to pass through, such that the inhabitants are constantly exposed to and cross between different tormenting and foreign experiences, yet with exciting cross-cultural capacity. Adding to this the 'whale' is a metaphor for the writers' movement, where their literary-lived practices relate to an indefinite cultural network between territories within the sea without national border restrictions and control. Again Stephanides' text is a perfect example of this movement and dwelling, when he states: 'shuttling between' the 'North' and 'South' sea 'sometimes I would hop and drop off into the Middle Sea, onto the island from which we all departed' ('Lips', 108). Ali and Adil also depict this middle sea site, enabling them, like a whale, to have total movement, a network and be shaped by multiple cultures without the need to define, locate or identify with a particular national territory. Thus, like the 'womb of space', the whale is a metaphor for a paradoxical site: the whale's belly symbolises tormenting experience of stagnation, entering and seeing the entire world as foreign, as well as a permeable site of activity, like Cyprus, that allows whatever debris – geographies, cultures, histories – the sea offers to enter. The whale's movement symbolises the writers' uncontrollable 'spatial practices', 'routes and routines' between territories and its people in the sea that together capture heterogeneous ambiguities to defy 'homogenous' cultural and national borders (Lefebvre, *Production*, 361).

Thus in identifying with the middle sea, balcony and the whale, the writers create a site to analyse and experience rhythms from multiple positions – geo-politically between the global north-south and local north-south; geo-nationally and culturally between Britain-Greece-Turkey Cyprus and beyond; historically between the British Empire, the Ottoman Empire, Ancient Greece, and inheritance beyond; ethno-religiously between Muslim-Turkishness, Orthodox-Greekness, and beyond; psycho-historically between 1950s anticolonialism, 1960s ethnic-conflict and 1964/74 partition – related to the Cypriot and global diaspora. They show that local Cypriot and global diasporic wanderers have mutually experienced, like those in the 'womb of space' and the whale, tortuous shifts between belonging to a familiar 'place' and longing in a foreign 'space'. The writers thus localise Boym's 'global diasporic solidarity' (Boym, 342) for Cyprus. This 'global diasporic solidarity' operates through diasporic intimacy, it is the mutual experience of uprootedness, defamiliarisation and longing without belonging between displaced people exploring ways of inhabiting places, spaces and time-zones (Boym, 252–54, xviii).

As true post-Linobambakoi rhythmanalysts in the 'womb of space', these authors position themselves on a 'balcony' and move like a 'whale' in the 'middle sea' so as to read and construct Cyprus. In this way they see and feel what they please, they capture tormenting experiences in opposing and unfamiliar territories, they expose contradictions and problems and they analyse rhythms as related to multiple positions that shape and are shaped by different Cypruses. To clarify and enhance the diaspora authors' practices, positioning and production via this 'whale of space', the remaining sections will provide examples of ways these post-Linobambakoi rhythmanalysts actively write, read, construct and experience five different positions and Cypruses – literary-lived Cyprus that shapes the marginal position; Colonial Cyprus that shapes childhood nostalgia position; British (post)colonial Cyprus for the british-cypriot position; partitioned Cyprus for the cypriotgreek-cypriotturkish border-crossing position; and transnational Cyprus for the Greek-Turkish-British broader-crossing position – that capture diasporic 'solidarity' with 'truths' for a differential Cyprus.

Marginal Position: Literary-Lived Cypruses

As post-Linobambakoi rhythmanalysts the writers use hospitable practices in their writing. Combining lived experiences and literary texts, they create a marginal literary form for marginal selves – I call this the marginal position determined by literary-lived Cypruses. Here Stephanides, Ali and Adil write their lived selves into literary texts, whilst also writing through other-selves and texts, whereby the writing, like them, becomes marginal, and the marginal is reclaimed. Here, they write through diasporic and Cypriot marginal narratives that expose dominant narratives, so as to produce differential literary-lived colonial, postcolonial and partitioned Cypruses.

For this marginal position and production, the diaspora writers focus on their own and other authors' literary-lived experiences with core moments in Cyprus, which engage with and expose the grand narratives that exclude them. As shown in this book, each moment in this literary narrative – British colonialism, anticolonialism, independence and conflict, partition and population transfer – is connected to a destination, which attempts to make sense of Cyprus' history through constructing Cyprus as ethnically and/or Cypriot-centrically exclusive and complete. The diaspora writers engage with these moments by revising, fragmenting and isolating them, particularly in the interest of a counter-narrative that reclaims the marginalised lived experiences of the silenced, outcast and forbidden. They show that, rather than having an escapist attitude with illusionary connection between moments striving towards a single destination, they thrive and perform between places, spaces, time-zones and energies without a destination, enabling a more inclusive understanding that deals with colonial, postcolonial and partitioned Cyprus. Here, for example, the diaspora writes their own and others' experiences of living through British-Cyprus, whilst performing between the bloody decolonial, postcolonial and partition moments, so as to capture mutual experiences of displacement that generates solidarity between conflicting diverse Cypriot groups.

Stephanides, Ali and Adil write these core moments by focussing on marginalised diasporic narratives, operating through absence-presence movement. For example, they show that all Cypriots are diasporic wanderers indefinitely moving between places, spaces, identifications and time-zones, including: the 1960s uprooting and dwelling in ethnic enclaves; the 1974 population transfer between the north-south divide; back and forth between the metropolitan centre London and periphery Cyprus; from Turkey or Greece to Cyprus. They expand on moments, like 1974 partition, to give presence to people absent from the moment itself and/or the dominant narrative: though they were physically absent they write themselves into 1974 through others who were present, where they dwell between actual lived and imagined literary partitioned Cyprus. They write for those physically and/or mentally stranded on the 'other' forbidden side of the borders by shifting between north and south. Thus, they expose dominant narratives so as to enable counter-narratives for marginal groups like themselves.

For these narratives they connect lived experiences with literary form, where together they are on the move, disruptive, transforming and experimental. They generate a new literary form with a personalised narrative style, voice and genre for and like the mutable-multiple selves: here they write these selves into a narrative that can accommodate diasporic and Cypriot literary-lived experiences; they write these marginal selves outside literary conventions, which simultaneously mirrors and enables an understanding of being the excluded Other outside borders and grand narratives. This marginal position is determined by literary-lived Cypruses, which now sets the stage to understand and meet the writers, their life and works.

Stephanides, Ali and Adil write diasporic and Cypriot experiences through narrating their own birth in the colonial moment, departure during the decolonial moment, and return to partitioned Cyprus. They write these Cypruses, first through an individual creative-critical positioning, so as poets, prose-writers, artists, film-makers, scholars, translators and/or activist; second through collective positioning, so working together and with other literary figures linked to marginal positions inside and outside Cyprus.

Stephanides was born in Trikomo. He moved to Britain when a child in 1958, where he remained until he completed university; during this period, he travelled between Britain, Cyprus, Formosa (Taiwan), Spain, Greece and beyond. After completing university, Stephanides dwelled in Guyana, which triggered his interest in the Caribbean, Indian diaspora and India. After years of mobility, Stephanides returned to and is now situated in Cyprus. Stephanides is a scholar, creative writer, translator and documentary film-maker, all of which figure here. Focus is mostly on his in-progress creative text *The Wind Under my Lips* – consisting of the already-published fragments 'The Wind Under my Lips', 'Winds Comes from Somewhere', 'Adropos Moves in Mysterious Ways' and 'a litany in my slumber' – that play with the characteristics of travel writing, autobiography and historiography, interspersed with fictional prose, poems and visuals. These fragments are about Stephanides' diasporic Cypriot experience, emphasising his dislocation between Cyprus-Britain-Formosa and geographies beyond, along with shifts between his first seven years in 1950s decolonial Cyprus, his departure to and dwellings between different spaces from 1958 onwards, and his return to partitioned Cyprus in 1991. I refer to *The Wind Under My Lips* as 'the text' because it has an experimental form with a supplementarity that moves beyond nameable literary conventions, wherein Stephanides himself contemplated what to name it.[8] This supplementation between different literary forms, fragments and styles parallels the supplementation between places, spaces and identifications with positions that provides an understanding of Stephanides' production of Cyprus. Also relevant is Stephanides' poetry collection *Blue Moon in Rajasthan*, his films and research on the Indian diaspora in Guyana, and his contribution to literary Cyprus via translation projects, edited collections and membership to movements, which relate mainly to border-crossing and broader-crossing positions.

Ali was born in Nicosia. She left Cyprus in the 1960s, lived in Britain and returned to Cyprus in 2003; she lives a life border-crossing between Britain-Cyprus, and north-south Cyprus and Britain, where she has a dwelling in all three locations. Ali is a prose writer, translator and a cultural activist. Her illicit moves are mirrored in her short stories, which are dispersed yet collected here, including a large selection from her collection *Pink Butterfly*, some from *Forbidden Zones*, from the magazine *Cadences* and various other collections.[9] These are her fictionalised lived stories, a literary-lived writing in a cinematic style that captures direct shots of diasporic Cypriot gendered experiences and mobility cross-cutting into 1950s decolonial Cyprus, her departures and dwellings between Cyprus-Britain, and her return and crossings to postcolonial partitioned Cyprus. Ali also contributed to literary Cyprus through translating and supporting moves, including Literary Agency Cyprus.

Adil was born in Nicosia. She lived in Turkey, Libya and Britain where she was (dis)located for the longest periods, and is now in Cyprus. She moves between Britain-Cyprus and north-south Cyprus, which is captured in her creative work. Adil is a poet-performer, artist and scholar, where her work dances between fictional prose, autobiography, artwork – including audio-visual installations and digital mediums such as photography, film and online projects – meeting various poetic forms – including film-poetry, performance-poetry and prose-poetry. The poetry collection *Venus Infers* divided into two sections – 'Dead Sister/1974 'and 'Venus Infers' that have characteristics of fiction, autobiography and prose, with the latter introduced as an 'autobiography' – captures an understanding of many positions and Cypruses. Whilst the film-poetry *Fragments from an Architecture of Forgetting*, and the web project 'Topography of a Text' capture the border-crossing and broader-crossing positions and Cypruses. Adil's writing, like herself, is always on the move, mirroring indefinite mobility and dwellings within and between her birth-arrival into decolonial Cyprus, adopted settlement in London, her death-like departure from partitioned Cyprus, and locations beyond. Through writing, Adil thrives and slips between her lived places of belonging and spaces of longing, diverse identifications and multiple time-zones that are in a constant state of nightmarish ambiguity. Through this a beastly beauty is born, a cinematic birth, with literary-lived sites hosted by Adil's ghostly 'twin', where together they breath truth.

Stephanides', Ali's and Adil's literary-lived Cyprus can be understood further through addressing their collaborations with renowned Anglophone, Turkophone and Hellenophone Cypriot authors. These authors offer Stephanides, Ali and Adil with diverse understandings of the marginal positions and the other four positions that enable the production of a differential Cyprus; they offer acute knowledge of movements between places, spaces and identifications related to diasporic Cypriot experiences in the margins of mostly Cyprus, oftentimes Britain, Greece, Turkey, sometimes the east Mediterranean and other times regions beyond. Some of these authors departed Cyprus for Britain never to return, other authors remained in or returned to Cyprus, thereby providing new meaning to being and becoming a displaced Anglophone, Turkophone, Hellenophone Cypriot in post-imperial Britain and in colonial, postcolonial and partitioned Cyprus, which develops a bi-/multi-communal national, cultural and lingual crossing.

Taner Baybars has been part of all literary identifications and constructions discussed in the book, a pioneer who materialises the negotiation and overlaps. With the ethnic-motherland nationalist he shaped anthologies like *Ilk Demet* appearing alongside Ozker Yasin; as a Cypriotist, he was influenced by Nazim Hikmet being the first to translate him into English in the 1960s, and he also translated Mehmet Yashin; as Turkish-Cypriotist he figures in literature curriculum; as Cypriot diaspora he is most influential Anglophone author and translator. In light of this, Baybars has been a wondering /wandering spectre haunting each chapter so as to display the Cypriot solidarity in a differential Cyprus. Born in Vassilia, he departed for Britain in 1955 where he resided most of his life, and then lived in France for his remaining years. Baybars is one of few authors who settled in his adopted-country without physically returning to his birth-country, which is reflected in his literary endeavours. Mostly produced between 1960 and 2009 in his adopted country, Baybars translated multiple collections including four of Hikmet's poetry, created masses of artwork, and authored five poetry collections and two prose texts. Baybars literarily returns to Cyprus in an autobiography, *Plucked from a Far Off Land: Images in Self Biography*, and some poems, including 'Letter to Homeland'.

Korkmazel, Selcuk and Marangou are well-known literary figures who mostly remained in Cyprus. Korkmazel was born in Paphos/Baf and lives in Cyprus; he is a Turkophone poet, prose writer and translator, and has published five poetry collections, two prose collections and three translation collections. Many of Kormazel's poems have appeared in English translation through collaboration with Stephanides and Ali.[10] Selcuk was born in Baf and lives in Cyprus; he is a Turkophone poet and translator and has published three poetry collections, a selection of which have been translated by Ali. Together with Korkmazel, Selcuk is part of Subconscious Group, which edited the underground literature and art journal *Isırgan*. Marangou was born in Limassol and lived in Nicosia; she was a Hellenophone poet, novelist, artist and owner of the Kochlias bookshop and publishing. She has five poetry collections, with *Nicosieness* and *Selections from the Divan* translated into English by Stephanides, and 13 prose pieces. Kochlias has published leading Cypriot works.

Such initiatives are expanded through collaborations with well-known Anglophone writers – such as Nadjarian, Hoplaros and Ierodiaconou – as part of *Cadences*, Literary Agency Cyprus and other projects. Nadjarian was born in Limassol and lives in Nicosia; she is a leading cypriotarmenian poet and prose writer; she has two prose collections and three poetry collection, where her short story 'Ledra Street' has received critical acclaim. Together with Stephanides, Nadjarian is on the editorial board for *Cadences*. Ierodiaconou was born in Cyprus and lives in France; she is a cypriotgreek poet and novelist, her novel *The Women's Coffee Shop* focusses on a village in decolonial Cyprus, and her bilingual poetry collection *Trawl* moves from colonial to partitioned moments. Hoplaros was born in Zimbabwe and lives in Cyprus; she is a cypriotgreek experimental novelist, *Mrs Bones* consists of short stories with visuals and the *Sign Maker* is the first Cypriot graphic novel. Both novels engage with her marginalisation between Zimbabwe and Cyprus.

These initiatives enable a new cypriotgreek-cypriotturkish-cypriotarmenian-cypriotbritish literary-lived Cyprus. Through collaborative and individual initiatives, Stephanides, Ali, Adil and other authors engage with multiple marginalised positions lived within and outside Cyprus, which meet marginalised literary form. They read, write and translate their words and worlds, collectively performed on stage and transformed into printed zines, as well as individually performed and published. In capturing the lived experiences shared amongst Cypriots in Cyprus and global territories, a disruptive literary form with a hybrid inter-generic network emerges. To clarify I interrupt this network by focussing on two common genres, including cinema and autobiography. This meditation shows how the Cypriot diaspora play with literary conventions so as to create a new literary form for the marginalised selves.

The Cypriot diaspora engage with cinema in two ways: first, through the moving-speaking image in audio-visual projects; and second, in the cinematic way they write moments in sharp writerly shots. The cinematic genre – both aspects of the term – is significant in diasporic and partition narratives because it captures a site from which a displaced people can speak, represent themselves, be seen, and become. Hall points to audio-visual cinema in Caribbean diasporic narratives: 'a form of representation which is able to constitute us as new kinds of subjects, and thereby enable us to discover places from which to speak [...] to recognise different parts [...] of ourselves' (Hall, 402). Salman Rushdie points to cinematic style in diasporic writing, which he calls 'CinemaScope and glorious Technicolor' (Rushdie, 10) to capture the experiences of straddling different territories and being distanced from the birth-country. Similarly, cinema is a core mode in partition narratives, which have been investigated in numerous studies on India. Kavita Daiya's *Violent Belongings*, for example, examines literary and film partition narratives in conversation, stating, 'I take them up [film] as literary texts that are experimenting with realistic and documentary form' (Daiya, 55). Thus, the

Cypriot diaspora experiment with cinema to capture the experiences – displacement, fragmentation, longing, loss and being silenced on the move – of their partitioned and diasporic Cypriot-selves; here successfully granting themselves a positionality, subjectivity and visual-auditory existence so as to re/produce these traumatised selves in realistic form.

This 'realistic' form points to the diaspora writers' engagement with autobiography, which relates to Bart Moore-Gilbert's 'postcolonial life-writing' made up of four 'thematics' – style, decentred selves, relational selves, located selves. The Cypriot diaspora adopt the thematic of 'style' characterised as 'inter-generic traffic and experimentation' between fiction, historiography and travel-writing. They show a consistent intersection between autobiography and fiction, which 'challenge[s] the epistemological status of autobiographical/authorial' and 'pact between author and reader' (Moore- Gilbert, xxii), especially through ambiguously identifying with real and imagined and/or absent and present positions. In this way they demonstrate their supplementation on behalf of a diverse and deferred understanding of identity/identification. They simultaneously use a historiographical narrative that shifts between timeframes, so as to re-write their own and others' personal, collective and national history, which 'remedies the deficiencies of western historiography or contests its conception of (parts of) the non-western world as being without, or even outside, history' (Moore-Gilbert, xxii). The diaspora show that they, like their literary predecessors, engage with collective concerns to write diasporic-selves/Cypriot-selves into the history that excluded them: here they contest both the British colonial notion that the Cypriots had no, or were outside of history, and the dominant nationalist Cypriot historiography that put the diaspora and Other Cypriots outside of history. Additionally they 'employ the travel-writing genre to stress the processual and unfinished nature of identity-formation' (Moore-Gilbert, xxii), where their writings are always on the move, confirming that self-knowledge and control of place, space and identification are never complete and whole, but always in process, ambiguity and becoming. They show these characteristics of 'travel-writing' by including another genre, the 'letter' or 'postcard', in their autobiographical narratives.

The literary identifications in Cyprus prioritise the letter: Papadopoulos' Greek-Cypriotist letter 'The Letter and the Road' relates to mobilising Greek-Cypriot sons in villages; the nationalist letters as in Montis' *Letter to the Mother* and Yasin's *Letter to Cyprus*, communicate between Baby Cyprus-Mother Greece or Turkey; Moleskis' Cypriotist letter 'A Letter to Gregory Afxentiou' maps the tears of Cypriot son into Mother Cyprus. The diaspora authors' letter or postcard narratives negotiate with these gendered letter-poems, to create a new letter that captures the Cypriot experience of being mobile and incomplete.

Stephanides focusses on letters he sent to his mother when he was in the UK in the 'North Sea', and she in Cyprus in the 'Middle Sea': 'Years would pass before I would receive a letter' ('Somewhere', 129). In the poem 'Letter to Homeland', Baybars also draws on the letters between birth and adopted locations; however, here he receives the letter but delays replying:

> Dear Father, you ask in your letter
> why for so long I have written no word.
> [...]
> Homesick?
> I am not because I've never had a home
> [...]
> Unhappy?
> Father you are persistent.
> I said I am not unhappy
> though I know I would unearth unhappiness
> in everything
> if I touched it (*Catch*, 19–20)

Baybars' letter-poem is a reply to his father in Cyprus, which shows his ambiguous attitude towards the birth and adopted country. Baybars repetitively claims that he is 'not unhappy' in his adopted country, but confirms he would unearth unhappiness if he confronted – 'touched'– the nostalgia towards the birth-country. Consequently, Baybars refuses to touch 'homesickness' or ideas of belonging to a birth home by writing himself out of Cyprus, 'I've never had a home', and prohibiting communication; however, in writing the letter, Baybars simultaneously writes himself into and communicates with Cyprus. Both Stephanides' and Baybars' 'letters' reflect on the communication and separation between parent and child, which symbolises their relationship between the birth and adopted home, whereby the parents are located and (not)writing from the writers' birth home, whilst the children, authors, are dwelling and (not) writing from the adopted home. The parent-child letter shows that the authors are separated, lack and long for communication with their parents, to suggest their separation from, and desire to belong in the birth home. The letter simultaneously shows that the writers confirm and long for the separation and detachment of communication from their parents, enabling them to escape the nostalgia towards the illusionary homeland and locate themselves in their adopted home. The letters express the authors' performance and mobility between their own birth and adopted country; they dwell and thrive between them in a place of belonging and a space of indefinite longing, which shapes the processual nature of their identification.

Adil's letter-poem, 'extract from a love letter on the run (unsent)', communicates between Cyprus and her adopted country. The poem is from the section 'Dead Sister/1974', which is about an ambiguous twin who is a major poetic concept for Adil; the twin symbolises multiple identifications that change as spatial perception changes. For the purpose of this section, let us take Adil's narrative on the twin in relation to Cyprus; she is located in Cyprus and is the Cypriot 'Woman I could have been, if 1974 hadn't happened and if I did not leave Cyprus'.[11] The letter is written whilst Adil is on the move: 'I'm writing this on the coach [...] Lover man you have come to kill me. So I'm forced to leave [...] I'm leaving because you are my dead sister' (*Venus*, 49). In addressing the letter to a lover who is simultaneously the 'dead twin sister', Adil is writing to Cyprus and her Cypriot self; here attempting to write herself out of Cyprus, where she confirms her departure from Cyprus and from her single Cypriot self by supplementing multiple selves – her twin, male lover and many more identifications – to show that her position is constantly in the process of becoming. Ali engages with letters as seen in poems she translates – i.e. 'unsent letters' by Nese Yashin. Nadjarian focusses on letters and postcards, including 'Postcard from Kyrenia'. Hoplaros' *Mrs Bones* set in Rhodesia from 1972 to 1985 during postcolonial failures is about a parent-daughter relationship and the immigrant experience, mainly depicted through letters she writes to her parents from boarding schools. Hoplaros' letters – including two handwritten childhood letters with parts crossed out in a section called 'censorship' (14); and other letters she writes in English to her dad, and in Greek to her mum in a section called 'unanswered mail' (21) – negotiate with homesickness in relation to dislocation and language, especially between boarding school and the family home, whilst negotiating with her positioning between mother/father-land and adopted land.

Thus the 'letter/postcard'[12] is a significant mode used by Cypriot authors, which creates a letter/postcard narrative genre. This genre, like travel-writing, shows Cypriot mobility, communication and ambiguous shifts between locations, which mirrors lacking control of a single identification and Cyprus. The letter/postcard captures places, spaces and identifications in an active process of being written, this is an unfinished dialogical-dialectical formation based on (in)complete transitional (be) longing that provides an understanding of being and becoming Cypriot and Cyprus.

Other than this thematic of 'style', the Cypriot diaspora focus on 'decentred selves', which reject the 'model of sovereign, centred unified Selfhood [and claims] models of dispersed and decentred subjectivity' (Moore-Gilbert, xviii). This has been touched on in the 'letter' analysis, where they adopt a decentred mutable self-shifting between birth and adopted locations, ending in an ambiguous hybridity and translation in a doubling identification with multiple positions. The 'relational selves' is also a pivotal thematic, wherein the diaspora claim 'a dialogical conception of Selfhood as something which is essentially social and relational' elaborated through 'links between themselves, their immediate circles and society more broadly' (Moore-Gilbert, xviii–xx). Again the 'letter/postcard' discussion show this, where self-conception is determined by relationships and communication between themselves and Cypriots – literary predecessors, community or families – in Cyprus; here 'selfhood' is determined by the writers' active intimacy, solidarity and conviviality in a socio-cultural environment within both Cypriot and global contexts. The final thematic of 'located selves' is on dislocation related to 'self, place and displacement' (Moore-Gilbert, xxi). Briefly shown in the 'letter/postcard' between birth and adopted home, this thematic, where they construct multiple selves through places and spaces, is the central to all diasporic narratives, this chapter and this book.

In this section I introduced the 'marginal position' shaped by literary-lived Cyprus. This is based on cohabitation between literary form – operating via a hybrid inter-generic traffic – with marginal diasporic and Cypriot experiences; this cohabitation is in a constant supplementation, 'a chain of supplements', where multiple genres and experiences indefinitely emerge, enabling authors to write themselves, and others, into an inclusive counter-narrative for the production of Cyprus. This 'marginal position' observes and obliterates homogeneous conventional order and control, whilst making room for a heterogeneous radical disorder; thus, analysing fully places, spaces and times with a 'right to difference' for the production of differential literary-lived Cypruses.

The 'marginal position' and literary-lived Cyprus is a significant supplement in the 'whale of space', where successfully carrying the weight of diasporic and Cypriot experiences, it connects with the other four 'positions' and Cypruses.

Childhood Nostalgia Position: Dual Archaeology of Decolonial Home

As post-Linobambakoi rhythmanalysts the authors adopt hospitable practices and positions that shift between the birth home and adopted adult home. In this process they analyse and experience rhythms through the notion of 'homeland', actively reading and constructing decolonial Cyprus, which determines the identification with the nostalgic position. This nostalgic position can be understood through Rushdie and Boym meeting Tuan and Lefebvre.

The writers rarely use terms like homeland, and they do not have a primary habitation. Instead they read and construct home through movement, consistently writing themselves into places, spaces, times and energies, with moments when focus is on their decolonial birth-homes, and other moments when they shift into their adopted-homes. This site between birth and adopted home is the diaspora authors' dwelling, where home is ambiguously a space, place, time of (be)longing (dis)location and (un)homeliness. This resonates with Rushdie's commentary on diasporic writings of home:

> we straddle two cultures. [...] But however ambiguous and shifting this ground may be, it is not an infertile territory for a writer to occupy [...] If Literature is [...] finding new angles at which to enter reality, then once again our distance, our long geographical perspective, may provide us with such angles. (Rushdie, 15)

Even though this site between the birth and adopted home is the Cypriot diaspora's fertile dwelling, enabling new readings and constructions of Cyprus, I interrupt this supplementary play to discuss the distinct characteristics and new angles separately. In some sections I focus on the birth home – i.e. here on decolonial Cyprus, and later on postcolonial partition Cyprus for border-crossing position; in other sections I focus on the play between birth and adopted homes that shapes the post(-colonial) hybrid position and transnational broader-crossing position. This fertile dwelling between homes can be enhanced through Boym's nostalgia:

> nostalgia is [...] a yearning for a different time – the time of our childhood, the slower rhythms. [...][T]he nostalgic desires to obliterate history and turn it into private or collective mythology, to revisit time like space (xv).
>
> [t]o unearth the fragments of nostalgia one needs a dual archaeology of memory and of place, [...] of illusionary and of actual practices (xviii)

The authors discussed in this book construct decolonial Cyprus by obliterating history and returning to the rhythms – places, spaces, times and energies – of 1930–1970s childhood; however, they each engage with 'archaeology' differently. The post-1964/74 Cypriotists and ethnic-nationalists construct Cyprus as restorative nostalgics, where, without dual archaeology, they recollect the memory and lost homeland via illusionary practices that dangerously 'confuse the actual home and the imaginary one' (Boym, xvi) so to make a single fantasy homeland they would die for. The diaspora authors construct Cyprus as reflective nostalgics, where, exposing the restorative nostalgics, they consciously adopt the dual archaeology shifting between memory and home and illusionary and actual practices, so as to inhabit multiple homelands in mutable time-zones. Here, they recognise we are 'nostalgic not for the past the way it was, but for the past the way it could have been. It is this past-perfect that one strives to realise in the future' (Boym, 351); they acknowledge that our construction 'of the past [is] determined by the needs of the present [that] impact on the realities of the future' (Boym xvi). Here, on the one hand, as reflective nostalgics consciously mirroring restorative nostalgics, they scrupulously 'detail' the past home, not the way it was but the way it could have been, consciously to cheat themselves and the reader into trusting this Cyprus as absolute truths. They recollect an imaginary secure homeland determined by their need for placement, so as to overcome the torment of their present postcolonial partitioned dislocations, enabling them to create a united fantasy for future Cyprus and selves. On the other hand, maintaining the spirit of reflective nostalgia, they write home to expose this single Cyprus, which Cypriotists, nationalist and many Cypriots consider real, as always and only an imaginary abstract home. In this way the diaspora capture the birth-home as actual homeland they lived in, and imaginary homeland that 'no longer exists or [one that] never existed' (Boym, xiii–xviii).

Boym's recipe relates to Rushdie's advice: 'if we do look back, we must do so in the knowledge [...] that we will, in short, create fictions, [...] imaginary homelands, Indias of the mind' (Rushdie, 10). The diaspora create imaginary homelands that are Cypruses of the mind and body, where they find new angles to enter reality that 'speak [or write] properly and concretely' (Rushdie, 12) about home. They create these Cypruses by claiming 'actual' concrete ways – dislocated and unhomely – childhood home was, whilst claiming that this decolonial home can never be 'actual' for two interrelated reasons. First, as Rushdie suggests, the diaspora writer is 'out-of-country [...] [confronted with] the physical fact of discontinuity, of his [her] present being in a different place from his [her] past, of his[her] being "elsewhere"' (Rushdie, 12); second, as shown by Boym, recalling memory and home is always subject to 'elsewhere' between other rhythms determined by past, present and future. Here constructing past Cyprus is determined by the needs in present Cyprus, meaning the present dislocation is implanted into the past; this results in an ambiguous actual and imagined past decolonial Cyprus that impacts on present and future postcolonial partitioned Cyprus.

Thus, in reading decolonial Cypruses through practices evoking Boym and Rushdie, the diaspora subject themselves and their readers to descend into the abyss of confusion and paradox. These paradoxical practices are enhanced via Tuan and Lefebvre. As advocated by Tuan they perform between a safe homely 'place' and foreign dangerous 'space'. Employing Lefebvre's 'representation of space', like architects, they conceive homes with codes, plans and details; adopting 'representational space' they live the social and memory sites, especially appropriating 'time (or times), rhythm (or rhythms)' of 'everyday activities [with] an origin [in] childhood' (Lefebvre, *Production*, 256 and 362); assuming 'spatial practice' they perceive physical routines between families and friends. In this process they produce Cyprus through Lefebvre's regressive-progressive approach, which 'acts retroactively upon the past, disclosing aspects and moments of it hitherto uncomprehend. The past appears in a different light, and hence the process whereby that past becomes the present also takes on another aspect' (Lefebvre, *Production*, 65). This dynamic between Rushdie's, Boym's, Tuan's and Lefebvre's spatial-temporal thoughts shows that the diaspora capture the truth of actual-concrete and imaginary-abstract times to produce differential decolonial Cypruses that shape diasporic nostalgic bodies and minds.

The writers remap their childhood homes – Baybars captures the 1930s, Ali and Stephanides 1950–1960s, Adil and Ierodiaconou 1960s–1970s – in decolonial Cyprus, through using visual imagery as well as detailed descriptive narratives; it is these located homes and moments that at first glance are considered actual real 'places'. In *Plucked*, Baybars scrupulously maps the childhood birth-home as a 'place' that provided him with a safety net united with his parents:

> Vassilia, a small mountain village west of Kyrenia. It was a fishing village too. The land between the hills and the sea was barely two miles wide. Our house was on a slope, tucked beyond the mosque without a minaret. (11)

Baybars narrates the compass point, then describes the surrounding area, and finally zooms in to detail and locate his birth village 'Vassilia' and 'house', which provide actual mappings of his home. Baybars also focusses on how he spent his childhood admiring and imitating Ibrahim, a friend a few years his senior, defined as the 'greatest artist on earth' because of 'his crayon drawings' that were 'marvellous scenes' of the village (13). Thus, Baybars maps fully his village through the detailed narrative of actual scenes he sees and through describing the drawings that he and Ibrahim created.

Similarly, yet three decades later, Stephanides maps his childhood home, 'easternmost island in the Middle Sea', to suggest the compass points of Cyprus, as well as Trikomo, the easternmost village in Cyprus. Stephanides maps Trikomo with scrupulous narrative detail: 'they [parents] lived together for two years in the house with the green balcony, overlooking the square with the coffee shops and the tiny renowned medieval church of Ayios Iakovos'. Like Baybars, this narrative mirrors the actual mappings in Trikomo, through which square and house can be found. This house with the green balcony has significance throughout Stephanides' narrative because it is symbolic of his birth 'place', his beginnings in a stable family homeliness. This potential beginning is recorded through detailing his parents' background and union that inform us the green balconied house was the first his parents lived in, which provided them with stability. Upon locating his parents, Stephanides locates himself: 'Katerina's body was my threshold into that room in the house with the green balcony' ('Lips', 102–106), to show that from the safety of his mother's womb he entered the same comforts in the green balconied room. Thus, Stephanides constructs this birth-home as a 'place' of belonging.

In the story 'Sefka'ba', Ali also recollects detailed mappings of her childhood neighbourhood in Nicosia: 'the three of them [Sefka'ba and siblings] lived in the corner house', and the location of her home: 'Our house was in between Pembe's and Havva's house' (*Pink*, 48–50). In the story 'Pink Butterfly', Ali zooms in to this childhood home, recording her childhood self with her siblings and mother, secure within the interior closed doors of the home. Ali narrates the home as a familial stable 'place' of inhabitancy, through the symbolism and reclamation of her mother's body. The opening of the story focusses on the mother's sexual groans and her bare breast with nipples compared to pink butterflies. In returning to the sexual female body through the butterfly, Ali symbolises her mother's actual metamorphosis towards freedom in settling, controlling and reclaiming her bodily self and the body of the home. The mother undergoes an actual metamorphosis from wife to 'widow', free to perform as she pleases in the sexual and domestic arena, without displaying or adapting it for a husband and the conventions the Cypriot, or otherwise, society bestows upon a woman. Through this narrative, Ali simultaneously reclaims the body of the female and of the domestic home, both of which are often confiscated from a woman's full control. This narrative relates to the moment of pregnancy, often the only moment when a woman is solely and fully responsible for her body, to provide a secure, safe and stable 'place' of dwelling for the child. This play between the mother's sexual and domestic body with the pregnant body suggests that Ali reclaims and compares the mother's control, stability and security of her body, 'womb', to that which she feels in the body of her birth home. This symbolic comparison between the mother's body – 'womb'– and the birth-home is the same as Stephanides' movement from his mother's womb to the green balconied room.

These birth-homes have significance for the writers because they are the actual family homes they were born into and inhabited in their first years of childhood. Like cartographers and architects, they all map these moments with narrative and/or visual detail in order to write and locate themselves into a stable childhood time and family home. At first glance these detailed descriptions suggest an actual reflection of the birth-homeland that is a 'place' of homeliness, fixity and stability; however, the narratives simultaneously mirror the confrontation and awareness that these depictions are manifestations of an imagined homeland. Like reflective nostalgics, they show the dual archaeology of home as an actual fixed 'place' they once inhabited, as well as an illusionary open 'space' with a comforting imagining in the interest of fixing themselves in their present and future.

The writers show that the birth-home is a comforting imagining by exposing the danger, dislocation and unsettlement they experienced within these homes; they show that they did not only inhabit these birth 'places', but they consistently moved inhabiting multiple 'spaces' in Cyprus. They expand upon this open imaginary 'space' through focussing on active memory, showing that in recalling the childhood moment they are in fact subject to and dwelling between unstable fragments of remembrance and forgetfulness, which ambiguously shift between times. In this process of reflection, the authors dwell in the 'space' of longing amidst multiple homes and time-zones, acknowledging that the stable home/homeland that is a closed 'place' does not, cannot and possibly never did exist.

Baybars interrupts the mappings of the stable family home in Vassilia by showing the multiple cities, towns and villages he inhabited in Cyprus. The autobiography is divided into three parts that mirror Baybars' actual dislocation, whereby each part relates to places or spaces Baybars spent his childhood: part one is set in Vassilia and framed around Baybars' first seven years in a stable family home; however, here Baybars records the threat he felt when informed he might be moving to the capital city, Nicosia; in part two Baybars records his short unsettlement in the village Minarelikoy; and in part three Baybars inhabits Nicosia. The fragmentary narrative structure shows not only multiple dwellings that determine and are determined by Baybars' present ruptured experience, but also displays the fragmentary nature of memory to confirm a stable, coherent or actual narrative of the past home/homeland is unattainable. Baybars' fragmentary structure draws attention to the fact that his narrative has been determined by splintered snapshots between times, 'places' and 'spaces': Baybars wrote the autobiography whilst in post-war Britain in the 1970s by travelling back four decades to the childhood moment in decolonial Cyprus; this recollection is a literary return between his present displacement in Britain and the ethnic bloodshed in Cyprus (1970s), the memory from the first anticolonial uprising (1930s), and his last vision of the armed struggle (1955) before his indefinite departure from Cyprus. Baybars remembers and recollects his childhood Cyprus without physically retuning.

Stephanides and Ali expand further on the dislocation by also writing about the memory of unsettlement, alongside the experience of an actual physical return. In Stephanides' narrative, the actual green balconied birth-home is transformed from located beginning place to a dislocated 'cross-road' space, where he, like Baybars, maps the multiple dwellings and indefinite movement he experienced. Moving from Trikomo to Nicosia and other locations in Cyprus, Stephanides writes: 'For the months ahead, I would be constantly on the move from town to village, sea to mountain, house to house, aunt to uncle, cousin to *koumbaro*, kith to kin' ('Somehwere', 130). Stephanides develops this indefinite wandering through commenting on his parents' divorce, where, without a stable family home, he inconsistently shifted between momentarily settlement with his father, his mother and sometimes without parents: 'When neither Katerina nor Demosthenes was there, it was no big issue for me as I knew one or the other would come' and 'In between, I was everybody's child' ('Lips', 108); often capturing scenes with his grandparents 'I lived with Katerina's parents, Pappou Chrisostomo and Yaya Milia, in the village of Trikomo', and other time capturing scenes with 'Wherever and whoever claimed me as their child' ('Somewhere', 130, 127). Throughout the narrative, Stephanides confirms lack of familial identification not only through these unsettlements, but also through referring to both parents 'Katerina and Demosthenes' by name, without using terms like mother and father. This ongoing wandering confirms Stephanides does not have a single family birth-home, but has adopted multiple birth homes and families in Cyprus.

Stephanides also confirms that the green balconied home is imagined. First, in stating 'their story was told to me with some colour and romance' ('Lips', 105), Stephanides shows that the stable home and familial experiences he is nostalgic for is an illusion he cannot remember, where he is only able to write it through fragmented memories of town folk and imaginary 'sibyls', through a polyphony of actual-imaginary voices from his childhood. Second, by physically returning to the home, where, as a reflective nostalgic, he retells the past with the difference that maps home as an actual place that exists and an imagined space that never existed. Stephanides' childhood home is in Trikomo in north Cyprus, and in the narrative his adult self 'crossed with many others for the first time in nearly thirty years' ('Lips', 107). Here he is referring to the opening of the borders in 2003, when he and numerous Cypriots border crossed to their past homes they departed from in 1974. Stephanides narrates the actual return to the green balconied house through the symbolism of the key ring: upon arriving into his village, Stephanides and the villagers search and find the man or the key-keeper who unlocks the door to the birth-home, and upon their departure from the home the key-keeper gives Stephanides a key-ring of an anonymous political party. The key-ring is symbolic of the present-absent key to home, which simultaneously enables entry into an actual existing place and illusionary non-existent space. The key is a tangible presence in the present that confirms an actual physical opening and entering into the house and green balconied room that Stephanides imagined for over four decades; the key is also absence in the past based on an illusionary stable childhood that never existed because when entering into the home he 'had no recollection of the inside of the room with the green balcony' ('Lips', 107). Stephanides departs from the house with only a key-ring that becomes his personal souvenir, reminding him that he has access to the actual house, yet he does not and will never have the key to return to a homely stable moment because all the obsessive yearnings of it were imagined and never existed. Stephanides' experience of return responds to the Cypriot 'key fetish'[13] related to partitioned Cyprus. It draws on the Cypriots' collective experience of being with and without keys to return to pre-1974 home: with key – most Cypriots have the key, with key fetish that promises return – because there is the possibility of physical return; without key because of the impossibility of permanent return to these homes, impossible because they are based on recollections and shifts between pre-1974, present and future time. These homes are and will always be illusions that never existed because, borrowing again from Boym, the Cypriots are not recalling the past the way it actually was, but recording the past the way it could have been, so they can write themselves into an un-partitioned located future. Stephanides' narratives on Cyprus enable him not only to confront and overcome such imaginings, but also to write himself into the truths of his and Cyprus' decolonial past and partitioned present and future.

Ali's stories also redefine the childhood home to capture Cyprus' ruptured present and future. In 'Pink Butterfly', Ali refers to the separation of her parents; however, whilst Stephanides draws on his dislocated space in-between the separation, Ali depicts the separation to claim the located-self settled within the domestic place and female body via her mother. Ali shows, however, that this stability is confiscated: the mother is displaced and loses control when the doors of her house are forcefully opened through the call 'Open the Door', and the entry of the 'Strange English soldiers'. Ali is referring to the 1950s anticolonial period, that 'curfew time soldiers fill[ed] the street' and raided the Cypriot houses in search of leads to allies of the anticolonial resistance. The colonial soldiers enter the childhood home:

> Click-click-click along the sitting room. Click-click…click-click… up and down the stairs. Look in the bedrooms, under the beds, in the wardrobes, beds. The butterflies are hanging on a nail behind the door. They are ruffled with the tip of a machine-gun barrel. (*Pink*, 103–104)

Ali recollects the 'clicking' footsteps of the English soldiers, who have taken control of her childhood home and her mother in the process. The butterfly, once symbolic of the metamorphosed and reclaimed body of home and mother, has been – 'hanged'– violated by the 'gun', suggesting that the mother's body and house have been put on display for the male soldiers. After a thorough search the soldiers leave and the houses' doors are closed: here the birth-home is symbolically transformed from a 'place' of secure inhabitancy to an open space of dislocated danger with her 'mother exhausted defeated [...] another authority has abolished my mother' (*Pink*, 107).

Ali's stories also emphasise actual physical dislocation from the birth-home in Nicosia, through narratives about her separation from her mother, when she also becomes someone else's child. In the story 'no granddad no', Ali and her siblings live with their grandparents, which she recollects as an unhomely hostile setting when voicing her grandmother's comments, 'they are half-orphaned after all', and the grandfather's complaints '[my daughter] gives birth to them and I am forced to look after them. She dumps them on me. She doesn't give a damn!' (*Pink*, 115–16).

Ali also narrates dislocation by physically returning to the actual childhood home to perform between times, where she, like Stephanides, confirms the childhood home is imagined because it is determined by her present dislocations and fragmented memories. In the story 'Sefka'ba', Ali recovers childhood moments through her neighbour:

> 'well, there were too many and my sister burned them'. Again another memory reaches me. They had burned their books, they were communist books [...] How strange that that comes back to me as I listen to her (*Pink*, 56)

Here Sefka'ba reports the moments when TMT undertook sudden searches in houses suspected communist, detailing how her brother had too many communist books so her elder sister burnt them to protect the family. Using Sefka'ba's account, Ali makes sense of the childhood moment through remembering fragments she had forgotten, whilst adding other fragments she had never recorded – people's names like 'Sefka'ba's brother who I now learn was called Mustafa', and details of the construction of her neighbourhood, 'I learn for the first time the date these council houses were built. And I had lived in them from 1951 to 1963' (*Pink*, 48). By this recollection, which shifts between times to collect – forgotten and unrecorded – fragments from childhood past, through narratives of the adult present, so as to reconstruct de/postcolonial Cyprus, Ali confirms the past home as inescapably a fragmented imagining that cannot attain a complete concreteness.

Stephanides, Baybars and Ali narrate a literary-lived return to the childhood moment that shifts between multiple times, fragmented memories and forgetfulness, place and space, located homeliness and dislocated unhomeliness, actual concrete realities and abstract imaginings, which collectively confirm that the birth-home they are nostalgic for exists without existing. Adil also narrates the birth-home in such terms, yet she does not return to a romanticised childhood nor engage with transitions between located homely and a dislocated unhomely Cyprus. Instead, Adil maps childhood Cyprus through a surreal imagining, where unfamiliar ghosts, doubles and mythical creatures inhabit and haunt both the birth and adopted home. Stephanides' childhood Cyprus is also haunted by spectres and sibyls: 'I heard ghosts speak to me' when wandering Nicosia streets as a child, and 'As I pass through [those streets] nowadays I wonder if the ghosts I used to hear are muted' ('Somewhere', 130). These spectral narratives of home relate to Boym's claims, 'the lost [birth] home and home abroad often appear haunted [...]with doubles and ghosts' (Boym, 251).

This supplement that I call 'nostalgia position' is shaped by the production of decolonial Cypruses. Here home ambiguously shifts between opposing categories – place-space, located-dislocated, imagined-actual, belonging-longing, homely-unhomely, INhabitancy-OUThabitancy, remembrance-forgetting, absence-presence, mind-body, conceived-lived, mental-social: home is the site between these hyphens. In this process the diaspora writers capture the 'truth of space': exposing restorative nostalgia to celebrate reflective nostalgia; exploiting the decolonial positions and Cypruses of their literary predecessors who select the former side of the hyphen, so as to confirm that both sides of the hyphen equally and inescapably produce decolonial Cyprus because of colonialism, postcolonialism and partition. The diaspora authors capture further this 'truth of space' through the british-cypriot position shaped by the (post)colonial birth-country of Cyprus and the adopted country of Britain – this is the third supplement.

(Post)colonial british-cypriot Sea Position: Hybridity and Translation in the Third Space

As rhythmanalysts the writers analyse colonial and postcolonial rhythms – places, spaces, times and energies – actively to read and construct Britain and Cyprus for the british-cypriot position; here as post-Linobambakoi, they are stranded between geographies, languages and cultures of Britain and Cyprus. This production of (post)colonial Britain and Cyprus determines the british-cypriot position, understood through Bhabha's 'third space of enunciation'[14].

Cyprus' legacy of being conquered, colonised and partitioned between different regimes exposes the inescapable operation of Bhabha's 'third space', an identification enabling new positions to emerge, which the writers make concrete through entering this contact zone reigned over by symbolic-concrete processes of 'cultural translation' and 'hybridity' between different cultures. The 'third space' can be unearthed in all the writings explored in this book because, as shown, each chapter elaborates on a different cultural position within the colonial and postcolonial moment; however, I address it here because the diaspora writers capture consciously the actual practices related to the 'third space'. They capture multiple palimpsestic cultural layers mapped by Western and non-Western imperial regimes, so as to emphasise the hybridisation and translation between the culture of Cyprus and of the Empires. Here I limit discussion to the culture of Cyprus within a British colonial and postcolonial context, because the diaspora writers often point to this condition as having major power in colonising and coercing Cyprus, yet this history has been largely obscured by dominant literary constructions of Cyprus. The ethnic-motherland nationalists replace British and all other cultural moments with Ancient/Modern Greece or the Ottoman Empire/Turkey. In doing so, they construct a hegemonic 'mental space' conceived as ethnically closed Greece-cyprus or Turkey-cyprus 'place' for ethno-religious selves. The post-1964/74 Cypriotists negotiate with the British regimes alongside all other regimes that shaped Cyprus, a process I coined 'Spatial Palimpsestic Archaeology'; however, through it they claim all occupying powers as equal without entering fully the contact zone, so making a 'Museum of the Palimpsest'. This serves to create a 'physical space' perceived as a pre-partition unified childhood 'place' that regulates the 'space' of foreignness for all Cypriot-selves. These literary constructs are limited illusionary practices because firstly they aim to empty Cyprus of the 'third space' by secreting or freezing the actual cultural palimpsestic layer, secondly, they empty the diasporic dimension by excluding their narratives; however, the cultural layers and Cypriot diaspora find positions and texts from which to write and construct Cyprus. The diaspora writers expose these limitations through making the 'third space' material, demonstrating full entry into a contact zone that shows the impact various cultures have had on Cypriot formation. As will be shown they enter fully the british-cypriot contact zone with all 'truths' that have been directly 'lived, conceived and perceived' in British colonial and postcolonial Cyprus.

The diaspora authors compulsively shift between Cyprus and Britain. They show that growing up in British decolonial Cyprus and migrating to the imperial centre, London, has resulted in them willingly entering this contact zone reigned over by processes of 'hybridity' and 'translation' between the British and Cypriot cultures. In this process they lose sight of the original essence because all meaning is generated through interruptive, reproductive and exchange practices with a tormenting negotiation and ambiguous doubling between the cultures. This, in turn, blurs the coloniser and colonised, or the British and Cypriot binary, to create a 'third space' that can accommodate the writers' british-cypriot-selves. Here the writers prioritise actual 'social spaces' that are directly 'lived spaces' within the (post)colonial moments, to expose the 'mental spaces' and 'physical spaces' (Lefebvre, *Production*, 38–41, 361–62, 371–72) related to the colonial moment, particularly problematising mappings by imperialists that claim Britain is culturally superior to Cyprus, the nationalists conceiving Greek or Turkish identification without Britishness, and the Cypriotists' restricted cultural entry. This 'truth of space' is captured through the diaspora authors' literary-lived geographic and language 'spatial/social practices' that are shaped by 'desires' and 'needs', which prioritise Lefebvre's 'representational space' and 'lived spaces' marked by conflicts between childhood-adulthood and dwelling-wandering (*Production*, 362–63). This truth is enhanced through Tuan's 'place' of paused childhood belonging and 'space' of moving adult longing between the cities and languages of Britain meeting the island and languages of Cyprus. In this way the writers capture the 'truth of space', where they prioritise actual lived human experiences for a differential British colonial and postcolonial Cyprus.

The writers produce a cultural geography through 'spatial/social practices', operating through self-destructive desires within and between Britain and Cyprus, where routes and routines are transformed from a competent-cohesive system to differential ambiguity related to movement in stagnation, difference in repetition, and wandering and dwelling (Lefebvre, *Production*, 362–95). These conflicts link to Tuan's experience between moving in space and paused in place. Stephanides' 'a litany in my slumber', for example, draws on his and Ali's routes between Cardiff and Nicosia, Ali's stories, mostly set in London and Nicosia/Famagusta, are based on routines between these locations, and Adil's *Venus Infers* captures the 'spatial/social practice' through the ambiguous 'twin sister' who proposes a sea network between probational dwellings in the London transportation zone and Cyprus historical time-zones, giving way to her creation of a third cultural geography.[15] Thus, these writers ambiguously swim between Britain and Cyprus without considering either as original, and the movement-pause between the probation dwellings provides the production of a third geography, a hybrid sea space, where together they grant their british-cypriot-selves indefinite leave to remain.

Language, especially the translation and transformation site between English and Greek or Turkish, also captures the british-cypriot position, shown by numerous writers – Baybars, Hoplaros, Ierodiaconou, Nadjarian, Stephanides, Ali and Adil. It is, however, Stephanides, Ali and Adil who expand fully on language in cultural translation and transformation within a postcolonial framework, where they generate meaning through interruptive practices between, for example, the colonisers' English tongue, and their mothers' (Cypriot) Greek or Turkish tongue in (post)colonial Cyprus. In this way, they construct a 'social space' based on conflicts between 'childhood-adulthood maturation' (Lefebvre, *Production*, 363) practices experienced as familiar homely place-unfamiliar foreign space.

The Cypriot diasporic practices with language expand on considerations by pioneering postcolonial writers. Like Chinua Achebe, they meditate on having no choice but to 'use' someone else's language and 'abandon' their mother-tongue (Achebe, 62), concluding that with/without choice they abandon-retain the mother-tongue. They consider a Ngugi wa Thiong'o style decolonial language programme,[16] which aims to replace the colonial master's English tongue with the abandoned pre-colonial mother-tongue, as impossible. In this process they use English to contest its agency, exposing that though it is their main communication, they have done more than just use it, they have transformed English. As Rushdie suggests, English 'needs remaking for our [diasporic] purpose' (17), and to personalise or 'cypriotise' Achebe's approach: this is a new Cypriot-English that carries the weight of their Cypriot and diasporic experience, still in communion with its ancestral home but altered to suit its new surroundings (62). This Cypriot-English operates within and between Cypriot (Greek or Turkish) and English, confirming the alienation and conflict between all three languages and cultures. This Cypriot-English shows that everyone linked to Cyprus is forced to experience a complex transformation and translation between the Cypriot and adopted English tongue as determined by place, space and time.

The diaspora writers show this transformation site between Cypriot and English, when the former is inescapably abandoned. Stephanides writes: 'he [Colonial officer Mr. Armstrong] taught me some English phrases' and 'pretending I could sing in English and I squeaked the words "Gwotever gwilbee gwilbee"' ('Somewhere' 131 and 135). Here Stephanides focusses on the decolonial moment when his childhood-self negotiated with the colonial master's dominating foreign tongue, ending in his and other adult selves abandoning their mother-tongue in postcolonial Cyprus, as displayed in this and other literary texts. Similarly, Baybars points to abandoning the mother-tongue in an illuminating interview, with questions posed in Turkish by Korkmazel, and his replies in English: 'Lycee was entirely in English [...] Eighteen months at the RAF introduced me to real spoken English, [...]in England, everything became English! [...] language is something like air you breathe in [...] You stop hearing the language you were born to' (Baybars, 'Interview', 119). More interestingly they show the transformative status of the mother-tongue, which leaves the diaspora and all Cypriots with no choice but to abandon it. Baybars explains the invention of Turkish that became foreign to the Cypriot diaspora who departed Cyprus in the 1950s–1960s, leaving them in diasporic possession of a mother-tongue – 'Osmanli Turkcesi' [Ottoman-Turkish] – considered outdated and foreign by Cypriots who remained. Stephanides expands this through narrating language via periphery-centre dynamics:

> Mr. Armstrong was British and he spoke Greek like an Athenian – or so said Demosthenes as I only understood the speech of the island and I had to concentrate to understand [...] Mr. Armstrong had studied Ancient Greek at a famous University called Oxford and he knew Greek better than we did. ('Somewhere', 131)

Here Stephanides points to the difference between standard 'Athenian Greek' used in Greece and in Cyprus' official setting, and the 'speech of the island' that is a distinct dialect used in unofficial familial/communal Cyprus. This is the same for Turkish usage in Turkey and Cyprus. In this way Cyprus disturbs the common binary proposed by postcolonial critics like Thiong'o regarding the mother-tongue 'associated with negative qualities of backwardness, underdevelopment, humiliation' (Thiong'o, 28) in comparison to English; in Cyprus users of the mother-tongue – Cypriot dialect or Ottoman-Turkish of the 1950/60s anticolonial moment – are considered backward, uneducated and of low status not in comparison to English users but in comparison to Greek and Turkish standards from the language centres. This also shows that the Cypriot diaspora possess a language of the anticolonial nationalising moment, which would usually be considered most fitting for decolonial national programmes, like Thiong'o's. In addressing these transformations, Baybars and Stephanides confirm that Cypriots have no choice but to abandon the mother-tongue, where they must select from the language moments, including: the anticolonial Cypriot tongue or postcolonial Turkish/Greek standard tongue; the Cypriot mother-tongue or English adopted-tongue.

Paradoxically the Cypriot diaspora also explore transformation to assert they have the choice to retain the mother-tongue, where they move between Cypriot (Greek or Turkish) and English in multiple ways. As example Baybars' first poetry collection, *That at the Tip of the Handkerchief* published in 1954, was written in Turkish when he lived in Cyprus. After migrating to Britain, Baybars' seven collections published from 1955 till his death in 2010 were written in English, yet throughout these years there were intervals, in 1997 for example, when he wrote in Turkish. Ierodiaconou writes in Greek and English as in her debut bilingual poetry collection *Trawl*. Other authors write only in English but interrupt the text with the Cypriot (Turkish or Greek) tongue: Adil's 'In Bars Late at Night' reads as follows: 'My dead sister speaks through the lips of strangers,/ sometimes in other tongues./ ruyalarim ruhsuz bir col'de danseder' (*Venus*, 29). Stephanides' text is interspersed with Cypriot (Greek) words, including: 'we chewed on *passatempo*' ('Lips', 109); 'parading and shouting *enosis-eleftheria*' ('Somewhere', 127). Ali's stories are consistently interrupted by Turkish words within sentences as in the story 'Sefka'ba': 'the *mucahitler* came here *kizim*' (*Pink*, 47). These shifts between the languages are not translated, which convey the diasporic community's common experience where they naturally perform between languages. In this process they transform both languages to make a hybridised new Cypriot-English for themselves.

This Cypriot-English is also enhanced via a translation site host to diverse experiences. For example, most narratives feature characters translating between the mother-tongue and English: in 'Breasts', Ali records her childhood translating from English to Turkish for her mother during a medical check for breast cancer (*Pink*, 136); in 'The Wind Under my Lips' Stephanides narrates the experience of his mother translating from English to Greek for his child self at the cinema. These examples capture a translation site that conveys dis/connection between mother and child tongue. This translation site is expanded through their narrative on the exchange between Cypriot migrants fresh from Cyprus to Britain, and their settled british-cypriot diasporic selves. For example, Ali's 'Emine fight' and 'daughter in law' are about Cypriot women who migrated to their british-cypriot husbands in Islington; these women suffer severe domestic abuse, they do not know English, and they get support from a charity founded by british-cypriot diasporic women. In both stories the british-cypriot diaspora translate for the abused women, shifting between both English and Cypriot (Turkish) languages and cultural experiences, where they reconnect with the mother-tongue, the Cypriot women, and Cyprus. Here Ali shows that translation enables the diaspora and Cypriot women to save each other, where the former reclaims the Cypriot mother-tongue and cultural experiences battered away from them. This generates a british-cypriot doubling between the women, where the diaspora connects with Cyprus and the new arrivals connect with Britain.

This british-cypriot doubling is also developed via actual translation between the Anglophone diasporic selves who departed Cyprus, and the Hellenophone or Turkophone Cypriot-selves who remained. For example: Baybars translated poetry from Turkish to English by Cypriot Turkophone poets, including: Mehmet Yashin's *Don't Go Back to Kyrenia* and Korkmazel's 'Kicking Butterfly'; Korkmazel translated Baybars' *Fox and the Cradle Maker* from English to Turkish. A further significant doubling is Stephanides' with Hellenophone poet Marangou, where he defines the translating process as a ritual catching fire on the original that he desired to join. By translating the collection *Nicosieness* and *Selections from the Divan* – including 'Roses', 'The Last Limassolian', 'As You Return from Egypt' and 'Festival at Menoika' – Stephanides connects with the ritual of the island and city in relation to Cypriot displacement. In exchange Marangou's bookshop published Stephanides' debut poetry collection about his external displacement. Similarly, Ali translated numerous Turkophone Cypriot works, including Nese Yahsin's poem 'unsent letters' and Filiz Naldoven's 'write songs about love' and 'flower identity' (Adamidou, 87 and 107) about being-becoming a Cypriot woman and child amidst postcolonial failures. In the past decade Stephanides', Ali's and Nadjarian's editorial work for *Cadences* show their commitment to translating Cypriot works into English, including: Stephanides' translation of Peonidou's 'In Autumn They Descend' (Peonidou, *Cadences*, 9), and the collaborative translation of

Korkmazel's 'Not poetry... Water' (*Cadences*, 46) 'The Pull of Moon' (*Cadences*, 32), 'Stravrogonno' (*Cadences*, 77).

Through this british-cypriot doubling, the diasporic writers show a process comparable with what Chantal Zabus calls 'reflexification', which is some sort of translation operating within the text that makes it a palimpsests where 'behind the scriptural authority of the target European language, the earlier, imperfectly erased remnants of the source of language are still visible' (Zabus, 103, 106). In the Cypriot diasporic texts, the source language is visible not from a linguistic perspective, as in the African case Zabus explores, but from a cross-cultural perspective. Here the moment narrated is experienced in the source language and culture – Cypriot (Turkish or Greek) – but the writers translate it into English; here reporting a Cypriot cultural experience that is unfamiliar to and disconnected from the English or British culture and language. For example Stephanides and Ali translate works by Peonidou, N. Yashin, Naldovan, Korkmazel and Marangou, which focus on Cypriot-specific experiences of partition borders and conflict. Stephanides translates the rituals that catch fire in Marangou's poems, where we taste Kleftiko, a Cypriot dish, and hear about EOKA struggles discussed in a village festival depicted in 'Festival at Menoika' (Marangou, *Divan*, 31); we experience being-becoming a divided Cypriot in Nicosia in *Nicossienses*; we see a strange spatial tripling of place names in 'Street Map of Nicosia' (Colette, 70–71); we feel spirits in the necropolis of Ledra in 'As You Return by Boat from Egypt'; we feel her retrieve Nicosia via greening and gardening in the poem 'Roses' (*Divan*, 19, 13). Stephanides also narrates Cypriot experiences in his own text: when he and his cousins, all children under eight, go up a shaky ladder to play and sleep 'on a rooftop' ('Somewhere', 135), a strange but common practice during summer nights in villages. Another Cypriot-specific event in Stephanides' and Ali's writing is the ritual of the 'quasi-mail bride' (Stephanides, 'Lips', 103), a metaphor for arranged marriages, where, upon the dowry payment, girls would be mailed from Cyprus to their husbands in Britain. In *Plucked*, Baybars narrates the custom of 'sunnet', circumcision, detailing being 'exhibited on camel back with a band of drums and flutes following' after being 'chopped off' (221). These examples demonstrate ways the diaspora claim English, a familiar language in the world, to convey unfamiliar Cypriot-specific experiences.

All of these language practices relate to Rushdie's commentary: 'Having been borne across the world, we are translated [wo]men' (17): the Cypriot diaspora settle in a transformative-translation site between Cypriot (Turkish or Greek) and English, so as to make a new hybrid Cypriot-English medium that captures diasporic and Cypriot familiar 'places' and unfamiliar 'spaces' of childhood-adulthood within (post)colonial Cyprus. This is a medium that can be written, read and felt by all people linked to pain of postcolonial partition, including Cypriots from across the divide residing in Cyprus or the globe; the citizens of Britain, Turkey, Greece and the postcolonial world; the Arab neighbours. This Cypriot-English can write (post)colonial partition Cyprus through negotiating between imperial centre London, ethnic centres Greece/Turkey and geographies beyond.

The diaspora writers' geographic and language practices between Britain and Cyprus exhibit Bhabha's claims on cultural hybridity and translation: here replacing the colonised-coloniser binaries based on ideas of original superior culture, with a british-cypriot doubling based on entering an indefinite negotiation with ambiguous shifts between the rhythms – familiar places-foreign spaces, colonial-postcolonial times and childhood-adulthood energies – shaped by Britain-Cyprus. This doubling can be understood through Derrida's supplementation that has two significations: something added to 'substitute' for something that is missing, and added as 'a surplus, a plenitude enriching another plenitude, the *fullest measure* of presence' (Derrida, *Of*, 144); it is 'maddening because it is neither presence nor absence' (Derrida, *Of*, 154).

This section has focussed on the 'british-cypriot sea position' that is a supplement for Britain-Cyprus operating via cultural hybridity and translation within the 'whale of space'. Here the diaspora writers are post-Linobambakoi rhythmanalysts who analyse rhythms related to both British and Cypriot positions, determined by the production of (post)colonial Britain Cyprus. The focus here has been on positions and productions related to marginalised diasporic selves in particular, whilst pointing to Cypriot-selves in preparation for the next sections that expand on the Cypriot 'border-crossing position' shaped by partitioned Cyprus, and 'broader-crossing position' via transnational Cyprus. For this the writers extend Bhabha's 'third space' because it is not sufficient to capture the truths of the partitioned and transnational positions and Cypruses.

Partitioned Border-crossing Position: Forbidden Zone

In this border-crossing position the writers compulsively focus on crossing the north and south border, where they enter, pause and play with various sites – especially the buffer zone with focus on crossing checkpoints along the green line – of partitioned Cyprus. In obsessively playing between this crossing, the writers name and claim these sites or contact zones as a forbidden zone, which is a personalised 'third space' where they maintain and extend its definitive qualities and operations through expanding the coloniser-colonised and british-cypriot hybridity and translation to a cypriotgreek-cypriotturkish understanding. The writers thrive between the north and south forbidden zone to generate a new – cypriotgreek-cypriotturkish – doubling that gives way to a – cypriotgreek-cypriotturkish-british – tripling in and for the reading and construction of partitioned Cypruses. This border-crossing position is again determined by Lefebvre's 'spatial/social practices', especially everyday routes and routines operating through ambiguities and self-destructive 'desires', which expose dominant 'mental space' that systematically divides (logos) to prioritise 'social and lived spaces' that overcome divisions (anti-logos) (Lefebvre, *Production*, 362–63, 391–95) related to north-south and cypriotgreek-cypriotturkish partition. This exposes the ways in which partition is a site of contradiction shaped by 'rhythms' of forbidden games, zones and desires, experienced as Tuanian 'place' and 'space'.

The writers capture, cross and blur partitioned Cyprus in various ways that operate between childhood-adulthood moments in relation to place and space. As shown in the 'nostalgia position', they map pre-partitioned decolonial Cyprus of their childhood through a fantasy past-perfect place of safe dwelling and wandering in a borderless order, as well as through actual past-imperfect spaces of dangerous dislocation and divisions in border-line disorder. Here they expand these moments through focussing on places and spaces of postcolonial partition. They capture fully literary-lived experiences of movement, pausing and crossing through the north-south divide, obsessively entering the UN-controlled buffer zone in Nicosia – mainly Ledra Palace crossing checkpoint – which they associate with the forbidden zone.[17] In obsessively entering and performing in this 'middle' forbidden zone between the north-south, the writers show that this zone is a Tuanian 'space' of dangerous movement and 'place' controlled on pause, ambiguously oscillating between Lefebvre's dominated 'social space' and dominant 'mental space', where the former often exposes the latter. The zone is at once an unfamiliar dangerous 'space' of dead ends, barriers, war, and a familiar childhood 'place'; it is a dominant and divided military-controlled 'mental' closed stagnant 'place', and a social 'space' of lived routines crisscrossing with a radical openness, freedom and negotiation beyond divisions. Through such ambiguous experiences with and desires for the forbidden zone, they destructively move between north-south without defining either side as the prior essence; here they Cypriotise Bhabha's hybridity and translation to a north-south and cypriotgreek-cypriotturkish understanding.

This cypriotgreek-cypriotturkish hybridity and translation is enhanced through the writers' play with an 'other' ethnic self, who is a personalised literary-lived double from across the divide that they self-destructively and obsessively live and write through. In 'the dedication', Ali introduces her double, Maro, a cypriotgreek childhood friend: 'Where are you Maro? My other self' (*Pink*, 90). In 'Pink Butterfly', Ali recollects when she exchanged school notes with Maro: 'I wanted to see what she had learned at school [...]. She had a blue Greek flag in her book, I a red Turkish flag. [...] She read the lesson, then I read it' (*Pink*,

109). Maro and Ali went to separate ethnic schools and these 'notes' are individual recordings from their ethnically motivated lessons during the reign of anticolonial nationalist contest in Cyprus. Similarly, Adil has Lysandros Pitharas, a cypriotgreek diaspora poet that she writes to and through, in the poem 'Beautiful Crows Mourn Apollo', and the film-poem, 'Memory and the Impossibility of Fidelity'. Stephanides has Korkmazel, a notable doubling, where they translate each other's poetry: Stephanides co-translated Korkmazel's 'Nicosia' and 'I Worshipped Too many Gods' (Colette, 31/33), 'Gravity of the Moon', 'Kiss my Corpse' (*Cadences*, 4–5, 10), 'The Flute', 'From the Radical' (*Cadences* 41, 44), and 'Mesaoria' (*Cadences*, 91). Korkmazel translated Stephanides' 'Jaya Devi' (*Cadences*, 40). In addition, Stephanides' poem 'Twice Born' (*Blue*, 29) speaks to Korkmazel's 'Kiss my Corpse' (*Cadences*, 11), and 'Water for Poetry' (Stephanides, *Blue*, 16) to 'Not Poetry...Water' (*Cadences*, 46). In 'Twice Born' Stephanides maps Famagusta through Korkmazel's body and words meeting Rumi's Sufism, suggesting that Cyprus is mapped with a theologically and culturally hospitable body and spirit, much like the Linobambakoi. These literary-lived doubles exhibit an actual negotiation and exchange of words and worlds between cypriotgreeks and cypriotturks, which expose the dominant mental 'place' experienced as a stagnant Greek-Cyprus or Turkish-Cyprus, so as to create an open processual social 'space' that is a cypriotgreek-cypriotturkish Cyprus. This doubling enables the diaspora writers to capture a cypriotturkish-cypriotgreek border-crossing position operating via hybridity and translation that grasps yet goes beyond bi-national and bi-communal north-south Cyprus.

The writers go beyond the hybridity and translation between two positions, as in Bhabha's third space, by expanding this cypriotgreek-cypriotturkish doubling to cypriotgreek-cypriotturk-cypriotbritish tripling. Here the Anglophone british-cypriot diaspora meet the Hellenophone and Turkophone Cypriot writers, where there is a crossing between three languages: as Ali states, this is 'poetry, in our three languages, Turkish, Greek and English' (Ali, *Pink*, 90), demonstrated in multiple projects. Ali and Adil were the first to animate such a tripling through events in London. This enhanced via projects in Cyprus, for example, as part of The Turkish Cypriot Union of Artists and Writers (CUAW), Stephanides and Korkmazel shaped events such as the 4th Annual Poetry Day in 2009, which consisted of a zine in three languages with Stephanide's 'Jaya Devi' translated from English to Turkish by Korkmazel, Korkmazel's 'Kicking Butterfly' translated from Turkish to English by Baybars, Marangou's 'Letter to Dionysus' translated from Greek to English and Turkish by Stephanides and Korkmazel respectively. Stephanides and Nadjarian have contributed further to this tripling via editorial work for *Cadences*, where their own works appeared alongside Hoplaros'and Ierodiaconou's in three languages. More recently Ali's and Adil's Literary Agency Cyprus (LAC) projects in collaboration with 15 women, provide a platform for three language: for example, 'Crossing North-South Checkpoints' culminated into zine 1 consisting of the Cyprus map plotted with English, Greek, Turkish poetry.

Beyond language, these three writers fixate on 'three' things. For instance, Stephanides and his parents are 'three islands, and the three of us would become three islands' ('Lips', 108). Adil shifts between the past, present and future. Meanwhile, Ali's stories are hosted by three familial generations, characters or objects in threes – in 'Pink Butterfly', for example, three British soldiers enter her childhood home, consequently she panics and hides three bullets in a box. Such tripling relates to Lefebvre in that he, like the writers and this chapter, fixates on all things three, a tripling that destroys binaries and divisions in order to capture 'truth of space' for a differential Cyprus.

The 'forbidden zone' is the term I give to this british-cypriotgreek-cypriotturkish tripling border-crossing position and production, which is, like the 'british-cypriot position', a tormenting experience shaped by destructive desires that the diaspora willingly enter to enable 'third' possibilities to emerge. This 'forbidden zone' expands Bhabha's third space not only through revising dualistic coloniser-colonised hybridity with a Cypriotised doubling and tripling, but through illuminating that this obsession with the 'forbidden' enables new possibilities to emerge. The diaspora authors disrupt dominant and official constructs set out by their Cypriot literary predecessors, or a nation generally, of a pure superior homogeneous 'identity' and 'place'. In this way, they submit themselves ambiguously to shift and be marked as traitors in contradiction, yet with pleasure they hybridise and translate themselves and the island through welcoming what is considered and erased by the Cypriot majority as the forbidden British imperial side and the other ethnic sides. This enables the writers to capture actual lived experiences of marginalised diasporic and Cypriot-selves considered to be on the forbidden side of the border,[18] which ambiguously transforms the dangerous excluded 'space' into a familiar homely 'place'. In this process, they expose that all Cypriots have experienced this ambiguous destructive desire because of postcolonial partition failures, when, for example, unfamiliar 'spaces' – the 1960s enclaves, pre-1974 houses the Cypriots departed from, post-1974 houses they arrived into, the other side – transformed into familiar 'places'. Most apparent in 2003, when border-crossings and forbidden zones transformed from a 'mental space' divided and experienced as a closed controlled 'place', to a 'social space' beyond divisions experienced as a 'space' of open freedom.

This section focussed on the 'border-crossing position' that is a supplement for partition Cyprus operating via the forbidden zone within the 'whale of space'. This forbidden zone captures the 'truth of space', exposing dominant north or south and cypriotgreek or cypriotturkish divisions, so as to prioritise secreted lived experiences with destructive desires that create postcolonial partitioned Cyprus. In this way the forbidden zone offers a solution beyond dominant nationalist binaries, where, acknowledging partition is here to stay, the diaspora deal with it by successfully crossing the north-south borders and the metropolitan/postcolonial divide via a doubling and tripling shifting between rhythms – towards transnational Cyprus.

Transnational Broader-crossing Position: Global Diasporic Solidarity

As post-Linobambakoi rhythmanalysts the diaspora writers analyse rhythms related to different national geographies that shape the broader-crossing[19] position. Like the Linobambakoi, the diaspora writers disrupt dominant constructions by adopting, crossing and thriving between opposing forces that produce transnational postcolonial partitioned Cyprus.

This position and production engage with and expand beyond Cyprus' geographic border and forbidden narratives, so to explore new kinds of broader-crossing positions that capture the truth of Cyprus. For this the diaspora authors analyse multiple Cypriot literary positions and productions, including particularly those discussed in the book, so to expose the broader-crossing possibilities that inevitably emerge within them. All Cypriot literary narratives are concerned with broader-crossing to Turkey or Greece: whilst Turkish-Cypriotists/Greek-Cypriotists and Ethnic-Motherland Nationalists construct Mother Greece or Turkey, the Cypriotist vehemently reject these ethnic Mothers for united Mother Cyprus. Through this analysis, the diaspora authors illicitly 'broader-cross' between Greece, Turkey and Cyprus, wherein the mother is always deferred and deterred, always becoming the mother and refusing to be a mother. Such diasporic practices expose that none of these constructs – Mother Greece, Turkey or Cyprus – have prime agency, but instead the actual production of Cyprus operates via a broader-crossing between the three, whilst interacting with the metropolitan centre (London, Britain). In this way the diaspora writers expose further that the 'Cyprus problem' is simultaneously a consequence of extreme fanaticism to cross or fanaticism to reject to cross into an ethnic centre. In analysing and exposing these competing narratives, the diaspora writers show the capacity for a 'forbidden zone' solution if these dominant narratives spoke to rather than prohibited and negated each other. To find the tool that enables negotiation between these competing positions and productions, the writers turn to the migrants of the world, another kind of broader-crossing, where they localise Boym's 'diasporic intimacy' for 'global diasporic solidarity' (Boym, 355, 342) and Gilroy's 'conviviality' to capture the truth of transnational Cyprus.

The writers 'social/spatial practices' are based on broader-crossing into national territories via a balcony poetics with a global network between Ottoman/ Modern Turkey, Ancient/Modern Greece,[20] Britain, Arab territories, and geographies beyond, which are, as Stephanides confirms, all within 'us' Cypriots ('Lips'). In this process they respond to nationalists and Cypriotists: expanding Cypriotist practices that make a static chronological 'Museum of the Palimpsest', they capture spatial history with all its fluid layers coming-into-being that have formative agency for the production of Cyprus. Here they map Cyprus from its ethnic-nationalist blood or spirit abstractions into a new mystical body with energies that are theologically, ethnically and culturally hospitable – thus adopting the post-Linobambakoi positioning and production. Both Adil and Stephanides expand this mystical body and energy through Sufism, in 'Twice Born', for example, Famagusta is mapped with Rumi's spirit meeting spatial history – i.e. the cumbez fig tree, the oldest living thing in Cyprus has witnessed many cultures; Saint Nicolas Cathedral built by the Franks; a Christian communion with half a loaf of bread; 'twenty thousand ghosts' of Ottoman martyrs. Stephanides expands spatial history in other poems: 'Broken Heart' maps Nicosia via a postcolonial flâneur unearthing traces of the old tombs of the Ottoman Bayraktar, the Venetian ramparts, the Byzantine saints and the hodjas, all meeting the spirit of community-communion feasting on Cyprus' local produce of citrus, milk and olives; in 'Rhapsody of a Dragoman' he is an Ottoman translator helping a woman visiting from Egypt. Stephanides expands fully the east Mediterranean spatial history in Cyprus via translating Marangou. For example, Marangou's 'At the Monetary of St John Lambadistis' writes about the Ottoman cartographer, Piri Reis' Kitab-i-BAHRIYE, so as to navigate through the weak Egyptians, Syrians and Turks who come to Cyprus to heal. In 'Letter to Dionysus' focus is on the feast of Saint Lazarus in Cyprus as related to Adonis' in Egypt. In 'Request For a Dream', we experience meetings between Hellene Egyptians in Ammochostos via the Arab poet Ismael Emre (Marangou, *Divan*, 45, 34, 14). In this way the writers engage with histories of dominant nationalist minds that construct a homogeneous 'place' and marginalised minds that construct a heterogenised 'space', so to hybridise and translate themselves and the island via its spatial history, analysing open spaces-closed places, different times and distinct energies to create Cyprus.

This spatial shift between Cyprus, Greece, Turkey and beyond shapes a network of rhythms for the post-Linobambakoi position, which deals with, rather than escapes, the truth – prioritising social concrete reality over mental abstractions – to produce transnational differential Cyprus. The writers capture the network and truth through broader-crossing into a global diasporic dimension, where a new crossing into the metropolitan centre, London, meets other crossings to centres and peripheries around the postcolonial world. In these crossings, they turn to the diasporic communities' energies, concurrently to claim a position for the thousands of displaced Cypriots and for the 'spatial/social practices' of the global diaspora in London. In 'London is my city', Ali states:

> Green Lanes is where Cypriots created 'Little Cyprus' along the 'Ladder' from Newington Green to Wood Green. While divisions and nationalist discourse raged in Cyprus, Cypriot men quietly drank coffee and played backgammon and cards in the sanctity of the mixed coffee houses, named after villages in the 'homeland'. (91)

Here the cypriotgreek and cypriotturkish diaspora move beyond Cyprus' territorial border narratives of a dominant mentally conceived Greece or Turkey Cyprus, intimately interacting in coffee shops with a village energy and desire that creates a socially lived 'Little Cyprus' in Green Lanes. Ali also captures other postcolonial little nations created by different diaspora communities: 'Bangla in Brick Lane, India and Pakistan in Green Street [...] Caribbean in Brixton' (87–88). In this process, Ali criticises ways these communities evince a 'lack of going "outside"' (93) their national communities, where they 'pause' in a closed 'place' refusing to 'move' towards open 'space'. This resonates with both Boym's and Said's individual commentaries that this type of broader-crossing has its limitations: '[the diaspora] reconstitute a mini-nation state on foreign soil, failing to see the diasporic dimension that feeds on their narrowly defined cultural intimacy' (Boym, 255). And for Said,

> the least attractive aspects of being an exile emerge: an exaggerated sense of group solidarity as well as a passionate hostility toward outsiders, even those who may in fact be in the same predicament as you. (Said, 'Mind', 51)

In scrupulously mapping and mixing together multiple postcolonial little nations, Ali displays and disrupts these limitations, where she negotiates with a Boymian-like evolution from a closed 'cultural intimacy' to an open 'diasporic intimacy' that captures the 'dimension' and 'predicament' shared between the diaspora communities in London. Ali shows Boym's 'diasporic intimacy', which captures shared experiences of uprootedness, defamiliarisation and longing without belonging that exist in migrant communities from different parts of the world (Boym, 252–354). Ali shows that the migrants in London have all been uprooted from a familiar homely 'place' and adopted an unfamiliar 'space', resulting in them reconstructing hostile, exclusive, little national 'places' that reduce longing and induce belonging, where they fail to go 'outside' their cultural intimacies to feel these diasporic intimacies. This exposure of diasporic intimacies, particularly mutual experiences that often escape the diaspora, gives way to the creation of 'global diasporic solidarity' (Boym, 342), which Ali captures and creates in her city of London. This London hosts conviviality via an extreme enclosure with processes of 'pause', and a 'radical openness [with] processes of cohabitation and interaction that have made multi-culture an ordinary feature of social life in Britain' (Gilroy, xi). Thus, the former colonial centre now accommodates multiple nations with the 'right to difference', where marginalised diaspora communities are a social force with an energy actively creating a differential London.

The diaspora writers also broader-cross into other nations around the globe, which expands the diasporic solidarity from differential London to other cities, countries and the world. Stephandies and Adil in particular draw attention to their own global diasporic dimension by engaging with others' diasporic experiences, especially through reflective nostalgia, where they are always on the move, inhabiting multiple places, spaces, times and energies around the globe. In and for this process they support Rushdie's comments regarding the Western writers 'raiding the visual storehouse of Africa, Asia, the Philippines [...] We must grant ourselves an equal freedom' (20). The writers grant themselves the same freedom, not to be masters who represent these nations, but to present their own/others' diasporic experiences of isolation, uprootedness and marginalisation, where together they are displaced and indefinitely longing without belonging to a single primary nation and geography. Here they raid the storehouse of globe, reading, writing and living through multiple geographies in translation and transformation between diasporic languages, religions, cultures and histories.

Many diasporic languages – including Greek, Arabic, Hindi, Urdu, Turkish, Spanish, French and beyond – reverberate in their English literary-lived production: Stephanides' poem 'ars poetica: pRoem' for example shifts between Hindi, Spanish, Greek, Turkish, English. Many types of diasporic moments and movements, where spectres of diverse traditions, expeditions, wars, myths and religions echo in their work. In *Venus Infers* Adil focusses on diasporic 'old stories' and new stories, often cross-cutting into the east Mediterranean: in 'Waiting for a Sign at Palmyra' (89) the imperial traveller Lady Hestor Stanhope wanders into the 'Bride of the Dessert' in Ancient Syria; in 'The Pharaohs Daughter' (73), Solomon's wife from the Hebrew script speaks; in 'I am hiding from her' (32) the heroin, Esher, from the Tanakh becomes Adil's sister; in 'The Source of Strength' (41), Adil questions if Samson Shimshon from the Book of Judges can help the dead girl; in '1974/Dead Sister' (19) her twin is a Bosnian in Palestine; in some poems 'one of the Islamic tradition's three perfect women, whisper' (10); in 'Perfect Falcon' (98) and her film-poem 'A Minute Taker at the Conference of Birds on Sufi Symmetry', Adil elaborates on Sufi mystics Rumi and Attar respectively. In her literary essays 'Another way of saying: A reverie on the poetry of al-Andalus', 'Nine Postcards, Nine Extracts' and 'The Aisha Project', Adil focusses on the golden age of Islam in the Mediterranean. Similarly, in *Blue Moon in Rajasthan*, Stephanides moves between Hindu, Islamic, Hellene traditions across cultural geographies. In his academic work *Translating Kali's Feast*, and film *Hail Mother Kali* Stephanides engages with Hindu practices of the Indian diaspora in Guyana. In many works, he elaborates on Greek diaspora and other displaced communities in the east Mediterranean, confirming identification:

> My dream was to embrace the whole of the Mediterranean, from Andalusia to Istanbul, from Tangier to Alexandria, Beirut, Damascus [...] [My grandfather] would sell pomegranates to Arab merchants who came to Famagusta. He liked talking to them in their language and on their ships about life in his beloved Alexandria. [...] I shared a legacy with Hermes Trismegistus who hailed from Alexandria like my grandfather. (Stephanides, 'litany', 3–4)

Stephanides' dream is materialised not only through his writing but also through his translation of Marangou's poetry in *Divan*, particularly through the symbol of 'ships'. In 'I Have Never Been in a Ship' the ships relate to being displaced and translated beyond. In 'for the sake of those' there is a translation between ships and writing in relation to displaced Greeks of Smyrna, Constantinople, Alexandria in the nineteenth century; in 'On the Road to Damascus' people move from Syria and Turkey like fire. In this process of reading, writing and living across the globe, the writers present their own/ others' diasporic experiences of colonialism, partition and conflict in longing without belonging, which confirms a diasporic intimacy and conviviality with global diasporic solidarity between these Others of the world, who comprise a social force with theologically and culturally hospitable energies actively to create a differential transnational city, Mediterranean and world.

These broader-crossing processes are localised for the reading and construction of Cyprus. Cyprus' legacy – Ottoman-Turkey, Greece, Britain, postcolonial ethnic-conflict, the 1964/1974 partition – has subjected all Cypriots, as in the global diaspora, to uprooting from their homes, constantly moving and entering unfamiliar 'space', where they long without belonging to a familiar 'place'. Cyprus is a site that hosts 'solidarity' between displaced Cypriots, who inescapably shift between multiple rhythms – radical openness and movement of space and enclosed paused place, times and energies – related to multiple 'positions' shaped by different Cypruses. Like the diaspora communities discussed by Boym and Said, however, most Cypriots fail to recognise these mutual diasporic experiences that feed on their narrowly defined fixed positions and Cypruses.

Closing Truth of Cypruses: Permanent Open Closures Indefinitely Moving to Remain They Wail: 'Whaled Into Space and Have a Whale of a Time in the Whale of Space'

This chapter has demonstrated the ways that the postcolonial Cypriot diaspora read and construct a multitude of literary and lived Cypruses. With the aid of Tuan and Lefebvre, the chapter has shown a range of readings and constructions of colonialism, postcolonialism and partition, ending with the production of differential Cyprus. For this production, the Cypriot diaspora position themselves as true post-Linobambakoi rhythmanalysts and worldly reflective nostalgics, collectively enabling them to operate through a theological, social, political, cultural and literary hospitality to analyse rhythms – conceiving, perceiving and living many places and spaces in colonial, postcolonial, and partitioned times-zones – relating to different positions and Cypruses. The chapter showed that they position themselves as post-Linobambakoi rhythmanalysts through the concept of middle sea, balcony and whale, resulting in a site I have termed the 'whale of space'. This is an in-between site host to practices that operate through a Derridean chain of supplements, where in a tormenting and maddening experience, the diaspora writers 'add' or 'substitute' various 'positions' and Cypruses that provides common ground between the islanders and their islands. It is a site that enables 'spatial/ social practices' operating via a desire to capture conflicts, especially related to movement and stagnation, which expose dominant 'mental' abstractions for the benefit of dominated 'social' concrete realities. It is a site enabling identification with multiple 'positions' and Cypruses operating through diasporic solidarity that captures the 'truth of space' for the actual production of Cyprus.

The chapter focussed on five 'positions' shaped by five Cypruses: the 'marginal position', displaying shared relationship between Cypriot and diasporic writers as related to their lived experiences and literary forms, is produced by literary-lived Cyprus. The 'nostalgia position', capturing intimacy based on shifts between imagined and actual places, spaces, time-zones and energies, is shaped by childhood decolonial Cyprus. The 'british-cypriot sea position' operating within a third space is shaped by a self-destructive childhood-adulthood wandering-dwelling between Britain and Cyprus within British colonial and postcolonial Cyprus. The 'border-crossing position', which Cypriotises the third space into a doubling and tripling called the 'forbidden zone', is shaped by self-destructive childhood-adulthood movement-pause between the past, present, and future in relation to post-1964/1974 partitioned Cyprus. The 'broader-crossing position', which extends from the 'forbidden zone' to localise Boym's 'global diasporic solidarity', is shaped by ephemeral-stable spatial histories and cultures of Greece-Turkey-Britain-Cyprus meeting nations far beyond. In this process the writers expose that without a single nation they blur dominant binaries – namely north-south or cypriotgreek-cypriotturk – in and for the production of a transnational differential Cyprus.

This production analyses multiple places, spaces, times, and energies with destructive desires mutually practised and experienced by all Cypriots. Here the writers respond to, rather than forbid, and show all the possibilities within, rather than depict an illusionary abstraction without, the concrete actualities of the Turkish-Cypriotist/Greek-Cypriotist, Ethnic-Motherland Nationalist, and Cypriotist identification produced by British-Greek-Turkish-beyond Cyprus. Here the writers reveal that the island and islander can never solidify or silence the dominant ethnonational binaries, escape from the permanence of the cultural palimpsestic, heterogeneous and hybrid realities, nor find a resolution by means of an imagined retreat, homogenisation and/or banishing of history. These actualities are here to stay, so the writers wail: deal with them by transforming and translating colonialism, postcolonialism and partition into 'the humanly-conceivable, humanly-evident, humanly-palpable!' (Lefebvre, *Production*, 399). Through this 'truth', they capture the 'right to difference', acknowledging all Cypriots and the diaspora without discrimination, which gives way to solidarity in and for a transnational differential Cyprus.

The site I have named the 'whale of space' enables us all to read and write not just Cyprus, but the Mediterranean and the world with a difference. This site has an open-door policy; there are no 'social contract' or entry visa necessities; anyone and anything, from literary form, timezone, country, culture, language, political standing, to literary group or individual, is welcome and has the agency to add a new position and new Cyprus, new position and Mediterranean, new position and world. Everyone has the agency to be part of the spatial position and production, the most powerful tool of thought, action, control and domination. This conviviality has been evidenced throughout the chapter; however, I personally experienced this throughout *Writing Cyprus*, this book, whereby the diaspora led me into their literary and lived space, place, time and energy; welcoming me to read, dwell and help construct a new 'position' and Cyprus, this book and particularly this chapter. This is a 'diasporic position' that started in 2009 with my journey from Kyrenia in the north, through the 'forbidden zone' where I was picked-up by a leading performer, scholar, writer of male belly dancing, to Limassol in the south, to an englishturkishgreek literary reading hosted by *Cadences*; we exchanged roses of recognition at first meetings at the London underground and/or national rail stations, and we shared our past-perfect in cinematic-poetic-prose by the second; we shared instant email intimacies about our future perfect literary, lived and spatial endeavours; we left our imprints and swam between the seas of London, Cyprus (north-south), Canterbury, Lebanon, Greece, Tibet, Malta, Egypt, Turkey, Myanmar, Palestine, Honduras.. ; we imagined and lived many places, spaces, times, energies and the people we, Cypriot or otherwise, could have been and could become.

Notes

1 A version of this chapter has appeared as 'Rhythmanalysts of the postcolonial partitioned diaspora: Writing differential Cyprus through Henri Lefebvre and Yi-Fu Tuan', *The Journal of Commonwealth Literature* (2019).

2 In this chapter I use binary labels 'cypriotturkish and cypriotgreek'; here the 'cypriot' and ethnic labels are lower case because, like me, the diaspora feel that such identifications should not be proper names because they lead to improper circumstances. On name game and identity, see Ch. 1.

3 See, Ali's *Identity*.

4 See, Stephanides' Culture/*Memory*, *Cypriana*. See also their contributions in Adamidou; Colette; Costello; Yashin's *Stepmother*.

5 See Ch. 1.

6 Literary-lived practices refer to the authors' biographies and texts, which is discussed in the next section.

7 *The Wind Under My Lips* is the working title for Stephanides' experimental text in-progress, made of four prose fragments alongside other fragments, which will be discussed in the next section.

8 In personal interviews in 2011 and 2012, Stephanides referred to the text as travel spatial writing, memory novel and an auto-psycho-graphy. *The Wind Under My Lips* has recently been released in book form in English and Greek, consisting of the four prose texts, 40 poems, and 20 visuals. Stephanides confirmed that though all fragments are together in book form, it is still in-progress. Given this book has just been released and my interest lies in its supplementation, I will not engage with it here but all texts thus discussed can be found there.

9 'Pass...port' in *Visa Stories*; 'Emine's Fight' in *Uncut Diamonds*; 'Daughter-in-Law' in *Crossing the Borders*, 'Caught Out' in *Diaspora City*.

10 Oya Akin has also translated numerous works by Korkmazel.

11 Stated in an interview in 2012, and in *Venus Infers*.

12 On postcards see also Stephanides' 'Postcards' and Adil's 'Nine'.

13 On Key Fetish, see Ch. 2.

14 See Bhabha *Location*, 'Interview'.

15 For more on the geographical social/spatial practices as related London transportation zones and Cyprus historical time-zones that create a British-Cyprus geography, see Kemal 'Rhythmanalysts'.

16 See Thiong'o *Decolonising*.

17 For more on the literary-lived experiences of the border-crossing position between north-south checkpoints, especially via Adil's film-poem 'A Small Forgotten War', and Ali's 'Pass...port control', see Kemal 'Rhythmanalysts'.

18 The writers' also cross different borders to claim various forbidden zones. As example they cross gender borders to dwell in marginalised 'forbidden zones' for unconventional women and LGBTQI+ Cypriots.

19 I use the word 'broader' rather than 'border' for various reasons. First, as practised by Anglophone Cypriot writers, this is a means to appropriate a new term that moves beyond, draws attention to and rejects the term

'border', *sinir* in Turkish and *sýnoro* in Greek. Second, I use border then broader so to demonstrate the difference and distinction between the border focus on crossing the north-south or cypriotgreek-cypriotturkish binaries in Cyprus, and broader focus on crossings between three or more positions, beyond the binary *border, sinir and sýnoro.*

20 For more on the broader-crossing position as related to Ottoman/Modern Turkey and Ancient/Modern Greece, especially illuminated in Adil's 'The Topography of the Text', see Kemal 'Rhythmanalyst'.

Bibliography

Achebe, Chinua. *Morning Yet on Creation Day*. London: Heinemann, 1975.

Adams, T.W. *AKEL: The Communist Party of Cyprus*. Stanford: Hoover Institution, 1971.

Adamidou, Tina, ed. *Weeping Island: A Collection of Cypriot Literature*. Nicosia: United Cypriot Friendship Association, 2001.

Adil, Alev. 'A Small Forgotten War,' 'Memory and the Impossibility of Fidelity' & 'A Minute Taker at the Conference of Birds on Sufi Symmetry.' *An Architecture of Forgetting: Journeys in the Dead Zone*. University of Greenwich CCMS Research Group, DVD, 2008.

———. 'Another Way of Saying: A Reverie on the Poetry of al-Andalus' Special Issue al-Adalusia. *Journal of Postcolonial Writing* 52.2 (2016): 218–24.

———. 'Nights of Destiny: A Fictional Autobiography.' *Critical Muslim Love and Death* 5 (2013): 207–21. Print.

———. 'Nine Postcards, Nine Extracts.' *Critical Muslim Reclaiming Al-Andalus* 6.2 (2013): 211–20. Print.

———. 'The Aisha Project.' *Critical Muslim Dangerous Free Thinkers* 12 (2014): online.

———. *The Archive of Lost Objects*. London: Limited edition, 2010.

———. 'The Topography of the Texts'. *MemoryMap*. The Secret Agent in the Apocalyptic Realm. 8 January 2011. 12 April 2012 www. memorymap.org. uk/projects/ topography- text

———. *Venus Infers*. London: NE Publications, 2004.

Alam, Javeed and Suresh Sharma. 'Remembering Partition.' *Seminar* 461 (January 1998): 98–103.

Ali, Aydin Mehmet. 'Bedtime Story.' *Cadences* 4 (2008): 54–68.

———. 'Caught Out.' *Diaspora City: The London New Writing Anthology*. Ed. Nick McDowell. London: Arcadia Books, 2003, 95–112.

———. 'Daughter-in-Law.' *Crossing the Border: Voices of Refugee and Exiled Women*. Ed. Jennifer Langer. Nottingham: Five Leaves, 2002, 135–39.

———. 'Emine's Fight.' *Uncut Diamonds: A Selection of New Writing*. London: MAIA, 2003, 173–83.

———. *Forbidden Zone*. London: Fatal, 2014.

———. 'My London.' *Cadences* 2.1/2 (2006):87–93.

———. 'Pass…Port.' *Visa Stories: Experiences between Law and Migration*. Eds. Bahriye Kemal et al. Newcastle: Cambridge Scholars, 2013, 123–134.

———. *Pink Butterfly*. London: Fatal, 2005.

Alexios, Alecou. *Communism and Nationalism in Postwar Cyprus, 1945–1955: Politics and Ideologies under British Rule.* New York: Palgrave, 2016.

Altay, H.S. Comp., *Kibris Turk Siir Antolijisi* [*Cypriot Poetry*]. Lefkosa: Maarif Dayresi, 1965.

Altbach, Phillip G. 'Education and Neocolonialism.' *Teachers College Record* 72.4 (1971): 543–58.

Altiok, Feriha. 'Ciktim Balkona Oturdum' [Balcony]. *Kibris Turk Edebiyati II* [*TCLII- Turkish Cypriot Literature II*]. Nicosia: K.T. Egitim Vakfi Yayinlari, 2008, 132–33.

Anderson, Benedict. *Imagined Communities.* London: Verso, 2006.

Angelides, Clair. 'Στερνός λόγος' [Last Words]. *Ανθολογία Κυπριακής Λογοτεχνίας για το Γυμνάσιο. [Cypriot Literature Anthology, Gymnasium].* Λευκωσία [Nicosia]: ΥΑΠ, 1998, 100.

———. *Literary Profiles Klairi Angelidou.* Ed. Naia Roussou. Nicosia: Cyprus Pen, 1994.

———. *Pentadakylos My Son.* Trans. Margaret Deyes. London: Trentham Books, 1994.

———. *The Mirror of The Soul.* Trans. Thom Nairn and Dionysia Zervanou. Edinburgh: Dionysia Press, 2010.

———. *The Streets.* Trans. Thom Nairn and Dionysia Zervanou. Edinburgh: Dionysia Press, 2003–04.

———. *Venerable Lady The Sea.* Trans. Constantine E. Evangelides. Nicosia: Angelides, 2000.

Angelopoulos, Andreas. 'Foreword.' *A Poetry and Prose Anthology of the 1955–59 EOKA Liberation Struggle.* Eds. Michalakisi I. Maratheftis and Roula Ioannidou-Stravrou. Trans. Irene Joannides Nicosia: Cyprus Ministry of Education and Culture, 2003, 11–12.

Anthias, Floya and Nira Yuval-Davis *Woman-Nation-State.* Eds. London: Macmillan, 1989, 150–67.

Anthias, Tefkros. *Literary Profile 51.* Ed. and Trans. Chrysanthos Chrysanthou. Nicosia: Cyprus Pen, 2009.

Afxentiou, Antonou. 'Today as I Laid Eyes on You.' *A Poetry and Prose Anthology of the 1955–59 EOKA Liberation Struggle.* Eds. Michalakisi I. Maratheftis and Roula Ioannidou-Stravrou. Trans. Irene Joannides. Nicosia: Cyprus Ministry of Education and Culture, 2003, 17.

Appadurai, Arjun. Chapter 2 'Disjuncture and difference in the global cultural economy.' and Chapter 6 'Number in the Colonial Imagination.' *Modernity At Large: Cultural Dimensions of Globalization.* Minnesota: University of Minnesota Press, 1996, 27–47 and 114–38.

Armstrong, John. *Nations Before Nationalism.* Chapel Hill: University of North Carolina Press, 1982.

Ashby, Eric. *Universities: British, Indian, African.* Cambridge: Harvard University Press, 1967.

Ashcroft, Bill, et al., eds. *The Empire Writes Back: Theory and Practice in Postcolonial Literature.* 2nd ed. London: Routledge, 2002.

———, eds. 'Language.' *The Postcolonial Studies Reader.* London: Routledge, 1995, 283–314.

———, eds. 'Place.' *The Postcolonial Studies Reader.* London: Routledge, 1995, 391–418.

———. *Post-colonial Studies: The Key Concepts.* 2nd ed. London Routledge, 2007.

Ashrawi, Hanan Mikhail. 'The Contemporary Palestinian Poetry of Occupation.' *Journal of Palestine Studies* 7.3 (Spring, 1978): 77–101.

Attalides, Michael. The Turkish Cypriots: Their Relations to the Greek Cypriots in Perspective. *Cyprus Reviewed*, Ed. Michael Attalides. Nicosia, Cyprus: The Association, 1977.

———. Cyprus, *Nationalism and International Politics.* New York: St. Martin's Press, 1979.

Baines, Jervoise Athelstane. 'The Census of Empire, 1911.' *Journal of the Royal Statistical Society* 77.4 (1914): 381–414.

———. 'Census Notes: The British Empire.' *Journal of the Royal Statistical Society* 75.8 (1912): 842–46.

Ball, John Clement. *Imagining London: Postcolonial Fiction and the Transnational Metropolis.* Toronto: University of Toronto Press, 2004.

Balman, Urkiye Mine. *Kibris Turk Yainin Ilk Kadin Sairlerinden Urkiye Mine Balman* [*First Woman Poet*]. Ed. Sevket Oznur. Nicosia: Gokada Yayinlar, 2003.

Barker, Dudley. *Grivas: Portrait of a Terrorist.* London: Cresset Press, 1959.

Baybars, Taner. *Plucked in a Far-off Land: Images in Self Biography.* Nicosia: Moufflon Publications, 2005.

———. 'Taner Baybars: Interview with Gur Genc.' *Cadences* 4 (2008):118–30.

———. *To Catch a Falling Man.* Suffolk: Scorpion, 1963.

———. *Mendillin Ucundakilar* [Handkerchief] Nicosia: Cardak, 1953.

———, Comp. and trans. *Nazim Hikmet The Day Before Tomorrow* Oxford: Carcanet Press, 1972.

———, Comp. and trans. *Nazim Hikmet A Sad State of Freedom.* Warrick: Greville, 1990.

———, Comp. and trans. *Selected Poems Nazim Hikmet.* London Jonathan Cape, 1967.

———, Comp. and trans. *The Moscow Symphony and Other Poems Nazim Hikmet.* London: Rapp & Whiting ltd, 1970.

Bedevi, Vergi. *Cyprus has never been a Greek Island.* Nicosia: Cyprus Turkish Historical Association, 1964.

Benitez-Rojo, A. *The Repeating Islands: The Caribbean and the Postmodern Perspective.* Trans. James E. Maraniss. Durham and London: Duke University Press, 1996.

Bernard, Anna. 'Forms of Memory: Partition as a Literary Paradigm.' *Alif: Journal of Comparative Poetics. No. 30, Trauma and Memory* / الذاكرة الجيعة و 33–9 :(2010).

Bhabha, Homi. 'Interview with Homi Bhabha The Third Space.' *Identity, Community, Culture, Difference.* Ed. Rutherford Jonathan. London: Lawrence and Wishart, 1990, 207–221.

———. *The Location of Culture.* London: Routledge, 1994.

Bhalla, Alok. *Partition Dialogues: Memories of a Lost Home.* New Delhi: Oxford University Press, 2007.

Bianchini, Stefano et al. *Partitions: Reshaping States and Minds.* London: Routledge, 2006.

Blom, Ida, et al., eds. *Gendered Nations: Nationalism and Gender Order in the Long Nineteenth Century.* London: Berg Publishing, 2002.

Blunt, Alison and Cheryl McEwan, eds. *Postcolonial Geographies*. London: Continuum, 2002.

Boletsi, Maria. 'Barbaric Encounters: Rethinking Barbarism in C. P. Cavafy's and J. M. Coetzee's *Waiting for the Barbarian*.' *Comparative Literature Studies* 44.1–2 (2007): 67–96.

Bongies, Chris. *Islands and Exile The Creole Identities of Post/colonial Literature*. Stanford: Stanford University Press, 1998.

Boym, Svetlana. *The Future of Nostalgia*. New York: Basic Books, 2001.

Brass, Paul. *Ethnicity and Nationalism: Theory and Comparison*. New Delhi: Sage Publication, 1991.

Braudel, Fernand. *The Mediterranean and the Mediterranean World in the Age of Philip II: Vol 1*. New York: Harper Perennial, 1975.

Bryant, R. 'An Education in Honour: Patriotism and the Schools of Cyprus.' *Cyprus and Its People: Nation, Identity, and Experience in an Unimaginable Community, 1955–1997*. Ed. Vangelis Calotychos. Boulder: Westview Press, 1998, 69–84.

———. *Imagining the Modern: The Culture of Nationalism in Cyprus*. London: I.B. Tauris, 2004.

———. 'The Purity of Spirit and the Power of Blood: A Comparative Perspective on Nation, Gender and Kinship.' *The Journal of Royal Anthropological Institute* 8 (2002): 509–30.

———, and Papadakis, Yiannis, eds. *Cyprus and the Politics of Memory: History, Community and Conflict*. London: I.B. Tauris, 2012.

Buckingham, C.F. 'The Turks of Cyprus.' *Journal of Royal Anthropological Institute of Great Britain and Ireland* 87 (1957): 165–74.

Butailia, Urvasho. *The Other Side of Silence: Voices from Partition of India*. Durham: Duke University Press, 2000.

Calame, Jon and Esther Charlesworth. *Divided Cities: Belfast, Beirut, Jerusalem, Mostar, and Nicosia*. Philadelphia: University of Pennsylvania, 2009.

Cahit, Neriman, Comp. *Female Poets and Writers in Turkish Cypriot Literature*. Nicosia: KT Egitim Vakfi, 2008.

Carrigan, A. *Postcolonial Tourism: Literature, Culture, and Environment*. London: Routledge, 2011.

Calotychos, Vangelis, ed. *Cyprus and its People: Nation, Identity, and Experience in an Unimaginable Community, 1955–1997*. Boulder, CO: Westview Press, 1998.

———. 'Introduction: Interdisciplinary Perspectives: Difference at the Heart of Cypriot Identity and Its Study.' *Cyprus and Its People: Nation, Identity and Experience in Unimaginable Community 1955–1997*. Ed. Vangelis Calotychos. Boulder: Westview Press, 1998, 1–32.

———. *Modern Greece: A Cultural Poetics*. Oxford: Berg Publishers, 2004.

———. '(Pre)occupied Spaces: Hyphens, Apostrophes and Over-sites in the Literary Imagining in Cyprus.' *Step-mother Tongue: From Nationalism to Multi-culturalism: Literatures of Cyprus, Greece and Turkey*. Ed. Mehmet Yashin. London: Middlesex University Press, 2000, 49–69.

———, Peter Hocknell and Yiannis Papadakis, eds. *Divisive Cities, Divided Cities: Nicosia*. Spec. Issue of *The Journal of Mediterranean Studies* 8:2 (1998): 1–228.

Carter, Paul. *The Road to Botany Bay*. London: Faber and Faber, 1987.

Cassia, S. Paul. 'Recognition and Emotion: Exhumations of Missing Persons in Cyprus.' *Divided Cyprus: Modernity, History, and an Island in Conflict.* Eds. Yiannis Papadakis, Nicos Peristianis and Gisel Welz. Bloomington: Indiana University Press, 2006, 194–13.

Cavafy, Constantine. 'Prayer.' *C.P. Cavafy Collected Poems.* Trans. Edmund Keeley and Philip Sherrard. Ed. George Savidis. London: Hogarth Press, 1975, 6.

———. *Constantine P. Cavafy – Poems.* Trans. Manolis. Ed. George Amabile. Surrey: Libros Libertad, 2008.

——— 'Thermopylae.' *C.P. Cavafy Collected Poems.* Trans. Edmund Keeley and Philip Sherrard. Ed. George Savidis. London: Hogarth Press, 1975, 12.

———. 'The God Abandons Antony.' *C.P. Cavafy Collected Poems.* Trans. Edmund Keeley and Philip Sherrard. Ed. George Savidis. London: Hogarth Press, 1975, 27.

———. 'Waiting for the Barbarians.' *C.P. Cavafy Collected Poems.* Trans. Edmund Keeley and Philip Sherrard. Ed. George Savidis. London: Hogarth Press, 1975, 14–15.

Cesaire, Aime. *Discourse on Colonialism.* Trans. John Pinkhan. New York: Monthly Review Press, 1972.

Chambers, Iain. *Mediterranean Crossing.* Duke: Duke University, 2008.

Chamboulides, Demetris. 'Song of the Resurrection.' *A Poetry and Prose Anthology of the 1955–59 EOKA Liberation Struggle.* Eds. Michalakisi I. Maratheftis and Roula Ioannidou-Stravrou. Trans. Irene Joannides. Nicosia: Cyprus Ministry of Education and Culture, 2003, 17.

Charalambides, Kyriakos. 'Την είδα' [I saw it]. *Ανθολογία Κυπριακής Λογοτεχνίας για το Γυμνάσιο.* [*Cypriot Literature Anthology, Gymnasium*]. Λευκωσία [Nicosia]: ΥΑΠ, 1998, 98–99.

———. *Literary Profile Kyriakos Charalambides.* Ed. Theodosis Pylarinos. Nicosia: Pen Cyprus, 2009.

Chatterjee, Partha. *The Nation and its Fragments.* Princeton: Princeton University Press, 1993.

Chrysanthi, Zitsea. 'Black-Garbed Mothers.' *A Poetry and Prose Anthology of the 1955–59 EOKA Liberation Struggle.* Eds. Michalakisi I. Maratheftis and Roula Ioannidou-Stravrou. Trans. Irene Joannides. Nicosia: Cyprus Ministry of Education and Culture, 2003, 126–27.

Cleary, Joe. *Literature, Partition and the Nation State: Culture and Conflict in Ireland, Israel and Palestine.* Cambridge: Cambridge University Press, 2002.

Cobham, D. Claude. *Excerpta Cypria: Materials for a History of Cyprus.* Cambridge: Cambridge University Press, 1908.

Cohn, S. Berhard. 'The Census, Social Structure and Objectification in South Asia.' *An Anthropologist among the Historians and Other Essays.* Delhi: Oxford University Press, 1987, 223–54.

Colette Ann, ed. *Cyprus* Spec. issue of *Kunapipi: Journal of Postcolonial Writing & Culture.* 33.1/2 (2011): 1–283. Print.

Conrad, L. I. 'Islam and the Sea: Paradigms and Problematics.' *Al-Qantara* XXIII.1 (2002): 123–54.

Constantinou, M. Costas. 'Aporias of Identity: Bicommunalism, Hybridity and the 'Cyprus Problem'.' *Cooperation and Conflict* 42.3 (2007): 247–71.

Crawshaw, Nancy. *Cyprus Revolt.* London: George Allen & Unwin, 1978.

Crosby, Alfred. *Ecological Imperialism: The Biological Expansion of Europe, 900–1900*. Cambridge: Cambridge University Press, 1993.

Daiya, Kavita. *Violent Belongings: Partition, Gender, and National Culture in Postcolonial India*. Philadelphia: Temple University Press, 2008.

Darwish, Mahmoud. *Unfortunately, It was Paradise*. Eds. and trans. Munir Akash and Carolyn Forche. Berkley: University of California Press, 2003.

Dawson, Graham. *Making Peace with the Past: Memory, Trauma and the Irish Troubles*. Manchester: Manchester UP, 2007.

Decavalles A, Comp. *Voice of Cyprus Anthology of Cypriot Literature*. New York: House Inc., 1965.

DeLoughrey Elizabeth and George B. Handley, eds. *Postcolonial Ecologies*. Oxford: OUP, 2011.

Deleney, Carol. *The Seed and the Soil: Gender and Cosmology in Turkish Village Society*. Berkeley: University of California Press, 1991.

Deliceirmak, Orbay. 'Bicaga Yumruk' [Punching a Knife]. *Kibris Turk Edebiyati II [TCL II- Turkish Cypriot Literature II]*. KKTC: K.T. Egitim Vakfi Yayinlari, 2008, 90–91.

Deleuze, Gilles and Felix Guattari. *A Thousand Plateaus Capitalism and Schizophrenia*. Trans. Brian Massumi. Minneapolis: University of Minnesota Press, 1987.

Demirag, Fikret. *Limnidi Atesinden Bugune Kitap 1[Limnidi]*. Lefkosa: Galeri Kultur Yayinlar, 1992.

———. *Huzun Ana Kitap 2 [Mother Grief]*. Lefkosa: Galeri Kultur Yayinlar, 1992.

———. *Siri Dokulmus Kokayna [Rootmirror], Yalnizlik, Gece Muzigi Kitap 3–4*. Lefkosa: Galeri Kultur Yayinlar, 1994.

Denizoglu, Nice. 'Zeytin Dali' [Olive Branch]. *Kibris Turk Edebiyati II [TCLII Turkish Cypriot Literature II.]*. KKTC: K.T. Egitim Vakfi Yayinlari, 2008, 139.

Denktash, R. Rauf. *The Cyprus Triangle*. Nicosia: K. Rustem & Brother, 1988.

Derrida, Jacques. *Monolingualism of the Other; or, The Prosthesis of Origin*. Trana. Patrick Mensah. Stanford: Stanford University, 1998.

———. *Of Grammatology*. Trans. Gayatri Chakravorty Spivak. Delhi: Motilal Banarsidass, 1994.

———. 'Psyche: Inventions of the Other.' Trans. Cathering Porter. *Reading de Man Reading*. Eds. Lindsey Waters and Wlad Godzich. Minneapolis: University of Minnesota Press, 1989, 25–65.

——— and Ferraris, *A Taste For the Secret*, trans. Giacomo Donis. Cambridge: Polity, 2001.

Deschaumes, Ghislaine Glasson and Rada Ivekovic, eds. *Divided Countries, Separated Cities: The Modern Legacy of Partition*. New Delhi: Oxford University Press, 2003.

Dimock Wai-chee and Lawrence Buell. *Shades of the Planet: American Literature as World Literature*. Princeton: Princeton University Press, 2007.

Dixon, William Hepworth. *British Cyprus*. London: Elibron Classic, 2005.

Dueck, Daniela. 'The Date and Method of Composition of Strabo's Geography.' *Hermes* 127.4 (1999): 467–78.

Dunbar, Gary Seamans. 'The Forests of Cyprus under British Stewardship.' *Scottish Geographical Journal* 99.2 (1983): 111–20.

Durrell, Lawrence. *Bitter Lemons*. London: Faber and Faber, 1957.
———. *Spirit of Place: Mediterranean Writing*. Ed. Alan. G. Thomas. London: Faber and Faber, 1998.
Durrell, Lawrence. Letter from Durrell to Freya Stark, December 1954.
———. *Cyprus Review* (1954–1956).
Dutton, Michael, Leela Gandhi and Sanjay Seth. *Watch this Space*. Spec. Issue of *Postcolonial Studies* 2.3 (1999): 227–436.
Edmond, Rod and Venessa Smith, eds. *Island in History and Representation*. London: Routledge, 2003.
Elmessiri, M. Abdelwahab. 'The Palestinian Wedding: Major Themes of Contemporary Palestinian Resistance.' *Journal of Palestine Studies* 10.3 (1981): 77–99.
Ersavas, Fahri, Comp. *Kibris Siirleri Antolojisi. [Cyprus Poetry]* Istanbul: Yagmur, [1952]1965.
Fanon, Frantz. *Black Skin, White Masks*. Trans. Charles Lam Macmann. London: Pluto Press, 2008.
———. *The Wretched of the Earth*. Trans. Constance Farrington. London: Penguin Books, 2001.
———. *Toward the African Revolution: Political Essays* Trans. Haakon Chevalier. New York: Grove Press, 1994.
Fisk, Robert. *Pity the Nation: Lebanon at War*. Oxford: Oxford University Press, 1990.
Fraser, Thomas G. *Partition in Ireland, India, and Palestine: Theory and Practice*. London: Macmillan, 1984.
Frazee, A. Charles. 'The Year of Revolution-1821.' *The Orthodox Church and Independent Greece1821–1852*. Cambridge: Cambridge University Press, 1969, 15–48.
Foley, Charles. *Island in Revolt*. London: Longman, 1962.
———. *The Memoirs of General Grivas*. New York: Preager, 1965.
Gandhi, Leela. *Postcolonial Theory: A Critical Introduction*. Edinburgh Edinburgh University Press, 1998.
Gazioglu, Ahmet C. *Cyprus the Island of Sustained Crises Volume 2*. Lefkosa: CYREP, 2002.
———. *Ingiliz Yonetiminde Kibris, Son Iki Yil (1958–1960): Enosis Cemberinden Kibris Cumhuriyeti*. Lefkosia: CYREP, 2000.
———. *The Turks in Cyprus: A Province of Ottoman Empire (1571–1978)*. Trans. London: K. Rustem & Brother, 1990.
Georghallides, George S. *A Political and Administrative Study of Cyprus 1918–1926*. Nicosia: Cyprus Research Centre, 1979.
Gilroy, Paul. *After Empire: Melancholia or Convivial Culture*. Oxfordshire: Routledge, 2004.
Given, Michael. 'Maps, Fields, and Boundary Cairns: Demarcation and Resistance in Colonial Cyprus.' *International Journal of Historical Archaeology* 6.1 (2004): 1–22.
———. 'Inventing the Eteocypriots: Imperialist Archaeology and the Manipulation of Ethnic Identity.' *Journal of Mediterranean Archaeology* 111 (1998): 3–29.
Gole, Suzan. *Cyprus on the Table: Maps of Cyprus in British Government Papers*. Nicosia: The Bank of Cyprus Cultural foundation, 1996.

Greenberg, Jonathan D. 'Divided Lands, Phantom Limbs: Partition in the Indian Subcontinent, Palestine, China, and Korea.' *Journal of International Affairs* 57.2 (2004): 7–27.

———. 'Generations of Memory: Remembering Partition in India/Pakistan and Israel/Palestine.' *Comparative Studies of South Asia, Africa and the Middle East* 25.1 (2005): 89–110.

Gritsi-Milliex, Tatiana, *Critique of Cypriot Literature*. Nicosia: Alpha-Omega Publications, 1970. [Greek]

Goddard, Stacie E. *Indivisible Territory and the Politics of Legitimacy: Jerusalem and Northern Ireland*. Cambridge: Cambridge UP, 2009.

Gregory, Derek *Geographical Imaginations*. London: Blackwell Wiley, 1994.

Gunnis, Rupert. *Historic Cyprus a Guide to its Towns and Villages, Monasteries and Castles*. Nicosia: Rustem, 1973.

Gunner, Liz, 'Names and the Land: Poetry of Belonging and Unbelonging, a Comparative Approach.' *Text, Theory, Space: Land, Literature and History in South Africa and Australia*. Eds. Kate Darien-Smith et al. London: Routledge, 1996, 115–30.

Hadjidemetriou, Katia. *A History of Cyprus*. Nicosia: I.G Kassoulides & Sons, 2007.

Hadjipieris, M., et al., Ed. *Nicosia*. Athens: Thegona Ltd, 1995.

Hakeri, Bener Hakki. *Kibris Tarihi [Cyprus History]*. Lefkosa: Hakeri Yayinlari, 1991.

———. 'Yigitler Ututulurmu?' [Can the Heroes be Forgotten?]. *Kibris Turk Edebiyati II [TCLII Turkish Cypriot Literature II]*. KKTC: K.T. Egitim Vakfi Yayinlari, 2008, 98.

Halil, Inalcik. 'Ottoman Methods of Conquest.' *Studia Islamica* 2 (1954): 103–29.

Hall, Stuart. 'Cultural Identity and Diaspora.' *Colonial Discourse and Post-Colonial Theory*. Eds. Patrick Williams and Laura Chrisman. Harlow: Longman, 1994, 392–403.

Harris, Wilson. *The Womb of Space: The Cross-Cultural Imagination*. Connecticut: Greenwood Press, 1983.

Harel-Shalev, Ayelet. *The Challenge of Sustaining Democracy in Deeply Divided Societies: Citizenship, Rights, and Ethnic Conflicts in India and Israel*. Lanham, MD: Lexington Books, 2010.

Hasan, Mushirul, ed. *Inventing Boundaries: Gender, Politics, and the Partition of India*. New Delhi: Oxford University Press, 2000.

Heise, Ursula. *Sense of Place, Sense of Planet: Environmental Imagination of the Global*. New York: Oxford University Press, 2008.

Herbrechter, Stan. *Lawrence Durrell, Postmodernism and the Ethics of Alterity*. Amsterdam: Rodopi, 1999.

Heraclidou, Antigone, *Imperial Control in Cyprus: Education and Political Manipulation in the British Empire*. London: IB Tauris, 2017.

Herodotus. *The History*. Trans. David Gren. Chicago: University of Chicago Press, 1987.

Hermes, Nizar. *The [European] Other in Medieval Arabic Literature and Culture, Ninth-Twelfth Century AD*. London: Palgrave, 2012.

Hikmet, Nazim. *Nazim Hikmet Butun Siirler [Complete Collection]*. Istanbul: Yapi Kredi Yayinlar, 2011.

Hill, George. *A History of Cyprus Volume IV*. Ed. Harry Luke. Cambridge: Cambridge University Press, 1952.

Hobbes, Thomas. *Leviathan*. Ed. Crawford Brough Macpherson. London: Penguin Classics, 1985.

Hochberg, Gil. *In Spite of Partition: Jews, Arabs, and the Limits of Separatist Imagination*. New Jersey: Princeton University Press, 2007.

Holland, Robert and Diana Markides. *The British and the Hellenes, Struggles for Mastery in the Eastern Mediterranean 1850–1960*. Oxford: Oxford University Press, 2006.

Homer. *Iliad*. Trans. Robert Fagles (Translator). New York: Penguin. 1998.

Hooker, Reginald, H. 'Modes of Census Taking in the British Dominion.' *Journal of the Royal Statistical Society* 57.2 (1894): 298–368.

Hoplaros, Miranda. *Mrs Bones*. Cyprus: Hoplaros, 2008.

Hoplaros, Miranda. *Sign Maker*. Cyprus: Hoplaros, 2015.

Horden, Peregrine and Nicholas Purcell. *The Corrupting Sea: A Study of Mediterranean History*. Oxford: Blackwell, 2000.

Howard-Johnston, Johnson. 'L'Islam et la mer: La mosquée et le matelot, VIIe–XXe siècle by Xavier de Planhol Review.' *The English Historical Review* 117.470 (2002): 118–20.

Huggan, Graham. 'Decolonizing the Map: Post-Colonialism, Post-Structuralism and the Cartographic Connection.' *Ariel* 20.4 (1989): 115–31.

——— and Helen Tiffin. *Green Postcolonialism*. Spec. issue of *Interventions International Journal of Postcolonial Studies* 9.1 (2007): 1–164.

———, eds. *Postcolonial Ecocriticism: Literature, Animals, Environment*. London and New York: Routledge, 2015.

Huggan, Graham and Ian Law, eds. *Racism Postcolonialism Europe: Postcolonialism across the Disciplines*. Liverpool: LUP, 2016.

Hutchins, David Ernest. *Report on Cyprus Forestry*. London: Waterlow & Sons Ltd, 1909.

Ierodiaconou, Andriana. *The Women's Coffee Shop*. Nicosia: CreateSpace, 2012.

———. *Trawl*. Nicosia: Moufflon, 2016.

Innes, Catherine Lynette. 'Virgin Territories and Motherlands: Colonial and Nationalist Representations of Africa and Ireland.' *Feminist Review* 47 (Summer, 1994): 1–14.

———, Comp. *Anthology of the EOKA Struggle*. Nicosia: I.M. Publications, 1973. [Greek].

———, Comp. *Face of an Island: 24 Short Stories from Cyprus*. Nicosia: Armida, 1997.

———, and Andreas Christofides, Comp. *Anthology of Cypriot Short-Stories*. Nicosia: I.M. Publications, 1969. [Greek].

Ismail, Sabahattin. *150 Soruda Kibris Sorunu [Problem in 150 Questions]*. Istanbul: Kastas Yayinevi, 1988.

Jabra, Ibrahim Jabra. 'In the Deserts of Exile.' *An Anthology of Modern Arabic Poetry*. Ed. and trans. Mounah Khouri and Hamid Algar. Berkley: University of California, 1975, 225–29.

JanMohammed, Abdul. *Manichean Aesthetic: The Politics of Literature in Colonial Africa*. Amherst: University of Massachusetts Press, 1983.

———. 'The Economy of Manichean Allegory: The Function of Racial Difference in Colonialist Literature.' *Critical Enquiry* 12.1 (1995): 18–23.

Jassal, Smita Tewari and Eyal Ben-Ari, eds. *The Partition Motifs in Contemporary Conflict*. New Delhi: Sage Publication, 2007.

Kappler, Matthias, 'Prolegomena for a Comparative Approach to Cypriot Literatures.' *Hellenic Studies: A Tribute to Cypriot Literature* 15.2 (2007): 49–54.

Karpat, H. Kemal. 'Ottoman Population Records and the Census of 1881/82–1893.' *International Journal of Middle East Studies* 9.3 (1978): 237–74.

Katsiaounis, Rolandos. *Labour, Society and Politics in Cyprus during the Second Half of the Nineteenth Century*. Nicosia: Cyprus Research Centre, 1996.

Katsourides, Yiannos. *History of the Communist Party in Cyprus: Colonialism, Class and the Cypriot Left*. London: IB Tauris, 2014.

Karakatsanis, Leonidas and Nikolaos Papadogiannis, eds. *The Politics of Culture in Turkey, Greece & Cyprus Performing the Left Since the Sixties*. London: Routledge, 2017.

Katzev, Suzan Wormer, 'The Ancient Ship of Kyrenia, Beneath Cyprus Seas.' *Great Moments in Greek Archaeology*. Eds. Pavos Valavanis and David Hardy. Oxford: University Press, 2007, 286–99.

Kaul, Suvir, ed. *The Partitions of Memory: The Afterlife of the Division of India*. New Delhi: Permanent Black, 2001.

Kazamias, Andreas and Erwin Epstein, eds. *School in Transition: Essays in Comparative Education*. Boston: Allyn and Bacon, 1968.

Kearney, Richard. *Myths and Motherlands*. Derry: Fieldday Publications, 1984.

Kechagioglou, George. 'Contemporary Cypriot Literature and the 'Frame' of Modern Greek Literature: A Provincial, Local, Marginal, Peripheral, Independent, Autonomous, Self- Sufficient or Self-Determined Literature?' *Journal of Mediterranean Studies* 2.2 (1992): 240–55.

Kemal, Bahriye. 'Writing Gifted Baby Cyprus: Anticolonial Ethnic Motherland Nationalist Literatures.' *Interventions International Journal of Postcolonial Studies* 19.18 (2017): 1088–111.

———. 'Rhythmanalysts of the Postcolonial Partitioned Diaspora: Writing Differential Cyprus through Henri Lefebvre and Yi-Fu Tuan.' *The Journal of Commonwealth Literature* Online First (2019): 1–24.

Khumar, Radha. *Making Peace with Partition*. India: Penguin Books, 2005.

———. The Partition Debate: Colonialism Revisited or New Policies? *The Brown Journal of World Affairs* 7.1 (Winter/Spring 2000): 3–11.

Kibris Turk Edebiyati: Baslangictan Bugune. [Turkish Cypriot Literature] KKTC Milli Egitim ve Kultur Bakanligi yayinlari. Kultur dizisi, 1989. [Turkish].

Killoran, Moira. 'Nationalism and Embodied Memory in Northern Cyprus.' *Cyprus and Its People: Nation, Identity, and Experience in an Unimaginable Community, 1955–1997*. Ed. Vangelis Calotychos. Boulder: Westview Press, 1998, 159–70.

———. 'Space and Nationalism.' *Stepmother Tongue from Nationalism to Multiculturalism: Literatures of Cyprus, Greece and Turkey*. Ed. Mehmet Yasin. London: Middlesex University Press, 2000, 129–146.

King, Ruby Hope and Mike Morrissey. *In Images in Print: Bias and Prejudice in Caribbean Textbooks*. Mona: Institute of Social and Economical Research, University of West Indies, 1988.

Kirkland, Richard. *Literature and Culture in Northern Ireland since 1965: Moments of Danger*. London: Longman, 1996.

Koutselini-Ioannidou, Mary. 'Curriculum as Political Text: the Case of Cyprus (1935–90).' *History of Education* 26.4 (1997): 395–407.

Kranidiotis, Nicos. *Cypriot Poetry*. Athens: Greek Editorial, 1969. [Greek].

———. 'Gregoris Afxeniou.' *A Poetry and Prose Anthology of the 1955–59 EOKA Liberation Struggle*. Eds. Michalakisi I. Maratheftis and Roula Ioannidou-Stravrou. Trans. Irene Joannides. Nicosia: Cyprus Ministry of Education and Culture, 2003, 39–40.

———. 'Μνήμη Κερύνειας' [Kyrenia Memory]. *Ανθολογία Κυπριακής Λογοτεχνίας για το Γυμνάσιο. [Cypriot Literature Anthology, Gymnasium]*. Λευκωσία [Nicosia]: ΥΑΠ, 1998, 96.

———, *The National Character of Cypriot Literature*. Athens: Greek Editorial Company, 1958 [Greek].

Murdered Militants in 1955–59. AKEL C.C. Press Office, 31 May 2018.

Korfioti, Vera, Comp. *Faces of an Island: 25 Poets from Cyprus*. Trans. Mona Saviddoi-Theodoulou Nicosia: Armida Publishing, 2000, 13–17.

Korkmazel, Gurgenc. 'Gravity of the Moon' & 'Kiss my Corpse'. Trans. Gur Genc and Stephanos Stephanides. *Cadence* 1.1 (2004): 5–6, 10–11.

———, Comp. *Kibrislirum Şiir Antolojisi*. [Cypriotgreek] Paloma: Istanbul, 2010.

———. 'Kicking Butterfly.' Trans. Taner Baybars. *Cadences* 6 Fall (2010): 11.

———. 'Not Poetry… Water.' Trans. Aydin M. Ali. *Cadences* 2.1 (2006): 46.

———. 'Mesaoria.' Trans. Gur Genc and Stephanos Stephanides. *Cadences* 3.1/2 (2007): 91.

———. 'Nicosia, I Worshipped to Many God's' The Pull of Moon.' Trans. Aydin M Ali and Stephanides. Spec. issue of *Kunapipi: Journal of Postcolonial Writing & Culture* 33.1/2 (2011): 31–32.

———. 'The Flute'& 'From the Radical.' Trans. Stephanos Stephanides and Korkmazel. *Cadence* 2.1/2 (2006): 41, 44.

———, Trans. Taner Baybars, Tilki ile Çobanaldatan / Toplu Şiirler 1951–2001. Yapi Kredi, 2007.

Kouyialis, Theoklis, ed. *27 Centuries of Cypriot Poetry*. PEN: Nicosia, 1981.

———, Comp. *Contemporary Cypriot Poetry*. Nicosia: Pen Publications, 1981.

Kusetoglu, Oguz. 'Kibris'im Bahtsiz Kizim' [Ill Fated Daughter]. *Kibris Turk Edebiyati II [Turkish Cypriot Literature II]*. KKTC: K.T. Egitim Vakfi Yayinlari, 2008, 98.

Kuzey Kibris Turk Cumhuriyet'inden Ulusal Siirler [National Poetry from the TRNC]. KKTC: Enformasyon Dairesi, 1985.

Kuzey Kibris Turk Milli Siirer Antologisi. [North Cyprus Turkish Poetry] Nicosia: Erenkoy Yainlar, 1971. [Turkish].

Kyprianou, Andreas. *Speech by the General Secretary of the C.C. of AKEL to Honour the* Laffan, Michael, *The Partition of Ireland, 1911–25*. Dundalk: Dundalgan Press, 1983.

Lavender, S. David. *The Story of the Cyprus Mines Corporation*. San Marino, CA: Huntington Library, 1962.

Lee, Dennis. 'Cadences, Country, Silence: Writing in Colonial Space.' *Boundary* 2 3.1 (1974): 15–168.

Lefebvre, Henri. *The Production of Space*. Trans. Donald Nicholson-Smith. Oxford: Blackwell Publishing, [1974] 1991.

———. *Rhythmanalysis: Space, Time and Everyday Life*. Trans. Stuart Elden. London: Continuum, 2004.
———. 'Theory of Moments'. *Critique of Everyday Life*. London: Verso.
———. *The Urban Revolution*. Trans. Robert Bonnono. Minneapolis: University of Minnesota, 2003.
Levent, Mehmet. 'Freedom and Peace Anthem.' *Kuzey Kibris Turk Cumhuriyet'inden Ulusal Siirler* [National Poetry from the TRNC]. KKTC: Enformasyon Dairesi, 1985, 1.
Lewis, Bernard. *The Emergence of Modern Turkey*. Oxford: OUP, [1969] 1989.
Loizides, G. Neophytos. 'Ethnic Nationalism and Adaptation in Cyprus.' *International Studies Perspectives* 8 (2007): 172–89.
———. *Designing Peace: Cyprus and Institutional Innovations in Divided Societies*. Philadelphia: University of Pennsylvania Press, 2015.
———. *The Politics of Majority Nationalism: Framing Peace, Stalemates and Crises*. Stanford, CA, USA: Stanford University Press. 2015.
Lucian of Samosata. *Lucian's True History*. Trans. Francis Hickes. London: Privately Published, 1894.
Lyndon, C. S. Way. 'The Local News Media Impeding Solutions to the Cyprus Conflict: Competing Discourse of Nationalism in Turkish Cypriot Radio News.' *Social Semiotics* Special Section 21.1 (2011): 15–31.
Maake, Nhlanhla. 'Inscribing Identity on the Landscape: National Symbols in South Africa.' *Text, Theory, Space: Land, Literature and History in South Africa and Australia*. Eds. Kate Darien- Smith, Liz Gunner, and Sarah Nuttall. London: Routledge, 1996, 145–55.
Macaulay, Thomas, B. 'Minute on India 1835.' *Speeches by Lord Macaulay*. Ed. George Malcolm Young. London: Oxford University press, 1935, 345–361.
MacNiven, S. Ian. 'Cyprus Paradise Regained and Lost.' *Lawrence Durrell: A Biography*. London: Faber and Faber, 1998, 385–442.
Mallinson, William. *Cyprus: A Modern History*. London: I.B. Tauris, 2005.
Marangou, Niki. *Nicosieness*. Trans. Stephanos Stephanides. Nicosia: R. Pakino leidykla, 2006.
———. *Selections from the Divan*. Trans. Stephanos Stephanides. Nicoisa: Kochlias, 2001.
Marx, Karl. *The Eighteenth Brumaire of Louis Bonaparte (1852)*. New York: International Publishers, 1984.
———. *Grundrisse: Foundations of the Critique of Political Economy*. Trans. Martin Nicolaus. London: Penguin Classics, 1993.
———. *Capital*. Trans. David Fernbach. London: Penguin, 1993.
Mavratsas, Caesar. 'The Ideological Contest and the Social Construction of Greek-Cypriot Identity.' *Ethics and Racial Studies* 20.4 (1997): 717–37.
McClintock Anne. *Imperial Leather: Race, Gender, Sexuality in Colonial Contest*. London: Routledge, 1995.
———. 'No Longer in a Future Heaven: Gender Race and Nationalism.' *Dangerous Liaisons: Gender, Race and Postcolonial Perspectives*. Eds. Anne McClintock et al. Minnesota: University of Minnesota, 1997, 89–112.
McLeod, John. *Postcolonial London: Rewriting the Metropolis*. London: Routledge. 2004.
Memmi, Albert. *The Colonizer and the Colonized*. Trans. Howard Greenfield. London: Beacon Press, 1965.

Michell Roland. 'A Muslim-Christian Sect in Cyprus.' *The Nineteenth Century Journal* 63 (1908): 751–62.

Mohanram, Radhika, ed. *Comparative Partitions* special issue of *Social Semiotics* 21.1 (2011): 53–55.

Moleskis, G. 'History and Poetry: Poetic Experiences on the Traumatic Landscape of Cyprus.' *Hellenic Quarterly* 5 (2000): 45–49.

———. *Literary Profiles: 21 Yiorgos Moleskis.* Ed Theoklis Kouyialis. Trans. Irene Joannides and Lisa Socrates. Nicosia: Cyprus Pen Publications.

———. *Poems.* Nicosia, 2004.

———. *Selected Poems.* Trans. and ed. Lisa Socrates. Nicosia: Livadiotis Press, 1991.

———, Trans. *CollaboNation* Spec, issue of *Cyprus Dossier*, 5 (2013): 66–71.

———. Comp., and Trans. *Contemporary Turkish Cypriot Poetry: Attempted Contacts.* [Greek]. Athens: Topos, 2010.

Montis, Costas. 'A Song for Our Older Brother.' *A Poetry and Prose Anthology of the 1955–59 EOKA Liberation Struggle.* Eds. Michalakisi I. Maratheftis and Roula Ioannidou- Stravrou. Trans. Irene Joannides. Nicosia: Cyprus Ministry of Education and Culture, 2003, 64.

———. *Closed Doors: An Answer to Bitter Lemons by Lawrence Durrell.* Trans. David Roessel and Soterios G. Stavrou. Minnesota: Nostos Books, 2004.

———. 'Grigoris Afxendiou.' Trans. Amy Mims. *Faces of an Island: 25 Poets from Cyprus.* Eds. Vera Korfioti, Vera and Mona Saviddoi-Theodoulou Nicosia: Armida Publishing, 2000, 13–17.

———. *Literary Profile Costas Montis.* Ed. Nicos Oprhanides. Nicosia: Pen Cyrpus, 1993.

———. *Moments.* Trans. Amaranth Sitas and Charles Dodd. Nicosia: Zavallis Press, 1965.

———, Christophides A., eds. *Anthology of Cypriot Poetry.* Trans. Mims A. Nicosia: Proodos, 1974.

Moore-Gilbert, Bart. *Postcolonial Life-Writing: Culture, Politics and Self-Representation.* London: Routledge, 2009.

Moon, Penderel. *Divide and Quit: An Eye-witness Account of the Partition of India.* Delhi: Oxford University Press, 1998.

Morgan, Austen. *Labour and Partition: The Belfast Working Class, 1905–1923.* London: Pluto Press, 1991.

Mukherjee, Pablo. *Postcolonial Environments; Nature, Culture and the Contemporary Indian Novel in English.* London: Palgrave, 2010.

Nadjarian, Nora. *Ledra Street.* Nicosia: Armida, 2006.

———. *Cleft in Twain.* Nicosia: Armida, 2003.

Nalbantoglu, Gulsum Baydar and Wong, Chong Thai, eds. *Postcolonial Space(s).* New York: Princeton Architectural Press, 1997.

Nairn, Tom. *The Break-Up of Britain: Crisis and Neo-Nationalism.* 3rd ed. Victoria: Common Ground Publishing, 2003.

Naldoven, Filiz. 'Yasamak' [Live]. *Kibris Turk Edebiyati II [TCLII-Turkish Cypriot Literature II].* KKTC: K.T. Egitim Vakfi Yayinlari, 2008, 134–35.

Nandy, Ashis. *The Intimate Enemy: Loss and Recovery of Self Under Colonialism.* Delhi: Oxford University Press, 1989.

Nasta, Susheila, ed. *Motherlands: Black Women's Writing from the Caribbean, Africa and South Asia.* London: Women's Press, 1991.

Notopoulos, A. James. 'Mnemosyne in Oral Literature.' *Transactions and Proceedings of the American Philological Association* 69 (1938): 465–93.

Noyes, John Kenneth. *Colonial Space: Spatiality in the Discourse of German South West Africa 1884–1915: Spatiality, Subjectivity and Society in the Colonial Discourse.* London: Routledge, 1992.

Oksuzoglu, Oguz. *Kitlik Tarlalar.* [Fields] Lefkosa: Yakin Yayinlari, 1966.

Oktay Oksuzoglu's 'Republic.' *Kuzey Kibris Turk Cumhuriyet'inden Ulusal Siirler [National Poetry from the TRNC].* KKTC: Enformasyon Dairesi, 1985, 2.

Olymbiou, Kika. 'Cypriot Poetry.' *Five Short Essays on Cypriot Literature.* Trans. John Vikers Lana Der Parthogh, Ed. Andreas Sophocleaous. Nicosial: Pen Publications, 1981, 29–46.

O'Shea, Helen. *Ireland and the End of the British Empire: The Republic and Its Role in the Cyprus Emergency.* London: I.B. Tauris, 2015.

Orr, Charles William James. *Cyprus under British Rule.* London: Robert Scott, 1972.

Ovid, *Metamorphosis.* Trans. A. D. Melville. Oxford: Oxford World Classic, 2009.

Padamsee, A. 'Uncertain Partitions: Undecidability and the Urdu Short Story.' *Wasafiri* 23 (2008): 1–5.

Panayiotunis, Panos. *Introduction to Cypriot Literature.* Nicosia: Thol, 1965.

Pandey, Gyanendra. *Remembering Partition.* Cambridge: Cambridge University Press, 2002.

———. 'In Defence of the Fragment: Writing about Hindu-Muslim Riots in India Today.' *Imperial Fantasies and Postcolonial Histories* Spec. Issue of *Representations* 37 (1992): 27–55.

Panteli, Stravos. *The History of Modern Cyprus.* New Barnet: Topline Publishing, 2005.

Papachrysostomou, Christodoulos. 'EOKA Hymn.' *A Poetry and Prose Anthology of the 1955–59 EOKA Liberation Struggle.* Eds. Michalakisi I. Maratheftis and Roula Ioannidou-Stravrou. Trans. Irene Joannides. Nicosia: Cyprus Ministry of Education and Culture, 2003, 71.

Papadakis, Y. *History Education in Divided Cyprus: A Comparison of Greek Cypriot and Turkish Cypriot Schoolbooks on the History of Cyprus.* Norway: PRIO, 2008.

———. 'Aphrodite Delight'. *Postcolonial Studies* 9 (2006): 237–50.

———, Peristianis, Nicos and Gisela Welz, eds. *Divided Cyprus. Modernity, History and an Island in Conflict.* Bloomington: Indiana University Press, 2006.

———. *Cyprus* Spec. issue of *Postcolonial Studies* 9.3 (2006): 227–342.

Papadopoulos, Yiannis. 'The Letter and the Road.' *A Poetry and Prose Anthology of the 1955–59 EOKA Liberation Struggle.* Eds. Michalakisi I. Maratheftis and Roula Ioannidou-Stravrou. Trans. Irene Joannides. Nicosia: Cyprus Ministry of Education and Culture, 2003, 74.

———. *Literary Profile 31. Yiannos Papadopoulos.* Ed. Yianis Peyiotis. Nicosia: Pen Cyprus.

Papaleontiou, Lefteris and Stephanos Constantinides, eds. *Hellenic Studies: A Tribute to Cypriot Literature* 15.2 (2007): 1–432.

Pappe, Ilan. *The Ethnic Cleansing of Palestine.* Oxford: Oneworld, 2006.

Parker, Andrew et al, eds. *Nationalisms and Sexualities*. New York: Routledge, 1992.

Pantelis, M. 'Osesilus.' Literary Profile. Ed. Nicos Orphanides. Trans. Rhea Frangofinou. Nicosia: Pen Cyprus, 1993, 12.

Peonidou Elli. Extracts from The Soil of Cyprus (1971), The Circle of Accusation (1977), Songs of Lost Mint (1979), Hours (1983), Hourglass 1987, Journeys (1997). *Literary Profile 16. Nicosia: Pen Cyprus, 2009.*

———. 'Illicit Lovers.' *Cultures of Memory / Memories of Culture*. Ed. Stepahnos Stephanides. Nicosia: University of Nicosia, 2007.

———. 'In Autumn They Descend', Trans. Stephanos Stephanides. *Cadences 5* Fall (2009): 9.

Pèrcopo, Luisa. 'Silent Lines and the ebb of Memory: Narratives of Our Wall in the Island of Cyprus.' *Social Semiotics: Special Issue* 21.1 (2011): 125–41.

Peristianis, Nicos. 'Left-Right, Greekcentrism-Cypriocentrism: The Pendulum of Collective Identification after 1974' N. Peristianis et al eds, *Anatomy of a Metamorphosis: Cyprus After 1974*. Nicosia, Intercollege Press. 1998.

——— and Hubert Faustmann, eds. *Britain in Cyprus. Colonialism and Post-Colonialism 1878–2006*. Mannheim/Möhnesee: Bibliopolis, 2006.

Pernaris, Andis. 'Mother of Cyprus.' *A Poetry and Prose Anthology of the 1955–59 EOKA Liberation Struggle*. Eds. Michalakisi I. Maratheftis and Roula Ioannidou-Stravrou. Trans. Irene Joannides. Nicosia: Cyprus Ministry of Education and Culture, 2003, 95–96.

———. *History of Cypriot Letters*. Nicosia: Bol, 1977 [Greek].

Persianis, K. Panayiotis. *Church and State in Cyprus Education: The Contribution of the Greek Orthodox Church of Cyprus Education during the British Administration (1878–1960)*. Nicosia: Violaris Printing, 1978.

———. 'The British Colonial Education 'Lending' Policy in Cyprus (1878–1960): An Intriguing Example of an Elusive 'Adapted Education' Policy.' *Comparative Education* 32.1 (1996): 45–68.

——— *The Political and Economical Factors as the Main Determinants of Education Policy in Independent Cyprus*. Nicosia: Prodos Press, 1981.

Petrovic, Drazen. 'Ethnic Cleansing – An Attempt at Methodolodgy.' *European Journal of International Law* 5.3 (1994): 342–60.

Philippou Niki Laddaki. *Anthology (1960–1992)*. Nicosia: 1994.

———. *Literary Profile Niki Ladaki Philippou*. Ed. Themis Theocharous. Nicosia: Cyprus Pen, 1994.

Pierides. T. 'Κυπριακή Συμφωνία I, II, IV' [Cyprus Agreement]. Ανθολογία Κυπριακής Λογοτεχνίας, Για το Λύκειο Μέρος Β΄. [CLALII- *Cypriot Literature Anthology Lyceum II*]. Λευκωσία [Nicosia]: Υ.Α.Π., 2001, 21–26.

Pitcher, L.M. 'The Divine Impatience': Ritual, Narrative, and Symbolization in the Practice of Martyrdom.' *Medical Anthropology Quarterly* 12 (1998): 8–30.

Planhol, Xavier. 'Islam and the Sea: The Causes of Failures.' *Interpreting Islam*. Ed. Donna Hastings. London: Sage, 2002, 130–149.

———. *L'Islam et la Mer: La Mosquée et le Matelot, VI–XX Siècle*. Paris: Librairie Académique Perrin, 2000.

Plutarch, *Plutarch's Lives, Volume 2*. Trans. John Dryden. Ed. Arthur Hugh Clough. Kansas: Digireads.com, 2009.

Politis, Linos. *A History of Modern Greek Literature*. Oxford: Clarendon Press, 1973.

Ramaswamy, Sumathi. 'Maps and Mother Goddesses in Modern India.' *Imago Mundi* 53(2001): 9–114.

Rappas, Alex, *Cyprus in the 1930s: British Colonial Rule and the Roots of the Cyprus Conflict*. London: IB Tauris 2014.

Reddaway, John. *Burdened With Cyprus: The British Connection*. London: K. Rustem & Bro. and Weidenfield &Nicholson, 1986.

Richmond, P. Olive. *Mediating in Cyprus: The Cypriot Communities and the United Nations (Series on Peacekeeping)*. Oxon: Frank Cass Publishers, 1998.

Roos Bonnie Roos, and Alex Hunt, eds. *Postcolonial Green: Environmental Politics and World Narratives*. Indiana: Indiana University, 2010.

Rose, J. Herbert. *Handbook of Greek Mythology*. London: Routledge, 2005.

Roessel, David. 'Something to Stand the Government in Good Stead': Lawrence Durrell and the Cyprus Review. *Deus Loci. The Lawrence Durrell Journal* 3 (1994): 37–50.

Roy, Parama. 'Partition's Other Avatars'. *Postcolonial Studies* 12.3 (2009): 365–69.

Rushdie, Salman. *Imaginary Homelands: Essays and Criticisms 1981–1991*. London: Granta, 1991.

Said, Edward W. *Culture and Imperialism*. London: Vintage Books, 1994.

———. 'Inventions, Memory, and Place'. *Critical Inquiry* 26.2 (2000): 175–92.

———. *Orientalism*. London: Penguin, 2003.

———. 'The Mind of Winter: Reflection on Life in Exile.' *Harpers Magazine* 269 (Sept.), 1984.

———. *The Question of Palestine*. New York: Vintage Books, 1992.

Samaddhar, Ranabir. 'The Undefined Acts of Partition and Dialogue' in *Partitions: Reshaping States and Minds*. London: Routledge, 2006.

Sanjay, Seth. 'Govermentality, Pedagogy, Identity.' *Beyond Representation: Colonial and Postcolonial Construction of Indian Identity*. Ed. Caspin Bates. New Delhi: Oxford University Press, 2006, 55–76.

Sarkar, Bhaskar. *Mourning the Nation: Indian Cinema in the Wake of Partition*. Durham: Duke University Press, 2009.

Sassen, Saskia. 'Cities as Frontier Zones: Making Informal Politics'. *16Beaver*. January 2013 www.16 beavergroup.org/ mtarchive/archives/002282.php

———. Leorke, Dale. 'Power, Mobility, and Diaspora in the Global City: An Interview with Saskia Sassen.' *Platform: Journal of Media and Communication* 1 (July 2009): 103–08.

———. 'When the Center No Longer Holds: Cities as Frontier Zones'. J. Cities January 2013 www.saskiasassen.com/PDFs/publications/when-the-center-no-longer-holds.pdf

Sayar and Percival, D.A. 'The Linobambakoi in Cyprus.' *Notes and Queries* 135.20 (1943): 115–16.

Schaeffer, Robert, *Warpaths: The Politics of Partition*. New York: Hill & Wang Pub, 1990.

Seferis, George. 'Helen'. *The Dark Crystal: An Anthology of Modern Greek Poetry by Cavafy, Sikelianos, Seferis, Elytis, Gatsos*. Trans. and eds. Keeley Edmund and Sherrard Philip. Athens: Denise Harvey & Co, 1981, 120–22.

———. *Complete Poems*. Trans. Edmund Keeley. London: Gardeners, 1993.

Serter, Zeki Vehbi. *Kibris Tarihi*. Nicosia: Kema Offset, 1999.

Shaw, Stanford J. *History of the Ottoman Empire and Modern Turkey: Volume 1*. Cambridge: Cambridge University Press, 1976.
Shirley, Rodney. *Kitchener's Survey of Cyprus 1978–1883*. Nicosia: The Bank of Cyprus Cultural Foundation, 2001.
Shlaim, Avi. *The Politics of Partition: The Politics of Partition: King Abdullah, the Zionists, and Palestine 1921–1951*. Oxford: Clarendon Press, 1999.
Siculus, Diodorus. *Histories Library of History (Loeb Classical Library)*. Trans. Charles Henry Oldfather. Harvard: Harvard University Press, 1933.
Smith, D. Anthony. *National Identity*. London: Penguin, 1991.
Sophocles, Ajax. *Trans Cambridge Greek Drama*. Cambridge: Cambridge University Press, 2001.
Sophocleous, Andreas. *Five Short Essays on Cypriot Literature*. Trans. John Vickers, Lana der Parthogh. Nicosia: Pen, 1981.
Spanos, Nicos, ed. *22 Contemporary Cypriot Prose-writers*. Nicosia: Cyprus Pen, 1981.
———. *Cypriot Prose-writers: From Antiquity to 1950*. Nicosia: Cyprus Pen, 1983.
Spivak, Gayatri Chakravorty. 'Can the Subaltern Speak?' *Marxism and the Interpretation of Culture*. Eds. Cary Nelson and Lawrence Grossberg. Basingstoke: Macmillan, 1988, 271–313.
———. 'Criticism, Feminism and Institution' Interview with Elizabeth Grosz.' *The Post-Colonial Critic: Interviews, Strategies, Dialogues*. Ed. Sarah Harasym. London: Routledge, 1990, 1–16.
———. 'Poststucturalism, Marginality, Postcoloniality and Value.' *Literary Theory Today*. Eds. P Collier and H. Geyer-Ryan. Cambridge: Cambridge Polity Press, 1990, 219–44.
———. 'Practical Politics of the open End' Interview with Sarah Harasym. *The Post-Colonial Critic: Interviews, Strategies, Dialogues*. Ed. Sarah Harasym. London: Routledge, 1990, 95–112.
Spyridakis, Constantinos. *The Education Policy of the English in Cyprus (1878–1954)*. Nicosia: Ethnarchy, 1954.
Stanek, Lukasz. 'Space as Concrete Abstraction: Hegel, Marx, and Modern Urbanism in Lefebvre.' *Space, Difference, Everyday Life: Reading Henri Lefebvre*. Eds. Stefan Kipfer et al. London: Routledge, 2008, 62–79.
Stevenson to Devonshire, Confidential, 24 December 1922, CO67/208/ 1091, NAUK.
Steffy, John Richard. 'The Kyrenia Ship: An Interim Report on its Hull Construction.' *American Journal of Archaeology* 38.1 (Jan. 1985): 71–101.
Stephanides, Stephanos. *Blue Moon in Rajasthan*. Nicosia: Kochlias Publication, 2005.
———. *Cultures of Memory/Memories of Culture*. Nicosia: University of Nicosia, 2007.
———. Excerpta Cypriana special issue of *91st Meridian*, University of Iowa 6:3. Iowa. http://iwp.uiowa.edu/91st/vol6_n3/articles/editorial.html. 2009.
———. *Hail Mother Kali*. Guyana: VHS, 1998.
———. 'Jaya Devi' trans Gurgenc Kormazel. 4th Annual International Poetry Days. *Zine*. Nicosia: The Turkish Cypriot Union of Artists and Writers, 2009.
———. *Kali in the Americas*. DVD. New York, 2003.
———. 'Litany in My Slumber.' *CounterText* 1.1 (2015): 105–30.

———. *Poets in No Man's Land*. Dir. Stephanides and Stephen Nugent. 2012. Video Documentary. YouTube. April 2013. 13 May 2013. www.youtube.com/watch?v=T-2GlFDZgu4

———. 'The Wind Under My Lips.' *Cadences* 5. Fall (2009): 102–11.

———. *Translating Kali's Feast: The Goddess In Indo-Caribbean Ritual and Fiction*. Amsterdam: Rodopi, 2000.

———. 'Winds Come From Somewhere.' *Kunapipi Journal of Postcolonial Writing and Culture* 33.1/2 (2012): 126–42.

———. *The Wind Under My Lips*. Athens: Rokakio, 2018.

——— and Anandana. 'Postcards from Cyprus (Made in India).' *Reenvisioning Cyprus*. Eds. Peter Loizos, Nicos Philippou, and Theopisti Stylianou-Lambert. Nicosia: University of Nicosia Press, 2010, 135–43.

Storrs, Ronald. *Orientations*. London: Nicholson & Watson, 1937.

Swedenburg, Ted. 'The Palestinian Peasant as National Signifier.' *Anthropological Quarterly* 63 (1990): 18–30.

Swiny, W. Helena and Micael L Katzev. 'The Kyrenia Shipwreck: A Fourth-century B.C. Greek Merchant Ship.' *Marine Archaeology*. Ed. David J. Blackman. London: Archon Books, 1973, 339–59.

Tansu, Ismail. *In Reality No One Was Asleep*. KKTC: Bolan Printing, 2007.

Terzis, Napoleon. 'Home.' Trans. Sevgul Uludag and Pavlos. *Yeni Duzen*. 23 September 2016.

Teverson, Andrew and Sara Upstone, eds. *Postcolonial Spaces: The Politics of Place in Contemporary Culture*. London: Palgrave Macmillan, 2011.

The Turkish Cypriot Political Parties. Nicosia: Press and Information Office, 1989.

Thiong'o, Wa Ngugi. *Decolonising the Mind: The Politics of Language in African Literature*. London: James Currey, 1986.

Thirgood, Jack. *Cyprus: A Chronicle of Its Forest, Land and People*. Vancouver: University of British Columbia Press, 1987.

———. *Man and the Mediterranean Forest*. London: Academic Press, 1981.

Thieme, John *Postcolonial Literary Geographies Out of Place*. London: Palgrave, 2017.

Tuan, Yi-Fu. *Space and Place: The Perspective of Experience*. Minneapolis: University of Minnesota Press, 1977.

Uckan, Mukadder. 'My Flag.' *Kuzey Kibris Turk Cumhuriyet'inden Ulusal Siirler [National Poetry from the TRNC]*. KKTC: Enformasyon Dairesi, 1985, 41.

Ulucamgil, Suleyman. *Suleyman Ulucamgil, Bütün Eserleri [Complete Works]*. Ed. Orbay Deliceirmak. KKTC: Milli Egitim ve Kultur Bakanlıgı, 1989.

———. 'Coban' [Shepherd]. *Kibris Turk Edebiyati II [Turkish Cypriot Literature II*]. KKTC: K.T. Egitim Vakfi Yayinlari, 2008, 93.

Uludag, Sevgul. *Cyprus: The Untold Stories*. Mannheim and Möhnesee: Bibliopolis, 2009.

———. *Oysters with the Missing Pearls*. Nicosia: Ikbe Bilban, 2005.

Unwin, Arthur Harold. *A Short Description of the Forests of Cyprus*. 2nd ed. Nicosia: Government Printing Office, 1927.

Upstone, Sara. *Spatial Politics in the Postcolonial Novel*. London: Ashgate Publishing, 2009.

Vanezis, Procopios Nichola. *Makarios: Faith & Power*. London: Abelard-Schuman, 1971.

Varnava, Andrekos. *British Imperialism in Cyprus 1878–1912*. Manchester: Manchester UP, 2009.

———, and Hubert Faustmann. *Reunifying Cyprus the Annan Plan and Beyond*. New York: IB Taurus, 2009.

———. 'The Minorities of Cyprus in the History of Cyprus Textbook for Lyceum Students: A Critique.' *The Minorities of Cyprus*. Eds. Andrekos Varnava, Nicholas Coureas and Marina Elia. London: CSP, 2009, 299–313.

——— and Stavroula Philippou. 'Constructions of Solution(s) to the Cyprus Problem: Exploring Formal Curricula.' *Reunifying Cyprus the Annan Plan and Beyond*. Eds. Andrekos Varnava et al. New York: IB Taurus, 2009, 194–212.

Varnavas, Panteles. *The Common Labour Struggles of Greek and Turkish Cypriots: Events through History*. Nicosia: Pancyprian Federation of Labour.

Viswanathan, Gauri. *Masks of Conquest: Literary Study and British Rule of India*. London: Faber and Faber, 1990.

Waterman, Stanley. "Partition and Modern Nationalism." *Community, Conflict, Partition and Nationalism*. Eds. Eleonore Kofman and Colin H. Williams. London: Routledge, 1989, 117–32.

Williams, Patrick and Laura Chrisman, eds. *Colonial Discourse and Post-Colonial Theory: A Reader*. London: Longman, 1994.

Williams, Raymond. *Marxism and Literature*. Oxford: OUP, 1977.

Wisker, Rina. 'Writing by Women from Cyprus'. *Post-Colonial and African American Women's Writing A Critical Introduction*. London: Macmillan, 2000, 336–45.

Wolford, Rick and Robert L. Miller, eds. *Women Ethnicity and Nationalism: The Politics of Transition*. London: Routledge, 1998.

WReC (Warwick Research Collective), *Combined and Uneven Development Towards a New Theory of World-Literature*. Liverpool: Liverpool University Press, 2015.

Yashin, Mehmet. 'Cypriot Literature and Indeterminable Identities.' *Current Matters* 68–70 (July 1998–March 1999): 321.

———. *Don't Go Back to Kyrenia*. Trans. Taner Baybar. Middlesex: Middlesex University Press, 2002.

———. 'Flowers for Peonidou.' *My Love the Dead Soldier*. Istanbul: Adam, 1997, 24.

———. *Kibrisliturk Siiri Antologisi. (Anthology Cypriotturkish)*. Istanbul: Yapi Kredi Yayinlari 1994.

———. *Stepmother Tongue from Nationalism to Multiculturalism: Literatures of Cyprus, Greece and Turkey*. London: Middlesex University Press, 2000.

———. 'Signaktan Cikinca' [Departing a Shelter]. *Kibris Turk Edebiyati II [Turkish Cypriot Literature II]*. KKTC: K.T. Egitim Vakfi Yayinlari, 2008, 127–28.

———. *The Series of Modern Turkish Cypriot Literature*. 1–8 vol. Girne Freebirds Yayincilik, 2009.

———. 'Three Generations, Three Identities, Three 'Parties' within Twentieth-century Cypriot Poetry.' *Cyprus and Its People: Nation, Identity and Experience in an Unimaginable Community, 1955–1997*. Ed. Vangelis Calotychos. Boulder: Westview Press, 1998, 223–33.

Yashin, Nese. *Sumbil ile Nergis* (Hyacinth and Narcissus). Istanbul: Cem Publications, 1978.

———. *Tears of Wars*. Istanbul: Yeni Turku Publications, 1980.

———. 'Unsent Letters.' Trans. Aydin M. Ali. *Weeping Island: A Collection of Cypriot Literature.* Ed. Tina Adamidou. Nicosia: United Cypriot Friendship Association, 2001, 101–110.

———. *Üzgün Kızların Gizli Tarihi.* Istanbul: Illetisim, 2015.

Filiz Naldoven. 'Write Songs about Love' & 'Flower Identity.' Trans. Aydin Mehmet Ali. *Weeping Island: A Collection of Cypriot Literature.* Ed. Tina Adamidou. Nicosia: United Cypriot Friendship Association, 2001, 88.

Yasin, Ozker. *Bayraktar Turkusu [Song].* Nicosia: Kibris Postasi Yayinlar, 1959.

———. *Kibris Benim Vatanim: Toplu Siirler I [Collected Poems I].* Istanbul: Cevre Yayinlar, 1986.

———. *Once Kuslar Uyanir: Toplu Siirler II [Collected Poems II].* Istanbul: Cevre, 1986.

Yildiz, Netice. 'The Vakf Institution in Ottoman Cyprus.' *Ottoman Cyprus: A Collection of Studies on History and Culture.* Eds. Michalis N. Michael, Matthias Kappler and Eftihios Gavriel. Wiesbaden: Harrassowitz Verlag, 2009, 117–59.

Yilmaz, Zubeyir and Ramazan Okum. *Kibris Turk Siir.* Istanbul: Milli Egitim Bakanligi, 1992.

Young, Robert. *Colonial Desire: Hybridity in Theory, Culture and Race.* London: Routledge, 1995.

Zabus, Chantal. *The African Palimpsest: Indigenization of Language in the West African Europhone Novel.* Amsterdam: Rodopi, 1991.

Zaphiriou, Lefkios. 'Pentadactylos.' Trans. Irena Joannides. *Faces of an Island: 25 Poets from Cyprus.* Eds. Vera Korfioti, Vera and Mona Saviddoi-Theodoulou. Nicosia: Armida Publishing, 2000, 85–88.

Magazines, Newspapers, Zines

Avgi (1955).

Birinci [First One] (1968).

Cadences: A Journal of Literature and the Arts in Cyprus (2003–).

Cardak [Pergola] (1955).

Cig (Raw).

Cyprus Review (1954–1956).

Cyprus Mail (1963).

Sanat Emegi [Art Work], 1–31 (1978–1981).

Haravgi (1978).

Hursoz (1963).

Ilk Demet (First Bouquet).

Ikink Demet (Second Bouquet).

In Focus Quarterly Magazine on Literature, Culture & the Arts in Cyprus. (2003) – Panos Ioannides.

Isirgan [Nettle] (2004-).

Kypriaka Chronika, [Cypriot Chronicles] 1960–1967.

Karanfil [Carnation] (1981).

Kultur *[Culture]* (1966).

Nea Epochi [New Age] (1960–).

Neos Anthropos [New Man].

Neos Democratis [NewDemocrats] (1955).

Nacak (1964).

Pirsos [Torch].
Philogiki Kypros [Literary Cyprus] (1960) – ed. Kypros Chrysanthis.
Pnevmatiki Kypros [Intellectual Cyprus] (1960) – ed. Kypros Chrysanthis.
Punch (1878).
Sanat Postasi (Art Post) (1966) ed. Demirag.
Themata Kritikis. [Subjects of Criticism] (1966) – ed. Kypros Chrysanthis.
The Cyprus Dossier (2011–).
Ucsuz [Pointless] (2017–).
Yasemin [Jasmine].
Yeni Duzen.
Zine 1 *Crossing South-North Checkpoints: Zine 1.* Bahriye Kemal Comp. Kent: Literary Agency Cyprus, 2014.
Zine 2 *White Flags: Bridges within and Between Lebanon and Cyprus.* Bahriye Kemal Comp Nicosia: Literary Agency Cyprus, 2015.
Zine 20 March 4th Annual International Poetry Days. Nicosia: The Turkish Cypriot Union of Artists and Writers, 2009.

Centre Publications:

The Peace Research Institute Oslo (PRIO) Reports – Led by Harry Tzimitras and Mete Hatay.
Cyprus PEN centre in English: Literary Profiles Series 1- (1993–2019) 1–53.
Costas Montis; Pantelis Mechanikos; Kypros Chrysanthis; Klitos Ioannides; Lina Solomonidou; Yiannis Katsouris; Panos Ioannides; Yiorgos Philippou-Pierides; Klairi Angelidou; Nayia Roussou; Theoklis Kouyialis; Iacovos Kythreotis; Niki Ladaki-Philippou; Achilleas Pyliotis; Andreas Christofides; Costas Proussis; Rina Katselli; Christakis Georgiou; Costas Vassiliou; Vera Korfioti; Nikos Orphanides; Yiorgos Moleskis; Mona Savvidou-Theodoulou; Sophocles Lazarou; Andreas Sofocleous; Nikos Nikolaides; Nikos Kranidiotis; Evgenia Palaiologou Petronda; Emilios Hourmouzios; Glafkos Alithersis; Michalis Pashiardis; Kyriakos Charalambides; Dina Katsouri; Niki Marangou; Theodosis Nikolaou; Tefkros Anthias; Theodosis Pierides; Christos Hadjipapas; Maria Pyliotou; Myrianthi Papaonisiforou; Roula Ioannidou Stavrou;Maroula Avraamidou; Andreas Pastellas; Yiannis Papadopoulos; Manos Kralis; Pitsa Galazi; Panikos Peonides; Elli Peonidou; Andreas Petrides; Petros Stylianou; Demetris Gotsis

Official Governmental Publications: Print

Afasd**

Republic of Cyprus Education

Ανθολογία Κυπριακής Λογοτεχνίας για το Γυμνάσιο. [CLAG-Cypriot Literature Anthology, Gymnasium 1,2,3]. Λευκωσία [Nicosia]: ΥΑΠ, 1998.
Ιστορία Νεοελληνικής Λογοτεχνίας Α΄Β΄Γ΄ Γυμνασίου, [History of Modern Greek Literature, Gymnasium 1,2,3.]. Αθήνα [Athens]: ΟΕΔΒ, 2006.
Κείμενα Νεοελληνικής Λογοτεχνίας Α΄ Γυμνασίου [Modern Greek Literature Text, Gymnasium 1]. Αθήνα: ΟΕΔΒ, 2006.
Κείμενα Νεοελληνικής Λογοτεχνίας Β΄ Γυμνασίου [Modern Greek Literature Text, Gymnasium 2.]. Αθήνα: ΟΕΔΒ, 2006.

Κείμενα Νεοελληνικής Λογοτεχνίας Γ΄ Γυμνασίου. [Modern Greek Literature Text, Gymnasium3] Αθήνα: ΟΕΔΒ, 2006.
Literature Concept Dictionary. Lyceum 1. OEDB. Athens. 2004.
Ανθολογία Κυπριακής Λογοτεχνίας, Για το Λύκειο, Μέρος Α΄ [CLALI- Cypriot Literature Anthology. Lyceum Part 1]. Λευκωσία[Nicosia]: ΥΑΠ, 1996.
Ανθολογία Κυπριακής Λογοτεχνίας, Για το Λύκειο Μέρος Β΄ [*CLALII- Cypriot Literature Anthology, Lyceum part* 2]. Λευκωσία [Nicosia]: Υ.Α.Π., 2001.
Νεότερη Ευρωπαϊκή Λογοτεχνία, Ανθολόγιο μεταφράσεων, Β΄ ενιαίου λυκείου (επιλογής), εκδ. β΄. [*Modern European Literature, Lyceum* 2]. Αθήνα [Athens] ΟΕΔΒ, 1999.
Κείμενα Νεοελληνικής Λογοτεχνίας Τεύχος Α΄, Α΄ Τάξη Ενιαίου Λυκείου, εκδ. γ΄ [*Text* of *Modern Greek Literature, Lyceum 1*]. Αθήνα [Athens]: ΟΕΔΒ, 2003.
Κείμενα Νεοελληνικής Λογοτεχνίας Β΄ Τεύχος, Β΄ Τάξη Ενιαίου Λυκείου, εκδ. Α΄ [*Text of Modern of Greek Literature, Lyceum 2]*. Αθήνα [Athens]: ΟΕΔΒ, 2001.
Κείμενα Νεοελληνικής Λογοτεχνίας Γ΄ Τεύχος (1945–2000), Γ΄ Τάξη Ενιαίου Λυκείου [*Text of Modern Greek Literature Text Lyceum 3*]. Αθήνα [Athens]: ΟΕΔΒ, 2004.
Ανθολογία Νεοελληνικής Ποίησης, Για την Τρίτη Λυκείου, [Anthology of Modern Greek Poetry, Lyceum 3]. Λευκωσία [Nicosia]: Υ.Α.Π., 2004.

Turkish Republic of Northern Cyprus

Kibris Turk Edebiyati I [TCLI -Turkish Cypriot Literature I]. KKTC: K.T Egitim Vakfi Yayinlari, 2008.
Kibris Turk Edebiyati II [TCLII- Turkish Cypriot Literature II] KKTC: K.T. Egitim Vakfi Yayinlari, 2008.

Official Governmental Publications: Electronic

Εκπαιδευτικό Υλικό Μέσης Εκπαίδευσης. [Education Material] Νέα Ελληνικά – Λυκείου [Modern Greek, Lyceum]. September 2009. Ministry of Education. 12 October 2009 www.schools.ac.cy/eyliko/mesi/themata/nea_ellinika/lyk_programmatismoi.html.
Εκπαιδευτικό Υλικό Μέσης Εκπαίδευσης. [Education Material] Νέα Ελληνικά – Γυμνασίου [Modern Greek, Gymnasium]. September 2009. *Ministry of Education*: 12 October 2009 www.schools.ac.cy/eyliko/mesi/themata/nea_ellinika/ gym_ programmatismoi.html.
Eurypedia – European Encyclopedia on National Education Systems. January 2010. European Commission. 12 January 2010 https://webgate.ec.europa.eu/fpfis/mwikis/eurydice/ index.php/ Greece: Overview.

Personal Interviews

Adil, Alev. Personal Interview. 15 March 2012.
———. Email Interview. 9 September 2012.
Ali, Mehmet Aydin. Personal Interview. 22 October 2010.
Angelides, Claire. Personal Interview. 18 April 2011.

Bozkurt, Ismail. Personal Interview. Institute of TMT Freedom-Fighters (Mucahitler Dernegi). 10 April 2011.

Dentash, R. Rauf. Personal Interview. 18 April 2011.

Gazioglu, Ahmet. Personal Interview. Turkish Cypriot Historian. 10 April 2011.

Lambros, Lambros. Personal Interview. Inspector of Literature at the Ministry of Education. 2 June 2009.

Lambros, Lambros and Stylianos Charalambous. Personal Interview. Inspectors of Literature at the Ministry of Education. 31 August 2010.

Moleskis, George. Personal Interview. 22 April 2011.

Montis, Stella. Personal Interview. 13 April 2011.

Muezzin, Cemay Onalt. Personal Interview. Teach and Textbook Author of Turkish Cypriot Literature. 2010.

Stephanides, Stephanos. Personal Interview. 16 April 2011.

——— Email Interview. 16 February 2012.

Index

Note: Page numbers followed by "n" denote endnotes.

Printed in Dunstable, United Kingdom

67042207R00179